THE

POLITICAL and SOCIAL IDEAS of

ST. AUGUSTINE

The POLITICAL AND SOCIAL IDEAS OF ST. AUGUSTINE

By HERBERT A. DEANE

COLUMBIA UNIVERSITY PRESS

NEW YORK AND LONDON

For
Dave, Ellie,
and Ted

PREFACE

For a number of years, in teaching undergraduate and graduate courses in the history of political thought, I have found that the problem of giving students an adequate grasp of the social and political ideas of St. Augustine presents unusual difficulties. In no single work by Augustine, comparable to Plato's *Republic,* Aristotle's *Politics,* Hobbes's *Leviathan,* or Hegel's *Rechtsphilosophie,* can his leading ideas about man, society, and the state be found. Nor can the student be sent to a work where Augustine expounds his entire philosophy, including his teachings on these subjects. He never produced a synthesis of his thought like the *Summa Theologica* of St. Thomas, which contains orderly, systematic treatments of such topics as law, justice, and obedience.

The usual recourse for the teacher is to ask the student to read Augustine's *The City of God.* This book, however, offers both too much and too little; too much, because it is a very long, discursive work, written over a period of thirteen years, which includes a great deal of material that is of only peripheral interest to the student of social and political ideas (e.g., the details of the polemic against pagan religion, or the frequent, extended discussions of purely theological issues); too little, because a number of crucial aspects of Augustine's thought, such as his views on the question of using the power of the state to punish heresy and schism, are not treated at all, or are treated only partially.

The key to the problem is, of course, the realization that St. Augustine, powerful and influential though his thought was, was not a system-builder. He wrote a great deal, and many of his writings, such as *The City of God,* the *De Trinitate,* the Commentaries on the Psalms, and the Commentaries on the Gospel and Epistle of St. John, are major works. But virtually everything that Augustine wrote—whether a very long, complicated work, a doctrinal treatise, a sermon, or a letter—was an occasional piece. Almost all his writings were polemical and controversial; as soon as an erroneous interpretation of Scripture or an heretical doctrine came to his attention, he immediately launched upon a criticism and a rebuttal. It is instructive to notice how many of his works bear the word *"Contra"* ("Against") in their titles; he produced treatises against the Manichaeans, the Donatists, and the Pelagians.

Never during the seventy-six years of his life was there a period of quiet and security, when, all the enemies of the Church having been vanquished, he could withdraw to write a nonpolemical, systematic treatise expounding his theology as a whole or his views about human nature and the social and political order. However, even had such an opportunity presented itself Augustine probably would not have produced a *Summa Theologica* like that of St. Thomas. Genius he had in full measure, but system-building and architectonic skill were not his forte; he is the master of the phrase or the sentence that embodies a penetrating insight, a flash of lightning that illuminates the entire sky; he is the rhetorician, the epigrammist, the polemicist, but not the patient, logical, systematic philosopher.[1]

To gain an adequate understanding of the social and political doctrines of a discursive thinker like Augustine, the student would have to read most of his writings. For many students this would be an impossible assignment. It would take months to read only the works that have been translated into English— about fifty treatises, hundreds of letters and sermons—to say nothing of the important works for which there are no English translations. Even if he were willing to undertake this task, the student of social and political thought might easily lose his way in the long stretches of Augustine's writings where little that is relevant to his concerns is discussed. These difficulties constitute the first reason for writing this book. Here the student will find in a single volume most of the important passages from the entire Augustinian corpus in which human nature, the social order, and the nature and functions of the state are discussed. To meet this need, as well as to give the reader a first hand acquaintance with Augustine's characteristic style of thinking, a large number of quotations from his writings have been included in the text and in the notes.

Yet I hope that the volume is more than an anthology, however useful such a work might be. Since Augustine possesses a powerful and markedly original intelligence, his views about man, society, and the state fall into coherent and consistent patterns, even though he is not a systematic theorist. The second aim of this book is, therefore, to organize the material from Augustine's writings and to elucidate the general point of view that permeates his reflections about social and political life. The danger inherent in this endeavor is the temptation to make his thought more systematic than it really is. Commentators have sometimes been drawn into this temptation by the striking manner in which he expresses his ideas; as a consequence, they have allowed themselves to reduce his complex insights to a simple, consistent theory.

Finally, this work is intended as a critical essay on Augustine's social and political doctrines. It seeks to demonstrate to the reader the connections between those doctrines and the general framework of his thought, to assess the coherence and validity of his ideas, and to call attention to the strengths as well as the limitations of the Augustinian approach. As far as I know, there is no work in English which presents a full treatment of Augustine's social and political ideas or a critical examination of them. The valuable bibliography appended to the third edition of Étienne Gilson's *Introduction à l'étude de saint Augustin,*[2] which lists the principal works written about Augustine up to 1943, refers, in the section on social and political doctrines, to only one book published in English, John Neville Figgis's *The Political Aspects of S. Augustine's 'City of God,'*[3] and I know of no volume that has been published since that time on this subject.[4] Although Gilson describes this work by Figgis as "excellent et très pénétrant,"[5] it is quite inadequate as a summary and analysis of Augustine's political thought, since it deals with only a single work, *The City of God.* Moreover, of the book's one hundred and nineteen pages only thirty are devoted to the central topics, the State (Chapter III) and the Church (Chapter IV).

Probably the best-known twentieth-century treatment of Augustine's social and political doctrines is Gustave Combès's *La doctrine politique de saint Augustin,*[6] which Gilson describes as "un répertoire systématique et détaillé des idées d'Augustin sur le 'gouvernement des nations.' "[7] Combès's work strikes the reader at first glance as a highly useful study, since it gives references to the entire corpus of Augustine's writings and deals with a number of important topics, such as authority, law, justice, war, and the relations between Church and State. Its usefulness to the student is marred, however, by many inaccurate quotations and references.[8] In addition, I find it difficult to accept many of the author's principal interpretations of Augustine's ideas. The value of Combès's book and of several other studies of Augustine's social and political ideas seems to me to be reduced because the authors give a Thomistic interpretation to his doctrines; as a result, they minimize or even disregard the differences between his philosophy and that of St. Thomas.

One final word should be added. I have occasionally called attention to similarities and differences between Augustine's ideas and those of other important political thinkers where it seemed that such comparisons might be illuminating to the reader. Less often, I have noted the contemporary relevance, either for political theory or for practice, of one or another of his insights. Some readers may feel that I ought to have pointed out, more frequently than I have, the places where Augustine's ideas conflict with or are supported by modern social and political theories, and the extent to which they are applicable to contemporary political and social problems. The only excuse I can offer is the stubborn, and possibly mistaken, conviction that we demonstrate an unwarranted "smugness of contemporaneity" when we congratulate a great thinker of another age if his conclusions happen to agree with the ideas fashionable in our own day, or when we chide him for his failure to achieve the level of wisdom and sophistication that we ourselves have attained. I think that the reader will be able to see for himself the relevance—or irrelevance—of most of Augustine's comments to both the perennial dilemmas of political life and the peculiar problems of our age. My chief concern, I freely admit, has been to understand what Augustine said and to communicate that understanding, as far as I could, to others.

ACKNOWLEDGMENTS

My fundamental obligation is to the two teachers who, almost fourteen years ago, first made me aware of the significance of the political thought of St. Augustine—Dino Bigongiari, whose knowledge and love of Augustine's writings are so great that it becomes almost an impertinence for his students to say or write anything on this subject, and the late Franz Neumann, who was profoundly impressed by Augustine's pessimistic realism and lack of sentimentality about politics.

This book would never have been written had I not enjoyed the generous encouragement and assistance of The Rockefeller Foundation, which by granting me a fellowship during the academic year 1958–59 made it possible for me to undertake the basic research and the early stages of the writing, and of the John Simon Guggenheim Memorial Foundation, whose fellowship award for the year 1960–61 permitted me to devote a full year to the completion of the work. I acknowledge my indebtedness to the Stanwood Cockey Lodge Foundation, whose generous grant made this publication possible.

One of the great advantages of academic life, which we often take for granted without realizing its importance, is the constant willingness of busy colleagues to devote time and energy to the task of reading and criticizing other people's writings. I am deeply grateful to those friends and colleagues who have read the manuscript and have given me the benefit of their comments and suggestions: Rosalie L. Colie, Robert D. Cumming, Julian

H. Franklin, Maurice M. Goldsmith, Moses Hadas, Reinhold Niebuhr, John Plamenatz, John B. Stewart, David B. Truman, and Neal N. Wood.

I am also indebted to the members of my graduate seminar at Columbia University in the year 1959–60. They not only tolerated my preoccupation with Augustine but also, by thoughtful questions and comments, contributed materially to the clarification of my ideas.

CONTENTS

A NOTE ON TEXTS AND TRANSLATIONS

For the three works by Augustine for which revised texts have recently appeared in the new series of Latin Christian authors, the *Corpus Christianorum, Series Latina* (Turnholti, Typographi Brepols editores Pontificii)—*The City of God* (*De Civitate Dei*), *The Commentaries on the Psalms* (*Enarrationes in Psalmos*), and *One Hundred and Twenty-four Tractates on the Gospel of John* (*In Ioannis Evangelium Tractatus CXXIV*)—I have quoted from and referred to the Latin texts in this series. For all other works by Augustine, I have used the Latin texts in the *Corpus Scriptorum Ecclesiasticorum Latinorum* (Vienna, Academy of Letters, 1866–) or in J.-P. Migne, *Patrologiae Latina* (Paris, 1854–66); since the former series does not yet include all the works in the Augustinian corpus, I have had to use and cite the Migne texts for the works which have not yet appeared in the Vienna edition.

The largest single collection of English translations of Augustine's works is found in the first eight volumes of the First Series of *A Select Library of the Nicene and Post-Nicene Fathers*, edited by Philip Schaff (reprinted by Wm. B. Eerdmans Publishing Company, Grand Rapids, Michigan, 1956). I have quoted and referred to these translations in this book, except for the works listed below. For *The City of God*, I have used the Marcus Dods translation as published in two volumes by the Hafner Publishing Company, New York (1948); aside from differences in pagination, this translation is identical with the Dods translation

found in Volume II of Schaff. For the *De Libero Arbitrio*, the
De Vera Religione, and the sections of the *De Diversis Quaestio-*
nibus ad Simplicianum that are included, I have used the translations by John H. S. Burleigh in Volume VI of *The Library of*
Christian Classics (Philadelphia, The Westminster Press, 1953).
For the *Confessions* and the *Enchiridion* I have used the translations by Albert C. Outler in Volume VII of *The Library of*
Christian Classics (Philadelphia, The Westminster Press, 1955).
For the *De Spiritu et Littera* and the parts of the *De Trinitate*
and of the *Tractates on the Epistle of John* that are included, I
have used the translations by John Burnaby in Volume VIII of
The Library of Christian Classics (Philadelphia, The Westminster Press, 1955).

English translations of a number of Augustine's works have
appeared in the series called *The Fathers of the Church* (New
York, Cima Publishing Co. Inc., 1948–). From this collection
I have used the translation of the *Contra Academicos* and the
De Ordine in Volume 1, the translation of the *Contra Julianum*
in Volume 35, and the translations of those letters of Augustine
which were not included in Volume I of Schaff; the five volumes
of Letters constitute Volumes 12, 18, 20, 30, and 32 of *The*
Fathers of the Church series, but they are also numbered as
Volumes I–V of the Letters of St. Augustine and I have referred
to them by these numbers, for example, FCL I indicates Volume
I of the Letters in *The Fathers of the Church* translation.

Where no English translation exists for a work by Augustine
or where I felt that the existing translation was incorrect or
seriously misleading, I have made my own translations of the
Latin text; in each case, I have added the phrase, "author's translation," after the citation to the Latin text.

Wherever the numbering of chapters or paragraphs of Augustine's works was different in the Latin text and in the English

translation, I have always given the numbering that is found in the Latin text; for example, in all references to the *Enarrationes in Psalmos* the numbers of the *Psalms* and of the sections of each Commentary are those found in the Latin text, and not the changed numbers given in the abbreviated version of the work that appears in translation in Volume VIII of Schaff.

THE

POLITICAL and SOCIAL IDEAS of

ST. AUGUSTINE

INTRODUCTION

Periods of disturbance

Important contributions to political and social philosophy have
been made more frequently in periods of political and social
disturbance than in more peaceful times. Our Western tradition
of political thought begins with the efforts of Plato and Aristotle
to understand and to deal with the crisis in the Athenian *polis*
and in the other Greek states, which resulted from the dissolution
during the fifth century of what has been called "the Inherited
Conglomerate" of traditional institutions and beliefs.[1] The crisis
was brought into sharp focus by the increasingly bitter conflicts
between rich and poor in most of the Greek states and by the
Peloponnesian War, in which the Athenians and their allies were
finally defeated by the Spartans and their allies. The political
writings of Machiavelli not only mirror the chaos and instability
of Renaissance Italy but seek to provide the key to the restoration
of order and security. In seventeenth-century England, civil war
called forth Hobbes's analysis of the foundations of society and
the state and his prescription of the ideas and institutions that
must be accepted if anarchy is to be banished in favor of peace
and the satisfactions of which peace is the condition precedent.
Rousseau's *Discourses* reflect the rejection and disgust which
the last stages of the *ancien régime* in France evoked in him and
in many other observers, while his *Social Contract* seeks to discover the principles of political right, the only true bases for a
just and legitimate society.

When a political and social system is running smoothly, and

when traditional arrangements and ideas are, on the whole, adequate to the problems that arise, there is little incentive to undertake a fundamental analysis of the nature and functions of society and the state, to ask basic questions about the grounds of political obligation or the citizen's duty to obey the commands of political authorities. In quiet times, men tend to take for granted the state and the order and security that it provides. After a period of stable government and security for life and property, they are tempted to regard peace and order as "natural" and "given" and to forget that, to a great extent, they are the results of elaborate, delicate contrivance.[2] If they think at all about fundamental problems of political and social order, they soon arrive at tolerably satisfactory answers which are couched in terms of the values and beliefs widely accepted as unquestionably true in their society.

When, however, men face serious difficulties which the traditional political and social system seems unable to solve, when conflicts between groups, classes, regions, or religious sects within the society become so intense that consensus evaporates, and, above all, when a crisis of the most fundamental kind undermines the body politic because traditional beliefs, attitudes, and values no longer command virtually automatic assent from most members of the society, thoughtful men are once more driven to the effort to examine the bases of social and political order and to suggest new answers to the questions of politics.

The age in which St. Augustine lived and wrote—the last part of the fourth century and the first decades of the fifth century—was a period of profound disturbances, marking the transition from the classical civilization of Greece and Rome to the Christian civilization of Western Europe. Augustine, heir to the classical tradition and great Christian philosopher and theologian, is the bridge between the thought of antiquity and that of the Middle Ages; indeed, he can be regarded as an important link between classical culture and the Christian civilization which, having dominated Europe from the fifth century until our own times, may now be coming to its end.

Of course, there is no neat break between classical and Christian civilizations, since many elements of Graeco-Roman culture passed over into the civilization of Western Europe. Even if we ignore the survival of the Roman Empire and of many elements of Graeco-Roman civilization in Byzantium for more than a thousand years after the end of the Western Empire, we now know that the Roman Empire did not "fall" in 410 when the city was sacked by Alaric, the Visigoth, or when the line of Western Emperors expired with the deposition of Romulus in 476. Many of the "barbarians" who migrated into Western Europe and created the "barbarian kingdoms" had been exposed to Roman culture and institutions long before they moved into the heart of the Empire, and they became much more Romanized after they had settled down in Italy, Gaul, or Spain. As long as there was a Roman Emperor in the West, their kings were contented, even eager, to accept such Roman official titles as *magister militum*. The barbarian rulers used the Roman bureaucracy until it gradually withered away with the decline in education and the increase of difficulties in communication. The authority of Roman law continued to be recognized for the subject peoples, although the conquerors retained for themselves their own Germanic laws. The sixth-century Merovingian kingdom of the Franks as well as Charlemagne's Frankish empire in the late eighth and ninth centuries demonstrate the extent to which Roman institutions, ideas, and culture survived in union with the Germanic elements brought in by the "barbarians."

Nevertheless, the end of the fourth and the beginning of the fifth century mark a significant point in the political, economic, and cultural disintegration of the Roman Empire in the West, which had been in process for more than a century. As the fourth century drew to a close, life ebbed away from the municipal institutions, and in increasing numbers the curials fled from the impossible burden of imperial taxation intended to support the army and the bureaucracy. In many areas of the Western Empire, large landholders retired to their country estates and built up for themselves power positions that were virtually immune from the control of the imperial state. After 380, when Catholic Christianity became the official religion of the Empire,[3] the practice of pagan religion was subject to disabilities and punishment of various kinds.[4] Although the triumph of Christianity was not immediate, the principal resistance to the Church came not from the older pagan cults but rather from such Christian heresies as Arianism, to which most of the Germanic invaders adhered, Nestorianism, Monophysitism, and, in Africa, Donatism. Both in thought and practice, paganism showed little vigor or tenacity when it was subjected to state persecution; the weakness of its hold upon the popular mind was made manifest by the ease with which the victory of Christianity was generally accepted. Finally, the novel spectacle of the barbarians—Visigoths, Ostrogoths, Vandals—not merely pressing across the frontiers of the Western Empire but overrunning its heartland—Italy, Gaul, Spain, and North Africa—and the sack of Rome itself offered dramatic proof of the decline of the Roman political, administrative, and military system.

The collapse of established institutions and beliefs, widespread and continued violence and war, and the new position of Christianity within the Empire impelled Augustine to examine anew the fundamental issues of social and political life. As a Christian philosopher and theologian, what materials did he have at hand to guide his reflections?

The attitude of the early Church toward society and the state has been the subject of extensive controversy. It has sometimes been argued that primitive Christianity was radically hostile to the political and economic institutions as well as the cultural and religious life of the Roman Empire; Christianity, it is said, was essentially a revolutionary protest of the underprivileged and enslaved against the economic, social, and political oppression to which they were subject. On this view the Church's gradual acceptance of traditional institutions such as the state, private property, and slavery constituted an abandonment of its original opposition to the world and an accommodation of its ethical teachings to the imperatives of social and political life.

I am convinced that this interpretation is so oversimple as to be seriously inadequate. Although the teachings of Jesus as recorded in the Gospels have relatively little to say about the proper attitude for Christians to adopt toward the social order and the state, certain fundamental principles are clearly established. On a number of occasions, Jesus warns His disciples against thinking of His kingdom as an earthly kingdom, to be established by a revolt of the Jews against Roman rule and maintained by ordinary political instruments. This hope for the advent of a Messiah who would reestablish the independence of the Jewish state and scatter its enemies was so deep-seated that it kept reappearing even among Jesus' closest followers until the very moment of His death and, indeed, after His resurrection.[5] Jesus not only insisted that His kingdom was not of this world and so discouraged His followers from thinking of Him as a Messiah who would be the temporal ruler of the Jewish people, but He also endeavored to draw His followers' attention away from interest in worldly matters such as the attainment of wealth or power over other men. Since His concern was for their salvation, the kingdom of God which He urged them to seek was an eternal kingdom based upon the double law of love—single-minded and total love of God and love of one's neighbor. It is fair to say that He encouraged His disciples to be indifferent to worldly concerns, including political power, but indifference is a far cry from rebellion, anarchism, or even hostility to the political order. He tells His disciples: "The kings of the Gentiles exercise lordship over them: and they that exercise authority upon them are called benefactors. But ye shall not be so." [6] He rebukes them for speculating about their relative precedence in the kingdom of heaven, and He reminds them that he who seeks to be first among them must follow His example by humbling himself to become the servant of the others.

However, Jesus never encouraged or permitted His followers to ignore or resist the commands of the established political authorities. He Himself acknowledged the legitimacy of Pilate's authority,[7] and He ordered Peter and the other disciples to abandon their plans for resisting the soldiers who were sent to arrest Him. Of central importance is His famous reply to the question about the lawfulness of paying tribute to Caesar—"Render therefore to Caesar the things that are Caesar's, and to God the things that are God's." [8] The obvious meaning of this command is that Christians are to obey the orders of the political authorities in all matters which do not involve neglect or disobedience of God's commands; as Parker says,[9] it is clear that the Church, from the beginning, understood Christ's injunction in this sense.

The Christian's conscientious duty to obey the commands of established political rulers is repeated and underlined in the famous passages in St. Paul's Epistle to the Romans and the First Epistle of St. Peter.[10] Although the Apostles maintain that political authority is divinely instituted, they demonstrate somewhat the same depreciation of and disinterest in political power that we have noted in Jesus' teachings.[11] According to Paul and

Rulers primary function

Peter, the ruler's primary function is the preservation of order by
the punishment of evildoers. This is a limited and negative task,
though not an insignificant one; further, the state's function is
not a matter of great concern to the Christian, since presumably
he will do good and avoid evil because he loves God and his
fellow man and not because he fears the punishments that rulers
and judges may inflict.

One other aspect of early Christian thought about the political
order deserves mention. In apocalyptic literature, and especially
in the Book of Revelation, a sharp contrast is drawn between
the kingdom of God and the kingdoms of this world, which are
part of the realm of Satan. All earthly thrones and powers are
destined to be destroyed when the world comes to an end (an
event which most Christians of the first century probably expected
to occur within a short time) and when Christ returns in triumph
to destroy the wicked and all their works. This apocalyptic attitude can only have served to strengthen the tendency in the early
Church to be more or less indifferent to the state and political
concerns and to regard the state as an instrument operated by
non-Christians for regulating and repressing the criminal actions
of other nonbelievers. Nowhere in the Gospels or in the Apostolic
teachings is it ever suggested that Christians have any obligation
to participate in the operation of the political system or that the
activities of the state have any real relevance to the conduct of
members of the Church or to their overriding concern—salvation
and participation in the kingdom of God. *Christian v. Greek*

The Christian view that the principal function of the state is *view of the state*
the repression and punishment of the wicked is at the opposite
pole from the classical, and especially the Greek, conception that
the purpose of the state is to promote the good life and to train
and educate its citizens so that they become good and virtuous
men.[12] Once eternal salvation and man's right relation to God

become the primary concerns, political activities, along with intellectual, cultural, and economic pursuits, become clearly secondary interests. Rebirth and salvation come through Christ and the Church that He established, and not through the activities or instrumentalities of the state. Christians may be good and obedient citizens of the state in which they live; they may follow the Apostolic injunctions to pray for their heathen rulers; but throughout the course of history they remain "strangers" and "pilgrims" in the cities of this world, men of "divided loyalties" whose primary allegiance is to God and His commands and whose closest ties are with their Christian brethren, Roman or Greek, bond or free, rather than with the fellow citizens of their city or nation. For good or evil, the spread of Christianity meant the introduction of a dualism in Western civilization that prevented a return to the conception of the state as the central focus of man's interests and activities or as the incarnation of man's highest values. Only with the rise of totalitarian societies in the twentieth century has a new general effort been made to bring all aspects of human life under the guidance and control of the state or the totalitarian party.

The persecutions of the Christian Church by the Roman State, which were carried on intermittently and with more or less vigor from the time of the Emperor Nero until the Decian persecutions in the middle of the third century and the final persecution, that of Diocletian, at the beginning of the fourth century, did not bring about any marked change in the Church's attitude toward the state.[13] On the one hand, the persecutions and the efforts of the state to compel Christians to renounce their faith in Christ and to do homage to the official divinities of the Empire, including the Emperor, kept alive during the second and third centuries the early Christian view that the state was a part of the "world," the devil's kingdom, from which as believers they had been set free by God's grace. Christians were not tempted to glorify a state which from time to time used its power and authority in efforts to destroy God's Church and to harass or kill His children. They had little incentive to modify the primitive view that the functions of the state, being primarily negative and repressive, had no positive value for the Christian. It is, perhaps, more surprising that the other aspect of Christian political doctrine—the belief that political authorities, as divinely ordained instruments for the punishment of the wicked, must be obeyed and, indeed, honored and never resisted or subverted—retained its vigor throughout the period of state persecution. Although true Christians refused, of course, to obey the state's commands to renounce their belief in Christ or to worship pagan deities, they continued to obey all other orders of the political authorities and to pay taxes, and they accepted punishment, even martyrdom, at the hands of the state without any attempt at resistance or rebellion.

Thus, despite its steady growth in membership and its increasing penetration of all classes of society, the Church in the second and third centuries was not compelled to undertake any major revision or clarification of its earlier attitudes toward the state. During the long intervals between the persecutions, the Church was able to maintain its original position of uninvolvement in the political order, combined with an acceptance of that order as a necessary instrument in this sinful world. As long as rulers and officials were pagans, Christians could retain their traditional stance of half-accepting, half-rejecting the state, while enjoying the benefits of the peace and order maintained by the state without their active participation.

The conversion to Christianity of the Emperor Constantine in 312, which came less than a decade after the Diocletian persecutions (303–305), the support and favor bestowed upon the Church by the Emperor, and the great influx of state officials and military personnel into the Church brought to a sudden and dramatic climax the steady penetration of Christianity into the pagan world. When Constantine died in 337, Christianity was one of the two official religions of the Roman Empire; although there were temporary setbacks for the Church during the reign of the Emperor Constantius, who was a partisan of Arianism, and during the brief renascence of paganism under the Emperor Julian (361–363), the triumph of orthodox Christianity was finally recognized in 380 when Theodosius the Great proclaimed Christianity as the official religion of the Empire.[14] He and his successors used the power of the state to support the Church and to punish its enemies—pagans, heretics, and schismatics. Its new situation forced squarely upon the Church the need to clarify and readjust its attitudes toward the world, and especially toward the state and its political, legal, and military activities. No longer was it possible to retain the antimilitarism and pacifism of such Christian writers as Tertullian and Lactantius,[15] and the official Church of the Empire could hardly say with Tertullian, "What has Athens to do with Jerusalem? [*Quid Athenae Hierosolymis?*]," or "Nothing is more foreign to us [the Christians] than the State."[16]

It is one of Augustine's great accomplishments that he formulated the Church's view of the state and political power in a manner which took into account both the traditional Christian attitudes which have been mentioned and the new situation in which the Church of the fifth century found itself. In his discussions of politics his penetrating insights could be given almost free rein, since there were only a few clear Scriptural texts to bound his thought and since none of the earlier Church Fathers had undertaken a detailed examination of the political order. The traditional view of the early Church that the state was an essential instrument for repressing the consequences of sin and that it was not the vehicle by which men could attain to true justice, true virtue, or true happiness was thoroughly congenial to Augustine's own leading conceptions—the sinfulness of human nature, salvation by unmerited divine grace, and the view that private property, slavery, and the political and legal systems are punishments and remedies for the depraved condition of mankind after the Fall. He was therefore able to accept, and then elaborate and refine, the traditional, but vaguely defined, beliefs of the Church. He made definite and clear the sharp cleavage between the Christian view of the nature and functions of the state and the classical doctrine that it was the highest and noblest form of human association, which existed to make possible the good life for its citizens and to form and educate them so that they might become truly human, that is, good and virtuous men who had realized their fullest potentialities.

Characteristically, Augustine did not simply ignore or discard this classical, and particularly Platonic, vision of the good society which embodies perfect justice and harmony and which gives its citizens complete happiness and fulfillment. The Platonic ideal is retained, but it is no longer an ideal that can be realized or even approximated in earthly societies. There is only one true republic in which perfect peace, harmony, justice, and satisfaction are assured to all the citizens; that society is the *civitas Dei,* which exists eternally in God's heaven and is the goal of God's elect while they sojourn as pilgrims in this sin-ridden, wretched earthly life. Only in that city "whose founder and ruler is Christ" is mutual love the ruling principle, so that there is no need for coercion, punishment, or repression. In that city alone can men realize the noble aims proclaimed by the philosophers of Greece and Rome—complete and unbroken peace, perfect concord and harmony, true self-realization, and perpetual happiness.

Once the classical vision of the state had been transferred to the heavenly city and the hope of embodying its ideals in any earthly society had been flatly rejected as impossible, Augustine was free to follow the lead suggested by the Christian tradition and to take a new, sharply realistic look at the actual states found in this world—to examine what they are intended to accomplish and what in fact they can accomplish, what they do and what they cannot do, and how in fact they perform the tasks that are set for them. Let us, in the chapters that follow, examine in detail the results of this fresh look at the workings of actual political institutions.[17]

CHAPTER I

THE THEOLOGY OF FALLEN MAN

When we consider St. Augustine's teachings about man, society, and the state, we must always remember that he was primarily a theologian or, more accurately, a pastor and a preacher, who was seeking to turn men away from themselves and the things of this world and to call them back to God, as the one true and ultimately satisfying center of man's life. The main theme of his preaching was not his own ideas about the good life for the individual or for the society, but the Word of God as revealed in the Scriptures. In his view, the task of the preacher is to set forth this divine message, to remind his hearers of God's commands, to explain and interpret the Scriptures, and to defend the true doctrine against enemies of the faith, whether pagans or heretics. Consequently, almost all of Augustine's writings are, in one form or another, commentaries on the Scriptures, and there is scarcely a book in the Bible on which he did not comment.

God was the focus of Augustine's life and thought to such a degree that he saw the hand of God in every event in the natural world and in every human action. The phrase applied to Spinoza —"a God-intoxicated man"—is perhaps even more apt as a description of Augustine. At the same time, his sense of God's omnipresence and omnipotence, of the universal sway of Divine Providence in every detail of the governance of the universe, does not lead him to ignore or neglect the part that men play in the world drama. He is a master psychologist, and the depth and subtlety of his insight into a wide range of human attitudes and motivations enable him to be extraordinarily perceptive when he surveys man's social and political situation.

At least a summary outline of certain aspects of Augustine's theology must be given before an attempt is made to discuss his psychological, moral, social, and political doctrines. Since his teachings about God, eternal life, and man's relation to God are the framework of his thought, we cannot hope to understand his attitudes toward the secular world without at least a general understanding of that framework. Indeed, it may be argued that if we have really understood his religious teachings, we can virtually deduce from them his views on the nature of man, society, and the state. At the least, an understanding of some of the major elements of his theology can save us from the error of attributing to him ideas about human nature and the social and political order which are fundamentally incompatible with his central religious beliefs.*

For Augustine, as for all Christians, the world and everything in it were created by God. The world is not eternal; it had a beginning, and the beginning of the world was also the beginning of time. The world will have an end—the Last Judgment—when heaven and earth shall pass away, and a new heaven shall appear, in which the saints will enjoy eternal peace and happiness with God and His angels. Between these two points, the creation of the world and its destruction, is played out the great drama of man's career on earth. The climax of the drama, the moment for

---

* The summary presented here of Augustine's doctrines of man's creation, his fall, and his redemption makes no claim to being complete —literally hundreds of works have been written dealing with various aspects of his theology—and it does not pretend to reveal anything new, although it is based directly on the writings of Augustine rather than on secondary works. The summary will serve its purpose if in a brief compass it gives the reader an outline of his views of the relations between God and man which does not do too grave an injustice to the subtleties and complexities of his teachings.

which all that went before was simply an anxious prelude, is the Incarnation, the appearance on earth of God in human form with the birth of Jesus Christ; "the Word became flesh and dwelt among us." In order to understand the significance of the Incarnation in the drama of man's salvation, we must return to the first act, to the Garden of Eden and the fall of the first human beings, Adam and Eve.

Like everything else that God created—the heavens, the earth, the seas, plants, and animals—the first man was created good; in *Genesis* we are told that after viewing each of His creatures God saw that it was good. Everything that He created was created out of nothing, *ex nihilo;* there was no eternally existing matter independent of God that He shaped or formed in the process of creation. Obviously, then, there is a clear difference between the Creator and the created. The Creator is unchangeably good, wise, and all-powerful by His very essence; God's goodness, wisdom, and power are not accidents or attributes separable from His being. Like all other created beings, man is good but not incorruptibly, absolutely, or necessarily good.[1] He is mutable and changeable, but as long as he acknowledges his dependence upon and his inferiority to God, his Creator, and obeys His commands, he will be good and happy.[2]

Moreover, man has been given the gift of free will, which no other earthly creature possesses; he can, if he wishes to do so, act in a manner contrary to God's command. He can choose to obey or disobey. If he disobeys and turns away from the source of his being, his life will be warped and stunted; the farther he removes himself from God the more wretched, miserable, and imperfect will he become.[3] Augustine adopts the neo-Platonic doctrine that evil has no substantial reality of its own, that it is simply the privation or loss of good. Consequently, evil can inhere only in that which is good but not perfectly good. And since evil is not a substance or a nature, but merely a privation, God is not its author or creator. A created being—a nature or sub-stance—becomes evil insofar as it falls away from its essence or nature and tends toward nonexistence, although by God's Provi-dence nothing in the universe is permitted to decline to the point of nonexistence.[4] Therefore, to the extent that man turns away from God, who is perfect being and goodness, he becomes less good and more evil. The choice is left to man, but, as we shall see, the consequences of the choice are eternally fixed and determined by God.

Man soon misused the free will that God had granted to him. The devil, the chief of the angels who had already fallen from heaven because of their perverse and prideful rebellion against God, tempted Eve to disobey God's command and to eat the fruit of the tree of the knowledge of good and evil, and Eve per-suaded Adam to join her in this rebellion against the Creator and Lord of the universe. Thus was committed that "original sin" of disobedience and rebellion against God, which had its root in man's pride and in his presumptuous desire, to which the devil adroitly appealed, to "be like God." "By craving to be more, man becomes less; and by aspiring to be self-sufficing, he fell away from Him who truly suffices him."[5]

It is important to understand clearly what Augustine means by "sin" and "original sin." Sin is to be clearly distinguished from sins, that is, particular acts that are wrong, unjust, or immoral; sin is a pervasive attribute or character of human beings. Sin is disobedience and revolt—man's turning away from God and from His will and His commands, and making himself and his own will and desires the center of his existence. Sin is man's refusal to accept his status as a creature, superior to all other earthly creatures but subordinate to God. So the root cause of sin, of falling away from God and from goodness and toward evil, is man's prideful self-centeredness. He attempts—although unsuccessfully—to ignore his Creator and his Ruler and to set up himself, his own will, as the hub of the universe. Refusing to acknowledge his lacks and limitations as a creature, he tries to upset the whole order of the universe by his perverse imitation of God.[6] In his egoistic arrogance and presumption, man vainly seeks to dominate all other men, who were created as his peers, and to use them—and even God—as instruments of his will. From that pride as a root stem all particular sins or violations of God's law.

Whence doth iniquity abound? From pride. Cure pride and there will be no more iniquity. Consequently, that the cause of all diseases might be cured, namely, pride, the Son of God came down and was made low. Why art thou proud, O man? God, for thee, became low.[7]

As a result of the Fall of Adam and Eve, as a consequence of and a punishment for their "original sin" of prideful, arrogant rebellion against God and against their own proper status as creatures, human life in this world became penal. Mortality, death, misery, suffering, crimes, the war of the flesh against the spirit, conflict among men—all these evils, which had no place in human nature as it was created—are the characteristics of fallen man. They are the necessary result and the totally just punishment of that "outrageous wickedness which was perpetrated in Paradise."[8] Moreover, the original sin of egoistic pride and disobedience and its necessary punishment were not confined to our first parents, Adam and Eve. In their sin the whole mass of the human race was condemned, and in all their descendants the originally good nature of man has been and remains radically vitiated and corrupted. Each man, from the moment he is born, is infected with the original sin of pride and the blasphemous desire to place himself at the center of the universe; "all men are a mass of sin [*massa peccati*]."[9] "But as man the parent is, such is man the offspring. . . . and what man was made, not when created, but when he sinned and was punished, this he propagated, so far as the origin of sin and death are concerned." [10] For Augustine, the human race is "sick and sore . . . from Adam to the end of the world. . . ." [11] And as every child born from this tainted root is marked with original sin, so its punishment— misery on this earth, and death as the end of this mortal life—is the lot of every human being born of Adam. Through his sin, Adam

subjected his descendants to the punishment of sin and damnation, for he had radically corrupted them, in himself, by his sinning. As a consequence of this, all those descended from him and his wife . . . all those born through carnal lust, on whom the same penalty is visited as for disobedience—all these entered into the inheritance of original sin. Through this involvement they were led, through divers errors and sufferings (along with the rebel angels, their corruptors and possessors and companions), to that final stage of punishment without end. [12]

But, even after the Fall, God did not entirely abandon his creature, man. Had He done so, man would have ceased to exist. Even in the misery of sinful existence, God continues to grant to all men the great blessings of His gifts—man's ability to live and to propagate his kind, his senses and his reason, the goods of nature, food and nourishment. [13] But in addition to these gifts, given to both the just and the unjust, God in His infinite mercy has conferred a priceless gift upon a small number of human beings. Since God is all-wise and since, in His knowledge, there is no past or future but only an eternal present, He knew, before the creation of the world and before the Fall, that man would sin and would be condemned to punishment. But His foreknowledge of what would happen did not compel man to sin. [14] Man's disobedience and his turning away from the perfect good were the result of his own free will. However, once man chose to sin rather than to remain subject to God, even his original freedom was lost. He was no longer able, of himself, not to sin, and his freedom was reduced to the choice between one or another sin.[15] He was, as St. Paul says, in bondage to sin, and what he thought was freedom was actually slavery to the devil and his works. From all eternity, however, God had determined to save a fixed number of these sinful, fallen men—a small minority of the human race.[16] This minority, the elect, were chosen to receive the gift of faith and, as a consequence, salvation and exemption from the just punishment of sin, without any regard to their future merits or good works.[17] By the operation of unmerited grace, those predestined to salvation are released from the just penalty inflicted on the whole mass of fallen mankind and are promised a life of eternal blessedness with God after the Last Judgment, the destruction of the world, and the resurrection of the body.[18] In many of his writings, and especially in the bitter controversies with the Pelagians that occupied the last twenty years of his life, Augustine insists again and again on the completely gratuitous character of God's gift of salvation to the few.[19]

Hence the whole mass of the human race is condemned; for he who at first gave entrance to sin has been punished with all his posterity who were in him as in a root, so that no one is exempt from this just and due punishment, unless delivered by mercy and undeserved grace; and the human race is so apportioned that in some is displayed the efficacy of merciful grace, in the rest the efficacy of just retribution. . . . But *many more are left under punishment than are delivered from it,* in order that it may thus be shown what was due to all.[20]

Augustine, like St. Paul, insists that God cannot be charged with injustice because He chose to bestow upon only a small number of men the grace which is the only means of salvation.[21] God is perfectly just in condemning *"the great majority"* of the sons of Adam [22] to eternal punishment as a consequence of original sin and of the additional sins that every man adds to that burden while he lives in this world. Indeed, God would have been perfectly just had He spared none of the sinful human race from this punishment. The fact that He wipes out the punishment for a few is an indication of His unfathomable goodness and mercy, and no more an injustice than if a creditor were to insist on repayment from most of his debtors, but were to remit the payment due from a few of them.[23] Since the latter would be an act of charity and grace, not of injustice, those who were compelled to repay what they had borrowed would have no basis for complaint.[24] On the other hand, those who, through no merit or desert of their own, are freed from the just punishment that they owe have no reason to glory in themselves or in their works.[25] Pride or a sense of superiority is utterly out of place; they can only be grateful to the God who has spared them from the universal penalty, and they must attribute all that they are and will be to Him and to His incomprehensible mercy.[26] One of the most frequently repeated texts in Augustine's writings is the seventh verse of the fourth chapter of St. Paul's First Epistle to the Corinthians: "For who maketh thee to differ from another? and what hast thou that thou didst not receive? now if thou didst receive it, why dost thou glory, as if thou hadst not received it?" The primary motive for Augustine's constant insistence that sinful man is absolutely dependent for his salvation upon God's free grace is, I believe, his conviction that pride is the root of sin, and that the most insidious form of pride is that of the man who attributes to himself and to his own efforts his good works or his progress in spiritual life. If pride is the root of sin, sin can be overcome only by complete humility and by attributing to God any good that man does. St. Paul's intention is "of a certainty sufficiently plain against the pride of man, that no one should glory in man; and thus, no one should glory in himself." [27]

If we ask why God chose some men to be saved and left all the others in their deserved punishment, the answer for Augustine, as for Job and St. Paul, is that we cannot hope to fathom the depths of God's mind and His purposes. All we know is that there is no injustice with God, and that the election of some men to salvation is a purely gratuitous act, which is not the consequence of their good deeds or even of God's foreknowledge of such deeds. In fact, their merits are the *result* rather than the *cause* of the grace that they have received. "What else but His gifts does God crown when He crowns our merits?"[28] It is clear that St. Paul's conceptions of salvation, election, and unmerited grace were definitive for Augustine's doctrine.[29] He studied the Pauline epistles even before his conversion, and certainly by 396 he had developed, in all essentials, the views on grace and predestination presented here. His bitter conflict with the Pelagians, who denied that man's salvation was completely dependent upon God's grace, only led him to sharpen and intensify his earlier teachings.

Augustine's deep-rooted sense that man was totally dependent upon God for his salvation was also based upon the events which St. Paul had experienced as well as the course of Augustine's own life. What merits did Paul, or, rather, Saul, have that "entitled" him to be selected for the gift of grace which he received in such full measure? All his energy and efforts were devoted to persecution of the followers of Christ and to attacks on His doctrines.[30] In the dramatic scene that took place on the road to Damascus, Christ "compelled" Paul to abandon his crusade against Him and to become one of His followers. Paul's strengths and merits as a teacher and preacher of the Word of God were all the result of that blinding flash and the voice from heaven that effected his conversion. He had not wanted to be saved; he had not been seeking God; God chose him and poured down His grace and power upon him.[31] Similarly, Augustine was certain that nothing in his own life before his conversion constituted a claim upon God for salvation.[32] For years he had been wandering in intellectual and moral error, as he graphically tells us in his *Confessions*. He was lost because he had turned away from God and was vainly seeking Him in material form, when he was a Manichaean, or in purely intellectual terms, during his Platonist period. Again, as in the case of St. Paul, it was an act of Divine Providence, an example of totally unmerited and undeserved grace, that effected, in highly dramatic fashion, Augustine's final conversion. As he lay prostrate in the garden, weeping over his inability to conquer his irresolution, the hold of the pleasures of the flesh, and his failure to give himself to God, he heard the repeated chanting of a child, *"Tolle lege, tolle lege."* ("Pick it up, read it; pick it up, read it.") Rushing into the house, he picked up the book that he had laid down a short time before—St. Paul's Epistles—and read the first words that caught his eye, "Not in reveling and drunkenness, not in debauchery and licentiousness, not in quarreling and jealousy. But put on the Lord Jesus Christ, and make no provision for the flesh, to gratify its desires." [33] The message was meant for him. His conversion, the return of his wandering soul to what he felt was its true source and light, God, was accomplished with no further delay or hesitation.[34]

At this point in my summary of Augustine's theological doctrines, we must return to the high point of the drama of salvation, the Incarnation. For the Incarnation, the assumption by God Himself of human flesh and His appearance on earth in the form of a man, born of woman and condemned to die like all other men, is the vehicle by which the salvation of sinful man is carried out. From the point of view of the neo-Platonists, the philosophers whose views of God and of reality came closest to those of the Christians,[35] the doctrine of the Incarnation, the assumption by the Logos of flesh and mortality, was the greatest possible scandal and stumbling block.[36] The neo-Platonist might find himself in agreement with the Logos doctrine set forth in the first chapter of St. John's Gospel, but when he came to the words of the fourteenth verse, "And the Word [*Logos*] was made flesh, and dwelt among us," he could only feel horror at the thought that pure Spirit and pure Reason should be contaminated by being incorporated into a material body and involved in suffering and death. And yet the Incarnation is *the* central doctrine of Christianity. Mankind was irretrievably lost in sin and held in bondage to the devil; for fallen man there was no possible way back to God. Or, more accurately, there was only one way—that God Himself should come to man, should take upon Himself the likeness of sinful flesh, and should Himself become the Mediator between man and God.[37]

The depth of God's humility and of His love for sinful men is indicated not simply by the Incarnation but by His willingness to undergo rebuffs, punishment, and, finally, the most ignominious of all deaths, death by crucifixion, in order to ransom the captives of sin and error.[38] Christ, by His death, broke the devil's bonds, in which men were held; when He, who was without trace of sin, was made to suffer death, the penalty for sin, men were released from the ancient thralldom and set free to become the sons of God and co-heirs with Christ of God's eternal kingdom. But here we must be careful to note a qualification. As we have seen, only a small minority of the human race is to be saved. While all those who are saved are saved only by virtue of Christ's mediatory sacrifice, not all men are destined for salvation. Not even the Incarnation and Crucifixion of God are, in the Augustinian theology, sufficient to accomplish the redemption of all men, although they provide the only way to rebirth and salvation for those whom God has predestinated to receive grace and eternal life. Augustine, in commenting on St. Paul's statement, "Who will have all men to be saved,"[39] explicitly says that this

does not mean that there is no one whose salvation he doth not will . . . but by "all men" we are to understand the whole of mankind, in every single group into which it can be divided: kings and subjects; nobility and plebeians; the high and the low; the learned and unlearned; the healthy and the sick; the bright, the dull, and the stupid; the rich, the poor, and the middle class; males, females, infants, children, the adolescent, young adults and middle-aged and very old; of every tongue and fashion, of all the arts, of all professions, with the countless variety of wills and minds and all the other things that differentiate people.[40]

So it is clear that for Augustine not all men who were alive at the time of the Incarnation or who have lived since that time are to be saved. Indeed, as we shall see, only a minority of those who are Christians, that is, baptized members of the visible, sacramental Church, will be saved.[41] Still another qualification must be introduced. Among those who have been predestined and chosen for salvation by God's grace are a number of men who lived before the Incarnation. This group includes the patriarchs and prophets of Israel, who believed, through God's grace, in the future coming of Christ and were saved by this faith; it also includes some non-Jews, such as Job the Idumean, who had the same faith.[42] These two qualifications make it absolutely impossible to identify the City of God, which contains the minority of the human race elected to salvation, with the visible Christian Church in this world.[43]

Before we examine the careers of the two divisions of mankind, the small minority destined for salvation and eternal life and the vast majority—the fallen and unredeemed men—doomed to eternal punishment, we must pause for a brief consideration of Augustine's doctrine of free will. If we are to avoid misunderstanding, we must distinguish carefully the various periods of man's history and the kind of free will that is characteristic of each period. Augustine sometimes confuses his readers because he uses the same terms, "freedom" and "free will," to refer to quite different things. Free will in the classic sense of freedom of choice, freedom to choose and to do good or evil, to sin or not to sin, is something that existed only in the brief period between man's creation and the Fall. But that freedom was lost when man misused his liberty and chose to follow the devil rather than God, to sin rather than to do good.[44] From that moment on, fallen man sins by necessity rather than by free choice; [45] his will is in bondage to sin, "for the law of sin is the tyranny of habit, by which the mind is drawn and held, even against its will," [46] and it is utterly impossible for him to do good or to live righteously.[47] Nor can man recover his free will by his own efforts; ". . . the grace of God liberates men from the misery inflicted on sinners, because man was able to fall of his own accord, that is, by free will, but was not able to rise of his own accord." [48] The mark of this servitude is delight in sinning, whereas liberty means that we find our delight in not sinning; [49] "because the will has sinned, the hard necessity of having sin has pursued the sinner, until his infirmity be wholly healed. . . ." [50]

The second important meaning of freedom of the will is, therefore, not the ability to choose between good and evil, but the will to do good, the will not to sin, taking pleasure in righteousness. This freedom of the will is completely lacking in fallen man; [51] if he has free will at all, and Augustine often indicates that he has, it is a freedom which is very different from the freedom of the good or righteous will.

We do not say that by the sin of Adam free will perished out of the nature of men; but that it avails for sinning in men subjected to the devil; while it is not of avail for good and pious living, unless the will itself of man should be made free by God's grace, and assisted to every good movement of action, of speech, of thought.[52]

When Augustine argues that he is not saying that free will "perished out of the nature of men" by Adam's sin, but rather that among the unredeemed free will avails only "for sinning," he seems to have fallen into an equivocation in the course of his argument against the Pelagians. Implicitly, at least, he is assigning yet a third meaning to the term "free will"—that is, fallen man is free to sin and to decide at any given moment whether or not to commit this or that particular sin. Just as he is obviously not forced to do good despite his will and inclination, so he is not "compelled" to sin by any force or power outside himself.

Certainly, fallen man does not have the "free will" that Adam had before the Fall—the choice between good and evil; it is, I assume, this freedom to which Augustine refers when he says that "sin which arises from the action of the free will turns out to be victor over the will and the free will is destroyed."[53] And, even more certainly, fallen man does not possess freedom of the will in the second sense of the good or righteous will. To put the matter briefly, and perhaps somewhat oversimply, Augustine asserts that everything that fallen man does on his own initiative and with his own powers is sinful and wrong. He is anxious to insist that fallen man has free will since he wishes to make it clear that he and he alone is responsible for all the evil and sin in the world. On the other hand, he insists that any good action performed by any human being is to be attributed not to his unaided will or inclinations but to the grace and love of God working in him. Only by holding fast to this belief can the man who is endeavoring to live righteously be saved from the sin of pride and self-congratulation.[54]

Only those who receive God's grace can be liberated from the bondage to sin, and even they, while they live in this world, cannot be said to have completely attained true freedom of the will, that is, a truly good and righteous will. The war within the mind between the law of God and the law of sin continues right up to the moment of death. Even when we know what we ought to do and what, perhaps, we want to do, we often find that we are not able to do it.[55] The truly free will is the good or pious will, the will that "is not the slave of vices and sins." [56] "For only if thy will is pious, will it be free. Thou wilt be free, if thou art a servant still,—free from sin, the servant of righteousness. . . ." [57] This true freedom, which is attained when a man takes pleasure in righteousness and does voluntarily that which is good and that which God commands, "is also devoted service in obedience to righteous precept." [58] To the man who is in bondage to sin "this liberty to do right" comes only through God's grace: "If the Son, therefore, shall make you free, then shall ye be free indeed." [59] Those who receive grace begin to enjoy this freedom even while they are in this life; that is, they begin to perform in the spirit of love those actions which other men do only because of fear, if indeed they do them at all.[60] By love, the gift of the Holy Spirit, shed abroad in their hearts, the redeemed move toward the state in which "a good work may be done not for fear, but for love; not for dread of punishment, but for love of righteousness. For this is true and sound freedom." [61]

However, since no one can say that he is without sin as long as he remains alive, even though he can and should attain to what Augustine calls "the first stage of liberty [prima libertas]," that is, being free from crime or grievous sin,[62] this "true and sound freedom" is possessed only in hope. It will be possessed completely—even by the saints—only after the resurrection of the body. In the bliss of eternal life, there will be "on the one hand, a permanent will to live happily, and, on the other hand, a volun-

tary and happy necessity of living virtuously, and never sinning."[63] Thus, the true freedom of the will that is to be attained
in heaven will be different from—and even better than—the first
freedom of the will that man possessed before the Fall. That first
freedom was a natural ability not to sin, but also an ability to sin,
whereas the final freedom of the will, which is to be the gift of
God and not a natural power, will be inability to sin, unfailing
delight in not sinning.[64]

But in the future life he [man] will not have the power to will evil;
and yet this will not thereby restrict his free will. Indeed, his will will
be much freer because he will then have no power whatever to serve
sin. For we surely ought not to find fault with such a will, nor say it
is no will, or that it is not rightly called free, when we so desire happiness that we not only are unwilling to be miserable, but have no
power whatsoever to will it. And, just as in our present state, our
soul is unable to will unhappiness for ourselves, so then it will be
forever unable to will iniquity.[65]

By God's free grace a small minority of mankind has been
chosen out of the mass of corruption and has been elected to
eternal salvation.[66] These men, together with the good angels
who never fell away from God, constitute the City of God, and
at the end of time, after the resurrection of the body, they will
live forever in perfect peace and happiness and in enjoyment of
God.[67] The rest of mankind, the vast majority, together with the
devil and his angels, are the citizens of the earthly city, which is
doomed to eternal punishment. The careers of these two cities
from the beginning of time until the end of the world and the
relations between their citizens are the theme not only of *The
City of God* but of a large number of Augustine's other writings.[68]

The City of God, the true Jerusalem, is the whole assembly of
the saints; it is identical with the Church of which Christ is the
Head and all the citizens are members, that is, the invisible
Church.[69] The human part of the City of God is a single society

that extends throughout the whole world and is made up of men of different eras.[70] It is of crucial importance to recognize that Christ explicitly stated that His kingdom, the City of God, is not of this world.[71] By this statement He made it perfectly plain to all men and to their earthly rulers that He had no intention of interfering with their temporal governance, and, more important, He made it clear that no earthly state, city, or association can ever claim to be a part or a representative of the City of God. Precisely because Christ's kingdom is the City of God, it exists eternally in heaven and is not embodied in any human or earthly institution. The commonwealth of the Hebrews, although it was directly established and ordained by God, was not a terrestrial incarnation of the City of God; rather, it was intended to "prefigure and fore-announce the city of God which was to be gathered from all nations." [72] Even the visible Church, which contains many of the reprobate along with the elect, is not an earthly division of the City of God, although, having been established by Christ Himself as the vehicle through which the elect are to be gathered together out of the world during the period from the Incarnation to the Last Judgment, it is more closely related to that City than any earthly state or society can ever be.[73]

The citizens of this kingdom of Christ pass through this world, but they are here only as pilgrims or wayfarers [*peregrini, viatores*];[74] their true country is in heaven, and while they are on the earth and share in the joys and sorrows common to all men, they live as sojourners in a strange land.[75] They are expatriates, who, in their "toilsome pilgrimage" here on earth, long for deliverance and for a return to the society of the holy angels, who have never been deprived of God's presence. From that heavenly city have been sent, for the guidance and solace of its pilgrim members, God's Word, as set forth in the Scriptures, and the King Himself in the person of Christ.[76] The human members of the City of God, of Christ's Church, are those men from Abel to the end of the world who, having been saved by God's grace, love God and do His will; God is the center of their affections and their actions. But no man, as long as he lives on the earth, can be certain that he is a member of this city or that he is destined for eternal life.[77]

The members of the earthly city, of the kingdom of the devil, are the fallen angels and the men from Cain to the end of the world "who wish to live after the flesh," [78] who place their affections and interest in this world and in temporal goods and honors.[79] They are the fallen and unredeemed men, the sinners, who have not been called back to God by His grace; their hearts are fixed only on material goods and earthly enjoyments, and at the end of time they will be consigned to eternal punishment. They are not strangers or pilgrims on earth; the city built by Cain "was not from home in this world [*non peregrinantem in hoc mundo*], but rested satisfied with its temporal peace and happiness. . . . the earthly city is dedicated in this world in which it is built, for in this world it finds the end towards which it aims and aspires." [80] Like the City of God, the earthly city extends over the entire earth and has an unbroken existence from Adam to the end of the world; and it, too, has its nonhuman members, the fallen angels, who are now demons, led by the arch-demon, the devil. For both reasons, it is difficult to make an identification between Augustine's "earthly city" and any particular earthly state or kingdom or all of them together. Yet it is clear that the relationship between the earthly city and what we call states is far closer than the connection between the City of God and any terrestrial group. The members of the earthly city, unlike the members of the City of God, are not pilgrims or sojourners on this earth; they are "at home" here, and it is here that they seek their ends and find their satisfactions. On a number of occasions

Augustine speaks of the states and kingdoms of this world as divisions or parts of the earthly city. He identifies the earthly city with "the society of mortals spread abroad through the earth everywhere, and in the most diverse places," and states that

among the very many kingdoms of the earth into which, by earthly interest or lust, *society is divided (which we call by the general name of the city of this world [ciuitatem mundi huius]),* we see that two, settled and kept distinct from each other both in time and place, have grown far more famous than the rest, first that of the Assyrians, then that of the Romans. First came the one, then the other. The former arose in the east, and, immediately on its close, the latter in the west.[81]

But even if the states of this world are in some sense regarded as parts of the earthly city, the members of those states and the members of the earthly city are not always identical. Some citizens of earthly states and even some of their rulers may, as individuals, be members of the City of God. These two cities cannot be separated and their members clearly identified as long as this world lasts. They are commingled on earth and are not to be separated until the end of time.[82] As a result, it sometimes happens that

certain men belonging to the city Babylon [the earthly city], do order matters belonging to Jerusalem [i.e., sinful men occupy positions of authority in the Church], and again certain men belonging to Jerusalem, do order matters belonging to Babylon [i.e., good men, members of the City of God, occupy positions of power and authority in earthly states].[83]

Nevertheless, throughout all time, the members of these two cities are always in opposition; "against each other mutually in conflict, the one for iniquity, the other for the truth." [84] There is a sharp line of division between the two cities, even though it is not visible to our eyes. No one can be a member of both societies; either God is loved with all the heart and all the soul and all the mind or the world is loved.

For he cannot love that which is eternal, unless he shall cease to love that which is temporal. Consider a man's love; think of it as, so to say, the hand of the soul. If it is holding anything, it cannot hold anything else. But that it may be able to hold what is given to it, it must leave go what it holds already.[85]

Between "the multitude of the impious," who are "lovers of the world" and, thus, "enemies of God," [86] and the small number of men who love and serve the one true God there can only be irreconcilable opposition;

even if they use the same tables and houses and cities, with no strife arising between them, and in frequent converse together with seeming concord: notwithstanding, by the contrariety of their aims, they [the wicked] are enemies to those who turn unto God. For seeing that the one love and desire this world, the others wish to be freed from this world, who sees not that the first are enemies to the last? For if they can, they draw the others into punishment with them.[87]

From the beginning of the world—from Cain and Abel—to the end of time the wicked persecute and harass the pilgrims from heaven.[88]

The members of the City of God, the sojourners and wayfarers in this world, who build no earthly dwellings but live in tents as they pass through the wilderness,[89] constitute the Jerusalem or Sion that longs for liberation from its captivity to Babylon, the earthly city, the city of confusion.[90] To these pilgrims Augustine says:

Ah! Christians, heavenly shoot, ye strangers on the earth, who seek a city in heaven, who long to be associated with the holy Angels; understand that ye have come here on this condition only, that ye should soon depart. Ye are passing on through the world, endeavouring to reach Him who created it. Let not the lovers of the world, who wish to remain in the world, and yet, whether they will or no, are compelled to move from it; let them not disturb you, let them not deceive nor seduce you.[91]

In this world the City of God is the "society of men, who live not according to man in contentment with earthly felicity, but according to God in hope of everlasting felicity." [92] Every city or society of men is held together by some law, and this city is held together by the law of Love. Its members obey the two great commandments, "You shall love the Lord your God with all your heart, and with all your soul, and with all your mind," and "You shall love your neighbor as yourself." [93] Since God is Love, he "who is full of Love, is full of God; and many, full of love, constitute a city full of God. That city of God is called Sion." [94] This heavenly Sion or Jerusalem is not a material city; the stones of which it is built are living stones, the souls of the saints.[95] And God's heaven is not the heaven that we see with our eyes, for "heaven and earth will pass away." Heaven is God's dwelling, that is, "all holy souls, all righteous souls. . . . all the holy Apostles, all the holy Virtues, Powers, Thrones, Lordships, that heavenly Jerusalem, wanderers from whence we groan, and for which we pray with longing; and there God dwelleth." [96] Since God dwells in His temple and the saints are His temple, the kingdom of heaven is within us; [97] "therefore thy faith in Christ is Christ Himself in thy heart." [98]

In this heavenly city are found everlasting peace and perfect harmony among the members, since self-love and self-will are completely replaced by "a ministering love that rejoices in the common joy of all, of many hearts makes one, that is to say, secures a perfect concord [concors]." [99] In the earthly city, on the contrary, there is constant conflict and strife, not only against the good but among the wicked themselves, since each man and each group seeks a larger share of material goods than the others and each strives for mastery and power over the rest.[100] During this life temporal goods and evils are distributed by God to the men of both cities in accordance with His plans for the world, and there is no correlation between a man's goodness and piety and his earthly happiness and prosperity. In fact, it sometimes seems that the good receive more than their share of misery and suffering.[101] The difference between the two types of man resides not in their fortunes or experiences in this life but in their attitudes toward the good or evil things that befall them.[102] The pilgrims of the City of God are not elated or made proud by earthly prosperity or success, nor are they shattered or broken by calamities or sufferings, which they regard as punishments for their sins or trials of their virtues. To the citizens of the earthly city, however, wealth, fame, and power are the highest goods, and they will do anything that is necessary to obtain them. They regard poverty, sickness, misfortune, and death as absolute disasters, which they will go to any lengths to escape or postpone, including prayers and sacrifices to demons. In a few words Augustine states the essential difference between these two classes of man: "The good use the world that they may enjoy God: the wicked, on the contrary, that they may enjoy the world would fain use God. . . ."[103]

As we come to the end of this outline of Augustine's views on sin and redemption, we must return to a subject that has already been mentioned briefly—the nature of the visible Church in this world, its membership, and its relation to the City of God, the true Church and Body of Christ. We have seen that Augustine never identifies the visible Church with the City of God. He clearly distinguishes the church on earth, "this kingdom militant," in which both good and wicked men are found, and the church in heaven, the kingdom of heaven, into which only the good will be permitted to enter.[104] In the course of his long-continued struggle with the Donatist sect in Africa,[105] he completely rejected the idea that it was possible or desirable to establish on earth a "church of the pure," made up only of men who, having received salvation through God's grace, were living blameless lives. The Donatists not only maintained that their sect was such a "church of the pure," but they insisted that the validity of the sacraments depended on the moral righteousness of the priests who performed them. Augustine, who saw great dangers to the universal church in this Puritan sectarianism, launched a vigorous attack on the Donatist doctrines. At the heart of his polemic is the assertion that as long as this life continues, no one, even if he has had the experience of "conversion," can be sure that he—or anyone else— is saved or that he will persist in his salvation until his death; [106] on the other hand, we cannot say with certainty that any man belongs to "the devil's party" as long as he is alive. This is a fact which is "a secret" to us, and "we cannot tell whether even the man who seems to stand shall fall, or whether he who seems to lie shall rise again." [107]

Although, after the Incarnation, no man can become a citizen of the heavenly city unless, before his death, he has become a member of the visible Church, some men who are now in the Church will not be in the City of God, and some who are now the worst enemies of that City will at the end be members of it.[108] Because wicked, depraved men, who were blasphemers and enemies of God, have often been converted to Christ, the Church prays for the salvation of all her enemies who still live in this world.[109] And good men, who were members of the Church, have frequently lapsed from their faith and fallen away into sin and wickedness.

According, then, to this divine foreknowledge and predestination, how many sheep are outside, how many wolves within! and how many sheep are inside, how many wolves without! How many are now living in wantonness who will yet be chaste! how many are blaspheming Christ who will yet believe in Him! how many are giving themselves to drunkenness who will yet be sober! how many are preying on other people's property who will yet freely give of their own. . . . In like manner, how many are praising within who will yet blaspheme; are chaste who will yet be fornicators; are sober who will wallow hereafter in drink; are standing who will by and by fall! These are not the sheep.[110]

If, in this world, we do not know who the saved and the damned are, it is obviously impossible to set up a visible Church composed only of saints and rigorously excluding sinners.[111] Moreover, any effort to do this is itself a great sin; it is a palmary example of the sin of pride—arrogating to oneself perfect virtue and sinlessness, and having the temerity to judge the unknown and unknowable hearts and minds of other men and to label them as irremediably sinful.[112] Over and over again in the course of his anti-Donatist sermons and writings, Augustine repeats the Gospel warnings against any attempt to separate the good and the bad in the Church before the end of the world and the Last Judgment, when Christ Himself, from whom nothing is hidden, will make the separation.[113] We must not try to separate the wheat from the tares before the time of the harvest, or the grain from the chaff before winnowing. Another oft-repeated figure is that of the good and bad fish who swim together in the nets of the Lord until the nets are brought ashore. In this wicked world there are many reprobate mingled with the good in the Church, "and in this world, as in a sea, both swim enclosed without distinction in the net, until it is brought ashore, when the wicked must be separated from the good, that in the good, as in His temple, God may be all in all." [114]

Augustine says,

For now we are separated, not by place, but by character, affections, desires, faith, hope, charity. Now we live together with the unjust, though the life of all is not the same: in secret we are distinguished, in secret we are separated; as grain on the floor, not as grain in the granary. On the floor, grain is both separated and mixed: separated, because severed from the chaff; mixed, because not yet winnowed. Then there will be an open separation; a distinguishing of life just as of the character, a separation as there is in wisdom, so also will there be in bodies. They that have done well go to live with the angels of God; they that have done evil, to be tormented with the devil and his angels.[115]

Both good and evil men within the Church receive the sacraments and attend the services; nothing in their outward behavior is a sure sign of election or of damnation. The "only final distinction between the sons of God and the sons of the devil" is love, and no one can say with certainty whether or not another man's actions are motivated by love.

All may sign themselves with the sign of Christ's cross; all may answer Amen and sing Alleluia: all may be baptized, all may come to church and line the walls of our places of meeting. . . . They that have charity, are born of God: they that have not charity are not. . . . Charity is that precious pearl, without which all that you have profits you nothing, and which suffices you if you have nothing else.[116]

Augustine frequently tells us that few of the members of the visible Church are among the saved; most of those who are found within the Church are and always will be unredeemed and sinful.[117] And as the end of the world approaches, it will be difficult to find even a handful of good men within the Church on earth; Scripture tells us that in those last days sin will abound and the love of many will wax cold.[118] Augustine notes that in his age there has been a great influx of people into the Church. With the end of the persecutions and the adoption of Christianity as the official religion of the Roman Empire, many men have come into the Church for reasons that have little if anything to do with love of God and of His commands. "Now that the Christian name has begun to be in such high dignity, hypocrisy, that is pretence, has increased; of those, I mean, who by the Christian profession had rather please men than God."[119] He also refers to "the enormous multitude that, almost to the entire subversion of discipline, gain an entrance [into the Church], with their morals so utterly at variance with the pathway of the saints." [120]

Many men come to Christ's Church only for the sake of temporal advantages.

One has a business on hand, he seeks the intercession of the clergy; another is oppressed by one more powerful than himself, he flies to the church. Another desires intervention in his behalf with one with whom he has little influence. One in this way, one in that, the church is daily filled with such people. Jesus is scarcely sought after for Jesus' sake.[121]

This influx of evil, worldly men into the Church has gone so far —now that it is no longer difficult or dangerous to be a professing Christian—that men even have the temerity to ask their Bishop for counsel and advice in their attempts to deprive others of their estates and property by lying and fraud.[122]

In all these statements Augustine demonstrates that he does not assume that growth in church membership or influence can be equated with an increase in the number of those men who truly love God. Indeed, as history draws to its close, the number of true Christians in the world will decline rather than increase. His words give no support to the hope that the world will gradually be brought to belief in Christ and that earthly society can be transformed, step by step, into the kingdom of God.

CHAPTER II

THE PSYCHOLOGY OF FALLEN MAN

Augustine believes that most men are unredeemed; this has always been true in the past and it will remain true until the end of the world. Therefore, the psychology of sinful or fallen man is crucially important if we are to understand the institutions of human society—property, the family, slavery, and, above all, the political order. Only a small minority of men are, during their earthly lives, converted by God's grace and changed from sinful to redeemed men, and this handful of saints cannot in this world be certainly distinguished from the crowd of sinners among whom they live, work, and die. It is therefore absolutely impossible to establish on earth a society or state made up of saints or true Christians. Thus, if we wish to understand how social, economic, and political life operate, and how, indeed, they *must* operate, we have to start with the assumption that we are dealing, for the most part, with fallen, sinful men. It is they who set the tone and fix the imperatives of earthly life and its institutions.

One of Augustine's favorite analogies involves a comparison of the relation between the soul and the body with that between God and the soul. The soul is the life of the body, its animating or energizing principle, even if it is foolish or unrighteous, and "it supplies vigor, comeliness, activity, the functions of the limbs to the body, while it exists in the body."[1] In like manner, God is the life of the soul, and while He is in it "He supplies to it wisdom, godliness, righteousness, charity." [2] God was the life of man's soul as long as man was obedient to Him and lived according to His commands, and He quickens and revives the dead soul of man when He sends His grace and His word into the heart of a sinner and turns him back to the true light. When, however, man abandoned God, the source of his life and his happiness, he tried to live according to himself and not according to God; as a result, "he lives according to a lie." [3] The more the soul is alienated from God, its true life, the more it becomes unlike Him and removed from Him. Instead of loving God, who is incorporeal, eternal, unchangeable, all-good, and all-wise, man finds himself loving objects that are temporal, mutable, and insubstantial.

If, then, one is nearer to God the liker He is to Him, there is no other distance from God than unlikeness to Him. And the soul of man is unlike that incorporeal and unchangeable and eternal essence, in proportion as it craves things temporal and mutable.[4]

So we arrive at the central principle of Augustinian psychology. Augustine follows Plato in the belief that love is the dynamic or energizing force of the human psyche. Just as Plato, particularly in the *Symposium,* regards *eros* as the ultimate power which, in different forms, moves and directs men's actions, so Augustine teaches that "my weight is my love." [5] Exactly as a body is impelled by its gravity to move in a particular direction, so the psyche or soul is moved by love. "By it I am carried wherever I am carried." [6] The soul moves toward and becomes like what it loves.[7]

Hold to the love of God, that you may stand fast for ever as God stands: *for the being of every man is according to his love.* Dost thou love the earth? To earth thou shalt turn. Dost thou love God? I would not dare to say, A god thou shalt be; yet we have the word of Scripture, "I have said, Ye are gods, and ye are all the sons of the Most High." [8]

If the soul is in its natural, healthy condition, it loves God and moves toward Him and becomes more like Him; it uses temporal, sensible things as this life requires, but it does not love them or set its course by its desire for them. When, however, the soul falls away from God, its actions are directed by the new object of its love, temporal goods, even though they are fleeting and unreal, and so cannot provide it with true or lasting satisfaction.

I say that there is no man who holds that there is nothing he ought to worship, who is not the slave of carnal pleasures, or seeks vain power, or is madly delighted by some showy spectacle. So, without knowing it, they love temporal things and hope for blessedness therefrom. Whether he will or no, *a man is necessarily a slave to the things by means of which he seeks to be happy.* He follows them whithersoever they lead, and fears anyone who seems to have the power to rob him of them. Now a spark of fire or a tiny animal can do that. . . . [T]ime itself must snatch away all transient things. Now since the world includes all transient things, *those who think to escape servitude by not worshipping anything are in fact the slaves of all kinds of worldly things.*[9]

And just as desire or love is "a forward movement of the mind," so fear is "the flight of the mind";[10] the good soul flees from what it fears—sin, evil, and alienation from God—and the wicked soul flees from God and attempts, unsuccessfully, to escape from temporal pain, misery, suffering, and death. The soul which is journeying in this world and has departed from God forgets its origin and its destination, and becomes enmeshed in the charms and pleasures of the sights and sounds seen and heard on the journey, while its

thoughts are diverted from that home whose delights would make us truly happy. . . . We have wandered far from God; and if we wish to return to our Father's home, this world must be used, not enjoyed . . . that by means of what is material and temporary we may lay hold upon that which is spiritual and eternal.[11]

The punishment imposed upon man as a result of his disobedience to God is altogether appropriate. The natural situation was that as God ruled the soul, so the soul ruled the body, and the understanding, enlightened by the truth that is of God, ruled the soul. After the Fall, the soul lost the command that it had formerly exercised over its inferior, the body.[12] Augustine expresses the same thought in a somewhat different manner when he says that the punishment for man's disobedience to God was man's "own disobedience to himself, so that in consequence of his not being willing to do what he could do, he now wills to do what he cannot." [13] Only the life of angels is heavenly; the life of beasts is earthly, that is, they seek only earthly pleasures, with "immoderate desires." "The life of men is midway between that of Angels and of beasts. If man lives after the flesh, he is on a level with the beasts; if he lives after the Spirit, he joins in the fellowship of angels." [14] Since fallen man has set his love on earthly things rather than on God and since his body no longer obeys all the commands of his soul, it is clear that he sinks to the level of the beasts, and, indeed, in his ferocity and malice toward other men he often sinks below the level of the animals. Even the good man, the pilgrim on this earth who yearns for his true home in heaven, is hardly able to live in this world without seeking some tangible, material goods as a place wherein his soul may pause to rest, if only temporarily.

The innocent man resteth in his house, his family, his wife, his children; in his poverty, his little farm, his orchard planted with his own hand, in some building fabricated with his own study; in these rest the innocent. But yet God willing us not to have love but of life eternal, even with these, though innocent delights, mixeth bitterness, that even in these we may suffer tribulation. . . .[15]

And even good men often abstain from reprimanding or correcting the wicked because, loving this present life more than they should, they are afraid of losing earthly possessions, safety, or reputation.[16]

If even the pilgrims are not completely immune from the love of worldly goods as long as they sojourn here on earth, and if the weak among them are troubled when they see that many wicked men abound in temporal goods and satisfactions, the sinful are completely captivated by worldly possessions and honors; they regard their attainment as the greatest possible good and their loss as the worst possible evil. They "worship" and "reverence" God only because they hope to be rewarded with temporal goods, which are their real god. They fail to see that while God is indeed the source of earthly goods and benefits, He is not to be worshiped with a view to obtaining these gifts, which He gives indifferently to the good and to the wicked, but with a view to receiving His really important gift, eternal life and heavenly blessedness.[17]

The pilgrims should use the goods of this life for the sake of attaining eternal life and should not enjoy them or be entranced by them.[18] Christ came to teach men to despise things temporal in comparison with things eternal, "that they should not esteem as a great matter whatever object evil men covet, that they should suffer whatever evil men fear."[19] However, Augustine does not advocate a completely negative, ascetic attitude toward the world; nor does he encourage the view that possessions and other earthly goods are *per se* evil. He frankly recognizes that, in addition to eternal blessings, there are temporal blessings, such as health, material possessions, honor, friends, a home, wife and children, and peace and quiet.[20] Temporal happiness is not to be scorned or shunned, but it is not to be regarded as the highest good or even as necessarily good; temporal goods sometimes profit and sometimes harm those who possess them.[21] Above all, they are never to be preferred to eternal blessings—eternal life with God and His angels, and blessed immortality of body and soul—and they are to be cheerfully surrendered, if it is necessary, for the sake of these eternal goods, which can only profit and never harm their possessor.

Goods

Always, Augustine's teaching is that the pilgrims must use the goods of this world and must not be "used" by them, that is, they must not love them or become immersed in or attached to them.

He who loves God is not much in love with money. And I have but touched on this infirmity, not venturing to say, He loves not money at all, but, He loves not money much; as if money were to be loved, but not in a great degree. Oh, were we loving God worthily, we should have no love at all for money! Money then will be thy means of pilgrimage, not the stimulant of lust; something to use for necessity, not to joy over as a means of delight. . . . *Use the world: let not the world hold thee captive.* Thou art passing on the journey thou hast begun; thou hast come, again to depart, not to abide. Thou art passing on thy journey, and *this life is but a wayside inn.* Use money as the traveller at an inn uses table, cup, pitcher, and couch, with the purpose not of remaining, but of leaving them behind.[22]

Augustine's view of the proper attitude for the pilgrims to adopt toward earthly goods has been stated in some detail in order to make clear the sharp contrast between their attitude and the outlook of the citizens of the earthly city. If love (*caritas*) is the root of the actions of the redeemed, lust (*libido*) is the fundamental quality of the unregenerate. For Augustine, lust is the generic term for all earthly desires; he defines it as "an appetite of the mind by which to eternal goods any temporal goods whatever are preferred."[23] Every earthly desire is a form of lust; anger is the lust for revenge, avarice the lust for money, and the urge to power the lust of ruling.[24] The common quality found in all members of the earthly city, all the "embittered ones" (*amaricantes*), as Augustine calls them, is that they share in the same end, that is, temporal and earthly happiness. It is this common end, this single motive which determines all that they do, that links them together in a single society, although the specific objects that they desire at different times are innumerable.[25]

Cupidity or avarice, the inordinate and insatiable appetite for material possessions, especially wealth, is one of the three primary forms of lust. There is no limit to sinful man's desire for material goods; his life consists in a restless quest for satisfaction by means of one object after another. The moment one desire is satisfied, another rises to demand fulfillment; so there is no rest or surcease for the anguished soul that is seeking happiness in material objects.

And it [the world] does not make good what it promises, it is a liar, and deceiveth. Therefore men never cease hoping in this world, and who attains to all he hopes for? But whereunto soever he attains, what he has attained to is forthwith disesteemed by him. Other things begin to be desired, other fond things are hoped for; and when they come, whatsoever it is that comes to thee, is disesteemed. . . . For for this cause are these things disesteemed, because they cannot stand, because they are not what He is. For nought, O soul, sufficeth thee, save He who created thee.[26]

The needs and wants of fallen man are countless,

for he pursues one thing after another, and nothing remains permanently with him. So what with his corn and wine and oil, his needs are so multiplied that he cannot find the one thing needful, a single and unchangeable nature, seeking which he would not err, and attaining which he would cease from grief and pain.[27]

By its very nature, this restless covetousness, this avarice, can have no bounds or limits.

Thou didst at first desire a farm; then thou wouldest possess an estate; thou wouldest shut out thy neighbours; having shut them out, thou didst set thy heart on the possessions of other neighbours; and didst extend thy covetous desires till thou hadst reached the shore: arriving at the shore, thou covetest the islands: having made the earth thine own, thou wouldest haply seize upon heaven.[28]

To the men engaged in this fruitless quest for happiness through the satisfaction of an infinite number of desires, constantly changing and unlimited in scope, to these men whom the world regards as men of great judgment and prudence, all means, all devices, for accumulating goods and money are legitimate and praiseworthy.

Like a shrewd man as you are, you leave nothing untried, whereby you may pile coin on coin, and may store it up more carefully in a place of secrecy. You plunder others; you guard against the plunderer; you are afraid lest you should yourself suffer the wrong, that you yourself do; and even what you suffer does not correct you.[29]

Nor is this boundless covetousness limited to the wealthy; it is rare to find an artisan "who does not practice his own art for the purposes of pecuniary gain."[30] Most poor men are not immune from the sins of avarice and cupidity; in their envy of the rich and their bitterness about their poverty, they desire and love temporal goods as much as, if not more than, the wealthy do.

This picture of man's restless striving for material satisfactions reminds us of Hobbes's portrait of natural man, who spends his entire life in the effort to satisfy one desire after another and never attains real repose or enduring satisfaction.[31] And Hobbes's graphic description of the *bellum omnium contra omnes* inevitably comes to mind when Augustine depicts the consequences of the fierce competition for inevitably scarce goods carried on by self-centered men, each one of whom is driven by infinite and insatiable desires. The earthly society is divided against itself and the strongest oppress the others "because all follow after their own interests and lusts, while what is longed for either suffices for none, or not for all, because it is not the very thing."[32] The world, that is, the earthly city, is compared to the bitter, stormy sea, "where men of perverse and depraved appetites have become like fishes devouring one another."[33] Each man, as he pursues his own satisfaction and profit, is ready to inflict loss and injury on every other man. If some men are too timorous to accomplish all the evil they would like to perpetrate, they never cease to hope that misfortune, failure, and even death will visit their enemies in the never-ending, ruthless struggle. And their enemies are all other men, including their relatives, their neighbors, and those whom they call their "friends."

Observe the evil sea, bitter sea, with waves violent, observe with what sort of men it is filled. Who desireth an inheritance except through the death of another? . . . By the fall of others how many men wish to be exalted? How many, in order that they may buy, desire for other men to sell their goods? [34]

In this struggle, success brings no real satisfaction and absolutely no assurance that the desired object can be retained, once it has been acquired by fair means or foul.[35] Hobbes's natural man is never free from worry and anxiety; since he must guard his possessions at every moment in a vain effort to prevent someone else from snatching them from him, he is never able to relax and to enjoy in quiet security what he has come to possess. Augustine's portrait of the condition of earthly men is fundamentally similar and equally striking. "How they mutually oppress, and how they that are able do devour! And when one fish hath devoured, the greater the less, itself also is devoured by some greater." [36] In another passage he varies the figures of speech but presents the same picture:

What then hast thou in hand? Gold. Keep it in hand, therefore: if thou hast it in hand, let it not be taken away without thy consent. But if through gold also thou art carried where thou wishest not, and if a more powerful robber seeketh thee, because he findeth thee a less powerful robber; if a stronger eagle pursue thee, because thou hast carried off a hare before him: the lesser was thy prey, thou wilt be a prey unto the greater. Men see not these things in human affairs: by so much avarice are they blinded.[37]

But at least these men harass and injure each other with the aim of obtaining the goods and money that they regard, however mistakenly, as the highest good. The depth of depravity is reached by those men whose desire to harm others no longer serves as a means to the end of material enrichment, but has become an end in itself. These men pursue wickedness for its own sake with no external advantage in view; they are wantonly and senselessly cruel.[38]

Whether they are more or less cruel or more or less rational in the conduct of this *bellum omnium,* these men of the earthly city are completely selfish and egotistical. A senseless pride is their fundamental vice. Each man, regarding himself and his own satisfaction as the center of the universe, struggles ceaselessly to acquire the objects that he hopes will satisfy his boundless appetites and will bring him happiness. However, the unbridled egoism and insatiable cupidity of earthly men are inevitably self-defeating. In the midst of the clash of conflicting egoisms and cupidities, very little satisfaction, even of material desires, is achieved; in fact, misery, suffering, and frustration are the usual lot of the participants in the conflict. The world in which these men live and struggle, despite its appearance of solidity and reality, is an empty, shadowy realm, far removed from the abode of true happiness and true satisfaction.

For they that have their joys from without sink easily into emptiness and are spilled out on those things that are visible and temporal, and in their starving thoughts they lick their very shadows. If only they would grow weary with their hunger and would say, "Who will show us any good?" And we would answer, and they would hear, "O Lord, the light of thy countenance shines bright upon us." [39]

If selfishness in the form of cupidity, the lust for money and possessions, is the first identifying characteristic of fallen man, his second and equally important quality is what Augustine repeatedly refers to as the passion for domination over other men or the lust for power (*libido dominandi*). This lust for power also has its root in the primal vice of pride, in the revolt against God and the insane desire to "be like God." By nature, man was given power over all other earthly creatures, but no man was given the right to dominate other men. Men were created as equals, and God alone was the superior and the ruler of mankind.[40] But the soul of fallen man, in "a reach of arrogance utterly intolerable," perversely seeks to ape God by aspiring "to lord it even over those who are by nature its equals,—that is, its fellow-men."[41] Actually, he succeeds only in imitating the devil, who was the first to forsake God as a result of his lust for power and his hatred of righteousness. Men imitate the devil

so much the more in proportion as they set their hearts on power, to the neglect or even hatred of righteousness, and as they either rejoice in the attainment of power, or are inflamed by the lust of it. . . . Not that power is to be shunned as though it were something evil; but the order must be preserved, whereby righteousness is before it.[42]

This lust for domination over other men is associated with the love of glory, honor, and fame, which men "with vain elation and pomp of arrogance"[43] seek to achieve by the subjection of others. Like avarice, this desire to exercise power and domination is not confined to a few men, although it is particularly strong in the ambitious and the arrogant; "there is hardly any one who is free from the love of rule, and craves not human glory."[44]

The *libido dominandi* is not completely separate from the *cupiditas* which I have already discussed, since men often use material possessions and wealth as weapons by which to secure or to maintain power over other men, and, conversely, they frequently utilize their power in order to plunder and steal the goods and property they covet. But these two great passions of earthly men are distinguishable; some individuals and some societies exhibit their greatest zeal in amassing wealth and property, while other men and other societies are peculiarly ridden by the lust for power and rule, even to the point of sacrificing material comforts and satisfactions.

As Augustine discusses the *libido dominandi,* we are again reminded of Hobbes's portrait of natural man and his "perpetual and restless desire of power after power, that ceaseth only in death." [45] However, there is a difference between the two thinkers. For Hobbes, man's desire for glory is secondary to his basic impulse—the drive for self-preservation and, therefore, for security—and to the acquisitive impulse which is one of the major vehicles by which this basic drive is satisfied. Augustine, on the other hand, regards the lust for domination and for glory as an independent drive, just as basic to man as cupidity. Naturally, this lust for power intensifies and exacerbates the *bellum omnium* that rages among earthly men. Even if we conjure up a situation in which material goods are so abundant that all the desires of egoistic men can be satisfied without conflict—the situation presumably envisioned by some Utopians—conflict, struggle, and war would not disappear, and the state, the instrument by which conflicts are held down and regulated, would never become unnecessary. For even if all material desires were satisfied, the lust for power and glory would still remain and would continue to drive men into personal and societal struggles and wars. The final irony of the human condition is that the earthly city, though it seeks for mastery and attempts to enslave the nations of the world, "is itself ruled by its lust of rule." [46]

Augustine frequently refers to the Romans as the principal example of a society of men whose master passions were the *libido dominandi* and the desire for glory. The intense zeal of the Romans, especially of the great heroes of the early period, for honor, praise, and glory was, strictly speaking, a vice, since their actions were motivated by a desire to win the applause and good opinions of men, rather than God's blessing or the approval of conscience. But, compared to the vices of the men of other nations or to the avarice, profligacy, and love of luxury characteristic of the Romans in the latter days of the Republic and in the Empire, the patriotic devotion and the love of glory of the ancient Roman heroes were at least quasi-virtuous, and indeed Augustine sometimes describes their qualities as "virtues" or "civic virtues." [47] For the sake of glory and love of their country, these ancient Romans suppressed their inferior egoistic impulses for wealth, material goods, and pleasure. "Glory they most ardently loved: for it they wished to live, for it they did not hesitate to die. Every other desire was repressed by the strength of their passion for that one thing." [48] They even longed for wars so that they might have occasions for displaying their valor and winning renown.

Augustine recalls Virgil's great tribute to the Romans in the *Aeneid, "Hae tibi erunt artes, Romani . . . ,"* [49] in which the poet extols as the Romans' special accomplishment "the arts of ruling and commanding, and of subjugating and vanquishing nations." [50] As a result of their devotion to patriotism, glory, and the love of power, the Romans conquered one city and one nation after another and gradually extended their empire until it included the entire civilized world. The great power and universal sway of this empire were granted to the Romans by God in furtherance of His own purposes and designs.[51] Thereby God demonstrated His justice; the lovers of dominion, power, and glory received their reward. They

despised their own private affairs for the sake of the republic, and for its treasury resisted avarice, consulted for the good of their country with a spirit of freedom, addicted neither to what their laws pronounced to be crime nor to lust. By all these acts, as by the true way, they pressed forward to honours, power, and glory; they were honoured among almost all nations; they imposed the laws of their empire upon many nations; and at this day, both in literature and history, they are glorious among almost all nations.[52]

God purposely granted this unparalleled domination to

such men as, for the sake of honour, and praise, and glory, consulted well for their country, in whose glory they sought their own, and whose safety they did not hesitate to prefer to their own, suppressing the desire of wealth and many other vices for this one vice, namely, the love of praise.[53]

If national pride, military glory, and a consuming zeal for the honor that men can confer have a magnificence that places them far above the ordinary vices of sinful man, they are, for Augustine, still vices. He never forgets the price of glory in misery and suffering, imposed on the bystanders even more than on the struggling "heroes," and he is aware that the lust for domination and for power can lead men to commit atrocious crimes. He reminds us that the fratricide committed by Cain, the founder of the earthly city, was repeated by Romulus, the founder of Rome. Both Romulus and Remus

desired to have the glory of founding the Roman republic, but both could not have as much glory as if one only claimed it; for he who wished to have the glory of ruling would certainly rule less if his power were shared by a living consort. In order, therefore, that the whole glory might be enjoyed by one, his consort was removed; and by this crime the empire was made larger indeed, but inferior, while otherwise it would have been less, but better.[54]

As we shall see when discussing Augustine's teachings about war,[55] he had no inclination to glorify war or military victory or to forget the sufferings and cruelties that are an inevitable part of wars between nations or between groups or classes within a society. His general verdict on the consequences of the lust for glory and power is that "this lust of sovereignty [*libido ista dominandi*] disturbs and consumes the human race with frightful ills." [56]

The worst crimes and atrocities are committed by men who are greedy for domination and power but do not possess that desire for glory that makes one eager to be praised and honored by other men;

he who is a despiser of glory, but is greedy of domination, exceeds the beasts in the vices of cruelty and luxuriousness. Such, indeed, were certain of the Romans, who wanting [i.e., lacking] the love of esteem, wanted not the thirst for domination. . . . But it was Nero Caesar who was the first to reach the summit, and, as it were, the citadel, of this vice; for so great was his luxuriousness, that one would have thought there was nothing manly to be dreaded in him, and such his cruelty, that, had not the contrary been known, no one would have thought there was anything effeminate in his character. [57]

The extent and glory of the Roman empire were intended by God not simply as a reward to the patriotic Romans for their "virtues," but as a reminder to the citizens of the heavenly city of "what a love they owe to the supernal country on account of life eternal, if the terrestrial country was so much beloved by its citizens on account of human glory." [58] When the pilgrims recall what the Romans endured, what great goods they despised, and what desires they suppressed for the sake of human glory and honor, which is "smoke which has no weight," [59] nothing but "empty pride and vanity, and peril of ruin," [60] and for the sake of a transitory earthly empire, they should feel no pride in the good works they may have done or the sufferings they may have endured for the sake of God's glory and His eternal kingdom which they will share. And they should feel ashamed and humbled if they see that the patriotic Romans were willing to do and to suffer more for the glory and grandeur of Rome than they are willing to do for the glory of God's eternal city. [61]

If covetousness and the lust for power are the two primary characteristics of fallen man, his third drive is his sexual lust. Like most of his contemporaries, Christian and non-Christian, Augustine sees little if any positive good in sexual attraction or in sexual activity. If some twentieth-century writers place so high a value upon satisfying sexual relationships that they sometimes seem to view sexual fulfillment as *the* end of human life, many of the early Christians, as well as the neo-Platonists, Gnostics, and Manichaeans, saw sexual activity as utterly evil and degrading and the sexual impulse as something to be repressed and excised if happiness or salvation was to be achieved. Augustine's attitude toward sex is undoubtedly negative, and at times he seems to be morbidly preoccupied with the subject.[62] But his denunciations of lust and concupiscence and his praise of chastity are not marked by the coldness and the resentment of other people's pleasures that frequently are so evident in the ascetic. His sexual career before his conversion had been extended and turbulent; so when he speaks of the violence of sexual emotions and of the misery that fills the life of the man whose sexual appetite is an overpowering force, it is clear that his thoughts are based upon his experiences and his memories of the bondage to lust, and not upon frustration or envy.

In any case, Augustine's asceticism is far less extreme than that of many of his contemporaries, for whom all sexual activity was completely sinful. His treatises on marriage and concupiscence— such as the *De Bono Coniugali,* the *De Virginitate,* and the *De Nuptiis et Concupiscentia*—make it plain that while virginity in God's service is the highest state, marriage and bearing children are morally good, provided only that concupiscence is restrained and sexual activity is engaged in only for the purpose of generating offspring.[63] He follows St. Paul in the concession that sexual intercourse between husband and wife, even if it is not strictly limited to the purpose of procreation, is permissible, although such sexual activity is not a good, and indeed is a sin. However, it is less sinful than adultery. And this might well follow if either of the marriage partners insisted, without the other's consent, upon a strict limitation of sexual activity to the "proper" purpose of conception.[64]

Augustine discusses at length the question of how sexual intercourse was carried on without lust or concupiscence before the Fall; the sexual members operated under the control of the will, and without resistance to it, as our hands and feet now move.[65] One of the punishments for man's disobedience to God was concupiscence or lust; his sexual members are now moved by lust and not by will. While our other bodily organs are within our power,

when it must come to man's great function of the procreation of children, the members which were expressly created for this purpose will not obey the direction of the will, but lust has to be waited for to set these members in motion, as if it had legal right over them, and sometimes it refuses to act when the mind wills, while often it acts against its will! Must not this bring the blush of shame over the freedom of the human will, that by its contempt of God, its own Commander, it has lost all proper command for itself over its own members? [66]

This domination of lust over the soul rages in the earthly man, who has not been redeemed by God's grace and aided to achieve chastity or continence in marriage.[67] Although lust and concupiscence are never completely eradicated while a man still lives in this world,[68] the good man does not allow these passions to gain control over his actions, but restrains and checks them by the bridle of reason.

In earthly men, however, lust is an ever-present drive, which leads those ensnared by it into immoralities and evils of every kind—adultery, promiscuity, abnormal sexual practices, bestiality.

Some earthly men are dominated by their sexual appetites; others restrain or limit their lust in order to further their pursuit of economic goods or of power and glory. Compared to the lover of glory, or the "economic man," the sexual profligate is the most degraded of men and the most miserable; his satisfactions are brief and violent, while his frustrations and sufferings never cease. As we have seen, concupiscence and the disobedience of the sexual impulse to the control of the will and of reason are the consequence and punishment of Adam's original sin of disobedience to God's commands; they do not, as some moderns seem to think, constitute the original sin.[69] Augustine does, however, link the transmission of original sin to all of Adam's descendants with the fact that every child born after the Fall, with the sole exception of Christ, who was immaculately conceived in the Virgin Mary by the operation of the Holy Spirit, is conceived in sin, that is, no child can be conceived without the operations of lust and concupiscence, even if his parents are among the redeemed.[70]

Augustine's picture of fallen man, ridden by avarice, lust for power, and sexual desire, is a somber and pessimistic portrait, which calls to mind the views of human nature expressed by his followers at the time of the Reformation, Luther and Calvin, and by Machiavelli and Hobbes. Augustine's grim realism about human nature is not modified or softened when he considers the behavior of new-born infants; there is no romantic coloring in his picture of the "innocent" child. In the *Confessions,* he gives us a vivid description of the young child's sense of frustration at his inability to communicate his desires to those around him, except by crying and by the unclear and feeble gestures of moving his arms and legs. With no trace of sentimentality he notes that, as an infant, he, like every other human being, desired immediate satisfaction of all his wants, and reacted with frustration, rage, and aggression to his inability to compel others to minister to his desires and to be subject to his *libido dominandi;*

and when I was not obeyed—either because I was not understood or because what I wanted was not good for me—I became indignant with my elders for not submitting to me, with those who were not my slaves for not serving me; and I avenged myself on them by crying. That infants are like this, I have myself been able to learn by watching them.[71]

A few paragraphs later he returns to this theme of the willfullness and jealousy of infants and their hostility toward those who will not gratify and obey their every whim and impulse. In a shattering phrase, he destroys the myth of the "innocence" and "purity" of the young child: "Thus, the infant's innocence lies in the weakness of his body and not in the infant mind." [72] He continues:

Nor was it good, even in that time, to strive to get by crying what, if it had been given me, would have been hurtful; or to be bitterly indignant at those who, because they were older—not slaves, either, but free—and wiser than I, would not indulge my capricious desires. Was it a good thing for me to try, by struggling as hard as I could, to harm them for not obeying me, even when it would have done me harm to have been obeyed? . . . I have myself observed a baby to be jealous, although it could not speak; it was livid as it watched another infant at the breast.[73]

Thus, the basic sinfulness of man is evident even in the infant who has just emerged from the womb; it is not simply a consequence of "bad environment" or "inadequate training." And "sinfulness" here means what it always means for Augustine— total egoism and self-centeredness, regarding oneself as the center of the universe. From this basic "sin" of unbounded egoism follow the sins of cupidity, the unlimited desire for material and sensual gratifications, the lust to dominate all other men, and the desire to injure anyone who refuses, even for our own good, to accept the role of a means or instrument for the satisfaction of our momentary and capricious desires.[74]

Nor is Augustine any more sentimental or idealistic when he discusses the attitudes and actions of typical parents. Parents and teachers punish children for their failure to "work" and for their desire to escape from lessons and chores and to spend their time at play. But these same grownups devote themselves to play and idling, which, however, they call "business."

> But the idling of our elders is called business; the idling of boys, though quite like it, is punished by those same elders, and no one pities either the boys or the men. For will any common sense observer agree that I was rightly punished as a boy for playing ball— just because this hindered me from learning more quickly those lessons by means of which, as a man, I could play at more shameful games? And did he by whom I was beaten do anything different? When he was worsted in some small controversy with a fellow teacher, he was more tormented by anger and envy than I was when beaten by a playmate in the ball game.[75]

Only those parents who have by God's grace been "converted" from this universal human self-centeredness and self-deification to a new life, based upon God as its center and focus, do not treat their children in this way—that is, as means to their own self-satisfaction. But such men and such parents are few and far between; the true Christian is a rare specimen. All children are born sinful and egoistic, and most of them have sinful parents who teach their impressionable offspring, by example even more than by precept, to become even more avaricious, vainglorious, and lustful. Even the infant who is born predestined to be saved and to become a citizen of the City of God,

> but meanwhile a prisoner for a time, when learneth he to love ought, save what his parents have whispered into his ears? They teach him and train him in avarice, robbery, daily lying, the worship of divers idols and devils, the unlawful remedies of enchantments and amulets. What shall one yet an infant do, a tender soul, observing what its

elders do, save follow that which it seeth them doing. Babylon then has persecuted us when little, but God hath given us when grown up knowledge of ourselves, that we should not follow the errors of our parents.[76]

It is no wonder, then, that

Boys when born speak somewhat like this to their parents: "Now then, begin to think of removing hence, let us too play our parts on the stage." For the whole life of temptation in the human race is a stage play; for it is said, "Every man living is altogether vanity."[77]

The outline I have given of Augustine's discussions of the psychology of fallen man has dealt only with his essential attributes—self-love, cupidity, love of power and glory, and concupiscence. I have not referred to Augustine's many other analyses of human nature, such as his extraordinarily subtle discussion of memory in the *Confessions*[78] or his intricate analyses of the relations among memory, understanding, and the will and of the analogies between those relations and the relations among the persons of the Trinity.[79] These discussions have been omitted, fascinating though they often are, because the psychological questions treated in them bear little direct relation to our main interest, the analysis of men's social, economic, and political activities and institutions.

Any thinker who, like Augustine, sees man as essentially selfish, avaricious, ambitious for power and glory, and lustful, cannot possibly be a cheerful optimist when he surveys the world and the human activities that go on in it. I have already noted the similarities between the Augustinian and Hobbesian analyses of man's fundamental drives, as well as the agreement between Augustine and Hobbes about the ruthless and never-ceasing conflict that is the natural consequence of the clashing appetites and ambitions of these self-centered men. Let us now go on to sketch in greater detail Augustine's grimly pessimistic picture of the evils and sufferings that inevitably mark the lives of men as they live, work, struggle, and die in this world.

When he tells us, as he often does, that the world is evil, miserable, or wretched, he is referring to the world of men and their actions and passions and not to the world of nature, the physical universe.

The world is evil, lo, it is evil, and yet it is loved as though it were good. But what is this evil world? For the heavens and the earth and the waters, and the things that are therein, the fish, and birds, and trees, are not evil. All these are good: but it is evil men who make this evil world.[80]

The world of nature is a good world, created by a perfectly good God; since material bodies and animal or human flesh are not *per se* evil, the neo-Platonists and such Christian Platonists as Origen are wrong when they say that the world was created in order to restrain and punish evil, and that bodies of all kinds are the prison-houses of souls which have committed sins of various kinds.[81] It is the human world, the world of men's misdirected wills, that is the world of sin, and as a consequence of sin life upon this earth has become penal and wretched. By God's "profound and just judgment" the life of demons and men, the two classes of sinners, "the one in the air, the other on earth, is filled with misery, calamities, and mistakes."[82]

Even for the saints this life is a time of sorrow and suffering. They must live among and suffer the persecutions of the unregenerate, and they share with the wicked the burdens and sufferings of mortality, sickness, ignorance, and temptation. Even in this world the redeemed possess a kind of felicity of which the damned have no knowledge or experience, but it is a felicity enjoyed in hope rather than in present actuality.[83] Real happiness will be the portion of the saints only after the corruptible body, death, and sin have passed away, and when eternal felicity in an incorruptible body is granted to them by God.[84] This world is "the land of the dead"; this life is "this hell upon earth." [85] For the wicked, the evils and misery of this life are the first installment of their punishment, to be continued after the resurrection in eternal punishment. For the good, the ills and sufferings of earthly existence are the just punishment for their sins, and a trial and test of their faith and of their virtues.[86]

In the land of the dead is labour, grief, fear, tribulation, temptation, groaning, sighing; here are false happy ones, true unhappy, because happiness is false, misery is true. But he that owneth himself to be in true misery, will also be in true happiness: and yet now because thou art miserable, hear the Lord saying, "Blessed are they that mourn." [87]

In this earthly life "there is but false pleasure, no security of joy, a tormenting fear, a greedy covetousness, a withering sadness." [88]

At the root of all the cruel ills that fill this life are the profound *ignorance* and *error* in which fallen men are engulfed, and the "*misplaced love* which is born with every son of Adam," the "love of many vain and hurtful things" and the failure to love the supremely good and completely satisfying Being, God.[89] This life is "so readily subject to vanity that we judge the false for true, reject the true for the false, and hold as uncertain what is actually certain." [90] Since men fix their love on other human beings, material goods, and earthly glory, all of which are mutable, insubstantial, and transitory, they inevitably suffer the pains of loss and disappointment—bereavement, losses, fraud, falsehood, false suspicions, and all the crimes and wicked deeds of other men.[91]

This is the infelicity of men; that for which they sin, they leave here when they die, and the sin themselves they carry with them. Thou dost sin for money, it must be left here; or for a country seat; it must be left here: or for some woman's sake; she must be left here, and whatsoever it be for which thou dost sin, when thou shalt have closed thine eyes in death, thou must leave it here; yet the sin itself which thou committest, thou carriest with thee.[92]

Every human society from the family to the empire is never free from slights, suspicions, quarrels, and war, and "peace" is not true peace but a doubtful interlude between conflicts. Treachery and deceit are found even within the family, and the larger social unit, the city, is filled with lawsuits and never free from the fear of insurrections and civil wars.[93] Our bodies are constantly a prey to sickness, physical and mental, accidents, and death. Even when we are asleep, our "repose" is sometimes disturbed by terrifying dreams and visions.[94] We never know at what moment disaster or tragedy may strike, even in the midst of what we call health, prosperity, and well-being. "What man can go out of his own house without being exposed on all hands to unforeseen accidents? Returning home sound in limb, he slips on his own door-step, breaks his leg, and never recovers." [95] A clear testimony to the miseries and the ills of this life is furnished by the very virtues which we strive to attain and which we regard so highly; the virtue of temperance is the instrument by which we wage war against our lusts, while prudence, justice, and fortitude are valued precisely because they help us to endure and to struggle against the violence of life's dangers and woes.[96] And the most terrible proof of the evils of human life is the fact that many men are so overwhelmed by them that they commit suicide, in spite of "the first and strongest demand of nature"— self-preservation and the avoidance of death in every possible way.[97]

Men in one generation after another pay the penalty for sin— never-ceasing temptations, sufferings, sickness, disappointments, anxieties, and the omnipresent fear of death.[98] Perhaps the saddest aspect of the human condition is that these miserable human beings are virtually "windowless monads," deprived even of the consolation of mutual understanding and sympathy in their wretched plight. Each of us is profoundly ignorant of the true character and motives of all other men. Each man knows himself far better than he can ever know anyone else, since, by introspection, he can obtain some idea of his own thoughts, desires, and goals. When we attempt to find out what others are thinking or feeling or wishing for, we have only their words and actions to go by, and so we are frequently mistaken in our opinions and judgments. "For what is so common to man as inability to inspect the heart of man; and therefore, instead of scrutinizing its inmost recesses, to suspect for the most part something very different from what is going on therein?" [99] The moral that Augustine draws is certainly a sound one:

And although in these dark regions of human realities, that is, of other people's inward thoughts, we cannot clear up our suspicions, because we are only men, yet we ought to restrain our judgments, that is, all definite and fixed opinions, and not judge anything before the time, until the Lord come, and bring to light the hidden things of darkness, and make manifest the counsels of the hearts; and then shall every man have praise of God. [100]

One of the most tragic consequences of this inability to read the true thoughts and feelings of other men is the precariousness of the great boon of friendship. We may believe that someone is a true friend, but we often find that our judgment has been faulty. Since we do not know how we ourselves will behave or feel tomorrow, we can have even less confidence in our knowledge of another person's character. [101] "The unfeigned confidence and mutual love of true and good friends" is "our one solace in human society, filled as it is with misunderstandings and calamities," and yet "in our present wretched condition we frequently mistake a friend for an enemy, and an enemy for a friend." [102] Moreover, the friends that we do have are a source of anxieties and fears as well as of solace; we not only fear that they may suffer from disease, famine, war, captivity, slavery, or death and are saddened when any of these evils actually afflicts them, but "we are also affected with the much more painful dread that their friendship may be changed into perfidy, malice, and injustice." [103]

Yet even in the depths of the misery of human life in this world, God has not completely abandoned the fallen human race. He fills our very misery with "rich and countless blessings"— the blessing of fertility, the constantly renewed gift of newly formed human beings, in whom body and soul are wonderfully joined together, the gift of the mind in which reason and understanding are inherent, the moral virtues and the astonishing practical arts and contrivances that are the fruit of human reason, the utility and beauty of man's body and of his senses and organs, and, finally, the beauty and utility of the rest of creation, sky, earth, and sea, "which the divine goodness has given to man to please his eye and serve his purposes, condemned though he is, and hurled into these labours and miseries." And "all these are but the solace of the wretched and condemned, not the rewards of the blessed. What then shall these rewards be, if such be the blessings of a condemned state?" [104]

The days that we spend on this earth are full of suffering and misery, and they are but passing shadows that have no true reality;

they are gone almost before they arrive; and when they are come, they cannot continue; they press upon one another, they follow the one the other, and cannot check themselves in their course. Of the past nothing is called back again; what is yet to be, is expected as something to pass away again: it is not as yet possessed, whilst as yet it is not arrived; it cannot be kept when once it has arrived. [105]

Although we all cry out that the days of our earthly lives are evil days, the final irony is that "no one is willing to end these same evil days, and hence men earnestly pray God that they may live long. Yet what is it to live long, but to be long tormented? What is it to live long, but to add evil days to evil days?" [106] Amidst all our anxieties and perplexities death is the only certainty, and we fear death more than any of the other evils and woes that we face. All the goods that we value are precarious, all our hopes and aspirations are doubtful;

whichever way you turn, all is uncertain, death alone is certain. . . . Amidst these uncertainties, where death alone is certain, while even of that the hour is uncertain, and while it alone is studiously guarded against, though at the same time it is in no way to be escaped, "every man living disquieteth himself in vain." [107]

Men dread to come to the end of this life, despite its troubles and misery; they love this life where they labor incessantly and suffer numberless evils, and which they know must come to an end sooner or later.[108] For the sake of prolonging this wretched life for a few days or weeks, men will sacrifice everything that they most love—wealth, honor, and reputation—and they will submit to great pain and suffering. When Rome was being laid waste by the barbarian invaders, "how many lovers of this temporal life gave everything they had been saving for the pleasure and adornment of life, not to mention its support and protection, in order to ransom it and to prolong its hapless and destitute existence!" [109]

Yet death is the common lot of all who are born; the most striking mark of the weakness of sinful man is that he cannot even live, let alone live as he wishes. "He wishes to live, he is compelled to die." [110] The moment a man is born he moves inexorably toward death; "our whole life is nothing but a race towards death," [111] and the only thing of which we can be certain is that we are at each moment one step closer to the inevitable end. And although we regard death as the greatest evil and vainly try every expedient to postpone its advent, we are so conscious of the

sufferings of this life that we would prefer to die rather than to
be born again as infants and repeat the whole experience. Augustine notes how appropriate it is that the infant weeps as he
comes into this world. "Our infancy, indeed, introducing us to
this life not with laughter but with tears, seems unconsciously to
predict the ills we are to encounter." [112]

Certainly no one would accuse Augustine of being idealistic
or romantic in his view of the human condition. His picture of
man's life on this earth is a somber one; life is indeed a hell on
earth, filled with suffering, sorrow, disappointment, strife, and
bitterness, and ended by death. Yet there is a difference between
the pessimism of Augustine and the sense of despair and futility
that marks so much of pagan philosophy in its later stages—Stoi-
cism, Epicureanism, neo-Platonism, Gnosticism. Augustine's pessimism is based upon a frighteningly clear-sighted realism about
men and their behavior. His dark portrait of human life has a
solid, factual quality that is vastly different from the sense of
weariness and decadence that marks the writings of the non-
Christian pessimist or the warped, bitter tone, often approaching
hatred and disgust for man and all his works, so often found
during the fourth and fifth centuries in the ascetic advocates of
flight from the world.[113]

Moreover, Augustine's pessimism and despair are not ultimate.
Men have been, are, and will always be as he describes them, and
misery and suffering will fill the world until the end of time. But
this is not the whole story. The evils and suffering of this life
are grimly real, but they are meaningful. The surest proof that
earthly miseries and calamities have a purpose and are not simply
the strokes of blind fortune is that God has foretold them and in
the Scriptures has warned men that sin and suffering will increase as the world moves toward its predestined end.[114] God has
also taught us that the sorrow and pain of earthly life, when seen

in their proper context, are the means by which the ultimate triumph of good is being accomplished. At least for the true Christian, the end of the drama is not death or futility, but the perfect peace and felicity of eternal life with God. Sufferings and temptations are an absolutely necessary element in the earthly life of the pilgrim who seeks to reach the heavenly city. Without the experience of strife, pain, and temptation, there can be no advance in self-knowledge, no development of spiritual and moral strength. "And, for the most part, the human mind cannot attain to self-knowledge otherwise than by making trial of its powers through temptation, by some kind of experimental and not merely verbal self-interrogation." [115]

For our life in this sojourning cannot be without temptation: because our advance is made through our temptation, nor does a man become known to himself unless tempted, nor can he be crowned except he shall have conquered, nor can he conquer except he shall have striven, nor can he strive except he shall have experienced an enemy, and temptations.[116]

The same experience of suffering or sorrow that destroys or embitters one man may be a means of furthering the growth or deepening the knowledge or compassion of another man.

Life is not "a tale told by an idiot"; no human action, no matter how cruel or wicked or lustful it may be, falls outside the control of God's Providence. God does not force men to sin or to commit evil deeds, but even the sinner is not permitted to do anything that runs counter to God's immutable will for the universe that He has created.

God willeth not that thou shouldest sin; for He forbiddeth it: yet if thou hast sinned, imagine not that the man hath done what he willed, and that hath happened to God which He willed not. . . . Thus whatever choice thou hast made, the Almighty will not be at a loss to fulfil His will concerning thee.[117]

Just as the entire natural world is ordered by God's wisdom, so the realm of human affairs is completely governed by His Providence, no matter how disordered and unjust events may seem to us as we observe them with our feeble, myopic vision.

For all men are ordered in their proper places; but to every man it seems as though they have no order. Do thou only look to what thou wouldest wish to be; for as thou shalt wish to be, the Master knoweth where to place thee. . . . [T]ake no care where He may order thee who cannot err, He knoweth where to place thee.[118]

All earthly goods, including possessions, wealth, honor, glory, and power, are under God's control. He gives them to, and takes them away from, evil men as well as good men, in furtherance of His unshakable purposes and designs, which we know only in part. But we do know that since God is perfectly good and just, everything that He does or permits men to do is part of a plan which is good and just; "a good man wills only what is commanded, and a bad man can do only what he is permitted, at the same time that he is punished for what he wills to do unjustly." [119] This absolute confidence in the universal dominion of God's Providence and in the justice and goodness of God is the ground for Augustine's ultimate optimism, which is the bedrock that lies beneath his realistic, pessimistic analysis of human nature and human conduct. It is this belief in the omnipotence and goodness of the God who rules the affairs of men that gives to his thought a positive, dynamic quality, a sense that there is meaning and purpose in history, that is far removed from the world-weariness and negativism that characterize so many of the writings of his period.

One of his favorite examples of God's Providence operating to control the actions of evil men as well as of the good is His granting temporal power and earthly rule to good and bad men and to various nations. It is God alone who has power to give kingship or domination over other peoples or to remove it; He gives and takes away temporal power according to His hidden counsel. The gift of power is not necessarily a blessing, nor is it inevitably a curse, and its removal does not make the man who loses it more or less blessed.[120] Even the most wicked, cruel, and tyrannical rulers receive their power from God alone; as we shall see,[121] this view has direct consequences for Augustine's doctrine that subjects owe complete obedience to their rulers. Repeatedly, he cites his favorite scriptural texts—"For there is no power but of God," "Who maketh to reign a man that is a hypocrite, on account of the perversity of the people," "Through me kings reign and tyrants hold the land through me," and "I gave them a king in my wrath"[122]—to show that even wicked rulers receive their power from God. Their tyranny and cruelty are a scourge to the evildoers and to the wicked, and a trial and a proof of the patience of the good.[123] After describing the extreme cruelty and depravity of the Emperor Nero,[124] Augustine concludes: "Nevertheless power and domination are not given even to such men save by the providence of the most high God, when He judges that the state of human affairs is worthy of such lords."[125] God's motives in giving power to one man or another, or in taking it away, or in assigning dominion to one nation or another, may be hidden from us, but we know that they are never unjust.[126]

When a country is overrun by invaders and is conquered by them, the motives of the conquerors may be only greed and the desire for empire; for their sins they, and they alone, are responsible, and, sooner or later, in this world or in the next, they are suitably punished for them. Nevertheless, through their wicked deeds God accomplishes what He wishes to perform— the chastisement of the wicked in the devastated country and a trial of the fortitude and fidelity of the good.[127] Inasmuch as every action, from the humblest to the most exalted, is "caused" both by men's wills, good or evil, and by God's Providence, each event can be analyzed from either of these perspectives. "He does even concerning the wills themselves of men what He will, when He will. . . . He has the wills of men more in His power than they themselves have. . . ." [128] In order to demonstrate that sacrifices to pagan deities were of no avail in preserving or securing earthly kingdoms, God brought about the defeat of the pagan Goth, Radagaisus, who attempted to capture Rome in 406, while four years later He allowed Alaric and his Visigoths, who were Arians and not Catholics and yet were hostile to pagan idols, to take Rome.[129] Perhaps the most striking example of Augustine's absolute confidence in Divine Providence is his statement that even the persecutors of the martyrs received their power from God, since the unintended consequences of their persecutions were the testing and correction of the righteous and the punishment of the wicked.[130]

When the ultimate problem of evil is raised—Why did God create angels and men who, as He foreknew, would sin and would have to be punished by countless miseries?—Augustine clings to his belief in God's perfect goodness and justice and stresses man's inability to see the entire design of Providence of which his life and his era form only a small part. He is aware that the faith of the weak believer is frequently shaken by the knowledge that in this world the wicked often flourish and the good suffer.

For thou regardest thy few days, and in thy few days thou dost wish all things to be fulfilled. What things? The condemnation of all the wicked: and the crowning of all the good: dost thou wish these things to be fulfilled in thy days? God fulfilleth them in His own time. Why dost thou suffer weariness? He is eternal: He waiteth: He is of long suffering.[131]

In addition, he uses the aesthetic argument that the wickedness of sinners serves the function of setting off and highlighting the good in the world. God knew how He would use the actions of sinful man on behalf of the good, and by this "opposition of contraries" the "beauty of the course of this world is achieved" and the course of the ages embellished, "as it were an exquisite poem set off with antitheses." [132]

Augustine's doctrine of Providence—God's unchanging plan for the universe and His unceasing activity in the affairs of men and societies—provides the framework for his conception of history. History is no longer viewed, as it was by many of the pagans, especially in late antiquity, as a series of recurring cycles, in which nothing of real novelty ever takes place, and where each final phase leads only to another round of the same cyclical pattern. As we have seen,[133] the Christian view of the history of the world is that it is a straight-line development, with a beginning, a climax, and an end, in which radical novelties, such as the Incarnation and the Crucifixion, take place and from which recurrent cyclical patterns are absent.[134] Augustine believes that the age of the world is less than six thousand years,[135] and that human history is divided into six ages or periods—the first, from Adam to Noah; the second, from Noah to Abraham; the third, from Abraham to David; the fourth, from David to the captivity in Babylon; the fifth, from the captivity to John the Baptist and the birth of Christ; and the sixth and last, the present age, from Christ's birth to "the hidden end of time." [136]

If we confine our attention only to the history of this world and do not look beyond it to the future kingdom of God's saints, we cannot call Augustine a believer in historical progress. In fact, he shares the view of the early Church that sin, error, and evil will increase as the world draws to its close. "As the end of the world approaches, errors increase, terrors multiply, iniquity increases, infidelity increases; the light, in short . . . is very often extinguished; this darkness of enmity between brethren increases, daily increases, and Jesus is not yet come." [137] At the end of the world, when the predicted reign of Antichrist will take place, the Church and her true children will suffer the most violent persecutions and tribulations that have ever been seen. In this period, which will last three years and six months,[138] the devil and his angels will be unbound and will wage a furious struggle against the saints until Christ comes again in glory to conquer the satanic hosts.[139] However, this period of unexampled trial and suffering for the Church does not necessarily mean that the earthly city, the persecutor, will be wracked by great wars and calamities in the last days of the world. For the wicked, the last hour may well be a time of prosperity and rejoicing, a feast suddenly interrupted by the triumphal return of the avenging and judging Christ.[140]

Although Augustine believes that certain events, such as the persecution of the Church by Antichrist and the reappearance on earth of the prophet Elias, who will bring the Jews to faith in Christ,[141] will signalize the end of the world, he denies that anyone can definitely state how many periods of persecution the Church will have to undergo, or the time of the final persecution.[142] Above all, no one is able to predict when the end of the world will take place, or to say that the calamities and sufferings of the present days indicate that the end of the world is imminent.[143] When we recall the despair and alarm felt throughout the civilized world when Rome fell to the barbarians, and the widespread belief that these disasters betokened the final apocalypse, we see that Augustine's unwillingness to assert that the last day was at hand or that it would soon arrive is striking testimony to his awareness of previous crises in human history and to his robust common sense.[144]

Like all good Christians, he naturally hopes that the day of the Lord is imminent, but he warns against disregarding Christ's teaching—"It is not for you to know the times or the seasons, which the Father hath put in his own power"[145]—and attempting to fix a date for the end of the world. Although it is safer to believe those who say that the Lord's coming will be delayed than those who say that it will soon take place, the safest position is to admit that we do not know which of these two views is correct.[146] He reminds one of his fellow bishops that St. Paul did not want his followers

to put their faith in those from whom they heard that the day of the Lord was at hand, lest, perhaps, when the time had passed within which they had thought He would come, and they saw that He had not come, they might think the other promises made to them were also false, and might despair of the mercy of faith itself.[147]

In the same letter he also observes that the present evils and disasters, which are thought to be ultimate and unprecedented and therefore to betoken the coming of Christ, are common to both kingdoms, that of Christ and that of the Devil, and afflict both good and bad, whereas the reign of Antichrist will be marked by the sufferings of the good and the seeming prosperity and security of the wicked.[148]

Augustine is not even willing to concede that the Roman Empire has finally collapsed; the city of Rome has fallen and the Empire is gravely menaced, but it may again be restored.[149]

Perhaps Rome is not perishing; perhaps she is only scourged, not utterly destroyed; perhaps she is chastened, not brought to nought. It may be so; Rome will not perish, if the Romans do not perish. And perish they will not if they praise God; perish they will if they blaspheme Him. For what is Rome, but the Romans?[150]

Of course, the world and everything in it, whether made by God or by man, will one day be destroyed, and "man himself, the city's ornament, man himself, the city's inhabitant, ruler, governor, comes on this condition that he may go, is born on this condition that he may die. . . ."[151] Every earthly kingdom or city perishes, and only Christ's heavenly kingdom is eternal. Each state has the life allotted to it by God, and then passes away; [152] so "what wonder then if some time or other there should be an end of a single city? And yet peradventure the city's end is not come now; yet some time or other come it will." [153]

Like St. Jerome and many others, Augustine is deeply moved by the fall of the world's greatest city, but his deepest sorrow is that many of the Romans have not profited from God's merciful scourging; indeed, they blame Christianity and the abandonment of pagan rites for the fall of Rome and for the other disasters that the Empire is suffering. While the whole world mourns for the calamity that has overtaken Rome, the Romans have remained unchastened and profligate. [154] In Carthage, many of the refugees from Rome flock to the theaters.

To those who murmur against God and His Church on account of the tribulations of the period, saying, "See, all things are perishing in Christian times," and who fail to see that God mingles "bitternesses with the felicities of earth" so that men may not love them but may seek for true felicity, Augustine replies: "What complaint is this! God hath not promised me that these things shall not perish; Christ hath not promised me this. The Eternal hath promised things eternal: if I believe, from a mortal, I shall be made eternal." [155]

Bad times! troublesome times! this men are saying. Let our lives be good; and the times are good. We make our times; such as we are, such are the times. . . . Wherefore are we sad, and blame we God? Evils abound in the world, in order that the world may not engage our love. Great men, faithful saints were they who have despised the world with all its attractions; we are not able to despise it even disfigured as it is. The world is evil, lo, it is evil, and yet it is loved as though it were good. [156]

In any case, the world is more dangerous to us in prosperity than in adversity, "in pleasant than in painful hours, and is to be guarded against more when it allures us to love it than when it warns and constrains us to despise it." [157]

Although Augustine refuses to predict the date of the end of the world and warns against seeing the calamities of his own period as certain signs that the last day is imminent, he shares with most of the early Christians the belief that Christ's coming initiated the last age of the world's history and that the world is growing old.[158] Five of the six epochs of human history were already completed when Christ was born, and in this final age, to which we cannot assign a fixed term of years, He "gradually withdraws His own people from a world that is corrupted by these vices, and is falling into ruins, to make of them an eternal city. . . ." [159] Christ was sent "in the world's old age."

Wonderest thou that the world is failing? Wonder that the world is grown old. It is as a man who is born, and grows up, and waxes old. There are many complaints in old age; the cough, the rheum, the weakness of the eyes, fretfulness, and weariness. So then as when a man is old; he is full of complaints; so is the world old; and is full of troubles. Is it a little thing that God hath done for thee, in that in the world's old age, He hath sent Christ unto thee, that He may renew thee then, when all is failing? . . . As a made, created, perishing thing, the world was now declining to its fall. It could not but be that it should abound in troubles; He came both to console thee in the midst of present troubles, and to promise thee everlasting rest. Choose not then to cleave to this aged world, and to be unwilling to grow young in Christ. . . .[160]

There is now no excuse for the Christian who still loves the world,

broken down as it is by such destruction that it has lost even the semblance of attraction. Those who disdained success, when everything in the world succeeded, deserve praise and commendation, but, in equal measure, those who delight in death, when the world is falling to ruin, are worthy of blame and censure.[161]

"When the world's day is drawing near its close, and the approaching consummation is heralded by the calamities which exhaust its energies," the true Christian, sensing the fulfillment of the prophecy that "heaven and earth shall pass away," should "only expect with increased confidence the everlasting blessedness of the heavenly city." [162] Just as men leave their homes and seek a more secure abode when the shaking of the walls indicates that the ruin of the house is at hand,

so ought Christians, the more that they perceive, from the increasing frequency of their afflictions, that the destruction of this world is at hand, to be the more prompt and active in transferring to the treasury of heaven the goods which they were proposing to store up on earth, in order that, if any accident common to the lot of men occur, he may rejoice who has escaped from a dwelling doomed to ruin; and if, on the other hand, nothing of this kind happen, he may be exempt from painful solicitude who, die when he may, has committed his possessions to the keeping of the ever-living Lord, to whom he is about to go. [163]

In the last two years of his life, Augustine saw the Arian Vandals under Genseric cross over from Spain and overrun his own province of Africa. When he died on August 28, 430, his own city of Hippo was under siege by the Vandals, who destroyed it not long after. The fall of Africa was to him a bitter blow, even more bitter than the fall of Rome, and he could not restrain his grief, although he still believed that God was good and just and that Africa's great calamities were the result of men's own sins. [164] In several letters written during the last two years of his life, he urges the clergy not to abandon their people and seek safety for themselves as the barbarians advance.

When, however, the danger of all, bishops, clergy, and laity, is alike, let not those who depend upon the aid of others be deserted by those on whom they depend. In that case, either let all remove together to fortified places, or let those who must remain be not deserted by those through whom in things pertaining to the Church their necessities must be provided for, and so let them share life in common, or share in common that which the Father of their family appoints them to suffer. [165]

In spite of his advanced age and his infirmity, Augustine practiced what he preached, and remained with his clergy and his people until he died.

About eleven months after Augustine's death, famine forced the Vandals to raise the siege of Hippo, which had lasted for fourteen months. Although they returned not long after and destroyed the city by fire, most of the inhabitants were able to escape during the brief period of respite. Since Hippo was only about a mile from the sea, they were able to reach the coast and thus escape to Italy.[166] During the long siege, the people of Hippo had frequently called upon the spirit of their dead Bishop to save them from the Vandals, and so it is not surprising that they attributed their escape to his intercession.

CHAPTER III

MORALITY AND JUSTICE, NATURAL

AND REMEDIAL

Despite its emphasis upon the individual soul and the unique relation between each soul and God, Christianity has also insisted, from the beginning, that man is naturally and inherently a social being. The *ecclesia* itself is regarded as a fellowship or society of believers, and the world outside the church is viewed as a community of sinners. The essence of Augustine's conception of two cities or two societies—the heavenly city and the earthly city—is found in the Christian tradition at least as far back as St. Paul.[1]

Augustine follows this traditional Christian doctrine that society and social life are natural to mankind, and hence are to be sharply distinguished from the state and the political and legal order. As we shall see,[2] the latter are not natural, but are remedial institutions ordained by God after the Fall in order to deal with the changed condition of sinful man. Even before the Fall, however, God intended man to be a social creature. As soon as He had created Adam, He saw that it was not good for man to be alone; He therefore formed Eve as a wife and companion for him. This bond between husband and wife, later extended to include their children, is the primary "natural bond of human society."[3] In addition, men are endowed with a great natural good, the power of friendship; by nature they are sociable beings who are inclined to love their fellow men. On several occasions

Augustine notes that God created one single man, Adam, as the source of the human race so that in this way men might learn how highly the unity of society and the bond of concord among men should be valued. "God willed to create all men out of one, in order that they might be held in their society not only by likeness of kind, but also by bond of kindred." [4] In any case, whether men love or hate their fellows, it is impossible for any man to avoid human society.

Wherever thou shalt be, there will gather them together other men, the desert with thee they will seek, will attach themselves to thy life, thou canst not thrust back the society of brethren. . . . For thou wilt not be able to be separated from mankind, so long as among men thou livest. [5]

Human sociability and friendship extend—or, rather, should extend—to the entire human race. The fact that every man is endowed with reason makes all men kin. So, when we are commanded to love our neighbor as ourselves, we are meant to apply this injunction to all men, and not simply to our relatives or friends. "There is accordingly no one in the whole human family to whom kindly affection is not due by reason of the bond of a common humanity, although it may not be due on the ground of reciprocal love. . . ." [6] Love and kindly affection are due to all men, even to our enemies, although it is true that we spontaneously feel greater affection for some persons than for others, and that we naturally have a greater obligation to aid and cherish our families and close friends than to assist strangers. [7] If "the most savage animals . . . encompass their own species with a ring of protecting peace . . . how much more powerfully do the laws of man's nature move him to hold fellowship and maintain peace with all men so far as in him lies. . . ." [8]

If men are naturally social beings, there must be certain norms or rules to govern their relations with one another. The essence of the Christian ethic is succinctly stated in the Gospel: "You shall love the Lord your God with all your heart, and with all your soul, and with all your mind," and "You shall love your neighbor as yourself." [9] On these two injunctions, the "great commandments," "depend all the law and the prophets." [10] Religion and morality—man's obligation to obey and love God and his duty to love and serve his fellow man—are thus indissolubly linked by Christian teaching. Just as there can be no purely individualistic and private relation between a man and God which does not issue forth in love and service to other men, so there can be no real love and service of other human beings that is not rooted in love and obedience to God. God alone is to be the object of men's love, and other human beings are to be loved *in* Him. This Christian ethic is clearly distinguished from any morality that is purely human or social, or from the conception that virtue resides in those actions and attitudes toward one's fellow men that are approved by individual reason or social tradition.

We have already seen that Augustine follows this Christian view when he insists that the patriotism, self-sacrifice, and devotion to the common good shown by the heroes of the early Roman Republic were not true virtues, although they can be described as "civic virtues" which, compared to the vices of other men, were at least relatively good.[11] Their good qualities were not true virtues because they were motivated by a desire for glory and honor, which depend upon the praise and admiration of other men. As a result, their heroism and their zeal for the good of the society were fatally infected with pride. And, as we have seen, the root of all human sin is pride, man's "craving for undue exaltation," his refusal to accept his status as a creature subject to God, and his attempt to revolt from God and to make himself the center of his world.[12] True virtue is attainable only by the man who, by God's grace, is turned from pride to humility, from love of self to love of God. If pride is the root of sin, true humility is the source of all virtue. In the dialectical manner that is so characteristic of his thought, Augustine tells us that "humility, by making us subject to God, exalts us. But pride, being a defect of nature, by the very act of refusing subjection and revolting from Him who is supreme, falls to a low condition." [13]

Augustine never tires of warning men of the danger of pride that lurks even in good works and virtuous actions, and of reminding them that false humility is even worse and more proud than open pride.[14] He tells the nuns of Hippo:

For every other kind of sin finds scope in evil works, so that by it they are done, but pride lurks even in good works, so that by it they are undone; and what avails it to lavish money on the poor, and become poor oneself, if the unhappy soul is rendered more proud by despising riches than it had been by possessing them? [15]

In another letter he writes: "All other vices are to be apprehended when we are doing wrong; but pride is to be feared even when we do right actions, lest those things which are done in a praiseworthy manner be spoiled by the desire for praise itself." [16] There is a close connection between the pride that waits to ensnare men even in their good works and the love of praise. The merit of any good work is lost when the motive for doing it is vanity and the desire for the applause and admiration of other men. Consequently, the "noble heathen" who appeared to live prudently, courageously, temperately, and righteously because they desired glory and praise among men did not, according to Augustine, possess true virtue.[17] When, on account of their "good" or heroic actions, they receive the praises of men, "they have reached their reward: vain men, and vain reward." [18]

Vices can be overcome, then, not by the desire for human

praise and glory—this course can only lead one to curb the greater vices by means of the lesser vices—but only by the love of God. Only that love, given by God Himself, can shift the whole center and focus of a man's life so that he acts righteously and shuns evil because he loves God and *therefore* desires to act as God wishes him to act, and not because he seeks the approbation of men.[19]

Therefore, where there is love, there of necessity will there be faith and hope; and where there is the love of our neighbor, there also of necessity will be the love of God. . . . Let us, therefore, be holding fast to this precept of the Lord, to love one another; and then all else that is commanded we shall do, for all else we have contained in this. But this love is distinguished from that which men bear to one another as such; for in order to mark the distinction, it is added, "as I have loved you. . . ." But those whose mutual love has the possession of God Himself for its object, will truly love one another; and, therefore, even for the very purpose of loving one another, they love God. There is no such love as this in all men; for few have this motive for their love one to another, that God may be all in all.[20]

If true righteousness, based on love of God, is quite different from that "virtue" which seeks to obtain praise of men, it is even farther removed from that semblance of virtue which consists in refraining from sin solely because one is afraid of the punishment, temporal or eternal, that may follow. In this case the will to sin is still present and is merely overborne by the fear of punishment.

How, then, can that man be called righteous who is such an enemy to righteousness that, if he had the power, he would abolish its authority, that he might not be subject to its threatenings or its penalties? He, then, is an enemy to righteousness who refrains from sin only through fear of punishment; but he will become the friend of righteousness if through love of it he sin not, for then he will be really afraid to sin.[21]

It necessarily follows, then, that the most that earthly states, with their rewards and punishments, can hope to accomplish is to maintain and enforce that semblance of virtue or righteousness which arises from the fear of punishment and the desire for praise, since these are the only motives to "good" actions that rulers can expect to find in most of their subjects.[22]   Virtue

Augustine defines virtue as "perfect love of God"; its four divisions—temperance, fortitude, justice, and prudence—are four forms of love.[23] Justice, for example, is "love serving God only, and therefore ruling well all else, as subject to man." [24]

"Christ the Virtue of God and the Wisdom of God" . . . giveth different virtues in this place, who for all the virtues which are necessary and useful in this valley of weeping shall give one virtue, Himself. For in Scripture and in many writers four virtues are described useful for life: prudence, by which we discern between good and evil; justice, by which we give each person his due, "owing no man anything," but loving all men: temperance, by which we restrain lusts; fortitude, by which we bear all troubles. . . . [F]rom these virtues we mount unto that other virtue. And what will that be, but the virtue of the contemplation of God alone? [25]

The perfection of virtue is attainable only in the life to come. As long as Christians live on this earth, no matter how virtuous they may be, they cannot say that they are without sin, and so each day they must pray, "Forgive us our trespasses." However, in the man in whom Christ has come to dwell are found the true virtues of this life of hardship and suffering—temperance, fortitude, prudence, and justice—even if his practice of them is not perfect. The unregenerate, on the contrary, possess only the false counterparts of these true virtues. The true justice of the Christian consists not only of equity and fair-dealing but of real benevolence—that is, love of and concern for his neighbor—which issues from the conscience of the heart.[26] He loves all men equally, even though he is not able to do good to all and is compelled to pay special attention to those with whom he is brought into closer connection "by the accidents of time, or place, and circumstance." [27] The true Christian does not envy any of his brethren who also love God; indeed, he seeks to bring to the love of God his household and his friends.[28] He does not return evil for evil, since to do so would be to make himself evil and unjust.[29]

Above all, he follows Christ's injunction to love his enemies, not only because he knows that God has commanded it, but because he realizes that

in no way can thine enemy so hurt thee by his violence, as thou dost hurt thyself if thou love him not. For he may injure thy estate, or flocks, or house, or thy man-servant, or thy maid-servant, or thy son, or thy wife; or at most, if such power be given him, thy body. But can he injure thy soul, as thou canst thyself? . . . For what good can thy neighbour's ill do thee? If he had no ill, he would not even be thine enemy. Wish him well then, that he may end his ill, and he will be thine enemy no longer. For it is not the human nature in him that is at enmity with thee, but his sin.[30]

Augustine thus accepts Plato's teaching that man's most precious possession is the health of his soul, and that the good man will not injure that highest good by doing evil in order to attain or safeguard any inferior possession.

What sort of justice is that which is retained for the sake of gold, as if gold were a more precious thing than justice herself, or as if when a man denieth the deposit of another man's goods, he to whom he denied them should suffer a greater loss, than he that denieth them to him. The former doth lose a garment, the latter fidelity.[31]

Augustine maintains that "there is nothing in all the dungeons of this world, nay, not even in hell itself, to surpass the dreadful doom of darkness to which a villain is consigned by remorse of conscience." [32] A clear external sign of the inward misery and dissatisfaction of the wicked man is his restless and fruitless search for repose and satisfaction in things outside himself.

For whoever is oppressed within his heart by a bad conscience, just as any man in consequence of the overflow of a waterspout or of smoke goeth out of his house, suffereth not himself to dwell therein; so he who hath not a quiet heart, cannot happily dwell in his heart. Such men go out of themselves in the bent of their mind, and delight themselves with things without, that affect the body; they seek repose in trifles, in spectacles, in luxuries, in all evils. Wherefore do they wish themselves well without? Because it is not well with them within, so that they may rejoice in a good conscience.[33]

Since Christianity enjoins upon its believers the virtues of justice, self-control, frugality, and conjugal fidelity, its morality, Augustine insists, is far superior to that described and extolled in pagan writings about the gods. If men imitate these deities, they are rendered "depraved" and "unfit to be good members of society," while

the Churches which are multiplying throughout the world are, as it were, sacred seminaries of public instruction, in which this sound morality is inculcated and learned, and in which, above all, men are taught the worship due to the true and faithful God, who not only commands men to attempt, but also gives grace to perform, all those things by which the soul of man is furnished and fitted for fellowship with God, and for dwelling in the eternal heavenly kingdom.[34]

Since Augustine insists that human fellowship and social life are natural to man, it is not surprising that he follows St. Paul and the Church Fathers in recognizing the existence of a law of nature, a basic moral law that is written in the hearts of all men, and that is distinct from human laws or divinely revealed laws.[35] The basic precept of this natural law, which should guide men in all their dealings with others, is the Golden Rule in its negative form, that is, "Do not unto others what you would not have others do unto you." Augustine states the precept in a number of ways, for example, "What thou wouldest not have done to thyself, do not to another," [36] "What thou art unwilling to suffer, be unwilling to do," [37] or "That which to thyself thou wouldest not have done, do not thou to another." [38] In this principle are embodied the basic moral rules that govern man's conduct toward others, such as the prohibitions against murder, violence, theft, fraud, and lying. It is by this law of nature that men judge whether any particular action is righteous or unrighteous, just or unjust, and this law is implanted in the conscience of every rational man, no matter how wicked his own conduct may be. He recognizes the law of nature and expects other men to observe it even if he flagrantly violates it himself.

Theft is punished by thy law, O Lord, and by the law written in men's hearts, which not even ingrained wickedness can erase. For what thief will tolerate another thief stealing from him? Even a rich thief will not tolerate a poor thief who is driven to theft by want.[39]

Since natural law or the law of conscience is innate in man, it has existed since the creation of Adam. Therefore, it precedes the Fall and the introduction of sin into the world,[40] and it antedates and is distinguished from the written law given directly by God to the Jews through Moses as well as the law of Christ in the Gospels.[41] The Ten Commandments and the Gospel precepts do not contradict or annul the law of nature; rather, they make it more explicit and overt and give it the greater force of God's direct commandment to men.[42] Although it is innate and not "learned," the law of nature is not perceived or recognized by the young child, but when a child has grown up he *discovers,* by the use of his reason, this law in his rational soul, that is, in his conscience.[43] The basic precept of the natural law—"That which therefore to thyself thou wilt not have to be done, do not thou to another" [44]—follows necessarily for any rational man from his unwillingness to suffer hurt or injury and from his recognition of the inevitable fact that he must live and work with other men.

Come, if thou art not willing to suffer these things, art thou by any means the only man? dost thou not live in the fellowship of mankind? He that together with thee hath been made, is thy fellow; and all men have been made after the image of God, unless with earthly covetings they efface that which He hath formed. . . . For thou judgest that there is evil in that, which to suffer thou art not willing; and this thing thou art constrained to know by an inward law; that in thy very heart is written.[45]

The natural law, since it is discoverable by all men by the use of reason, without special revelation, is a universal law, and by it the Gentiles, to whom the law of Moses was not given, are judged and found to be transgressors.[46]

Augustine also speaks of this law of nature as "the eternal law of God [*lege Dei aeterna*]," written in "the hearts of the godly," and says that from this eternal law was copied the law given to the Jews through Moses.[47] The law of nature is God's eternal law because the source of these rules that rational men discover in their consciences is God's Truth.

Where indeed are these rules [*regulae*] written, wherein even the unrighteous recognizes what is righteous, wherein he discerns that he ought to have what he himself has not? Where, then, are they written unless in the book of that Light which is called Truth? whence every righteous law [*omnis lex justa*] is copied and transferred (not by migrating to it, but by being as it were impressed upon it) to the heart of the man that worketh righteousness; as the impression from a ring passes into the wax, yet does not leave the ring.[48]

Augustine distinguishes this law of nature or law of conscience from a very different "law of nature," which, he says, "has never been violated, and which is common to us with the beasts";[49] this law is essentially the law of self-preservation, by which "we love ourselves, and what is beneath us but connected with us." [50] Inasmuch as this latter natural law is not only innate but instinctual, it does not require reason for its discovery or application.[51] This natural and proper love of self or instinct of self-preservation is clearly different from the unnatural self-love that is characteristic of the sinful man who attempts to make himself rather than God the center of the universe. Since by nature, men, like all animals, love themselves and their own bodies, the law of conscience and the law of Moses, which is based upon it, did not directly command us to love ourselves, but rather gave us injunctions in regard to our conduct toward God and toward our fellow men. The first three commandments of the Decalogue enjoin us to love God, and the next seven precepts relate "to the love of our neighbor, which is the bond of human society." [52] However, as Augustine observes, "when it is said, 'Thou shalt love thy neighbor as thyself,' it at once becomes evident that our love for ourselves has not been overlooked." [53] Like the other Church Fathers, he does not regard the ceremonial law of the Old Testament as binding after the coming of Christ, but he insists that the moral law of the Old Testament, especially as set forth in the Ten Commandments, is still "necessary for us for the right ordering of our life." [54] The only element in the Decalogue which is no longer binding is "the carnal observance of the Sabbath," that is, literal adherence to the prohibition against any form of labor on the seventh day of the week.

How, then, are the law of nature—the eternal law of God written in men's hearts—and the law of God given in the Old and New Testaments, related to human laws and customs? Augustine distinguishes sins against nature, such as the offenses of the Sodomites, sins against custom, and sins against the laws.[55] Offenses against nature and against the unchanging law of God, which is the standard of judgment employed by "true inner righteousness," are always and everywhere crimes and should be punished. But customs and laws, being human institutions, based on convention and agreement among men, may differ from time to time and from place to place. For example, "a plurality of wives was no crime when it was the custom; and it is a crime now, because it is no longer the custom."[56] Human laws and customs are, however, binding upon all men who dwell in a particular city or nation at a given time, whether they are citizens or strangers, unless God's commands overrule these laws or customs. "When God commands anything contrary to the customs or compacts of any nation, even though it were never done by them before, it is to be done; and if it has been interrupted, it is to be restored; and if it has never been established, it is to be established."[57] Any action that contravenes God's law cannot be just.[58] When Augustine says that God's commands take precedence over human "customs or compacts," it seems clear that he is referring to those commands of God that have been directly revealed to men in the Scriptures, such as the prohibition against idol-worship.[59]

In one of his earliest works, the first book of the *De Libero Arbitrio,* written in 388, Augustine says that although it would be right for a public-spirited people to be permitted to choose its own magistrates, it would also be right to transfer that power to one good man or a few good men if the people became corrupt. He then goes on to comment that

there is nothing just or legitimate in temporal law save what men have derived from the eternal law [*in illa temporali nihil esse iustum atque legitimum quod non ex hac aeterna sibi homines derivaverint*]. For if the people we have been speaking of at one time bestowed honours justly and at another time unjustly, the change in question belongs to the temporal sphere, but the judgment as to justice or injustice is derived from the eternal sphere in which it is abidingly just that a serious-minded people should bestow honours, and a fickle people should not. . . . Briefly to express in words as best I can the idea of eternal law as it is stamped upon our minds [*aeternae legis notionem, quae impressa nobis est*] I should say this: it is just that all things should be in perfect order.[60]

In another early work, the *De Vera Religione,* written about 390, he says that the legislator, if he is a good and wise man, will frame the laws that he is making for a particular people at a given time in accordance with the eternal law of God.

In the case of temporal laws, although men make judgments regarding them when they institute them, nevertheless when they have been instituted and confirmed, it is not lawful for a judge to pass judgment upon them, but only to give judgment in accordance with them. So too the framer of temporal laws, if he is a good and wise man, takes into consideration that very eternal law upon which no soul is permitted to pass judgment, so that in accordance with its immutable rules he may determine for the time in question what is to be commanded and forbidden. Therefore, what the eternal law is pure souls may know, but they may not pass judgment upon it.[61]

As far as I have been able to discover, in none of the works written during the remaining forty years of his life does Augustine ever state that positive law must conform to God's eternal law or to the law of nature if it is to be valid. Even in the passage just quoted from the *De Vera Religione* he carefully states that the lawmaker, *"if he is a good and wise man,"* decides what actions he will enjoin or forbid by taking into consideration the "immutable rules" of the eternal law. He does *not* say that if the ruler is unwise or evil and fails to take the eternal law into account when he frames temporal laws, these laws have no validity and the subjects have no obligation to obey them; nor does he say that the subjects have the right to determine for themselves, by reference to the natural or eternal law, whether or not such a temporal law is valid and is to be obeyed. Therefore, I cannot agree with Combès when he says that Augustine holds.

that if a positive law is unjust, that is, if it does not conform to the natural law or the eternal law, "elle n'est plus qu'une formule inerte et vide, incapable de dicter un devoir et de commander l'obéissance," and that Augustine "enseigne qu'une loi injuste n'est pas une loi et que le citoyen doit lui refuser l'obéissance." [62]

The varieties and alterations that we find in human laws and customs do not mean that justice itself or God's law is subject to change or alteration. Just as we must recognize that "in one man, one day, and one house, different things are fit for different members," [63] so we should admit that a thing that was formerly lawful may at a later time become unlawful, and something that is permitted or even enjoined in one place may be justly prohibited somewhere else.

Therefore, it is not true to say that a thing rightly done once should not be changed. Obviously, right reason demands a change in what was right to do at some earlier time, if the time circumstance is changed, so, when these objectors say it is not right to make a change, truth answers with a shout that it is not right not to make a change, because then it will be right both ways, if the change accords with the variation in time.[64]

Is justice, then, variable and changeable? No, but the times over which she presides are not all alike because they are different times. But men, whose days upon the earth are few, cannot by their own perception harmonize the causes of former ages and other nations, of which they had no experience, and compare them with these of which they do have experience; although in one and the same body, or day, or family, they can readily see that what is suitable for each member, season, part, and person may differ.[65]   *Details may change*

In other words, God's law, the basic principles of morality and justice, is eternal and unchanging, but the specific, detailed customs and positive laws that govern men's relationships may differ from time to time and from place to place in accordance with circumstances and needs, and these different laws or customs may all conform to what is right and just.

One man in the east understands justice, another man in the west understands justice; is justice which the one understands a different thing from that which the other understands? In body they are far apart, and yet they have the eyes of their minds on one object. The justice which I, placed here, see, if justice it is, is the same which the just man, separated from me in the flesh by ever so many days' journey, also sees, and is united to me in the light of that justice.[66]

The reason why justice and righteousness are always and everywhere the same is that Christ, the Wisdom and Word of God, is everywhere present and eternally unchanging.

Augustine recognizes that many men, seeing the wide variety of human customs and precepts and their changes through time, have concluded that "there was no such thing as absolute right, but that every nation took its own custom for right; and that, since every nation has a different custom, and right must remain unchangeable, it becomes manifest that there is no such thing as right at all." To these early exponents of cultural relativism in morals, he answers: "Such men did not perceive, to take only one example, that the precept, 'Whatsoever ye would that men should do to you, do ye even so to them,' cannot be altered by any diversity of national customs." [67] He is also aware of the danger of changing customs unless there is a pressing need for their revision; "mere change of custom, even though it may be of advantage in some respects, unsettles men by reason of the novelty: therefore, if it brings no advantage, it does much harm by unprofitably disturbing the Church." [68]

Augustine's insistence upon the fact that men are by nature social creatures bound together by ties of equality and fraternity, and his frequent references to the natural law of moral conduct which man can discover by the use of reason may seem difficult to reconcile with his description of human life in this world as "this hell upon earth" and with his graphic portrayal of the strife and conflict that result from the clash of men's avaricious and ambitious strivings.[69] We must always remember that when he says that "the laws of man's nature move him to hold fellowship and maintain peace with all men so far as in him lies," [70] he is talking about the natural state of man before the Fall and the introduction into the world of sin and its consequences. Once the nature of man has been corrupted by sin each man seeks to gain possessions and wealth at the expense of others and each seeks to gain mastery over others. When we observe their actions and attitudes, we may well be forgiven for forgetting that these creatures are brothers descended from the same parents and that they were intended to live together in concord and harmony. Augustine's comment on the hatred and conflict that rage among men is bitterly sorrowful: "For there is nothing so social by nature, so unsocial by its corruption, as this race." [71] Into such enormities of sin—cruelty, murder, war—has man fallen that

even the beasts devoid of rational will . . . would live more securely and peaceably with their own kind than men, who had been propagated from one individual for the very purpose of commending concord. For not even lions or dragons have ever waged with their kind such wars as men have waged with one another.[72]

Only among the small number of men who have been redeemed by God's grace do we find the true unity and concord that are natural to man. They are made one by Him in Himself, and become members of the one Body of which Christ is the Head. Among them are found true love of and service to others, since each of them loves God and makes Him the center of his life and each loves other men as sons of God. Left to themselves, fallen men are, in contrast, incapable of unity and concord, "separated as they are one from another by divers pleasures and desires and uncleannesses of sin. . . ." [73]

Moreover, sin and unrighteousness have almost effaced from men's hearts the natural law that God has implanted, although some faint traces of that law still remain.[74] Ignorance and misguided will, the two primary defects of fallen man, make it difficult for him to know what he ought to do and impossible for him to do what he may know that he should do. Even in his corrupt state man retains some ability to ascertain what is right and wrong, just and unjust, and he can see the force of the fundamental precept of the natural law—"What thou wouldest not have done to thyself, do not to another"—especially when he is observing and judging the actions of other men.[75] But he has an extraordinary capacity to ignore this voice of conscience and to fail to apply the moral law when he is contemplating an action of his own or considering it after the event. He usually manages to distinguish his own case from the general rule and to rationalize as necessary or even praiseworthy actions which he would instantly condemn if another man were to perform them. When he is about to act, he listens to the clamorous demands of cupidity, pride, lust, and hatred and ignores the small voice of conscience and God's eternal law. He treats other men as instruments for the satisfaction of his own desires and often employs treachery, deceit, and coercion in his dealings with them. In a word, he reverses the central precept of the natural law by treating other men in exactly the manner in which he does *not* want to be treated by them.[76]

Once sin entered the world through Adam's disobedience and radically corrupted all his descendants, it became absolutely impossible for any man to lead a good life or to attain salvation by attempting to carry out the precepts of the law of nature.[77] As St. Paul said, even the law of God given to the Jews through Moses cannot bring fallen men to true virtue or to salvation; indeed, it simply adds to the burden of man's sin by adding to the original evil action the crime of transgressing God's law.[78] The natural law is even less capable of serving as the vehicle of salvation. If either the natural law or the law of Moses could lead men to eternal life, then, in St. Paul's phrase, "Christ died in vain." "If, however, Christ did not die in vain, then human nature cannot by any means be justified and redeemed from God's most righteous wrath—in a word, from punishment—except by faith and the sacrament of the blood of Christ." [79] Without faith, faith in Christ, it is impossible to please God and to be saved. Therefore, no unbeliever can ever attain true virtue by means of a perfect obedience to the precepts of natural law. As long as we remain unregenerate we do not do what we know we ought to do or what, in a sense, we may want to do, since there is another law—the law of sin and lust—that overcomes the law of God within us. Only faith in Christ, given by God's grace, can bring us to repentance and to a new life, in which we die to sin and begin to carry out the commandments of God.[80] In his polemic against Julian and his semi-Pelagian doctrines, Augustine says: "You introduce a race of men who can please God by the law of nature without the faith of Christ. This is the chief reason why the Christian Church detests you." [81]

Since the fraternity and concord natural to human society have been shattered by the egoism of sinful men, and the natural law regulating human relations has been all but effaced from the human heart, how is society—which is essential to man's existence—to be maintained? God's grace which brings regeneration and ransom from the captivity to sin cannot serve as the basis for social organization since, as we have seen, it liberates only a small minority of the mass of sinners.[82] Since most men —whether they are heathen or nominal Christians—are unredeemed and will be so until the end of the world, new means must be provided to introduce a measure of order, stability, and peace in the midst of the strife and conflict that mark earthly life. Even to disobedient, prideful man God has been most merciful;

He has established new institutions, adapted to the new conditions of sinful existence, in order to keep a check on human greed and violence and to prevent society from collapsing into complete anarchy and chaos. These institutions, such as private property and the entire legal and political order, are divinely ordained as both punishments *and* remedies for the sinful condition of man.[83] Although they provide an element of order, stability, and peace in social life that would be completely absent without them, the earthly peace and order that they make possible are no longer natural and spontaneous, but must be maintained by coercion and repression.

In view of the condition of sinful man, the peace, concord, and justice that are maintained by these economic, legal, and political institutions are supremely important. Yet they are only imperfect images or reflections of the natural, uncoerced peace, order, and justice that existed in Paradise or of the true and abiding concord, peace, order, and justice that will reign for all eternity in the heavenly city, the society built upon the love of all its members for God and for one another in God. As we have already seen, Augustine says that even the godless are able to make some moral judgments, judgments about what is right and wrong and about how men ought to behave, despite the fact that their own lives and minds are unrighteous. He also says that the ideas or norms of justice and righteousness which enable them to make such judgments are "images" or "impressions" of God's Truth and Righteousness.[84] If the image of God and the law of God were completely obliterated from man's soul by sin, if no "faint outlines" of the original remained, men would have no conception of justice, righteousness, or peace to use as the foundation of the human standards of equity, fair-dealing, and order that are the pillars of civilized society.[85]

Obviously, man cannot of himself renew or re-form the image

of God or the law of God that was implanted in him, although he was able to deform that image. "Through sin, righteousness [*justitiam*] and holiness of truth were lost; wherefore this image has become deformed and faded. The mind receives it again, when it is re-formed and renewed." [86] But even without the reformation that comes only through God's grace, some "traces" or "vestiges" of true or heavenly justice [*supernae justitiae*] remain imprinted upon the minds of sinful men, and it is these "traces" that form the basis for the human ideas of justice that are embodied in economic, legal, and political institutions. Without these "vestiges" of true justice, there would be no justice among men,[87] and yet "the old or exterior or earthly man"—that is, sinful or unredeemed man, who is a lover of earthly things—can never rise above the level of what Augustine calls "servile justice," [88] although he may, and often does, transgress the rules of this earthly justice. Even the commercial transactions of men, the "transactions of giving and receiving" which knit men together into human society, have a kind of equity, although it is only an "image" of God's equity.

No one can be charged with unrighteousness who exacts what is owing to him. Nor certainly can he be charged with unrighteousness who is prepared to give up what is owing to him. This decision does not lie with those who are debtors but with the creditor. This image [*imago*] or, as I said, trace [*vestigium*] of equity [*aequitatis*] is stamped on the business transactions of men by the Supreme Equity.[89]

These "vestiges," "semblances," or "images" of justice, mutual trust, and equity are the shadowy, though essential, bases of the measure of peace, harmony, and order that human society can achieve. Moreover, as we shall see, earthly peace and order must also be defended by the heavy hand of coercion and punishment in order to prevent them from being destroyed by the powerful forces of sin—human selfishness, pride, covetousness, ambition, and lust.[90] Augustine takes pains to point out that the entire fabric of human civilization and earthly governance rests upon order, predictability, and peace, while these in turn are based upon the invisible and intangible foundations of human reason and understanding and men's conceptions of justice, equity, and mutual confidence.

> Observe this whole world arranged in the same human commonwealth, with what administrations, with what orderly degrees of authority, with what conditions of citizenship, with what laws, manners, arts! The whole of this is brought about by the soul, and yet this power of the soul is not visible.[91]

Without some degree of mutual understanding and good faith, without some traces of justice and concord, no human association would survive more than a few hours. No matter how imperfect and fragile the order, concord, and equity may be, they are essential if a community is to be constituted from a collection of individuals, whether the community be a family, a city, a nation, or a band of robbers. As Socrates had pointed out to Thrasymachus many centuries before Augustine, completely unrestrained egoism would destroy the basis for cooperative action that even thieves must preserve among themselves.[92]

It is essential to keep in mind the fact that Augustine uses terms like "justice," "harmony," and "peace" in two quite different senses, which are sometimes blurred and confused by his commentators. "True" or "genuine" justice, peace, and concord are found only in the City of God, and to a degree among its pilgrim members during their sojourn on this earth. In earthly institutions, whether social, economic, or political, we find only the shadows or traces of these supernal qualities. The images differ from the originals in kind as well as in degree. Some commentators use the term "relative justice" or "relative righteousness" when they refer to the justice found in earthly societies and states.[93] While I do not object seriously to it, the term itself is not Augustine's; as we have seen, he speaks of the "image," "trace," or "impression" of justice that exists even among sinful men. Whatever terms we use, we must remember that Augustine is referring to the elements of order, justice, and peace embodied in human society and in its institutions. Without these elements society would collapse into anarchy, and yet earthly peace and justice are always imperfect and always unstable and precarious; they are maintained by coercion and are constantly endangered by the disintegrating forces of self-seeking, greed, and lust for power.[94]

Peace is one of Augustine's favorite themes, and his discussions of peace graphically illustrate the twofold usage to which I have just referred. True peace is the absence, not only of overt conflict, but of all resistance, contradiction, and opposition. It is clear that as long as we live in this world, true peace is completely unattainable; the life of the wicked is a life of strife and conflict, and even "the saints and faithful ones" must constantly wrestle with the devil, with the law of sin in the flesh, and with the troubles and desires of this world. "Find me anything by which thou art refreshed, wherein if thou continue thou dost not again become weary. What peace then is that which men have here, opposed by so many troubles, desires, wants, wearinesses? This is no true, no perfect peace."[95] Perfect and eternal peace will be found only in the City of God.

Who would not long for that City whence no friend goeth out, whither no enemy entereth [*unde amicus non exit, quo inimicus non intrat*], where is no tempter, no seditious person, no one dividing God's people, no one wearying the Church in the service of the devil. . . . There shall be peace made pure in the sons of God, all loving one another, seeing one another full of God, since God shall be all in all. We shall have God as our common object of vision, God as our common possession, God as our common peace. . . . Our joy, our peace, our rest, the end of all our troubles, is none but God: blessed are "they that turn their hearts unto Him." [96]

Even the pilgrims from the City of God cannot enjoy this full and perfect peace as long as they live on this earth. Although they are strengthened by the hope of eternal peace, the peace which they have in this life "is rather the solace of our misery than the positive enjoyment of felicity."[97] They have "a certain kind of peace [*pax aliqua*]" inasmuch as they love one another and thus have mutual confidence in one another. However, this is not a true or complete peace,

for we see not the thoughts of one another's hearts; and we have severally better or worse opinions in certain respects of one another than is warranted by the reality. And so that peace, although left us by Him, is our peace: for were it not from Him, we should not be possessing it, such as it is; but such is not the peace He has Himself. And if we keep what we received unto the end, then such as He has shall we have, when we shall have no elements of discord of our own, and we shall have no secrets hid from one another in our hearts.[98]

God has called us to concord and commanded us to have peace among ourselves, "but at present we are at strife, very often with those whose good we are seeking." [99] We are in conflict with heretics, pagans, false brethren; on every side there are countless necessities of strife. Often the Christian becomes weary of this struggle and seeks to withdraw from the battle by retiring within himself; but there, too, he finds strife and conflict.

Very often one is overcome with weariness, and says to himself, "What have I to do with bearing with gainsayers, bearing with those who render evil for good? I wish to benefit them, they are willing to perish; I wear out my life in strife; I have no peace. . . . Let me return to myself. . . ." Do return to thyself, thou findest strife there. . . . What strife, sayest thou, do I find? "The flesh lusteth against the Spirit, and the Spirit against the flesh." [100]

Repeatedly, Augustine warns the faithful that Christ has not promised "peace in this world, and repose in this life. . . . Every man doth seek repose; a good thing he is seeking, but not in the proper region thereof he is seeking it. *There is no peace in this life; in Heaven hath been promised that which on earth we are seeking: in the world to come hath been promised that which in* this world we are seeking." [101] "Whoever hopes for this so great good [i.e., peace] in this world, and in this earth, his wisdom is but folly." [102]

If true peace is not attainable by God's children in this world, it is obvious that the children of the devil, the lovers of this world, are even further removed from genuine peace and concord. To them peace means exemption from the annoyance of wars and lawsuits, so that they may enjoy the things of this world in which they place their love. Since each of these earthly men seeks his own satisfaction, there can be no real harmony among them, and consequently no true peace. And between them and the righteous no true peace is possible, since their hearts and wills are completely at variance. "For as one is called a consort who unites his lot [*sortem*] with another, so may he be termed concordant whose heart has entered into a similar union [*quomodo enim consors dicitur, qui sortem iungit, ita ille concors dicendus est, qui corda iungit*]." [103]

Yet there is a universal desire among men for peace, and even the wicked seek to create a peace and order of their own, unjust though it may be. They

wage war to maintain the peace of their own circle, and wish that, if possible, all men belonged to them, that all men and things might serve but one head, and might, either through love or fear, yield themselves to peace with him! It is thus that pride in its perversity apes God. It abhors equality with other men under Him; but, instead of His rule, it seeks to impose a rule of its own upon its equals.

It abhors, that is to say, *the just peace of God, and loves its own un-just peace; but it cannot help loving peace of one kind or other.* For there is no vice so clean contrary to nature that it obliterates even the faintest traces of nature.[104]

Even those who make war desire nothing but victory, that is, peace with glory.

It is therefore with the desire for peace that wars are waged, even by those who take pleasure in exercising their warlike nature in command and battle. And hence it is obvious that peace is the end sought for by war. *For every man seeks peace by waging war, but no man seeks war by making peace.* For even they who intentionally interrupt the peace in which they are living have no hatred of peace, but only wish it changed into a peace that suits them better. They do not, therefore, wish to have no peace, but only one more to their mind.[105]

Thus, even among the children of this world there is a temporal peace, the peace of the earthly city, Babylon. It is not the true peace of God nor even the approximation to it known by the pilgrim members of the City of God. It is not always just; perhaps it is rarely just. It is often broken. And it is primarily a negative peace—the absence of overt conflict and hostilities—maintained by restraint, coercion, and discipline. In all these ways, earthly peace is different from the heavenly peace of which it is the blurred image. In the state, which is the primary instrument for maintaining this temporal peace and order, there is found "the well-ordered concord of civic obedience and rule [*imperandi oboediendique concordiam ciuium*]." [106] The end or aim that the earthly city seeks by means of this peace or "well-ordered concord" is "the combination of men's wills to attain the things which are helpful to this life [*ut sit eis de rebus ad mortalem uitam pertinentibus humanarum quaedam compositio, uoluntatum*]." [107] The state and the peace that it maintains are viewed as instruments which minimize and regulate overt conflict and so allow men to live and work together; by their cooperative efforts all men can promote their long-term interest in obtaining the goods and services that they require during this mortal life. The principal mechanism through which the state secures this temporal, external peace and concord is the legal system. The laws and the penalties attached to them punish overt crimes or breaches of the peace—although they are powerless to change the basic motives or the wills of evil men—and they deter some men from crime through fear of punishment. By these laws of the earthly city "the things necessary for the maintenance of this mortal life are administered." [108]

While the members of the City of God wander as pilgrims on this earth, they must be concerned with at least the necessities of life. So they, too, must participate in the legal and political order which sustains "the peace of Babylon," that is, "the temporal peace which the good and the wicked together enjoy." [109] As long as the two cities are mixed together, that is, until the end of the world, this mortal life is common to both cities, and so there is a certain harmony between them with respect to the necessities of that life.

Even the heavenly city, therefore, while in its state of pilgrimage, avails itself of the peace of earth, and, so far as it can without injuring faith and godliness, desires and maintains a common agreement among men regarding the acquisition of the necessaries of life, and makes this earthly peace bear upon the peace of heaven.[110]

Therefore, its members do not hesitate to obey the laws of the earthly city, provided only that those laws do not require them to deny the commands of God; thus, they cooperate in maintaining the precarious and inferior, yet all-important, peace of Babylon. Unlike the wicked, the wayfarers from God's kingdom do not *need* to be regulated and repressed by the laws of the earthly city, since they refrain from crime and immorality because they love God and not because they fear punishment, but they acknowledge and abide by the laws and make no effort to claim exemption from them. When earthly rulers are friendly to the cause of Christianity, the Church in all parts of the world uses the temporal peace which they provide "for the work of building houses after a spiritual fashion, and planting gardens and vineyards." [111]

At this point I shall not undertake any further discussion of the state and the temporal peace that it maintains through its instruments of coercion and repression, since in the chapters that follow I shall analyze in detail Augustine's teachings about the political and legal systems.[112] Instead, let us turn to an examination of his treatment of the economic order. Like the state, the institutions of private property, private wealth, and slavery are consequences of the Fall and of the sinful condition of fallen man. Since they did not exist in the natural order that preceded the Fall, they must be regarded as both punishments and remedies for human sinfulness. Property and slavery form part of that earthly or temporal order which preserves external peace and sustains that earthly justice which is a vestige of God's true and immutable justice. Since these institutions are absolutely essential to man's life on this earth under the conditions created by sin and pride, they must be guarded and respected even by those true Christians whose interest in earthly goods and possessions is minimal.

When Augustine discusses property, riches, usury, and slavery, he follows, with no great changes, the doctrines set forth by the earlier Church Fathers.[113] In general, Patristic theory held that private property and the resulting differences in men's possessions were not natural. According to the law of nature, the earth and all that it produces were the common possession of mankind. Christian writers often associated this common ownership of things with the state of man in Paradise before the Fall, just as the

Stoics had connected it with the "natural" condition of mankind during the vanished Golden Age. Private property appears on the scene after the Fall, or, in the Stoic version, with the passing of the Golden Age. It is one of the conventional institutions which are necessary for social life in view of the sinful state of fallen man.[114] One important consequence of this doctrine was the view that private property and the rights that go with it are not founded on the law of God or on natural law in its original form. It is human or positive law that assigns property rights to men. What human law has conferred it can modify or take away, and so the Patristic theory allows for changes in property arrangements by human action and gives no ground for a claim to God-given, inalienable, "natural" rights to property, immune from social or political control and regulation.

Augustine does not elaborate a detailed theory of property, but in several passages in which he is defending state confiscation of property belonging to the Donatists, he sets forth the major principles of a doctrine of property, principles which follow the lines of the Patristic theory to which I have referred. He clearly states the doctrine that the property and possessions of every man are his only by human right, and not by divine right, and that political rulers—kings and emperors—are the authorities who determine the human rights, including the right to property, of their subjects.

By what right does every man possess what he possesses? Is it not by human right [*iure humano*]? For by divine right [*iure diuino*], "The earth is the Lord's, and the fullness thereof." The poor and the rich God made of one clay; the same earth supports alike the poor and the rich. By human right, however, one says, This estate is mine, this house is mine, this servant is mine. By human right, therefore, is by right of the emperors. Why so? Because God has distributed to mankind these very human rights through the emperors and kings of this world. Do you [i.e., the Donatists] wish us to read the laws

of the emperors, and to act by the estate according to these laws?
. . . But what is the emperor to me? thou sayest. It is by right from
him that thou possessest the land. Or take away rights created by
emperors, and then who will dare say, That estate is mine, or that
slave is mine, or this house is mine? If, however, in order to their
possessing these things, men have received rights derived from kings,
will ye that we read the laws? . . . Do not say, What have I to do
with the king? as in that case, what have you to do with the possession? *It is by the rights derived from kings that possessions are enjoyed.* Thou hast said, What have I to do with the king? Say not
then that the possessions are thine; because it is to those same human
rights, by which men enjoy their possessions, thou hast referred
them.[115]

Since the Donatists, like all other men, owe their property
rights to the actions of the emperor, it is perfectly just for the
emperor to deprive them of some or all of those rights as a
punishment for their impiety and evil deeds. Since human right,
the basis of the right to possessions, "is in the jurisdiction of the
kings of the earth, you are mistaken in calling those things yours
which you do not possess as righteous persons, and which you
have forfeited by the laws of earthly sovereigns. . . ."[116] However, Augustine strongly disapproves of anyone who, by taking
advantage of the imperial edict confiscating the property of the
Donatists,

covetously seeks to possess himself of your property. Also we dis-
approve of anyone who, on the ground not of justice, but of avarice,
seizes and retains the provision pertaining to the poor, or the chapels
in which you meet for worship, which you once occupied in the name
of the Church, and which are by all means the rightful property only
of that Church which is the true Church of Christ.[117]

In one of his letters Augustine says that "lawfully" [*iure*]
means "justly" [*iuste*] and "justly" means "rightly" [*bene*]; therefore, "he who uses his wealth badly possesses it wrongfully, and
wrongful possession means that it is another's property [*omne*

igitur, quod male possidetur, alienum est, male autem possidet, qui male utitur]." [118] In the light of this statement and the comment that "money is wrongly [*male*] possessed by bad men while good men who love it least have the best right to it," [119] it is sometimes argued that Augustine held that a man's property rights are limited by the use to which he puts his possessions, that he who uses his property badly has no real claim to it, and that, at least *de jure,* property belongs to the good.[120] Clearly, however, this is a misinterpretation of his intent. He has already told us that the property rights of individuals are determined by kings and rulers. Any such system of positive legal rights to property would be thrown into complete chaos and confusion by the rule that evil men have lost their title to their property by their bad use of it and that only those who use possessions well have a rightful claim to them.[121] The confusion disappears when we observe that Augustine is making a moral judgment and not formulating a legal rule when he says that those who use property badly possess it wrongfully. In the same letter from which we have just quoted, he clearly states that the legal order cannot possibly take into account the goodness or badness of those who own property or of the uses that they make of their possessions, although those who use their property for evil purposes and who insist that they have an absolute right to do what they will with their own are guilty of immoral behavior. All that the laws can do is to prevent men from appropriating property that legally belongs to others and to punish anyone who commits theft or fraud. "*In this life the wrong of evil possessors is endured* and among them certain laws [*iura*] are established which are called civil [*ciuilia*] laws, not because they bring men to make a good use of their wealth, but because those who make a bad use of it become thereby less injurious." [122]

As we have already seen in the discussion of avarice and cupidity,[123] Augustine's attitude toward possessions and wealth is neither favorable nor completely hostile. The ethic that he espouses is far removed from what Max Weber has described as the capitalist spirit; he would consider it a grave sin for a Christian to devote his energies to the accumulation of ever larger amounts of goods and money. In his eyes, great wealth is a danger both to the soul and to the body, and the man who possesses a moderate amount of this world's goods is in a far happier situation.

Money is nought; not thence will ye have aid. Many have been cast headlong down for money's sake, many have perished on account of money; many for the sake of their riches have been marked out by plunderers; they would have been safe, had they not had what made men hunt for them. Many have presumed in their more powerful friends: they in whom they presumed have fallen, and have involved in their ruin those who trusted in them.[124]

On the other hand, it is clear that Augustine does not regard wealth or possessions as *per se* evil, or poverty as good in itself.[125]

For Christians, the most admirable course is to renounce all ownership of earthly goods and to hold in common the material things that are necessary for the support of life. In practice, however, this way of life, like that of complete chastity, is demanded only of those Christians who, as priests, monks, or nuns, have taken special vows; just as marriage is good and honorable, although a less exalted state than holy virginity, so the ownership of wealth and property can be good and honorable, even though renunciation of property in God's service is a higher calling.[126] But even the Christian who has not renounced the world and possessions must be careful to use his wealth and power in the service of God and not to love his money and his possessions so that he becomes their servant.[127]

Take heed that ye presume not in money, in a friend, in the honour and the boasting of the world. Take away all these things: but if thou hast them, thank God if thou despisest them. But if thou art puffed up by them; think not when thou wilt be the prey of men; already thou art the Devil's prey.[128]

Augustine insists that it is far better for a man to have fewer wants and desires than to have great wealth, extensive possessions, and high rank as means for the satisfaction of a large number of wants.

For as for riches and high rank, and all other things in which men who are strangers to true felicity imagine that happiness exists, what comfort do they bring, seeing that it is better to be independent of such things than to enjoy abundance of them, because, when possessed, they occasion, through our fear of losing them, more vexation than was caused by the strength of desire with which their possession was coveted? Men are not made good by possessing these so-called good things, but, if men have become good otherwise, they make these things to be really good by using them well.[129]

The fetters with which men have been bound by God as a consequence of their sins are mortality and the corruptibleness of the flesh. In a striking phrase, Augustine says:

Whenever men in the world will to be rich, for these fetters they are seeking rags. But let the rags of the fetters suffice: seek so much as is necessary for keeping off want, but when thou seekest superfluities, thou longest to load thy fetters. In such a prison then let the fetters abide even alone.[130]

The true Christian, whether he is rich or poor, should love God alone, and put his trust only in Him and not in any earthly good. He must, therefore, be prepared to sacrifice any temporal good—even life itself, to say nothing of riches—rather than to deny Christ or to disobey His commands. The true Christians who happen to be wealthy "possess riches" but "are not possessed by them";

they have renounced the world in truth and from their heart, and
. . . put no hope in such possessions. These use a sound discipline in
training their wives, their children, and their whole household to
cling to the Christian religion; their homes, overflowing with hospi-
tality, "receive the just man in the name of a just man that they may
receive the reward of a just man"; they deal their bread to the hun-
gry, they clothe the naked, they ransom the captive. . . . If it happens that they have to suffer the loss of their money for the faith of
Christ, they hate their riches . . . finally, if there is question of an
agreement with their adversary about the very life of their body,
they go so far as to hate their own life, rather than risk being forsaken by a forsaken Christ.[131]

In his interpretation of the Gospel teaching that "it is easier
for a camel to go through the eye of a needle than for a rich
man to enter the kingdom of God," [132] Augustine maintains that
Christ was condemning covetousness, not wealth, the *desire* for
money and goods, *not* their *possession,* and that poor men can
be just as guilty of these sins as rich men.

And that ye may know, that not money in a rich man, but covetousness is condemned, attend to what I say; Thou observest that rich
man standing near thee, and perchance in him is money, and is not
covetousness; in thee is not money, and is covetousness. . . . In order
that thou mayest know, that not riches are blamed; Abraham had
much gold, silver, cattle, household, was a rich man, and unto his
bosom Lazarus, a poor man, was borne up. Unto bosom of rich man,
poor man: are not rather both unto God rich men, both in cupidity
poor men? [133]

It is not true that God "does not hear those who have gold and
silver, and a household, and farms, if they happen to be born to
this estate, or hold such a rank in the world." [134] Only let the
wealthy remember St. Paul's admonition: "Charge them that are
rich in this world, that they be not highminded." [135] Their riches
can, of themselves, do them no good, and they should take care
lest their wealth lead to their ruin; "what certainly profiteth is a
work of mercy, done by a rich or a poor man: by a rich man, with
will and deed; by a poor man, with will alone." [136] The rich

man who was tortured in hell, while Lazarus, the poor beggar, was taken up into Abraham's bosom, was punished for his pride and not for his wealth. Above all, the wealthy should remember not only that they should use their riches to accomplish good works, but that they should "attribute their good works to the grace of God, not to their own strength."[137]

When Augustine is asked whether the rich must give away all their possessions or how much they should give away, he answers that St. Paul said, "Let them communicate,"[138]

not "Let them give the whole." Let them keep for themselves as much as is sufficient for them, let them keep more than is sufficient. Let us give a certain portion of it. What portion? A tenth? . . . The Scribes and Pharisees gave the tenth. How is it with you? Ask yourselves. Consider what you do, and with what means you do it; how much you give, how much you leave for yourselves; what you spend on mercy, what you reserve for luxury.[139]

His greatest indignation is poured out on those who believe that they can propitiate Christ for their "most damnable sins" by giving to the poor a small part of the wealth they acquire by extortion and spoliation. They think that in this way

they have bought from Him a licence to transgress, or rather do buy a daily indulgence. . . . We ought therefore to do alms that we may be heard when we pray that our past sins may be forgiven, not that while we continue in them we may think to provide ourselves with a licence for wickedness by alms-deeds.[140]

Augustine always couples his admonitions to the rich not to trust in their wealth nor to love their possessions with warnings to the poor not to trust in their poverty. The man who has "a full house, rich lands, many estates, much gold and silver," but knows that he must not put his trust in them, and so does good with them and humbles himself before God, is counted among God's poor. On the other hand, the poor man who views his poverty as a curse and burns with the desire for wealth and possessions is guilty of avarice and covetousness.

"God doth not heed the means a man hath, but the wish he hath, and judgeth him according to his wish for temporal blessings, not according to the means which it is not his lot to have." [141]

In any case, wealth is an uncertain and undependable good. "For what is so uncertain as a rolling thing? It is not unfitly that money itself is stamped round, because it remains not still." [142] Possessions, money, estates—all these are not true riches, and

if thou dost call them riches, thou wilt love them: and if thou love them, thou wilt perish with them. . . . They are full of poverty, and liable ever to accidents. What sort of riches are those, for whose sake thou art afraid of the robber, for whose sake thou art afraid of thine own servant, lest he should kill thee, and take them away, and fly? [143]

Money and other temporal goods, such as wife, children, health, or "the world's dignity," cannot be true goods, since we see that evil men have them as well as good men.[144] So Augustine admonishes the poor to refrain from plundering and to bridle their desires.

Seek only for a sufficiency, seek for what is enough, and do not wish for more. All the rest is a weight, rather than a help; a burden, rather than an honour. "Godliness with sufficiency is great gain. . . ." Avarice is the wishing to be rich, not the being rich already. This is avarice. Dost thou not fear to be "drowned in destruction and perdition"? Dost thou not fear "avarice the root of all evil"? [145]

The poor should remember that "the poverty of the industrious is never in itself a crime; nay, it is to some extent a means of withdrawing and restraining men from sin." [146]

To Augustine it is clear that usury is absolutely prohibited by God's command in the Scriptures, and, like most of the Fathers, he uses the term "usury" to cover any lending of money at interest, no matter what the rate may be. He refers to the text, "He that putteth not out his money to usury," [147] and denounces the practice in the strongest terms: "And how detestable, odious, and execrable a thing it is, I believe that even usurers themselves

know." [148] The fact that there may even be members of the
clergy who are guilty of this sin constitutes no excuse for the practice of usury.[149] The only permissible "usury" is to give to the
poor, and thus to give to Christ, who will repay far more than
you give.

He is pleased to borrow upon interest. He promiseth more than thou
hast given. Give the rein now to thy avarice, imagine thyself an
usurer. If thou wert an usurer indeed, thou wouldest be rebuked by
the Church, confuted by the word of God, all thy brethren would
execrate thee, as a cruel usurer, desiring to wring gain from other's
tears. But now be an usurer, no one will hinder thee.[150]

Augustine insists that all Christians, whether rich or poor, masters or slaves, rulers or subjects, are brothers, since all call on
God as "our Father," "an expression which they cannot justly
or piously use, unless they recognise that they themselves are
brethren." [151] The rich and powerful should not behave arro-
gantly or proudly toward their poor and humble brethren.[152]
This fraternity among Christians, based on their equality before
God, does not mean, of course, that the distinctions in this world
between masters and slaves or lords and servants are erased by
Christianity. St. Paul clearly teaches Christian slaves to be subject to their masters, and to be good servants rather than bad
ones, whether their masters happen to be good men or evil men,
Christians or pagans.

It hath been thy lot to become a Christian, and to have a man for thy
master: thou wast not made a Christian, that thou mightest disdain
to be a servant. . . . Behold, he hath not made men free from being
servants, but good servants from bad servants. How much do the
rich owe to Christ, who orders their houses for them! . . . If the
Lord of heaven and earth, through whom all things were created,
served the unworthy, asked mercy for His furious persecutors . . .
how much more ought not a man to disdain, with his whole mind,
and his whole good will, with his whole love to serve even a bad
master! Behold, a better serveth an inferior, but for a season.[153]

Slavery and the domination of man by man are not natural. According to the order of nature, God's plan for the universe, men were free and equal; man was to have dominion over the beasts but not over other men. Slavery is "a name, therefore, introduced by sin and not by nature. . . . But by nature, as God first created us, no one is the slave either of man or of sin." [154] Slavery, like private property and the state, is thus not "natural," but, given the circumstances of fallen man, it is a necessary remedial institution. Its "prime cause" is "sin, which brings man under the dominion of his fellow,—that which does not happen save by the judgment of God, with whom is no unrighteousness, and who knows how to award fit punishments to every variety of offence." [155] Slavery is penal; it is both the just punishment for man's sin and a remedy for sin. It is "appointed by that law which enjoins the preservation of the natural order and forbids its disturbance; for if nothing had been done in violation of that law, there would have been nothing to restrain by penal servitude." [156] Augustine states that the practice among the Jews of freeing slaves after they had served for six years does not apply to the case of Christian slaves, as St. Paul's admonition makes clear.[157]

It is far worse to be in bondage to sin than to be in bondage to another man. The slave can be free from the heavier bondage if he lives righteously and serves his master "not in crafty fear, but in faithful love, until all unrighteousness pass away, and all principality and every human power be brought to nothing, and God be all in all." [158] On the other hand, many masters are wicked men; although they have religious men as their slaves, they are themselves in bondage.

And beyond question it is a happier thing to be the slave of a man than of a lust; for even this very lust of ruling, to mention no others, lays waste men's hearts with the most ruthless dominion. Moreover, when men are subjected to one another in a peaceful order, the lowly position does as much good to the servant as the proud position does harm to the master.[159]

The only true Lord in the universe is God, since He does not need any of His creatures, while all of them need Him. Therefore, the human master is not the true lord of his servant; since both are men, both need God. In addition, there is a relationship of mutual need between master and servant.

He needs the good you provide for him in feeding him, and you need the good he provides for you by his service. For yourself you cannot do all the drawing of water, the cooking, the running before your carriage, the grooming of your beast. You are in want of the good your servant furnishes, you are in want of attendance; and inasmuch as you want an inferior, you are no true lord.[160]

Although Augustine recognizes that by law slaves are treated as items of property, which can be bought and sold and can be the subjects of lawsuits, he does not believe that it is right for a Christian to treat a slave as if he were an inanimate possession. "For a Christian ought not to possess a slave in the same way as a horse or money: although it may happen that a horse is valued at a greater price than a slave, and some article of gold or silver at much more." [161] Therefore, Christ's command that if a man sues you for your cloak, you should give him your coat in addition, does not necessarily apply to the slaves that you happen to own.

But with respect to that slave, if he is being educated and ruled by thee as his master, in a way more upright, and more honourable, and more conducing to the fear of God, than can be done by him who desires to take him away, I do not know whether any one would dare to say that he ought to be despised like a garment. For a man ought to love a fellow-man as himself, inasmuch as he is commanded by the Lord of all . . . even to love his enemies.[162]

CHAPTER IV

THE STATE: THE RETURN OF ORDER

UPON DISORDER

In the last chapter I analyzed Augustine's conceptions of temporal peace and earthly justice as distinguished from "true" or "real" peace and justice, found only in the City of God. We saw that although earthly peace and order are frequently disturbed by conflict, and the justice they provide is often imperfect, they are essential conditions for man's continued existence and must, therefore, be maintained by a political and legal system furnished with powers of coercion. So we come at last to the central theme —Augustine's analysis of the state, its tasks, and its powers. The state operates in this world, and most of its citizens are (and always will be) those sinful men whose characteristics we have already discussed.[1] In any earthly state a small number of the citizens may be men who have been converted by God's grace; since these men have died and been born anew, their loves, their aspirations, and their behavior are completely different from those of the great mass of the unredeemed. However, as long as this world lasts, there will never be a society or a state made up solely or even predominantly of the saved. Since the two cities are inextricably bound together until the Last Judgment, every earthly state will be composed primarily of sinners, with perhaps a scattering of saints living in their midst.[2] The political and legal system must, therefore, be set up and operated on the assumption that it is dealing with fallen men. The motives upon which it relies when it makes laws and imposes penalties must be the drives that impel such men to action, and its expectations should never outrun the characteristics that they can be presumed to possess.

As we have seen, the state, for Augustine, is an external order; the peace that it maintains is external peace—the absence, or at least the diminution, of overt violence. The state is also a coercive order, maintained by the use of force and relying on the *Coercive* fear of pain as its major sanction for compliance to its commands. It has no weapons by which it can mold the thoughts, desires, and wills of its citizens; nor is it really concerned to exert such influence. It does not seek to make men truly good or virtuous. Rather, it is interested in their outward actions, and it attempts, with some success, to restrain its citizens from performing certain kinds of harmful and criminal acts. We have also observed that the state is a non-natural, remedial institution; like private property, slavery, and other forms of domination of man over man, it is a consequence of the Fall. It is both a punishment for sin and a remedy for man's sinful condition; without it anarchy would reign, and self-centered, avaricious, power-hungry, lustful men would destroy one another in a fierce struggle for self-aggrandizement. This external, coercive, repressive, remedial order—and its main virtue is that it *is* an order—is clearly distinguished by Augustine from the order or hierarchy found among the angels and in the whole City of God; the latter is a spontaneous order of love and not an order of coercion or domination.[3]

The reader of this brief summary of Augustine's doctrine of the state may wonder whether I am talking about Augustine, or about Hobbes or Machiavelli. Certainly, this conception of the state strikes us as essentially "modern," and we may be surprised to find it in a Christian philosopher of the fifth century. Since this formulation of the gist of Augustinian political theory is one to which some of his commentators might take exception, it will be our task to show, by explicit statements from Augustine as well as by deductions from his views of the nature of man, that it is an accurate summary and that it does not do violence to what Augustine himself says throughout the whole corpus of his writings.

Let us turn first to his discussion in *The City of God* of the definitions of a people (*populus*) and of a commonwealth or state (*res publica*) given by Scipio in Cicero's *De Republica*. He first refers to these Scipionic definitions in Book II, where he notes that according to Scipio a people is not "every assemblage or mob, but an assemblage associated by a common acknowledgment of law [i.e., an agreement about right or justice], and by a community of interests [*Populum autem non omnem coetum multitudinis, sed coetum iuris consensu et utilitatis communione sociatum esse determinat*]."[4] He promises that at a later point he will demonstrate that, according to this definition, there was never a people (*populus*) in Rome, and, consequently, that Rome was never a state or commonwealth (*res publica*), since true justice never had a place in it, and Scipio—and Cicero—has made an agreement about justice (*consensus iuris*) essential to the existence of a people and a state. This, to Augustine, is an absurd conclusion; so he adds, "But accepting the more feasible [i.e., "more probable" (*probabiliores*)] definitions of a republic, I grant there was a republic of a certain kind, and certainly much better administered by the more ancient Romans than by their modern representatives [*Secundum probabiliores autem definitiones pro suo modo quodam res publica fuit, et melius ab antiquioribus Romanis quam a posterioribus administrata est*]."[5] To make it quite clear that no other earthly state—whether pagan or Christian, ancient or modern—possessed true justice and was therefore a commonwealth according to Scipio's definition, Augustine immediately adds: "But the fact is, true justice has no existence save in that republic whose founder and ruler is Christ [*uera autem iustitia non est nisi in ea re publica, cuius conditor rectorque Christus est*]."[6]

In Book XIX, Augustine fulfills his promise to return to the consideration of the Scipionic definitions of a "people" and a "commonwealth." Again he notes that, according to Scipio, "a common acknowledgment of right [*consensus iuris*]" is essential to the existence of a people and of a commonwealth; this means

that a republic cannot be administered without justice. Where, therefore, there is no true justice there can be no right. . . . Thus where there is not true justice there can be no assemblage of men associated by a common acknowledgment of right, and therefore there can be no people, as defined by Scipio or Cicero; and if no people, then no weal of the people [*res populi*], but only of some promiscuous multitude unworthy of the name of people. Consequently . . . most certainly it follows that there is no republic where there is no justice.[7]

After citing the traditional definition of justice as "that virtue which gives every one his due,"[8] Augustine proceeds again to show that true justice was never present in the Roman commonwealth, whether we look at its early, heroic period or its later phase of decay and degeneration. "Where, then, is the justice of man, when he deserts the true God and yields himself to impure demons? Is this to give every one his due?"[9] If a man does not serve God,

what justice can we ascribe to him, since in this case his soul cannot exercise a just control over the body, nor his reason over his vices? And if there is no justice in such an individual, certainly there can be none in a community composed of such persons. Here, therefore, there is not that common acknowledgment of right which makes an assemblage of men a people whose affairs we call a republic.[10]

Once more, Augustine is insisting that true justice can be found only in a community or commonwealth made up of individuals who serve and love God and, *as a result,* possess true justice.

However, there is only one such community—the City of God —and it has no earthly representative; so neither the Roman State nor any other state can possibly possess true justice. If, then, in agreement with Scipio, we make justice a constitutive element in the definition of the state, we will be forced to the conclusion that no state or commonwealth has ever existed or will ever exist on this earth.

At this point it is no doubt clear that I cannot accept the interpretation of these passages from *The City of God* that is offered, for example, by Professor Charles H. McIlwain in his well-known work, *The Growth of Political Thought in the West*.[11] Professor McIlwain, in his criticisms of Figgis and Carlyle, admits that Augustine states that a kingdom (*regnum*) or a city (*civitas*) may exist without justice, and that he defines both of them without including the element of right or justice in the definition.[12] McIlwain then goes on to argue that Augustine meant to confine these statements to *regna* and *civitates,* and did not intend them to apply to states or commonwealths (*res publicae*). For a true *res publica* there must be the bond of justice and law which Cicero required; but if there is to be true justice, God must be worshiped and given His due. Therefore, only a Christian state can be just and, as a result, a true *res publica.* Augustine's remarks about *regna* and *civitates* are now confined to heathen states, and the way is open for McIlwain's conclusion that, for Augustine,

justice and justice alone is the only possible bond which can unite men as a true *populus* in a real *res publica*. The great states before Christianity were *regna* but they were not true commonwealths because there was no recognition in them of what was due to the one true God, and without such recognition there could be no real justice, for justice is to render to *each* his due. . . . [A *populus*] must be united *consensu juris,* by consent to law, and that law must include the law of God as well as the law of man. Such law and such justice there cannot be in any state in which the just claims of the one true God are denied. No heathen state can ever rise quite to the height of a true commonwealth.[13]

A number of difficulties must be faced by anyone who accepts McIlwain's interpretation, in which Augustine is said to have espoused exactly that Ciceronian definition of the state or *res publica* that he seems to reject. First, McIlwain ignores Augustine's clear statement, to which I have already referred, that "true justice has no existence save in that republic whose founder and ruler is Christ,"[14] that is, in the City of God. This statement surely means that no earthly state, whether a *res publica,* a *regnum,* or a *civitas,* whether ostensibly heathen or Christian, can possess true justice, unless one proposes to identify the City of God with a so-called Christian state—an identification which Augustine would never dream of making, since he will not even allow an identification between the City of God and the Church Militant.

In addition, McIlwain ignores another important statement by Augustine, where he repeats at greater length the same idea that the only true *res publica* in the Ciceronian sense is the City of God; here alone is found in *all the citizens* and therefore in the community as a whole that true justice whereby God is served and, as a consequence, the soul rules the body and reason the vices. Certainly it would be very difficult for anyone to argue that when the Roman Empire or any other state became officially "Christian," all its citizens or even all its Christian citizens became truly just and righteous in Augustine's sense of these terms. The passage from Augustine is worth quoting in full; it comes just before he gives an alternative definition to replace the Scipionic definition that he is rejecting.

And therefore, where there is not this righteousness [*iustitia*] whereby the one supreme God rules the obedient city according to

His grace, so that it sacrifices to none but Him, and whereby, in *all the citizens* of this obedient city, the soul consequently rules the body and reason the vices in the rightful order, so that, as the individual just man, so also the community and people of the just, live by faith, which works by love, that love whereby man loves God as He ought to be loved, and his neighbour as himself,—there, I say, there is not an assemblage associated by a common acknowledgment of right, and by a community of interests. But if there is not this, there is not a people, if our [lit., "this" (*haec*)] definition [i.e., the Scipionic definition] be true, and therefore there is no republic; for where there is no people there can be no republic.[15]

Immediately Augustine proceeds to give his alternative definition of a *res publica,* which he had promised in Book II when he said that, "accepting the more feasible definitions of a republic, I grant there was a republic of a certain kind" [16] in Rome. Chapter 24 of Book XIX opens with this alternative definition, which is startling to so many readers, including McIlwain, since it completely omits the idea of justice from the definition of the state. It is a completely amoral account of what a *populus* or a *res publica* is, and it is an elastic definition that permits us to include under it a wide variety of peoples and states with different goals and interests.

But if we discard this definition [i.e., the Scipionic] of a people, and, assuming another, say that a people is an assemblage of reasonable beings bound together by a common agreement as to the objects of their love [*populus est coetus multitudinis rationalis rerum quas diligit concordi communione sociatus*], then, in order to discover the character of any people, we have only to observe what they love. Yet whatever it loves, if only it is an assemblage of reasonable beings and not of beasts, and is bound together by an agreement as to the objects of love, it is reasonably called a people; and it will be a superior people in proportion as it is bound together by higher interests, inferior in proportion as it is bound together by lower. According to *this definition of ours,* the Roman people is a people, and its weal is without doubt a commonwealth or republic.[17]

This passage presents insuperable difficulties for any commentator who, like McIlwain, is trying to prove that Augustine really accepted Cicero's definition of the state in terms of justice. McIlwain attempts to meet these difficulties by expressing serious doubt as to whether this alternative definition represents Augustine's own opinion; he argues that Augustine simply assumes it as a hypothetical definition in his attempt to argue for Christianity and against heathenism.[18]

It is difficult to see how this interpretation fits the facts. For, in the first place, Augustine had, in Book II, promised his readers "more feasible" definitions of a "people" and a "commonwealth" to replace the Scipionic definitions. It is this promise that he now fulfills by giving a careful, precise definition from which "justice" is eliminated, so that we will have a definition of the state which can be applied to the states which exist in this world, rather than one which applies to only one commonwealth, the City of God in heaven. Second, in the quotation itself, he speaks of this new definition as "this definition of ours [*istam definitionem nostram*]." Third, the definition fits perfectly with Augustine's emphasis upon love as the determining element in human action; as we have seen,[19] "my weight is my love" is the central principle of his psychological analysis. It is therefore natural and fitting that he should define and differentiate states by reference to the different objects of love which the members of each state pursue. Fourth, and perhaps most important, the definition is repeated in all its essentials in a number of other places in Augustine's writings.[20]

It is significant that Augustine nowhere makes the distinction between heathen and Christian states that is central to McIlwain's argument.[21] At no time does he say—or suggest—that while pagan states could not possibly exhibit true justice Christian states necessarily are, or at least may be, truly just. When he speaks of the possibility that all or most of the members of a state—rulers and subjects—might actually behave like Christians, he always uses the form of a condition contrary to fact; for example,

If the kings of the earth and all the peoples, if the princes and all the judges of the earth, if young men and maidens, old and young, every age, and both sexes; if they whom John the Baptist addresses, the tax collectors and the soldiers, *were all together to hear and observe* [*audirent atque curarent*] *these precepts* [of the Christian religion] regarding justice and honesty of character, *then would the republic* [*res publica*] *adorn the lands of this life with its own felicity,* and mount the pinnacle of life eternal to reign most blessedly. But *because* this man listens, and that man scoffs, and *most are enamored of the evil blandishments of vice rather than of the beneficial severity of virtue, the servants of Christ*—whether they be kings or princes or judges, soldiers or provincials, rich or poor, bond or free, male or female—*are enjoined to endure even the most wicked and most vicious commonwealth, if so it must be* [*tolerare Christi famuli iubentur . . . etiam pessimam, si ita necesse est, flagitiosissimamque rem publicam*], that so they may by this endurance purchase for themselves an eminent place in that most holy and august parliament of the angels and in the celestial republic, where the will of God is law [*caelestique re publica, ubi Dei uoluntas lex est*].[22]

It is clear that Augustine is here speaking of his own period, when the Empire is "Christian," and not of the pagan past or of the period of the persecution of the Church by the State. Although he assumes that it is possible that emperors or kings, princes or judges may, as individuals, be Christians, this does not lead him to speak of the state as good or just or Christian. Indeed, the conclusion of his argument is almost the reverse; true Christians must be prepared "to endure even the most wicked and most vicious commonwealth."

The Emperor Constantine had been converted to Christianity almost a century before Augustine wrote *The City of God,* and it was about forty years since Theodosius I, Gratian, and Valentinian II had issued the Edict of Thessalonica (February 27, 380), in which they established Christianity as the official religion of the Roman Empire.[23] So, had Augustine wished to make the distinction between pagan and Christian states that McIlwain tries to impose upon him he could easily have done so. His failure to say that Christian states, in contrast to pagan states, are or can be truly just, when taken together with his statements that true justice exists only in the City of God, appears to be powerful evidence on the point.[24] This evidence is strengthened when we recall that he was convinced that not even the Church, to say nothing of the state, could ever be an association composed solely of men who are redeemed and, therefore, good and just. If the number of the saved is always a small minority, it is impossible to establish and maintain an earthly society made up only of men who love and serve God and who are, as a result of that love, truly just.

One of the possible sources of Professor McIlwain's difficulties in dealing with Augustine is the failure to make the distinction, so crucial to understanding his thought, between "true justice" (*vera justitia*), found only in God's kingdom, and the much inferior but still important "image of justice" or "temporal" or "earthly" justice found in all ordered earthly states, whether they are called *res publicae, civitates,* or *regna*.[25] A state or earthly city, for Augustine, can be called "just" only in the sense that it is what he refers to as "well-ordered" (*bene ordinata*) [26] or "well-constituted" (*bene constituta*).[27] It has, that is, a certain harmony and concord among its citizens, and a measure of temporal peace —"what the vulgar call felicity"—is secured in it. Rulers, whether kings or princes, and laws are the major elements in securing this measure of order, peace, and earthly justice, and, therefore, a well-ordered state. "For without these things no people can be well-ordered, not even a people that pursues earthly goods. Even such a people has a measure of beauty of its own." [28] On the other hand, no state or society in this world can be called "just" in the sense of embodying true justice, that is, giving to each his due. For a city or a state would be just only if the men who make up the community—king, court, ministers, and people— were just; for "individual men . . . are, as it were, the elements and seeds of cities." [29]

Since the great majority of the members of any society are men who belong to the earthly city, who place their love in the world and in the things of the world, it necessarily follows that they will be unjust as each strives to outdo the others in the unceasing struggle for material goods, power, and glory.

For when those things are loved which we can lose against our will, we must needs toil for them most miserably; and to obtain them, amid the straitnesses of earthly cares, whilst each desires to snatch them for himself, and to be beforehand with another, or to wrest it from him, must scheme injustice.[30]

When Augustine speaks of the ungodly or the wicked, he never confines these terms to pagans or to non-Christians, but always insists that many members of the visible Church are included in the ranks of the unredeemed; this will continue to be true as long as this world lasts.[31] Even if the unredeemed have "virtues," such as modesty, continence, or civic virtue, these are not true virtues, and their justice is not true justice,[32] although they may have a certain "uprightness," sufficient to maintain an earthly state.[33]

One of Augustine's most shockingly realistic discussions of earthly states is the famous fourth chapter of Book IV of The City of God in which he draws the comparison between kingdoms and robber bands. It is possible to raise questions about the meaning of certain phrases in this passage, but the sense of the chapter as a whole is clear beyond any doubt. A number of different translations and interpretations can be given for the first words of the opening sentence—*"Remota itaque iustitia quid sunt regna nisi magna latrocinia? quia et latrocinia quid sunt nisi parua regna?"* "And so, justice removed, what are kingdoms but great robber bands? And what are robber bands but small kingdoms?" Does Augustine mean, "If true justice is absent— and it need not be—kingdoms are nothing but large robber bands"? That this cannot be the meaning is clear from what we have said about the impossibility of finding real or true justice in any earthly state. Or is he saying that a kingdom which does not have even earthly or temporal justice—the shadow or image of real justice—is nothing but a great robber band? Or does he perhaps mean that since all kingdoms are unjust they are nothing but great bands of robbers? [34] Perhaps the best course is to set aside the question of the correct meaning of this initial sentence and go on to consider the rest of the paragraph. After the flat statement that robber bands are nothing but small kingdoms, Augustine continues:

The band itself is made up of men; it is ruled by the authority of a prince; it is knit together by the pact of the confederacy; the booty is divided by the law agreed on. If, by the admittance of abandoned men, this evil increases to such a degree that it holds places, fixes abodes, takes possession of cities, and subdues peoples, it assumes the more plainly the name of a kingdom, because the reality is now manifestly conferred on it, *not by the removal of covetousness* [*cupiditas*], *but by the addition of impunity* [*impunitas*].[35]

At every point there is a parallel between the robber band and the kingdom: both are composed of men, both are ruled by the authority of a leader or prince; both are held together by a *pactum societatis,* a pact of association; in both the spoils are divided in accordance with the rules agreed to by the group. By these means—authority, a fundamental agreement, and operating rules—both maintain a kind of order, harmony, and even "justice." The points of identity are startling enough, but we are even more surprised when Augustine points out the differences between the robber band and the kingdom. Here, if anywhere, we would expect him to tell us that it is the presence of justice that distinguishes the state from the band of robbers. If this is our expectation, we are completely disappointed. The kingdom is larger than the robber band both in numbers and in territory occupied, and it has a fixed abode. As the robber band increases in size and settles down, it assumes the more plainly the name of a kingdom, not because its cupidity has been taken away but because it now possesses the priceless advantage of the "impunity" of a "sovereign state." Kingdoms are no less avaricious than robber bands, but whereas the band of robbers may be punished by the state, there is no super-state or international police force to punish the state for its misdeeds or its depredations.[36] The somber message of the chapter is pointed up by the anecdote that Augustine relates with approval in the final sentences.

Indeed, that was an apt and true reply which was given to Alexander the Great by a pirate who had been seized. For when that king had asked the man what he meant by keeping hostile possession of the sea, he answered with bold pride, "What thou meanest by seizing the whole earth; but because I do it with a petty ship, I am called a robber, whilst thou who dost it with a great fleet art styled Emperor." [37]

A few pages later Augustine returns to this comparison when he is discussing the wars waged by Ninus, king of the Assyrians, in order to extend his empire. "But to make war on your neighbours, and thence to proceed to others, and through mere lust of dominion to crush and subdue people who do you no harm, what else is this to be called than great robbery?" [38] The similarity between the robber and the king or prince is again pointed out

when he says that even the thief and murderer who is unwilling
to have any associates or accomplices wants his wife and children
to obey his commands, and thus he shows that he desires to have
peace in his home.

And therefore, if a city or nation offered to submit itself to him, to
serve him in the same style as he had made his household serve him,
he would no longer lurk in a brigand's hiding-places, but lift his
head in open day as a king, *though the same covetousness and wickedness should remain in him.* And thus all men desire to have peace
with their own circle whom they wish to govern as suits themselves.
For even those whom they make war against they wish to make their
own, and impose on them the laws of their own peace.[39]

Once more, the point is driven home that the king is distinguished from the robber not by the absence of wickedness or
cupidity but rather by his exalted position, his impunity, and his
acceptance by the group over which he rules.

It is important to get a clear picture of what Augustine is saying about political power and about temporal rulers. He is *not*
saying that all kings are wicked, evil men; indeed, in his arguments against the Donatists he clearly rejects their contention
that all kings are the enemies of the righteous, and insists that
many kings have proved to be the friends of the godly.[40] In
many earthly commonwealths we find citizens of the City of
God among its rulers and magistrates who conduct its affairs.
Since the two kingdoms, the two types of man—the lovers of
earthly things and the lovers of heavenly things—are mingled
together as long as this world lasts,

we see now the citizen of Jerusalem, citizen of the kingdom of
heaven, have some office upon earth: to wit, one weareth purple, is
a Magistrate, is Aedile, is Proconsul, is Emperor, doth direct the
earthly republic: but he hath his heart above, if he is a Christian, if
he is a believer, if he is godly, if he is despising those things wherein
he is, and trusteth in that wherein he is not yet. . . . Despair we
not then of the citizens of the kingdom of heaven, when we see them

engaged in any of Babylon's matters, doing something earthly in republic earthly: nor again let us forthwith congratulate all men that we see doing matters heavenly; because even the sons of pestilence sit sometimes in the seat of Moses. . . .[41]

Men are fortunate indeed if their rulers happen to be individuals who possess true piety and, therefore, true virtue. "But there could be nothing more fortunate for human affairs than that, by the mercy of God, they who are endowed with true piety of life, if they have the skill for ruling people, should also have the power."[42] Since God, in the furtherance of His plans, grants power and dominion to both the good and the wicked, it is obvious that individual kings and rulers can be good and pious men. Augustine also says that good men who have a talent for governing have an obligation to assume the burdens of rule.[43] He frequently exhorts rulers to remember their subordination to God and their heavy responsibilities and duties toward their subjects,[44] and he gives a detailed portrait of how the pious, just ruler ought to behave. When we say that certain Christian emperors were happy, we are not referring to their long reigns, their victories at home and abroad, or their succession by their sons.

But we say that they are happy if they rule justly; if they are not lifted up amid the praises of those who pay them sublime honours, and the obsequiousness of those who salute them with an excessive humility, but remember that they are men; if they make their power the handmaid of His majesty by using it for the greatest possible extension of His worship; if they fear, love, worship God; if more than their own they love that kingdom in which they are not afraid to have partners; if they are slow to punish, ready to pardon; if they apply that punishment as necessary to government and defence of the republic, and not in order to gratify their own enmity; if they grant pardon, not that iniquity may go unpunished, but with the hope that the transgressor may amend his ways; if they compensate with the lenity of mercy and the liberality of benevolence for whatever severity they may be compelled to decree; if their luxury is as much restrained as it might have been unrestrained; if they prefer to govern depraved desires rather than any nation whatever; and if they do all these things, not through ardent desire of empty glory, but through love of eternal felicity, not neglecting to offer to the one true God, who is their God, for their sins, the sacrifices of humility, contrition, and prayer. Such Christian emperors, we say, are happy in the present time by hope, and are destined to be so in the enjoyment of the reality itself, when that which we wait for shall have arrived.[45]

This portrait of the ideal Christian ruler, which is sometimes taken as Augustine's description of how Christian kings *do* behave rather than as his view of how they *ought* to act, and is therefore used as proof that he believed that a Christian state could be truly just, is obviously in the tradition of the large body of literature known as the "Mirror of Princes." These treatises, which first appear in the Hellenistic period and continue to be produced both in the West and in Byzantium throughout the Middle Ages, are addressed to rulers by philosophers. They all assume that kingship is the best, if not the only, form of government, and they confine their efforts to giving advice and counsel to the king under the guise of painting a highly idealized portrait of the king's benevolence, magnanimity, temperance, and justice.[46] In the Hellenistic period many of these treatises on kingship were written by Stoic teachers. Seneca's *De Clementia*, addressed to Nero and praising his many virtues, is perhaps the most famous example of the genre; there is bitter irony in the fact that Nero is here presented to the world as the model of the just and merciful ruler. Augustine was certainly familiar with this kind of political writing, and his own portrait of a good and wise Christian emperor is an obvious reworking of traditional materials.

One of the elements in Augustine's picture of the ideal Christian emperor requires special comment. We see that he urges the ruler not only to be pious and humble before God, but also to

make his power the handmaid of God's majesty "by using it for
the greatest possible extension of His worship." [47] The good
Christian ruler is bound to use his royal power to promote true
religion and the worship of the one true God. In a letter written
about 414 to Macedonius, Vicar of Africa, Augustine tells him:
if you employ your prudence, fortitude, temperance, and justice
only with the aim that "those whose welfare you have at heart
may be safe in body and secure from the dishonesty of anyone,
that they may enjoy peace" and material prosperity, "in that case,
yours are no true virtues, and theirs no true happiness." [48] If, he
continues, your actions have only the aim "that men may suffer
no undue distress according to the flesh," and if you think that

it is not incumbent on you that they should make a return for that
tranquility which you try to secure for them, that is, . . . that they
should worship the true God in whom is all the fruition of the
peaceful life, such effort on your part will bring you no return in
true happiness.[49]

How, it may be asked, can these injunctions to a Christian
ruler be reconciled with Augustine's general view that it is the
task of the state and of its rulers to preserve external peace and
to maintain an imperfect earthly justice among sinful men?
First, it is evident that absolute consistency and complete harmony are not to be expected among the hundreds of statements
about the state and its functions which are scattered throughout
Augustine's writings—his doctrinal and moral treatises, his sermons, and his letters—and which he never brought together into
a systematic theory of the state. We can discover a generally consistent point of view, and it is this which we are trying to
elaborate here, but we should not be surprised if we find certain
elements or emphases that are not easily harmonized with the
main thesis. Second, the question now being discussed—the
Christian ruler's use of the state's power and authority for the

support and extension of true religion—is a problem with which Augustine wrestled for many years, and in the course of the struggle against the Donatist heretics in Africa he answered the question in a number of different ways. Since we shall, at a later point, examine in detail his treatment of this issue of the use of state power against schism and heresy,[50] let us postpone any further consideration of the role of the Christian ruler with respect to religious worship and doctrine or of the tensions between Augustine's views on this subject and his more general theories about the state's functions. Here we need only remember that, for Augustine, the maintenance of earthly justice and temporal, external peace and order—the peace of Babylon, that is, the maintenance of "the combination of men's wills to attain the things which are helpful to this life," [51] of "a common agreement among men regarding the acquisition of the necessaries of life" [52] —is always the basic and fundamental task that the state is expected to perform. When he tells a Christian ruler or magistrate that he ought to use his power not only to secure peace and prosperity for the people but also to promote and foster true religion and piety among them, he is reminding him of his duties as a Christian who is seeking to win eternal salvation—he is not discussing what a state must do if it is to be a state, nor is he advising the ruler to neglect the fundamental functions of the political and legal order.

If some kings are true Christians, many more are ordinary sinful men who are exposed to more than their share of temptations to pride and arrogance, and some are wicked and cruel rulers, whom God sends to punish men for their sins. For every good ruler such as Constantine or Theodosius, who aided the church "by most just and merciful laws . . . [and] indeed, he rejoiced more to be a member of this church than he did to be a king upon the earth," [53] one can mention a number of evil emperors, such as Diocletian, Julian, and that most impious of men, Nero. The important thing for us to remember is Augustine's insistence that it will *never* be true that the world will be ruled by the wise and the godly. Life on this earth would be far happier

if the chief rule and government of human affairs were in the hands of the wise, and of those who were piously and perfectly subject to God; but *because this is not the case as yet* (for it behoves us first to be exercised in this our pilgrimage after mortal fashion, and to be taught with stripes by force of gentleness and patience), let us turn our thoughts to that country itself that is above and heavenly, from which we here are pilgrims.[54]

Moreover, we must never forget that the wicked or unjust man who exercises rule is in every way as legitimate and as much entitled to absolute obedience as the most pious or just ruler.[55] The goodness or badness, piety or impiety, justice or injustice of the ruler has nothing at all to do with his title to rule and to be obeyed.

Even more important is Augustine's view that while this or that man who happens to be a ruler or an official may be pious and just, the state itself—the political order—can never be truly just. Since rulers have to deal with subjects many of whom are sinful, wicked men, the actions of the state cannot be a direct embodiment of Christian precepts of righteousness. As we have seen, the state deals with its citizens only on the level of outward, external behavior. It imposes penalties upon those who violate its laws, but it and its agents have no way of affecting the hearts and wills of men or even of knowing what men's true characters and motivations are.[56] Its main weapon—fear of punishment—cannot make men good or virtuous, but only less harmful to their fellows. The state cannot know whether the punishment imposed is too heavy or too light for the man who has committed this particular crime in these circumstances, and it is never sure whether those who are punished are improved or made worse by the punishment.[57] The judge can never be sure that he is not condemning an innocent man; like all other men, he is prone to regard his suspicions as knowledge and to view as true the facts that seem credible to him.[58] Frequently his judgment is distorted even further by the pride that overcomes him because he has the power to decide the fate of other men and to judge whether they are guilty or innocent.[59] And when he employs torture in order to extract the truth from suspected criminals or from witnesses, he never knows whether the confession or the testimony that he obtains may not be false, extorted from an innocent man by torture or by the fear of it.

What shall I say of *these judgments which men pronounce on men, and which are necessary in communities, whatever outward peace they enjoy?* Melancholy and lamentable judgments they are, since the judges are men who cannot discern the consciences of those at their bar, and are therefore frequently compelled to put innocent witnesses to the torture to ascertain the truth regarding the crimes of other men. What shall I say of torture applied to the accused himself? He is tortured to discover whether he is guilty, so that, though innocent, he suffers most undoubted punishment for crime that is still doubtful, not because it is proved that he committed it, but because it is not ascertained that he did not commit it. Thus the ignorance of the judge frequently involves an innocent person in suffering. And what is still more unendurable . . . is this, that when the judge puts the accused to the question, that he may not unwittingly put an innocent man to death, the result of this lamentable ignorance is that this very person, whom he tortured that he might not condemn him if innocent, is condemned to death both tortured and innocent. . . . And when he has been condemned and put to death, the judge is still in ignorance whether he has put to death an innocent or a guilty person, though he put the accused to the torture for the very purpose of saving himself from condemning the innocent; and consequently he has both tortured an innocent man to discover his innocence, and has put him to death without discovering it.

If such darkness shrouds social life [In his tenebris uitae socialis], will a wise judge take his seat on the bench or no? Beyond question he will. For human society, which he thinks it a wickedness to abandon, constrains him and compels him to this duty.[60]

And he thinks it no wickedness that innocent witnesses are tortured regarding the crimes of which other men are accused; or that the accused are put to the torture, so that they are often overcome with anguish, and, though innocent, make false confessions regarding themselves, and are punished; or that, though they be not condemned to die, they often die during, or in consequence of, the torture; or that sometimes the accusers, who perhaps have been prompted by a desire to benefit society by bringing criminals to justice, are themselves condemned through the ignorance of the judge, because they are unable to prove the truth of their accusations though they are true, and because the witnesses lie, and the accused endures the torture without being moved to confession. These numerous and important evils he does not consider sins; for *the wise judge does these things, not with any intention of doing harm, but because his ignorance compels him, and because human society claims him as a judge.* But though we therefore acquit the judge of malice, we must none the less condemn human life as miserable. And if he is compelled to torture and punish the innocent because his office and his ignorance constrain him, is he a happy as well as a guiltless man? Surely it were proof of more profound considerateness and finer feeling were he to recognise the misery of these necessities, and shrink from his own implication in that misery; and had he any piety about him, he would cry to God, "From my necessities deliver Thou me." [61]

It is inescapable dilemmas like these that make it impossible for a state to be truly just, no matter what the character and personality of its rulers may be at any particular moment. The justice that emerges in the well-ordered state is a most imperfect replica or image of true justice, no matter how good the intentions of the rulers may be. Most overt crimes are punished; but some are never detected and others are never solved; sometimes the wrong man is punished, and the guilty go scot free.[62] The rulers and the citizens are only men, fallible, prejudiced, and

ignorant of much that they need to know. Even when they do
the best that they can, their best is far from true justice; and,
often, what they do is far from their best.[63] Rulers are, as St.
Paul said, God's ministers, avengers against those that do evil.
But a province or a state can only be ruled by instilling fear in
those who are ruled, and the fear of punishment can never
produce true righteousness or justice. By their fear of the laws
and of the punishments attached to them, men can be kept from
performing certain injurious actions, but they cannot be made
good or righteous by these means. Civil laws do not "bring men
to make a good use of their wealth," but "those who make a bad
use of it become thereby less injurious." [64] Augustine states the
kernel of the problem in one sentence: "But, ruling a province
is different from ruling a Church; the former must be governed
by instilling fear, the latter is to be made lovable by the use of
mildness." [65]

Of course, these dilemmas would not exist and this very imperfect, rough "justice" of the state would be converted into true
justice if not only the rulers but all the subjects were truly pious
and just men, who obeyed the commandments of Christ, and,
as a consequence, preferred common interests to their egoistic,
private interests.[66] If this were possible, we could have the "Christian state," the truly just society, based on God's law, that some
commentators seem to think that Augustine regarded as feasible
or necessary.[67] It is perfectly clear, however, that the conditions
sine qua non for the existence of such a state can never be realized
on this earth. Moreover, if they were to be realized, the result
would not be a Christian or truly just state but rather the complete absence of the state as we know it. Since the entire apparatus
of law, punishment, coercion, and repression that constitutes the
heart of the state would be totally unnecessary, the state would
indeed "wither away" and be replaced by the anarchist's paradise

—a spontaneous, noncoercive order of love, which would embody true justice, true peace, and true harmony, with no need for armies, courts, policemen, judges, jailers, and hangmen.[68]

In other words, a truly just society would be the City of God brought down from heaven to earth, and that for Augustine is an absolute impossibility. Even when he is defending Christianity against pagan charges that it is incompatible with patriotism and the well-being of the state, he is careful to retain the contrary-to-fact conditional form in speaking of the possibility of a state made up of true Christians.

> Wherefore, let those who say that the doctrine of Christ is incompatible with the State's well-being, give us an army composed of soldiers such as the doctrine of Christ requires them to be; let them give us such subjects, such husbands and wives, such parents and children, such masters and servants, such kings, such judges—in fine, even such taxpayers and tax-gatherers, as *the Christian religion has taught that men should be,* and then let them dare to say that it is adverse to the State's well-being; yea, rather, let them no longer hesitate to confess that *this doctrine, if it were obeyed, would be the salvation of the commonwealth.*[69]

Augustine is perfectly explicit about the purpose of the earthly state and of the coercion and punishment it employs. The heavy hand of the state and its dreadful instruments of repression are necessary because they are the only methods by which sinful men can be restrained; the fear of punishment is the only safeguard of general peace and security. Only by such means can the wicked be kept from destroying one another as their competing egoisms clash, and discouraged from open assaults upon the minority of good and pious men.

> Surely, it is not without purpose that we have the institution of the power of kings, the death penalty of the judge, the barbed hooks of the executioner, the weapons of the soldier, the right of punishment of the overlord [*dominantis*], even the severity of the good father.

All those things have their methods, their causes, their reasons, their practical benefits. *While these are feared, the wicked are kept within bounds and the good live more peacefully among the wicked.* However, men are not to be called good because they refrain from wrongdoing through their fear of such things—*no one is good through dread of punishment but through love of righteousness*—even so, it is not without advantage that human recklessness should be confined by fear of the law so that innocence may be safe among evil-doers, and the evil-doers themselves may be cured by calling on God when their freedom of action is held in check by fear of punishment.[70]

By the laws that it enforces the state protects from the encroachments of other men the things that each citizen properly regards as "his"—his body and bodily goods, his liberty (that is, his right as a free man to have no master), his household, his citizenship, and his possessions. The function of the temporal law is to insure that "men may possess the things which may be called 'ours' for a season and which they eagerly covet, on condition that peace and human society be preserved so far as they can be preserved in earthly things."[71] The law determines what the citizen may lawfully possess,[72] and then by its sanctions it secures to each citizen the enjoyment of his proper "possessions." Thereby, it moderates the intensity of the inevitable conflict among earthly men for goods and for glory, and prevents the clash of egoistic interests from totally disrupting the peace and harmony of society. The law operates through the instrument of fear.[73] It has no effect on the men who are subject to it except through the medium of those very goods and possessions that it exists to protect and regulate. In other words, the sanction by means of which the state attempts to insure conformity to the conduct prescribed by the laws consists in the ability to deprive the offender of one or more of these possessions—his property, his liberty, his citizenship, or, in the last resort, his life. Since the men of the earthly city regard these possessions as the highest good, they are afraid of being deprived of any or all of them. Therefore, each man somewhat restrains his unlimited desire to acquire more possessions and more power at the expense of other members of the society, because he feels that the chance of greater gain and satisfaction is outweighed by the deprivations that he will suffer if he is punished for violating the law that protects the property of all.

It is sufficient to see that the authority of this law in punishing does not go beyond depriving him who is punished of these things or of some of them. It employs fear as an instrument of coercion, and bends to its own ends the minds of the unhappy people to rule whom it is adapted. So long as they fear to lose these earthly goods they observe in using them a certain moderation suited to maintain in being a city such as can be composed of such men [*quendam modum aptum vinculo civitatis, qualis ex huiuscemodi hominibus constitui potest*]. The sin of loving these things is not punished; what is punished is the wrong done to others when their rights are infringed.[74]

Augustine sees that the legal system with its sanctions and punishments does not change, and does not attempt to change, the basic desires and attitudes of the men whose conduct it seeks to regulate. In fact, the system works precisely because these lovers of earthly goods are *not* transformed into lovers of real or eternal goods; unless they continued to place their affections in the things of this world, the law and its punishments would inspire no fear in them and so would have no effect on their behavior. The law can effectively punish only those men who love the possessions that can be taken from them against their will. "You see also that there would be no punishment inflicted on men either by injury done them or by legal sentence if they did not love the things that can be taken from them against their will." [75]

These reflections about the state's purpose—the maintenance of external peace and order—and about the means that it employs

to achieve this end—punishment and the deprivation of possessions, liberty, and life—exhibit one of the most characteristic fea-
tures of Augustine's thoughts about man and his life on earth—
his keen awareness of the paradoxes and ironies that mark every
aspect of the human condition, and especially of political life.
There is a constant danger that men will destroy one another as
they seek to accumulate more and more possessions and power by
robbing, cheating, or injuring their fellows. They are kept from
this mutual injury and annihilation only by being threatened
with the loss of the goods that they love and seek to acquire. The
very sin of loving earthly goods thus supplies, to some extent, its
own corrective and remedy, with the result that human society,
which is essential to man's survival, is not completely dissolved
and at least a minimum of security and peace is maintained.

Throughout the entire course of the world, order is imposed,
through God's Providence, even upon the willful actions of evil
men who seek to disrupt or destroy the natural order.[76] Acts of
political governance and the penalties imposed by the legal system represent striking examples of this process whereby order
is recreated and restored out of disorder.

Some man, for instance, has chosen to be a house-breaker: the law
of the judge knows that he has acted contrary to the law: the law
of the judge knows where to place him; and orders him most properly. He indeed has lived evilly; but not evilly has the law ordered
him. From a house-breaker he will be sentenced to the mines; from
the labour of such how great works are constructed? That condemned
man's punishment is the city's ornament.[77]

The same point is made even more strikingly when Augustine
refers to the "cruel and ferocious" hangman who is, nevertheless,
an indispensable element in the order of a well-regulated state.

What more hideous than a hangman? What more cruel and ferocious
than his character? Yet he holds a necessary post in the very midst
of laws, and he is incorporated into the order of a well-regulated

state [*bene moderatae ciuitatis*]; himself criminal in character, he is nevertheless, by others' arrangement, the penalty of evil-doers.[78]

The state's legal and punitive system does not *require* good and just men as its legislators, judges, jailers, or executioners;[79] this is fortunate since only a small minority of its officers can be expected to be truly good. If true Christians happen to occupy these offices, they will punish evildoers not with vengeance but with the love and good will "which a father has towards his little son, whom by reason of his youth he cannot yet hate."[80] Since the correction of evildoers is a duty, especially for those who are magistrates or hold other public posts, the imposition of legal penalties upon those who have violated the law does not contravene the Gospel precepts which forbid us to recompense evil for evil and which command us to turn the other cheek.[81] Provided that the Christian keeps patience and benevolence in his heart as he punishes and disciplines the criminal for his own good and for that of society, he commits no sin "in correcting with a certain benevolent severity, even against their own wishes, men whose welfare rather than their wishes it is our duty to consult; and the Christian Scriptures have most unambiguously commended this virtue in a magistrate."[82] Just as fathers and heads of households have a duty to correct by admonition or punishment their children and their servants so that, if possible, they may be improved and domestic harmony may be maintained, or, at least, they may be restrained from further crimes and others may be deterred from evil actions, so those who have political or judicial authority must punish those citizens who violate the law.[83] But judges and law-enforcement officers must, if they are Christians, remember that they themselves are sinners who need God's mercy; they must therefore show mercy to those whom they have the authority to punish or even to kill.[84] Also, rulers and judges should remind themselves that power and exalted

office, no less than great wealth, bring with them special dangers
to the eternal well-being as well as the earthly happiness of their
possessors.[85]

The state and its instruments of coercion and punishment are,
in Augustine's view, divinely ordained institutions designed as
remedies as well as punishments for the sinful condition of
fallen man. God uses the evil desires of fallen man as means for
the establishment of earthly peace and order and for the just
punishment of his vices. The state is thus a gift of God to man,
despite the inadequacies and imperfections that necessarily mark
the peace and justice that it can maintain among the unredeemed.
The authority of the ruler over his subjects is therefore derived
from God. The king or prince is established by God, no matter
how wicked or unjust he may be, and Augustine allows no scope
for any limitations of his power by his subjects or for any disobedience or resistance to his commands.

One of his favorite texts is the famous thirteenth chapter of
St. Paul's Epistle to the Romans:

Let every person be subject to the governing authorities. For there is
no authority except from God, and those that exist have been instituted by God. Therefore he who resists the authorities resists
what God has appointed, and those who resist will incur judgment.
For rulers are not a terror to good conduct, but to bad. . . . But if
you do wrong, be afraid, for he does not bear the sword in vain; he
is the servant of God to execute his wrath on the wrongdoer. Therefore one must be subject, not only to avoid God's wrath but also for
the sake of conscience.[86]

Any one who resists "duly constituted authority" resists "the
ordinance of God." [87] In order to make clear the divine origin of
political power Augustine also refers to Christ's statement to
Pilate: "You would have no power over me unless it had been
given you from above." [88] Christians therefore have a solemn
duty to obey the laws and the commands of the rulers and to

submit to all taxes and imposts.[89] They owe to rulers, no matter
how wicked or tyrannical they may be, not only obedience and
reverence but respect and love, and they are obliged to see to it
that their families, servants, and friends refrain from lawbreaking
and crime.[90] When Christians render obedience to rulers they are
really obeying God rather than men, since it is God who estab-
lishes rulers and who orders that they be obeyed.[91]

One of the primary reasons why Augustine insists so strongly
on the divine origin of political authority and on the subjects'
duty of absolute obedience to it is that, like Hobbes, he is so
keenly aware of the need for a strong power to restrain the
boundless appetites and ceaseless conflicts of men. He would
agree with Hobbes's warning that any suggestion that resistance
or disobedience to established rulers may be permissible or desirable in certain circumstances would serve as an invitation to
anarchy. Factious, self-seeking individuals and groups would use
such doctrines in order to rationalize their own desires to evade
the laws, to escape punishment for their evil deeds, and to acquire domination for themselves. Once egoism and ambition are
unleashed in this way, the intricate fabric of social peace and
order is in danger of being rent apart, and the dreadful specter
of unending civil strife roams the land.

So all men, including Christ's saints, "are enjoined to be subject to the powers that are of man and of earth." [92] The seventy-
year period of the captivity of the Jews in Babylon signifies and
prefigures this subjection of mankind to the kings of this world.
Only at the end of time will this need for human authority and
for absolute obedience to it come to an end. Only then will the
Church "be delivered from the confusion of this world" and pass
over from this world with its sufferings and its coercive, remedial
order to the heavenly kingdom of perfect bliss and an order based

upon perfect freedom and perfect love. In the meantime, all men must give absolute obedience to God's ministers, the kings and rulers of this earth, no matter how impious or wicked they may be. It is God who sends men tyrannical and cruel rulers in furtherance of His own designs.[93] He uses the evil actions of wicked rulers, for which they alone are responsible and which hurt only themselves, to punish the transgressions of the sinful and to try the patience and fidelity of the good. The fact that a king may "rage with tyrannical cruelty" provides no excuse for condemnation of "the order of royal power"[94] or for disobedience to his commands, just as the fact that a usurper may rule with benevolence and justice does not mean that his rebellion against the constituted authority is to be praised.

If wicked, sinful men occupy positions of power and authority as judges or kings, they are to be obeyed and their cruelty is to be accepted as divinely ordained discipline and punishment, while "the honour due to their power must needs be shown them."[95] If anyone attempts to rebel against the established ruler, he is not to be aided but rather opposed and, if possible, punished, even if he seems to be a better and wiser man than the present king. However, it is God who, by His control over human actions, even over the actions of wicked men, determines the destinies of states and of rulers.[96] It is a logical consequence of this belief in Providence that if a rebellion is successful and the former ruler is killed or routed, the usurper becomes the rightful ruler. He is then to be obeyed and honored as his predecessor was, although his act of usurpation and rebellion is not thereby rendered right or meritorious. Nevertheless, even his sinful action would not have been successful had God not chosen to use him and his wickedness as a way of punishing the previous ruler or of chastening the people, and as a demonstration that He can, when He will, humble the mighty and the proud who fail to recognize that their power is from Him and that they are His ministers.

The kings and princes of the earth, those who occupy "exalted stations" in this world, are sometimes good powers and fear God and sometimes evil powers and fear not God; but in either case they are to be obeyed and honored as long as they retain their authority. In this life the pilgrims from the City of God often have to endure as superiors men who are their inferiors;

we endure those whom we would not, we suffer for our betters those whom we know to be worse. . . . And it is a good thing to consider ourselves to be sinners, and thus endure men set over our heads: in order that we also to God may confess that deservedly we suffer. . . . God seemeth to be wroth, when He doeth these things: fear not, for a Father He is, He is never so wroth as to destroy. When ill thou livest, if He spareth, He is more angry. In a word, these tribulations are the rods of Him correcting, lest there be a sentence from Him punishing.[97]

Indeed, Augustine insists that the Christian ought to show to evil rulers a respect even greater than the deference exhibited to them by sinful, earthly men.[98]

While Augustine does not use the phrase *legibus solutus* to describe the power of the king or ruler of a state, he recognizes that kings possess sovereignty (*imperium*), which he refers to as "the highest point of his [man's] desire,"[99] and he seems to regard a king as free to enact any laws that he believes to be necessary for the preservation of the peace and good order of the society over which he is ruling. He explicitly states that in making law the king is not limited by the precedents of his own prior enactments or those of his predecessors.

For it is lawful for a king, in the state over which he reigns, to command that which neither he himself nor anyone before him had commanded. And if it cannot be held inimical to the public interest to obey him,—and, in truth, it would be inimical if he were not obeyed, since *obedience to princes is a general compact of human society* [*generale quippe pactum est societatis humanae oboedire regibus suis*]—how much more, then, ought we unhesitatingly to obey God, the Governor of all his creatures![100]

Since obedience to rulers is clearly in the public interest, all the laws promulgated by the ruler must be obeyed by all citizens, with the sole exception of laws or commands that run contrary to God's ordinances.[101] Although Augustine believes that such laws are impious and wicked and insists that the Christian must not obey them, he never argues that the Christian has a right not to be punished when he refuses to obey a law or an order of this kind. The ruler has the right to punish anyone who refuses to obey his commands, whether the refusal is motivated by criminality, self-interest, or obedience to God, but only the man who refuses to obey because the order is contrary to God's ordinance is justified in his disobedience. Even this man, however, cannot claim a right not to be punished for his failure to comply with the law.

Christians owe the same obedience and honor to non-Christian kings that they must render to Christian rulers. Augustine notes that St. Paul taught us to make "supplications, prayers, intercessions, . . . for all men, for kings and for all who are in high positions, that we may lead a quiet and peaceable life, godly and respectful in every way."[102] If even the rulers who persecuted the faithful were to be obeyed, honored, and prayed for, how much more are obedience and devotion due to those Christian kings who aid and cherish the Church and provide "the secure quiet of peace," so that "the Churches might be built up, and peoples planted in the garden of God, and that all nations might bring forth fruit in faith, and hope, and love, which is in Christ."[103]

Nevertheless, God, as the highest Power in the universe, must be obeyed, no matter what kings or rulers command. Since there is a hierarchy of authorities in the world, in case of conflicting orders the command of the superior authority is to be obeyed. Just as parents are to be obeyed in all that they command as long as they do not order their children to contravene the wishes of superior authorities such as the state or God, so the rulers of the state are to be given absolute obedience provided that they do not command us to do what God forbids or to omit what God enjoins.[104] If the powers ordained command you to do what God forbids,

in this case by all means disregard the power through fear of Power. Consider these several grades of human powers. If the magistrate [*curator*] enjoin anything, must it not be done? Yet if his order be in opposition to the Proconsul, thou dost not surely despise the power, but choosest to obey a greater power. Nor in this case ought the less to be angry, if the greater be preferred. Again, if the Proconsul himself enjoin anything, and the Emperor another thing, is there any doubt, that disregarding the former, we ought to obey the latter? So then if the Emperor enjoin one thing, and God another, what judge ye? Pay me tribute, submit thyself to my allegiance. Right, but not in an idol's temple. In an idol's temple He forbids it. Who forbids it? A greater Power. Pardon me then: thou threatenest a prison, He threateneth hell.[105]

In an interesting foreshadowing of the later Gelasian doctrine of the Two Swords,[106] Augustine states that since we consist of body and soul, we must, as long as we are in this life, be subject with respect to our bodies to the powers of this world to whom is granted "the governance of temporal affairs [*rerum temporalium gubernatio*]," while as far as our souls and their eternal salvation are concerned we must be subject only to God and not to any man who contravenes God's law.[107] We must follow the rule which the Lord Himself prescribed:

Render therefore to Caesar the things that are Caesar's, and to God the things that are God's.[108]

If therefore anyone thinks that because he is a Christian, he is not obligated to pay taxes or imposts or does not have to render the honor due to those powers which deal with these matters, he is seriously mistaken. Likewise, if anyone thinks that he must be subject in such a manner that the man who excels with a certain majesty in the administration of temporal affairs is thought to have power even over his faith, he falls into an even greater error.[109]

Even when we refuse to obey the orders of the temporal ruler because they clearly conflict with God's commands (e.g., His prohibition against the worship of idols), we have no right to *resist* the state's commands or to *rebel* against the constituted authority. Our only recourse is to follow the example of the holy martyrs, that is, to refuse to obey the ruler's sacrilegious commands and to accept quietly, without resistance, even joyously, whatever punishment he may impose upon us for our failure to obey.[110] Even death is to be accepted without any effort to resist or subvert the political authority. This kind of passive disobedience with complete acceptance of the consequences of not obeying the state's commands is the only kind of disobedience that Augustine will sanction, and it is permissible only when the ruler commands his subjects to do something that clearly contravenes God's laws.[111] In everything else, he must be given complete obedience, even if he is himself a pagan idolater, an enemy of the Church, and a wicked and impious man.

Julian was an infidel Emperor, an apostate, a wicked man, an idolater; Christian soldiers served an infidel Emperor; when they came to the cause of Christ, they acknowledged Him only who was in heaven. If he called upon them at any time to worship idols, to offer incense; they preferred God to him: but whenever he commanded them to deploy into line, to march against this or that nation, they at once obeyed. They distinguished their everlasting from their temporal master; and yet they were, for the sake of their everlasting Master, submissive to their temporal master.[112]

Did not Christ Himself pay tribute, and have not His Apostles commanded us to be subject unto the higher powers and to pray for the kings of this earth? "How then have the Christians offended against them? What due have they not rendered? in what have not Christians obeyed the monarchs of earth? The kings of the earth therefore have persecuted the Christians without a cause." [113] Moreover, Christians, insofar as they follow the precepts of Christ, are truly virtuous men, who refrain from crime and sin not simply because they are afraid of human punishment but because they fear God, who knows the innermost thoughts of men, and also love God and wish to do what He commands. No ruler could ask for a better or more virtuous citizen than the true Christian. [114]

Christianity teaches kings to be humble before God and to seek the good of their peoples, while it counsels the peoples to be subject to their kings. [115] The desire to win or to retain positions of honor and power is proper if they are sought for the sake of the benefits that can be conferred upon the governed, rather than "for the empty gratification of pride and arrogance, and for a superfluous and pernicious triumph of vanity." [116] Rulers ought to practice humility before God since their eminence and exaltation make them particularly prone to fall into the sin of pride.

And therefore the more exalted kings are in earthly eminence, the more ought they to humble themselves before God. . . . Let not then the kings of the earth be proud, let them be humble. Then let them sing in the ways of the Lord, if they be humble: let them love, and they shall sing. . . . Sing what? that "great is the glory of the Lord," not of kings. [117]

Emperors and kings, though they rightly enjoy great power and honor among men, are, nevertheless, men, who are, in God's sight, the equals of other men. Like other men, they are mortal, frail creatures, subject to the same vicissitudes and sufferings that mark the lives of ordinary mortals. They are also sinful, condemned creatures, unless and until they have been redeemed by God's grace, and that grace is certainly not given on the basis of earthly power or eminence.

When one considers human frailty, one may rightly "despise the falling pinnacles of an earthly kingdom"; [118] all the pomp, majesty, and power of temporal rule are trivial and ephemeral when compared to God's eternal kingdom. And for the sake of that kingdom, the only kingdom "which does not totter like all temporal dignities, but stands firm on eternal foundations," [119] "the opposition of all earthly kingdoms should be patiently borne." [120] Augustine notes that although the imperial office has lasted for a long time, each of its occupants has held it only briefly, and during his brief tenure each emperor has been subject to heavy cares and burdens; the office has been "filled by a constant succession of dying men." [121] The powerful and mighty ones of this world, no less than their subjects, are merely creatures of a brief moment, "dying men."

The fact that this earth is a land of "dying men," all mortal and all subject to sin, suffering, and misfortune, is at the root of Augustine's political and social quietism. There is little room in his thought for the idea that power may be used to improve the lot of man on earth or to lessen his misery, and certainly no room at all for the view that one form of government should be abolished or a particular ruler replaced so that a better social and political order may be instituted. A relatively peaceful society and good rule are gifts of God to men; social disturbances, cruel and tyrannous rulers, and civil and foreign wars are punishments that He visits upon men when He sees that they require such chastisements. Since everything that takes place, whether "good" or "bad," is part of God's plan for the world and is, therefore, ultimately good, there is little or no impulse toward social or political reconstruction or amelioration. This life is only the anteroom to eternal life, a place of suffering and punishment for sin and a testing-ground for the virtues of the faithful. The institutions of social, economic, and political life have no real positive value. Their essential contribution is that they hold down the dark passions of sinful men and provide a measure of peace and stability. The breakdown of social and political order through disobedience or rebellion is therefore the worst of all possible earthly evils.

As long as the rulers do not force their subjects into impiety or disobedience to God, they should be obeyed quietly and without complaint.

For, as far as this life of mortals is concerned, which is spent and ended in a few days, *what does it matter under whose government a dying man lives,* if they who govern do not force him to impiety and iniquity [*quid interest sub cuius imperio uiuat homo moriturus, si illi qui imperant ad impia et iniqua non cogant*]? [122]

We should not worry too much about the fact that we may be in bondage to evil rulers, or to evil masters if we are slaves, for both king and subject, master and slave, are on this earth for only a brief period, and the only really important concern is man's eternal salvation. Servitude to the devil and his angels is to be feared far more than temporal—and temporary—servitude to men; the former is servitude of the mind and soul and will last unto all eternity, while the latter is merely servitude of the body in this life.[123] Moreover, no matter how we may be treated by human rulers and masters, we have "inner freedom," freedom of our thoughts and minds and souls.

Anyone can easily see that under a human lord we are allowed to have our thoughts free. We fear the lordship of demons because it is exercised over the mind in which is found our only means of beholding and grasping the truth. Wherefore, though we be enchained and subjected to all the powers given to men to rule the state, provided we "render unto Caesar the things that are Caesar's and to God the things that are God's," there is no need to fear lest anyone should exact such service after we are dead. The servitude of the soul is one thing, the servitude of the body quite another.[124]

Finally, it should be noted that when Augustine is discussing the relations between rulers and subjects he often expresses a strongly paternalistic view of the position of the ruler. The ruler is not simply a man who occupies an office that is necessary and useful; he is, almost literally, "the father of his people," and it is for him to decide what they should do and how they should do it. He does not ask the people what they want, any more than a father tries to ascertain the desires of his young children before he tells them what they must do. Augustine reveals—perhaps unconsciously—his paternalistic conception of political authority by his frequent use of the analogy between the ruler and the father who regulates and punishes the behavior of his children. The king may be a good and wise father, or a cruel and tyrannous father, but in either case his subjects must not only obey but honor and respect him. Augustine does not conceive of the citizens as mature, rational persons who have a right to be consulted about their wishes. Most of them are willful, passionate children, who must remain permanently under the firm tutelage of a stern master. In one of his letters he argues that

we confer a benefit upon others, not in every case in which we do what is requested, but when we do that which is not hurtful to our petitioners. *For in most cases we serve others best by not giving, and would injure them by giving, what they desire* [*nam pleraque non dando prosumus et noceremus, si dedissemus*]. Hence the proverb, "Do not put a sword in a child's hand. . . ." We are convicted of unfaithfulness towards those whom we profess to love, if our only care is lest, by refusing to do what they ask of us, their love towards us be diminished—and what becomes of that virtue which even your own [i.e., pagan] literature commends, in the ruler of his country who studies not so much the wishes as the welfare of his people [*et ubi est, quod et uestrae litterae illum laudant patriae rectorem, qui populi utilitati magis consulat quam uoluntati*]? [125]

CHAPTER V

WAR AND RELATIONS AMONG STATES

In none of Augustine's writings on the subject of war can we find a trace of militarism or of glorification of the struggles that states and groups wage against each other with so much ferocity. Almost every one of his references to civil or international war is bitterly sorrowful; he always remembers the suffering and misery that war brings in its wake, especially for its innocent victims. Like most of his contemporaries, he was profoundly shocked by the sack of Rome by the Visigoths under Alaric in 410, although he recovered to write *The City of God* to defend Christianity against pagan charges that the fall of the city was a result of Rome's abandonment of its own gods and its adoption of Christianity. We have noted that in the last years of his life he watched the barbarian hordes advancing across North Africa, and when he died in 430 his own city of Hippo was under siege by the Vandals, who destroyed it not long after.[1]

His own experiences and the age of plundering and slaughter in which he lived left him with a deep hatred of war and a great scorn for those who thought that conquest and military victories were glorious and noble accomplishments. In discussing the war waged by the early Romans against their mother-city, Alba, he charges that "this vice of restless ambition was the sole motive to that social and parricidal war," and he cries out with passion, "Why allege to me the mere names and words of 'glory' and 'victory'? Tear off the disguise of wild delusion, and look at the naked deeds: weigh them naked, judge them naked."[2] The price of "glory" in human suffering and cruelty revolts him.

For I do not see what it makes for the safety, good morals, and certainly not for the dignity, of men, that some have conquered and others have been conquered, except that it yields them that most insane pomp of human glory, in which "they have received their reward," who burned with excessive desire of it, and carried on most eager wars. For do not their lands pay tribute? Have they any privilege of learning what the others are not privileged to learn? . . . Take away outward show [iactantiam], and what are all men after all but men?[3]

At the same time Augustine follows Athanasius and Ambrose in rejecting the pacifism and antimilitarism of many of the Church Fathers, such as Tertullian, Origen, and Lactantius. Christians are not compelled by the Gospel precepts to abstain from the use of force or from killing if they are acting in a public capacity; therefore, they may serve in the army and fight against the enemies of the state.[4] Wars are inevitable as long as men and their societies are moved by avarice, greed, and lust for power, the permanent drives of sinful men. It is, therefore, self-delusion and folly to expect that a time will ever come in this world when wars will cease and "men will beat their swords into ploughshares." "Whoever hopes for this so great good [i.e., peace] in this world, and in this earth, his wisdom is but folly. . . . [F]or in the very great mutability of human affairs such great security is never given to any people, that it should not dread invasions hostile to this life."[5] "As to wars, when has the earth not been scourged by them at different periods and places?"[6] The prophecy in the Psalms that God "maketh wars to cease unto the end of the earth" is not yet fulfilled, and will not be fulfilled until this world comes to an end. Until that day, there will be wars among nations, classes, and sects; some just wars, many more unjust. "This not yet see we fulfilled: yet are there wars, wars among nations for sovereignty [*pro regno*]; among sects, among Jews, Pagans, Christians, heretics, are wars, frequent wars, some for the truth, some for falsehood contending. Not yet then is this fulfilled . . . but haply it shall be fulfilled." [7]

As this last quotation suggests, Augustine believes not only that wars are inevitable, given the sinful state of fallen man, but also that some wars, at least, are just wars and therefore defensible. His analysis of war closely parallels his discussion of punishment and earthly justice within the state.[8] The just war is the punishment imposed upon a state and upon its rulers when their behavior is so aggressive or avaricious that it violates even the norms of temporal justice. Other states then have not merely the right but the duty to punish these crimes and to act in the same fashion as the judge, policeman, jailer, and executioner act within the state. In both cases, however, the punishment can only be rough justice; the innocent will suffer with the guilty. And in the case of war, since there is no impartial judge who stands aside from the protagonists, it is easy for punitive action to pass over into unjust desires for revenge, booty, or conquest. Neither within a state nor in relations among states can punishment be avoided if the most flagrant injustices are to be prevented and a minimum of justice is to be preserved in the world, but the punishment is a grim and horrible necessity. War is always an evil, though on some occasions it may be necessary in order to prevent worse evils.

But, say they, the wise man will wage just wars. As if he would not all the rather lament the necessity of just wars, if he remembers that he is a man; for if they were not just he would not wage them, and would therefore be delivered from all wars. For it is the wrong-doing of the opposing party which compels the wise man to wage just wars; and this wrong-doing, even though it gave rise to no war, would still be matter of grief to man because it is man's wrong-doing. Let every one, then, who thinks with pain on all these great evils, so horrible, so ruthless, acknowledge that this is misery. And if any one either endures or thinks of them without mental pain, this is a more miserable plight still, for he thinks himself happy because he has lost human feeling.[9]

God is no more to be held responsible for the wars that rage among men than for any of the other evils that are the consequence of man's sin. War is not God's doing; it is rooted in the war that rages within every man between flesh and spirit.[10] Thus, war is "a work of men, and that not one which is considered desirable by them." [11] Nevertheless, wars, like all other human actions, no matter how evil or unjust, do not escape the net of God's Providence. Just as God does not force men to sin—to rob, to kill, to injure one another—and yet regulates and uses their sinful actions so that they become instruments for carrying out His eternal designs for the world, so He permits states and rulers, even if they are acting unjustly, to wage war only insofar as their battles and campaigns contribute to His ends—the punishment of the wicked and the testing and the training of the good.[12] He regulates the durations and the issues of wars in accordance with His changeless and inscrutable judgments, but this does not mean that victory always goes to those whose cause is more just. Like all temporal goods, victory and conquest are bestowed by God on both the good and the evil, although in either case the outcome must be ultimately just and right and must contribute to His righteous plans for the world, or it would not take place. In God's power "it lies that any one either subdues or is subdued in war; that some are endowed with kingdoms, others made subject to kings." [13]

Most of the wars that are waged between states are in no sense just; they are internecine quarrels within the earthly city. Each side seeks to impose its will upon the other, and peace is the end sought for by war.[14] But the peace which the conquerors impose upon the vanquished is little more than a temporary truce in which the victors satisfy their greed, avarice, lust, and ambition at the expense of the conquered. Even this earthly city, which

is itself, in its own kind, better than all other human good . . . desires earthly peace for the sake of enjoying earthly goods, and it makes war in order to attain to this peace; since, if it has conquered, and there remains no one to resist it, *it enjoys a peace which it had not while there were opposing parties who contested for the enjoyment of those things which were too small to satisfy both.* This peace is purchased by toilsome wars; it is obtained by what they style a glorious victory.[15]

The peace that is obtained by such wars is either self-destroying or short-lived, a truce between wars. Each section of the earthly city that goes to war against another section seeks to conquer and triumph over others, while it is itself conquered and in bondage to its vices—cupidity and the lust for domination. The victorious party may be made proud and arrogant by its victory; if so, nemesis will pursue it, since its very arrogance will arouse the enmity of the conquered peoples and of other nations. Or the victors may be anxious and nervous about the difficulties and dangers that they now face in dealing with the conquered. Although their attitude is more realistic, their fears of future danger and defeat rob them of any satisfaction in their triumph.

If, when it has conquered, it is inflated with pride, its victory is life-destroying; but if it turns its thoughts upon the common casualties of our mortal condition, and is rather anxious concerning the disasters that may befall it than elated with the successes already achieved, this victory, though of a higher kind, is still only short-lived; for it cannot abidingly rule over those whom it has victoriously subjugated.[16]

If the king or ruler happens to be a truly good man, he will refrain from wars of aggression, conquest, and plunder; he will wage only just wars. Both in the conduct of the war and in the making of the peace he will strive to attain a just peace, which will punish the evildoers and the aggressors without being cruel, vengeful, or avaricious, and which will consider the interests of the conquered as well as those of the victors.[17]

Think, then, of this first of all, when you are arming for the battle, that even your bodily strength is a gift of God; for, considering this, you will not employ the gift of God against God. . . . Peace should be the object of your desire; war should be waged only as a necessity, and waged only that God may by it deliver men from the necessity and preserve them in peace. For peace is not sought in order to the kindling of war, but war is waged in order that peace may be obtained. Therefore, even in waging war, cherish the spirit of a peacemaker, that, by conquering those whom you attack, you may lead them back to the advantages of peace. . . . As violence is used towards him who rebels and resists, so mercy is due to the vanquished or the captive, especially in the case in which future troubling of the peace is not to be feared.[18]

Always, Augustine regards war and the bloodshed it entails as dire calamities, even if the war is just and necessary. The ruler or official who makes peace or prevents the outbreak of war by negotiation and agreement deserves greater honor and glory than the just warrior.

Those warriors are indeed great and worthy of singular honour, not only for their consummate bravery, but also (which is a higher praise) for their eminent fidelity, by whose labours and dangers, along with the blessing of divine protection and aid, enemies previously unsubdued are conquered, and peace obtained for the State, and the provinces reduced to subjection. But it is a higher glory still to stay war itself with a word, than to slay men with the sword, and to procure or maintain peace by peace, not by war. For those who fight, if they are good men, doubtless seek for peace; nevertheless it is through blood. Your mission, however, is to prevent the shedding of blood. Yours, therefore, is the privilege of averting that calamity which others are under the necessity of producing.[19]

We have noted that Augustine believes that a war is just if it is necessary in order to punish a state that openly flouts the standards of earthly right and justice. "Those wars are normally called just which avenge injuries [*iusta autem bella ea definiri solent quae ulciscuntur iniurias*]."[20] The objective to be sought in a just war is not conquest, glory, or wealth, but rather the punishment of those who have committed injuries and compelling them to make restitution for the wrongs that they have done. "Now, when victory remains with the party which had the juster cause, who hesitates to congratulate the victor, and style it a desirable peace?",[21] even though such a peace is far inferior to the peace found only in the heavenly city.

What criteria does Augustine offer for determining whether or not a war is just? First, a defensive war is obviously a just war, since it aims only to prevent or to punish the unjust actions of the aggressor. In this case, as in the case of a law that allows a person to kill in defense of his life or in order to prevent rape, a lesser evil is allowed in order to prevent worse evils from being committed.[22] Without fully committing himself to accepting the argument, Augustine observes that the claim has been made that some of the wars waged by the Romans, especially in their early history, were defensive wars, in which they had to fight to protect life and liberty against the envious assaults of their neighbors.[23] Second, he maintains that an offensive war may be a just war in one of two situations: war may be waged against a state if it refuses to make reparation for wrongs committed by its citizens, or if it fails to return property that has been wrongfully appropriated.[24]

Augustine thus narrowly limits the scope of offensive wars that can be regarded as just, and he knows that few of the conflicts between nations in human history fall within these limits. Yet, particularly in his arguments in defense of the Old Testament against the Manichaeans, he does cite examples of offensive wars that were just.

It should be noted then how just wars were waged. For the right of innocent passage was refused [to the Jews by the Amorites], a right which they should have granted by virtue of the equitable conventions of human society. God, then, in order to fulfill His promises, at this point came to the aid of the Israelites, to whom it was appropriate that the land of the Amorites be given.[25]

Against the doctrinaire pacifism of the Manichaeans, he argues that when God commanded Moses to carry on wars, He "acted not in cruelty, but in righteous retribution, giving to all what they deserved, and warning those who needed warning." [26]

The pacifist who regards death as the great evil involved in war is ready to buy life at the price of subjection to injustice.

What is the charge brought against war? Is it that some men, who will in any case die sooner or later, are killed so as to establish order for people who will live in peace? To make such a charge is the part not of religious minds, but of timorous minds. The real evils in war are the love of violence, revengeful cruelty, fierce and implacable enmity, wild resistance, and the lust of power, and such like; and it is generally to punish these things, when force is required to inflict the punishment, that, in obedience to God or some lawful authority, good men undertake wars, when they find themselves in such a position as regards the conduct of human affairs, that right conduct requires them to act, or to make others act in this way.[27]

Always, Augustine's central point is the same—war is evil and dreadful, and yet, like the work of the jailer and the hangman in any society, it is sometimes necessary if wrongdoing and rank injustice are not to be permitted to flourish.[28] Anarchy and open flouting of the rules of human society are the worst evils. On the international scene, peace and order must be reestablished among the nations if some country has committed aggression or flagrant injustice. The wrong must be righted and reparation made for the damage, either by pacific means or, if these fail, by the arbitrament of war.

Who is to decide that a state has so flagrantly violated the code of justice that it must be punished by a just war waged against it? In the case of retaliation against an aggressive attack, the answer is fairly simple, though Augustine does not discuss the difficulties that are involved in determining which of the two parties is really the aggressor, or which one actually began the military operations. When an offensive war is to be waged against a state that has refused to act justly, the decision is even more difficult. On one point Augustine is perfectly clear: it is the monarch, the chief of state, who has both the right and the duty to decide that a just war is to be undertaken. To him and to him alone belongs the responsibility of judging whether another country has so seriously violated the rules of just dealing that it must be punished by waging war against it. If he decides that war is necessary, he has the right to begin hostilities, and the soldiers and citizens under his command must obey his orders, whether or not they agree with his judgment.

The major difficulty in this solution of the problem is, of course, that the ruler is one of the parties to the dispute, and yet he must also act as the judge who decides whether or not the other state is guilty of injustice and whether its wrongdoing is great enough to warrant the infliction of punishment. It is difficult for the most conscientious ruler to make this decision without being swayed by personal, dynastic, or national interests, by emotion, or by misinformation or inadequate information. However, Augustine can see no other solution to the problem.

A great deal depends on the causes for which men undertake wars, and on the authority they have for doing so; for the natural order which seeks the peace of mankind [*ordo tamen ille naturalis mor-*

talium paci adcommodatus] ordains that the monarch should have the power of undertaking war if he thinks it advisable, and that the soldiers should perform their military duties in behalf of the peace and safety of the community. When war is undertaken in obedience to God, who would rebuke, or humble, or crush the pride of man, it must be allowed to be a righteous war; for even the wars which arise from human passion cannot harm the eternal well-being of God, nor even hurt His saints; for in the trial of their patience, and the chastening of their spirit, and in bearing fatherly correction, they are rather benefited than injured.[29]

Once the war has been declared by the ruler, the soldier must simply obey his leaders. He is not guilty of wrongdoing if he fights in obedience to the commands of his rulers, even if the justice of the war that is being waged is doubtful or even if it is clear that the monarch has acted unjustly and sacrilegiously in undertaking a "just war." [30] Even if the king's command is unrighteous, "the soldier is innocent, because his position makes obedience a duty." [31] Here, as in the case of the citizen's duty to obey the laws and the commands of the state, Augustine leaves no room for disobedience based upon the citizen's or soldier's individual decision that the command he receives is unjust or illegitimate. To do so would invite anarchy and desertion of duty and would throw a state or an army into utter confusion.

The soldier who has slain a man in obedience to the authority under which he is lawfully commissioned, is not accused of murder by any law of his state; nay, if he has not slain him, it is then he is accused of treason to the state, and of despising the law. But if he has been acting on his own authority, and at his own impulse, he has in this case incurred the crime of shedding human blood. And thus he is punished for doing without orders the very thing he is punished for neglecting to do when he has been ordered.[32]

As late as the fifth century, there were Christians who still adhered to the teachings of the early Church, which forbade Christians to participate in the army or in war or to serve as state officials if their duties made it necessary for them to use coercion against other men. In all his discussions of war and of punishment, Augustine endeavors to persuade his readers that his approval of inflicting pain and even death on criminals and his defense of just wars do not contradict the Gospel precepts that enjoin Christians to "Resist not evil," and "Turn the other cheek." [33] His principal argument is that it is our duty to punish evildoers for their sake and for the good of others; we punish them so that we may instill fear into them and into others like them and so keep them from doing further wrong. In acting in this way, we are doing them a service. Therefore, our action, if taken with no desire for revenge and no pleasure in inflicting pain, is an act of love and benevolence, which is not a violation but rather a fulfillment of the commandments of Christ.

When, however, men are prevented, by being alarmed, from doing wrong, it may be said that a real service is done to themselves. The precept, "Resist not evil," was given to prevent us from taking pleasure in revenge, in which the mind is gratified by the sufferings of others, but not to make us neglect the duty of restraining men from sin. [34]

Christ's teachings require us to maintain patience and good will toward other men in our hearts even when we are correcting and punishing their misdeeds; they do not enjoin upon us absolute pacifism and passivity in the face of evil. Christ Himself did not literally obey the commandment, "Turn the other cheek," when He was struck on the face when being examined by the High Priest.

Our Lord Jesus Himself, our perfect example of patience, when He was smitten on the face, answered: "If I have spoken evil, bear witness of the evil, but if not, why smitest thou me?" If we look only to the words, He did not in this obey His own precept, for He did not present the other side of his face to him who had smitten Him, but, on the contrary, prevented him who had done the wrong from adding thereto; and yet He had come prepared not only to be smitten on the face, but even to be slain upon the cross. . . .[35]

Thereby, He demonstrated to us

that these precepts pertain rather to the inward disposition of the heart than to the actions which are done in the sight of men, requiring us, in the inmost heart, to cherish patience along with benevolence, but in the outward action to do that which seems most likely to benefit those whose good we ought to seek. . . .[36]

Just as it is possible—and right—to take action against those who do evil, by admonishing, punishing, or even killing them, while retaining benevolence and love toward them in our hearts, it is possible—and wrong—to refrain from action intended to correct and discipline the evil, while cherishing anger and hatred toward them within ourselves. In his discussions of war and in his many references to punishment of the Donatists,[37] Augustine often uses, as an example of punishment and stern discipline imposed not only with love but because of love for the wrongdoer, the correction and chastisement imposed upon a son by a loving father.

For in the correction of a son, even with some sternness, there is assuredly no diminution of a father's love; yet, in the correction, that is done which is received with reluctance and pain by one whom it seems necessary to heal by pain. . . . For the person from whom is taken away the freedom which he abuses in doing wrong is vanquished with benefit to himself; since nothing is more truly a misfortune than that good fortune of offenders, by which pernicious impunity is maintained, and the evil disposition . . . is strengthened.[38]

Once again, the argument is that the punishment of criminal men or nations is justified not only because it protects the innocent but also because it prevents the offender from continuing to misuse his liberty and from adding further crimes to his previous offenses. Augustine agrees with Plato that the most unhappy and unfortunate man is he who by successfully evading the punishment that is due him continues unchecked his life of crime and wrongdoing.

In conducting wars and in peacetime relations with other states, rulers and military leaders should fulfill and guard the agreements, treaties, and conventions made with their friends and with their enemies. "For, when faith is pledged, it is to be kept even with the enemy against whom the war is waged, how much more with the friend for whom the battle is fought!"[39] This fidelity to promises and engagements is a sacred obligation. Yet, with his usual realistic insight into human affairs, Augustine realizes that a situation may occur in which a state is compelled to make the agonizing choice between fidelity to its treaties and engagements and its own self-preservation. He discusses at length the bitter fate of the Saguntines in Spain who, during the Second Punic War, were destroyed because of their fidelity to their treaty of alliance with the Romans.[40] After a siege of eight or nine months, "this opulent but ill-fated city, dear as it was to its own state and to Rome, was taken, and subjected to treatment which one cannot read, much less narrate, without horror."[41] To escape falling into the hands of Hannibal, those Saguntines who had survived siege and famine killed their dependents and then threw themselves into the flames of a massive funeral pyre. Thus it was shown that the pagan gods could not or would not interfere to preserve a city closely allied to the Romans and completely faithful to the obligations of that alliance, although these gods were the guarantors and mediators of the treaty.

When Augustine returns to this subject in Book XXII of *The City of God,* he notes that according to Cicero's argument in Book III of the *De Republica,* a state will not engage in a war except for honor or for safety. Death for a state is not natural, since a state should be so constituted as to be eternal. "But when a state is destroyed, obliterated, annihilated, it is as if (to compare great things with small) this whole world perished and collapsed." [42] Augustine agrees with Cicero's view that a state must engage in war if it is necessary in order to preserve its existence and to prevent destruction—*salus populi suprema lex.* However, he then goes on to ask whether the Saguntines acted correctly when they chose to perish as a nation rather than to break faith with the Romans. He does not say that their decision was wrong; indeed, he clearly admires them for the nobility of their choice. He insists, however, that a state may have to face the dilemma of choosing between fidelity to its obligations and safety and preservation, and that one or the other of two terrible evils—breaking faith or self-destruction—may have to be accepted.

But I do not see how they could follow the advice of Cicero, who tells us that no war is to be undertaken save for safety or for honour; neither does he say which of these two is to be preferred, if a case should occur in which the one could not be preserved without the loss of the other. For manifestly, if the Saguntines chose safety, they must break faith; if they kept faith, they must reject safety; as also it fell out. [43]

In this world of sin, imperfection, and suffering, men and states are sometimes confronted with dreadful choices, and they cannot refuse to choose because they do not like either of the alternatives. If a statesman feels—and he may well do so—that his primary duty is to secure the existence and safety of the state whose affairs he is directing, he may have to act in a manner that is morally objectionable, in ways in which he would never think of acting in his personal relations. There is only one city which is never forced to make this terrible choice between safety and keeping faith, and that is the City of God. "But the safety of the city of God is such that it can be retained, or rather acquired, by faith and with faith; but if faith be abandoned, no one can attain it." [44]

Although Augustine recognizes the advantages that have been the result of the far-flung Roman Empire and of the *pax Romana* that it has imposed upon the Mediterranean world, he is well aware of the enormous costs of building that Empire and of the ultimately self-defeating character of imperialist expansion. He sees the diversity of men's languages as a symbol and also as a cause of the conflicts and misunderstandings that divide the human race. The division of mankind into nations with different and mutually unintelligible languages was God's punishment for the arrogance and presumption of those who sought to build the Tower of Babel. The punishment was altogether appropriate.

As the tongue is the instrument of domination, in it pride was punished; so that man, who would not understand God when He issued His commands, should be misunderstood when he himself gave orders. Thus was that conspiracy disbanded, for each man retired from those he could not understand, and associated with those whose speech was intelligible; and the nations were divided according to their languages, and scattered over the earth as seemed good to God, who accomplished this in ways hidden from and incomprehensible to us. [45]

Ever since that time, this diversity of language has been a grave impediment to understanding and communication among men.

For if two men, each ignorant of the other's language, meet, and are not compelled to pass, but, on the contrary, to remain in company, dumb animals, though of different species, would more easily hold intercourse than they, human beings though they be. For their common nature is no help to friendliness when they are prevented by diversity of language from conveying their sentiments to one another; so that a man would more readily hold intercourse with his dog than with a foreigner. [46]

Rome has endeavored to overcome this diversity of languages and the other grounds for strife among the nations by imposing upon the subject peoples "not only her yoke, but her language, as a bond of peace, so that interpreters, far from being scarce, are numberless."[47] The order and unity thus provided by the Empire have been real goods, "but how many great wars, how much slaughter and bloodshed, have provided this unity!"[48]

In spite of the great extent of the Empire there have always remained beyond its borders hostile nations against whom wars have had—and still have—to be waged. But even if we suppose that there were no peoples left outside the Empire, it would not follow that peace would reign throughout the world. "The very extent of the empire itself has produced wars of a more obnoxious description—social and civil wars—and with these the whole race has been agitated, either by the actual conflict or by the fear of a renewed outbreak."[49] After the destruction of Rome's great rival, Carthage, the removal of fear and anxiety led, as Scipio had feared, to a decline in the morals of the Romans and to a weakening of the bonds of internal concord so that seditions and bloody civil wars followed in rapid succession. At the time of Pompey's conquest of the Jews,

Rome had already subdued Africa and Greece, and ruled extensively in other parts of the world also, and yet, as if unable to bear her own weight, had, in a manner, broken herself by her own size. For indeed she had come to grave domestic seditions, and from that to social wars, and by and by to civil wars, and had enfeebled and worn herself out so much, that the changed state of the republic in which she should be governed by kings, was now imminent.[50]

The final term of this process of internal conflict and civil war was the collapse of the republic and of the liberty of the Romans, and the rise of dictators, such as Pompey, Marius, and

Caesar, and, at last, autocratic rule by the Emperor Augustus and his successors. The *libido dominandi,* the lust for rule, the vice that was most characteristic of the Romans, was now turned inward, and a few men subdued the weary masses of the people. "That lust for rule which among the other vices of mankind was found more concentrated among all the Romans, after it had prevailed in the case of a few more dominating men, subdued under the yoke of slavery the others, worn out and wearied." [51] Augustus, who completely deprived the Romans of their liberty, "infused as it were a new life into the sickly old age of the republic, and inaugurated a fresh *régime.* . . ." [52]

Since the price of the great expansion of the Roman Empire was constant conflict and bloodshed and unceasing anxiety and lust, the Romans and the other nations of the world would have been happier had the Empire never grown to such a size.

I. should like first to inquire for a little what reason, what prudence, there is in wishing to glory in the greatness and extent of the empire, when you cannot point out the happiness of men who are always rolling, with dark fear and cruel lust, in warlike slaughters and in blood, which, whether shed in civil or foreign wars, is still human blood; so that their joy may be compared to glass in its fragile splendour, of which one is horribly afraid lest it should be suddenly broken in pieces. That this may be more easily discerned, let us not come to nought by being carried away with empty boasting, or blunt the edge of our attention by loud-sounding names of things, when we hear of peoples, kingdoms, provinces.[53]

Everyone will admit that a man "of middling circumstances" who is contented with his small estate, is at peace with his family and neighbors, and enjoys health and a good conscience is far happier than a very rich man who is never free from anxious fears, insatiable covetousness, and "most bitter cares." [54] So, too, the citizens of a small, prosperous state are far more fortunate than the citizens of a vast and powerful empire. "Why must a kingdom be distracted in order to be great? In this little world of man's body, is it not better to have a moderate stature, and health with it, than to attain the huge dimensions of a giant by unnatural torments, and when you attain it to find no rest, but to be pained the more in proportion to the size of your members?" [55] Augustine would thus prefer a world made up of small states, each of which would be satisfied with its moderate territory and power so that all of them might live in harmony and peace. Had the iniquity of Rome's neighbors not provoked the Romans into waging just wars against them and, thereby, into extending their empire, "human affairs being thus more happy, all kingdoms would have been small, rejoicing in neighbourly concord; and thus there would have been very many kingdoms of nations in the world, as there are very many houses of citizens in a city." [56]

However, if there was to be a world empire, it would have been better, both for the Romans and for the peoples that they conquered, had the advantages of unity and common laws been imposed with the consent of the nations concerned rather than by conquest and slaughter.

Had this been done without Mars and Bellona, so that there should have been no place for victory, no one conquering where no one had fought, would not the condition of the Romans and of the other nations have been one and the same, especially if that had been done at once which afterwards was done most humanely and most acceptably, namely, the admission of all to the rights of Roman citizens who belonged to the Roman empire, and if that had been made the privilege of all which was formerly the privilege of a few, with this one condition, that the humbler class who had no lands of their own should live at the public expense—an alimentary impost, which would have been paid with a much better grace by them into the hands of good administrators of the republic, of which they were members, by their own hearty consent, than it would have been paid with had it to be extorted from them as conquered men? [57]

CHAPTER VI

CHURCH, STATE, AND HERESY

St. Augustine developed no detailed, systematic theory of the proper relationship between Church and State or of the way in which their respective spheres of activity should be separated and marked off. As we have already noted,[1] some of his statements foreshadowed the later Gelasian formula of the "Two Swords," the standard medieval doctrine that royal power and priestly power were two separate but cooperating authorities divinely established to govern men's lives in this world; the State was to deal with human, temporal concerns while the Church was charged with responsibility for man's eternal salvation and for the worship of God. We have also seen that Augustine's view of the relation between men's obligations to temporal rulers and their higher duties to God[2] is based on Christ's injunction: "Render therefore to Caesar the things that are Caesar's, and to God the things that are God's."[3] In commenting on the Jews' objections to the inscription placed upon the cross when Jesus was crucified—"Jesus of Nazareth, the King of the Jews"—and on the chief priests' statement to Pilate, "We have no king but Caesar,"[4] he says that the Gospel story applies to all peoples and not only to the Jews.

They [the Jews] openly rejected Christ as their king. Even Caesar is a king, a man over men for human concerns, but there is another king for divine concerns; one king for temporal life, another for eternal life; one an earthly king, the other a heavenly king; the earthly king is under the heavenly king, the heavenly king is over

all. Therefore, their sin was not that they said that they held Caesar
as king, but that they refused to hold Christ as king.[5]

The State is a physical authority which operates through force
and fear, while the Church is a moral authority which operates
through teaching and the ministration of the sacraments.[6] The
penance that Ambrose, Bishop of Milan and Augustine's mentor,
had imposed upon the Emperor Theodosius for his massacre of
the Thessalonians had made it clear to Augustine that not even
the Emperor was immune from being "coerced by ecclesiastical
discipline" when he violated the moral law.[7]

Augustine was well aware that the Church had entered a new
period of its earthly existence when the centuries of state persecution ended with the conversion of Constantine and the adoption of Christianity as the official religion of the Empire. He
believed that the attitude of the Church toward the State and
its rulers could not remain unchanged as the ancient ties with
pagan deities and cults were abandoned and as the Emperor and
many of his officials became members of the Christian community.[8] He saw that if its new position brought benefits to the
Church it also brought grave dangers. Now that it was no longer
perilous but rather advantageous to be a Christian, many men
whose faith was, at the best, lukewarm and whose morals left
much to be desired were flocking into the Church; many of
them sought the aid and protection of bishops and clergy in
order to promote their worldly interests.[9] Likewise, many priests
were more interested in the power, wealth, and honor now
attached to clerical offices than in their religious duties. Augustine's letters and sermons are full of references to the heavy burden of civil administration which he and other bishops had to
bear; bishops had to adjudicate and arbitrate many legal dis-
putes, and they aided the civil authorities by participating in
the guardianship and education of orphans and by regulating

the right of sanctuary.[10] As the Empire grew weaker, the Church and her clergy became more and more involved in daily tasks of administration and in acting as a prop for the faltering regime. At the same time, the Church called upon the State to use its coercive powers to punish heretics and schismatics as well as pagans.

In a sense, the whole description that Augustine gives in *The City of God* of the two cities, the earthly city and the City of God, is the foundation of his analysis of the relationship between Church and State. Until the end of the world there is unceasing hostility between those who love themselves and the world and those who love God; true justice, true felicity, and true peace are found only in the heavenly city and not in any earthly state. Since, however, the Church in this world cannot be identified with the City of God, and since a minority of the citizens of earthly states are pilgrim members of the heavenly city, we cannot directly deduce Augustine's ideas about Church–State relations in this world from his sharp contrast between the two cities. It is to his writings dealing with the Donatist schism in Africa that we must turn for an understanding of his views about the role of the State and its rulers in relation to the Church. From 391, when he was ordained a priest, until about 417, the campaign against the Donatists and the effort to reestablish the shattered unity of the Church in Africa occupied most of his attention. In the course of these controversies he had to face the problem of whether it was right for the Church to call upon the State to use its coercive power to force schismatics and heretics to return to the fold. During the long campaign he gradually shifted his position from opposition to the use of state power and compulsion against schism and heresy to approval of these methods. In dealing with this problem he was compelled to consider many aspects of the relationship between the Church and the State.

Before turning to Augustine's writings on this subject, I must give at least a brief outline of the nature and history of the Donatist schism.[11] A forty-year period of peace for the Church had been broken by the persecutions of Diocletian in 303–305. During these persecutions some of the leaders of the Church in Africa were accused of avoiding punishment or martyrdom by obeying the commands of the political authorities to surrender the sacred writings. After the persecution, some of the bishops and priests admitted the charge of having been *traditores,* surrenderers of the Scriptures; others said that they had not surrendered the sacred books but had turned over to the authorities other writings, sometimes those of heretics, in order to escape prosecution; still others denied the charges completely. To many African Christians, who fervently admired the martyrs of the past, such as the great Cyprian, and who believed that every true Christian ought to be eager to die for his faith in Christ, the sin of denying Christ under persecution and of surrendering God's Holy Word seemed particularly heinous. In 312, after peace had been restored, Caecilian was chosen Bishop of Carthage by the presbyters and was acclaimed by the citizens, although he was not liked by the lower classes. He was consecrated by Felix, Bishop of Aptungi, and two other bishops. Immediately, opposition broke out among the rigorists in Carthage; they disliked Caecilian and his predecessor, Mensurius, who had followed a lenient policy toward those who had lapsed during the persecution. This opposition group constituted the beginning of the Donatist sect. With the aid of about seventy bishops from Numidia (some of whom had themselves been guilty of *traditio* and other crimes) they held a synod at Carthage in 312, con-

demned Caecilian's consecrator, Felix, as a *traditor,* and elected
Majorinus as Bishop of a schismatic church at Carthage.

Late in that year or early in 313 the Emperor Constantine, recently converted to Christianity, ordered his officials in Africa
to support Caecilian and to give him financial aid and exemption for his clergy from municipal levies.[12] Immediately, the dissidents sent an appeal to the Emperor, accusing Caecilian of
being a *traditor* and asking Constantine to submit the dispute to
the adjudication of the bishops of Gaul. The Emperor appointed
three Gallic bishops to judge the case, under the presidency of
the Bishop of Rome, Miltiades, who brought in fifteen Italian
bishops as assessors. In October this synod acquitted Caecilian of
the charge of having been a *traditor* and recognized him as lawful bishop of Carthage. In 314 the proconsul in Africa, Anulinus,
was ordered to hold an inquiry into the conduct of Felix of
Aptungi during the persecution; as a result, he, too, was found
innocent of the charge of *traditio.* When the party of Majorinus
again appealed to the Emperor against the decision of the synod
of Rome, he remitted the appeal to the Council of Arles, "which
was a more or less general council of the Western Patri-
archate";[13] it met early in August, 314, and once more Caecilian
and Felix were found innocent and the latter's accusers were
excommunicated. The Majorinists or Donatists still refused to
accept this verdict and appealed to the Emperor to try the case
in person. Late in 316 the Emperor announced his decision—
Caecilian was completely innocent and his opponents were
"calumniators."[14] The churches of the Donatists were ordered
confiscated, and some of the leaders were exiled. However, in
321 Constantine, who had become concerned about the security
of Africa in the event of war with his fellow-Emperor, Licinius,
permitted the exiles to return and granted toleration to the
Donatists, who grew stronger with every year that passed. From

313 on, they were led by Donatus "the Great," who held the post of schismatic Bishop of Carthage for more than forty years. Donatism appealed to the rigorists and purists in the African Church, and to the many Africans, especially in the rural areas of Numidia, whose language was not Latin or Punic but Libyan, the direct ancestor of the modern Berber. They were hostile to Roman culture, Roman soldiers, administrators, and tax-collectors, and Roman landlords, and they regarded the Catholic Church as the ally of their enemies, especially of the political authorities.[15]

From about the middle of the fourth century there appeared on the scene the marauding bands of Circumcellions or armed brigands, who were primarily of peasant origin and of Libyan speech.[16] They were fanatical Donatists who were often led by Donatist bishops, such as the notorious Optatus of Thamugadi. Their name and their war-cry, *Deo laudes,* became a terror to their enemies. In their zeal for Donatism, intensified by opposition to Rome and to the Romanized coastal regions of Africa, they attacked the persons, churches, dwellings, and farms of Catholics and pagans. In 347 and 348 under the Emperor Constans the State undertook a campaign of severe repression of the Donatists; some of their bishops fled, others were exiled, and many of their churches were seized. Many of them committed suicide or forced the authorities to kill them and so to make martyrs of them. However, with the accession of the pagan Emperor Julian in 361, Donatism was tolerated, perhaps encouraged, in the hope that Christianity would thus be weakened in Africa. The result was a new outburst of Donatist violence against Catholics. After Julian's reign, which lasted only two years, his Christian successors again attempted to repress the Donatists, with little success. When Donatus died (probably in 355), he was succeeded as Bishop of Carthage by Parmenian, a man of Spanish or Gallic origin, who held this post until his death in 391 or 392; during this time, "Donatism grew to be about as strong as the Church in Africa, and in Numidia was definitely stronger." [17]

From 363 on, Donatism was plagued by the appearance of several splinter groups, but these sects seem to have been no less opposed than the parent church to the Catholics. The Donatists were aided by the revolts against the Empire in Africa led by Firmus, a Moor (372-375), and by his brother, Count Gildo (397-398), in alliance with the Donatist Bishop, Optatus of Thamugadi. However, after each of these revolts was finally crushed, the authorities issued a series of edicts against Donatism and confiscated some of their property. In 366 or 367, St. Optatus, Catholic Bishop of Milevis, wrote a long anti-Donatist treatise, *De Schismate Donatistarum,* in which he defended the Catholic position and criticized the Donatists. This work provided a great deal of historical material for Augustine in his polemics against the Donatists, as well as some of the fundamental bases of his arguments against them.

In spite of all the efforts of the Empire to restrain the violence of the Donatists and to curb their drive to enlarge the sect by the practice of rebaptizing former Catholics, the movement was stronger in 391, when Augustine became a priest, than it had ever been before.

The years 391 to 392 may be regarded as decisive in the history of the two Churches. Up to this moment, the Donatists had not only succeeded in drawing the mass of fanatical Christianity in the bazaars and villages to them, but on the whole they had produced the abler and more learned leadership. They could claim with some justice to be the true successors of the primitive Church and of Cyprian. . . . The Catholic Church, on the other hand, had shown little power of attraction.[18]

Donatism was particularly strong in Augustine's diocese of Hippo. From 392 to 395 the Emperor Theodosius and his sons promulgated one edict after another against the Donatists, but the laws seem to have been laxly enforced in Africa and had little effect on the flourishing sect. In these same years, however, a new split took place in the Donatist ranks, which resulted in a bitter struggle between the majority, known as Primianists, and the minority, called Maximianists. During this conflict the majority provided ammunition for the attacks of their Catholic opponents by appealing to the State to use compulsion against their enemies and by receiving back into communion some of the dissidents, both actions being contrary to fundamental Donatist principles.

In 395 Augustine became a bishop and began an extended campaign against the Donatists in Hippo and throughout Africa. In 398 he produced a work in three books, *Contra Epistulam Parmeniani,* and about 400, a long treatise in seven books, *De Baptismo contra Donatistas,* and after that a treatise in three books, *Contra Litteras Petiliani;* a number of letters and sermons in which Donatism is discussed and analyzed also belong to this period, 395–400. In 399, in a rescript in response to a complaint from the African Church, the Emperor Honorius ordered that existing laws against heretics be applied to the Donatists, who up to this time had been regarded as schismatical rather than heretical. In 404 the Catholic bishops of Africa, assembled at the ninth Council of Carthage, sent two of their number, Evodius and Theasius, to ask Honorius for protection of the Church and its clergy against violence and for selective enforcement of the laws against heretics that Theodosius had enacted.[19] Even before their arrival the Emperor had issued a severe decree against the Donatists, and, later, he issued further decrees against them, as

well as the famous first Edict of Unity of February 12, 405.[20]
Although the severe penalties imposed upon the Donatists by this
Edict seem to have effected numerous conversions to Catholicism,
especially at Carthage, there is little evidence that the Donatist
strongholds in Numidia were appreciably weakened as a result
of the state persecution. At about this time Augustine published
another important anti-Donatist treatise, the *Contra Cresconium,*
in four books.

In 410, after several reversals in Imperial policy, a new anti-
Donatist decree was issued, and the Emperor ordered Marcellinus
to go to Carthage to preside over a conference to discuss the
entire problem of the schism in the African Church.[21] Two
hundred and eighty-six Catholic bishops and two hundred and
eighty-four Donatist bishops were present at the Conference,
which began on June 1, 411; the case for each side was presented
by seven *actores* or disputants, aided by seven assessors and four
clerks. Augustine was one of the *actores* for the Catholics. After
days of argument Marcellinus handed down a judgment against
the Donatists, which was upheld by the Emperor in a constitution, or Edict of Unity, of January 30, 412, in which all the
repressive laws against the Donatists were confirmed.[22] The next
year the Donatists were overjoyed by the downfall of Marcellinus;
he and his brother were denounced, presumably falsely, to the
authorities for having aided in the revolt of Count Heraclian, and
despite Augustine's attempts to save them they were secretly
executed. However, during the next six or seven years the campaign for the suppression of the Donatists in accordance with the
imperial constitutions and edicts went forward throughout Africa
with some measure of success. Under the pressure of legal sanctions some of their clergy and laity returned to the Catholic
Church, and the depredations of the Circumcellions were
checked. Augustine was active in bringing to the notice of

Catholics and Donatists the proceedings and the results of the Conference of 411; prominent among his anti-Donatist writings in this period are the *De Correctione Donatistarum* (*Ep.* CLXXXV) of 417, and his last major work dealing with the controversy, the *Contra Gaudentium* in two books, written in 420. When the Vandals, who were Arians, arrived in Africa in 429, both Catholics and Donatists were persecuted by the invaders, although the decline of the Catholic Church seems to have been more rapid and more marked than that of its Donatist rival. The Donatist communities appear to have survived in the villages of Numidia, and as late as the end of the sixth century (some sixty years after the Byzantine reconquest of North Africa), we find Pope Gregory urging the Numidian Catholics as well as the Emperor and his officials to take firm action against the Donatist heretics.[23]

Before we turn to Augustine's teachings on the subject of the use of state power and legal coercion against the Donatists, let us briefly note the main arguments used by the Donatists against the Catholic Church in Africa. The Donatists claimed to be rigorists in matters of church discipline; they insisted that the visible Church should be a church of the pure, that is, that it was possible as well as desirable to exclude from the Church anyone who was guilty of sinful or immoral conduct. In practice, they tended to focus most of their attention on one aspect of morality—How had believers behaved during the persecutions of the early fourth century? If members of the Church had compromised in any way with the persecuting state in order to avoid punishment or martyrdom, and especially if they had been guilty of *traditio*—the surrender of the sacred Scriptures to the authorities—they had irrevocably cut themselves off from the Christian community. Any priest or bishop who was guilty of *traditio* or of any other sin lost his power to administer valid sacraments. As a result, the Donatists argued, the Catholic Church in Africa after the persecution of Diocletian was no longer a true church. Its bishops and priests had been ordained and consecrated by men like Felix or Caecilian whom they regarded as *traditores*. Thus they insisted that the Catholic clergy had not received valid ordination or consecration, and that the sacraments which they then administered—such as baptism, the Eucharist, or ordination—were also without validity.

Once the Christian Churches in other countries refused to accept the Donatists' claim to be the only true church in Africa, they went on to claim that they now constituted the only true Christian Church in the world. By continuing in communion with the Catholics of Africa all other churches had been stained by their sins and had forfeited their right to call themselves Christian. Since the Donatists did not recognize the validity of the sacraments administered by Catholics, they insisted on rebaptizing any Catholic who was, by persuasion or force, brought over to their sect. To Augustine this practice of rebaptism, based upon the argument that the sacrament of baptism was efficacious only if the priest who administered it was morally unspotted, was the most sacrilegious act of the Donatists.

On the historical questions involved in the dispute Augustine insisted that the Donatists had been proved to be in error in the charges of *traditio* that they had leveled against Felix and Caecilian; indeed, some of their own leaders had been shown to have committed the very crime which they charged against others. When the Donatists objected to the efforts of the Catholics to gain protection from the Emperor and the State against their illegal and violent actions, Augustine replied that the Donatists were thoroughly dishonest when they attacked the State and the Emperor and when they insisted that the secular authorities had no right to interfere in matters of the organization and discipline of the Church. He reminded them that it was they who had first appealed to the State when they asked the Emperor Constantine to judge their case, and that it was only after he and his successors had ruled against them that they had adopted their anti-state and anti-imperial policy. However, it should be noted that he does not mention that the original Donatist appeal to Constantine came after the Emperor had already ordered that his officials support the Caecilianists against the Donatists.[24] Augustine also reminded his opponents that they had been quite willing to accept state aid and protection from the apostate Emperor Julian, and that they had frequently appealed to the State and to its legal machinery when they wanted to proceed against the dissident groups, such as the Maximianists, which had splintered off from their sect.

Augustine did not rest his case against the Donatists only on these factual grounds. He leveled a fundamental attack on their conception of a church of the pure and on their view that the validity of the sacraments depended upon the moral purity of the individual priest or bishop who administered them. Since the visible Church was—and would always be—a mixture of good and evil men, it was impossible and blasphemous to attempt to make a final separation of the good and the wicked before the end of the world and the Last Judgment.[25] Of course, church discipline had to be maintained, and overt and notorious sinners had to be corrected and, if necessary, expelled from the Church. But this did not mean that in this world any group of men could take upon themselves the responsibility of separating God's elect from the sinners, and of setting themselves up as a church of the pure and holy. The attempt to make such a discrimination involved the claim of being able to read the hearts and innermost thoughts of men and to render final judgment upon them, a sacrilegious pretension to usurp the functions reserved for God alone.

Against the Donatists, Augustine argued that the sacraments—baptism, in particular—were Christ's sacraments and not man's, and that any attempt to make the validity of baptism depend upon the goodness or holiness of the celebrant would lead to a complete disintegration of the Church. Any priest who administered the sacrament of baptism according to the traditional rite and in the name of the Father, the Son, and the Holy Spirit conferred valid baptism, no matter what his hidden sins or imperfections might be. The priest was only the minister of the sacrament; its power came from Christ. Therefore, no Christian had to worry lest his baptism be rendered invalid by the discovery of moral laxity in the celebrant. Since Augustine regarded Donatist rebaptism as a blasphemous procedure, he insisted that persons who had been baptized in the Donatist sect should not be rebaptized when they returned to the Catholic Church. They had received valid baptism, although it only began to be profitable rather than damning to them when they abandoned schism and returned to the unity, peace, and charity of the universal Church. Above all, Augustine rejected the Donatist claim that theirs was the only true Church in the world. Since Christ had promised that His Church would extend from Jerusalem unto all the kingdoms of the earth, universality was one of the principal marks of the Catholic Church.

During the period of Augustine's priesthood, 391–395, and the first two or three years of his episcopate, he was gravely concerned about the Donatist schism, especially in his own city of Hippo. He frequently warned his congregation of the dangers of the sect, and, in 393, he composed an alphabetical psalm to be sung to the people, the *Psalmus contra partem Donati,* so that even the

most unlearned members of his congregation might be made
aware of the Donatists' errors and of the Church's answers to
them. During the years from 391 to 400, he also wrote a number
of letters to Donatist bishops and laymen, in which he tried
to persuade them by argument and by citations from Scripture
that their tenets were mistaken. The tone of these letters is
friendly; in almost every case he urges his correspondent to
agree to meet with him or with other Catholics for a peaceful discussion of their differences in the hope of achieving agreement
and reunification of the Church in Africa.

In this first phase of his campaign against the Donatists, that
is, from 391 to about 398, Augustine flatly rejects the suggestion
that compulsion of any sort be applied to force the Donatists to
renounce their errors and to return to the Church. He denounces the violence of the Circumcellions and the forcible conversions carried out in many areas by the Donatists, but he insists that their use of force and compulsion does not justify the
use of counterforce by the Church or an appeal to the civil
authorities to apply legal punishments to the schismatics. The
only authority to which appeal should be made by either of the
conflicting parties is the word of God, as set forth in the
Scriptures. Where men disagree about the interpretation of
the Scriptures they must investigate the question, see what the
Church in other lands and in earlier ages has received as the correct answer, and deal with one another by rational argument
and persuasion and not by force or threats of force.

In a letter written in 392 to Maximinus, Donatist Bishop of
Sinitum, near Hippo, Augustine says:

I do not propose to compel men to embrace the communion of any
party, but desire the truth to be made known to persons who, in
their search for it, are free from disquieting apprehensions. *On our
side there shall be no appeal to men's fear of the civil power;* on

your side, let there be no intimidation by a mob of Circumcelliones. Let us attend to the real matter in debate, and let our arguments appeal to reason and to the authoritative teaching of the Divine Scriptures, dispassionately and calmly, so far as we are able.[26]

Four years later, in 396, he reiterates this aversion to any use of compulsion:

my desire is, not that any one should against his will be coerced into the Catholic communion, but that to all who are in error the truth may be openly declared, and being by God's help clearly exhibited through my ministry, may so commend itself as to make them embrace and follow it.[27]

In the next year, 397, he wrote a treatise in two books, the *Contra partem Donati,* which is not extant. However, in his discussion of the work in the *Retractations,* he tells us that in it he referred to the possibility of appealing to the State to use its power to reunite the Church in Africa, but that at that time he was unwilling that any such appeal be made.

In the first of these books I said that I was not in favor of schismatics being forcibly constrained to communion by the force of any secular power. And indeed at that time I did not favor that course, since I had not yet discovered the depths of evil to which their impunity would dare to venture, or how greatly a careful discipline would contribute to their emendation.[28]

In the same year he noted in a letter to a number of Donatists that "they [the Donatists] refuse to have these errors corrected by constituted human authorities, applying penalties of a temporal kind in order to prevent them from being doomed to eternal punishment for such sacrilege." [29] But he did not at this time go on to argue that they ought to be punished by the State for their errors.[30]

His position seems to remain unchanged in a letter written to the same persons in 398, in which he reports the results of a debate with the Donatist Bishop of Tubursi, Fortunius. He says:

For I granted that no example could be produced from the New Testament of a righteous man putting any one to death. . . . Among other things it was alleged that our party was still intending to persecute them; and he [Fortunius] said that he would like to see how I would act in the event of such persecution, whether I would consent to such cruelty, or withhold from it all countenance. I said that God saw my heart, which was unseen by them; also that they had hitherto had no ground for apprehending *such persecution, which if it did take place would be the work of bad men,* who were, however, not so bad as some of their own party. . . .[31]

Ten years later, in 408, when Augustine was discussing his change of heart on this question of using state power against the Donatists, he summed up his original position and the reasons why he held it in these words: "For originally my opinion was, that no one should be coerced into the unity of Christ, that we must act only by words, fight only by arguments, and prevail by force of reason, lest we should have those whom we knew as avowed heretics feigning themselves to be Catholics."[32]

One of Augustine's favorite arguments against the Donatists when they complained of being persecuted by the State at the instigation of the Catholics was to remind them that they had frequently used judicial processes and the force of the State to punish their own dissidents, the Maximianists, and to expel them from their churches. One of the first occasions on which he used this argument was a letter written in 399 or 400; it is noteworthy that he here neither accepts nor rejects the thesis that it is right for the Church to appeal to the authorities for aid.

Again, you are wont to reproach us with persecuting you by the help of the civil power. . . . I take up this position: if this be a crime, why have you harshly persecuted the Maximianists by the help of judges appointed by those emperors whose spiritual birth by the gospel was due to our Church? Why have you driven them, by the din of controversy, the authority of edicts, and the violence of soldiery, from those buildings for worship which they possessed, and in which they were when they seceded from you?[33]

The *Contra Epistulam Parmeniani,* which most authorities date at about 400,[34] shows the first clear indication that Augustine is moving toward approval of the principle of state intervention. He notes that the civil power punishes pagans for their false and harmful religion, and that this action is generally approved. In addition, the civil power punishes many of the "works of the flesh" mentioned by St. Paul in *Galatians* v, 19-21, including poisoning: Is it powerless to punish hatred, violence, emulations, wrath, strife, seditions, and heresies, all of which are mentioned in the same context? [35] In the same work Augustine also rejects the Donatist argument that anyone who suffers persecution by the State for religious reasons is, *ipso facto,* a martyr. Only those who suffer persecution "for righteousness' sake" are glorified, and the Donatists are obviously not included in this group.[36]

There are several references to the problem of state intervention against heresy in the *Contra Litteras Petiliani,* also written about 400, in which Augustine replies to a letter addressed by Petilian, the Donatist Bishop of Cirta, to his priests and deacons. After referring to the savage attacks on the Church by the troops commanded by Optatus, he states that it was violence of this kind that made it necessary to ask the authorities to punish the Donatist leaders by imposing upon them a fine of ten pounds of gold, an extraordinarily mild punishment, considering the enormity of their crimes.

It was this that first made it necessary to urge before the vicar Seranus that the law should be put in force against you which imposes a fine of ten pounds of gold, which none of you have ever paid to this very day, and yet you charge us with cruelty. But where could you find a milder course of proceeding, than that crimes of such magnitude on your part should be punished by the imposition of a pecuniary fine? . . . But what else was it, save such deeds as these of yours, that made it necessary for the very laws to be passed of which you complain? The laws, indeed, are very far from being proportionate to your offenses; but, such as they are, you may thank yourselves for their existence.[37]

Augustine seems to be limiting the use of state punishment to the leaders of the schism, and especially to those who have been guilty of organizing and carrying out violent attacks on the Catholics. Although he defends the imperial laws that provide for punishment of heretics, we note that he does not seek to have the penalty provided by the law—a fine of ten pounds of gold—actually levied even upon the few Donatist leaders who have been tried and found guilty. He seems to view the law and its penalties as a threat rather than as a direct punishment of heresy.[38] The laws enacted against you, he says to the Donatists, do not compel you to do well; they only prevent you from doing ill.

No one is indeed to be compelled to embrace the faith against his will; but by the severity, or one might rather say, by the mercy of God, it is common for treachery to be chastised with the scourge of tribulation. . . . For no one can do well unless he has deliberately chosen, and unless he has loved what is in free will; but the fear of punishment . . . at any rate keeps the evil desire from escaping beyond the bounds of thought.[39]

In accordance with his general doctrine of punishment, which I have already discussed,[40] Augustine insists that it is not only right for the public authorities to punish wrongdoing, since in so doing they are acting as ministers of God, but that such punishment is an act of love which is intended to lead to the correction and reform of those who are punished. The punishment itself does not change a man's evil will or improve his conduct, but it may serve as a warning to him and as an inducement to change his attitude and his way of life. He sees no necessary conflict between free will and the warnings that are given by the correction of the laws; if a man sees that it is unrighteousness for which he suffers, he may be induced, from the consideration that he is suffering and being tormented most fruitlessly, to change his purpose for the better, and may at the same time escape both the fruitless annoyance and the unrighteousness itself. . . . And so you, when kings make any enactments against you, should consider that you are receiving a warning to consider why this is being done to you.[41]

In replying to the Donatist argument that any appeal by Christians to the State to employ its coercive power to punish evil is wrong, Augustine charges them with insincerity in view of their own actions against the Maximianists. He also makes a strained effort to find a basis in the Gospels for coercive punishment of enemies of true religion by reminding the Donatists that "Christ persecuted even with bodily chastisement those whom He drove with scourges from the temple. . . ."[42] You console yourselves for your small numbers, he tells them, "not by the rod and staff of the Lord, but by the cudgels of the Circumcelliones, with which you think that you are safe even against the Roman laws,—to bring oneself into collision with which is surely nothing less than to walk through the valley of the shadow of death."[43] Augustine's vehement disapproval of disobedience to law and established authority, and his view that such disobedience is a grave sin are not, as we know, views that he adopted in order to strengthen his position in this controversy. They express his general doctrine that it is necessary to give absolute obedience to the State's commands, except where they openly conflict with God's commands.[44] If kings threaten us with fines or confiscation of property because we abide in the true Catholic faith and are not Jews or pagans, we must not follow their commands; we must be willing to give up everything that we possess if they choose to take our wealth or goods from us. "But if kings threaten you with loss or condemnation, simply on the ground that you are heretics, such things are terrifying you not in cruelty, but in mercy; and your determination not to fear is a sign not of bravery, but of obstinacy." [45] Augustine ridicules the Donatists' claim that they are holy martyrs and that their persecution at the hands of the State proves the rightness of their cause; being punished by the Emperor is certainly no proof of righteous conduct, as the Donatists themselves must admit if they reflect upon the case of the Maximianists. [46]

After the Emperor had issued the first Edict of Unity and had ordered his officials in Africa to impose severe penalties on the Donatists, [47] Augustine, in accordance with the decision taken by the tenth Council of Carthage in August, 405, wrote to the provincial governor, Caecilianus, congratulating him for the measures he had taken, with remarkable success, throughout the rest of Africa "on behalf of Catholic unity," and expressing his sorrow

because the district of Hippo and the neighbouring regions on the borders of Numidia have not enjoyed the benefit of the vigour with which as a magistrate you have enforced your proclamation, my noble lord, and my son truly and justly honourable and esteemed in the love of Christ. . . . If you condescend to acquaint yourself with the extremities to which the effrontery of the heretics has proceeded in the region of Hippo . . . I am sure you will so deal with this tumour of impious presumption, that it shall be healed by warning rather than painfully removed afterwards by punishment. [48]

Here again, as in the letter to Crispinus mentioned above, [49] the suggestion is that if the authorities proclaim the Emperor's edict and enforce it against a few of the leaders of Donatist violence, most of their followers will heed the warning and so will not have to be punished.

In a letter to Emeritus, Donatist Bishop of Caesarea, which may have been written in the same year, [50] Augustine gives what is perhaps the clearest statement of his views on the question of using state power against heresy during the period that I have been discussing, that is, from 399 to 405. Even if we admit, he says, that Christians ought not to persecute even the wicked, we surely cannot say that the state authorities, ordained for the very purpose of punishing evildoers, should fail to carry out their mission. And he insists that the Catholics have asked for help from the civil power *"not to persecute you, but to protect themselves against the lawless acts of violence perpetrated by individuals of your party,* which you yourselves, who refrain from such things, bewail and deplore." [51] He implies that the Church has not asked the State to inflict punishment on schismatics or heretics simply because of their schism or heresy, but that she has only asked for protection for herself and for her priests and laymen against the illegal acts of violence committed by some of the Donatists and especially by the Circumcellions. At the same time Augustine warns Emeritus that the Emperors, on their own initiative,

whatever the occasion of their becoming acquainted with the crime of your schism might be, frame against you such decrees as their zeal and their office demand. For they bear not the sword in vain; they are the ministers of God to execute wrath upon those that do evil. Finally, if some of our party transgress the bounds of Christian moderation in this matter, it displeases us.[52]

Again, in the next year, 406, in writing to Januarius, Donatist Bishop of Casae Nigrae, Augustine repeats the argument that it was only the violence and crimes of the Donatists that compelled the Catholics to have the imperial decrees against them revived and applied again.

You have therefore no ground for complaint against us: nay more, the clemency of the Catholic Church would have led us to desist from even enforcing these decrees of the emperors, had not your clergy and Circumcelliones, disturbing our peace, and destroying us by their most monstrous crimes and furious deeds of violence, compelled us to have these decrees revived and put in force again.[53]

He goes on to reject the Donatist complaints that they are being persecuted, and vigorously reminds them that it is the Catholics who are being killed, blinded, and robbed.

You say that you are persecuted, while we are killed with clubs and swords by your armed men. You say that you are persecuted, while our houses are pillaged by your armed robbers. You say that you are persecuted, while many of us have our eyesight destroyed by the lime and acid with which your men are armed for the purpose. . . . They take no blame to themselves for the harm which they do to us, and they lay upon us the blame of the harm which they bring upon themselves.[54]

He contrasts with these outrages the mildness of the Catholic treatment of the Donatists who fall into their hands, and the orders given by the Catholic clergy that the Donatists should not be injured but brought to the priest or bishop for instruction. Even if

they refuse to be reconciled to the unity of Christ, they are allowed to depart, as they were detained, without suffering any harm. We also exhort our laity as far as we can to detain them without doing them any harm, and bring them to us for admonition and instruction. Some of them obey us and do this, if it is in their power: others deal with them as they would with robbers, because they actually suffer from them such things as robbers are wont to do.[55]

He again replies to the Donatist argument that the State and the Emperor have no authority in matters of religion by reminding them that it was their predecessors who began the appeal to the civil power by their repeated efforts to secure from the Emperor Constantine the condemnation of Caecilian and Felix.[56]

In the same year, 406, in a letter to the layman, Festus, Augustine insists that it is "reasonable and right" for Catholics "to labour constantly and with energy not only in the defence of those who are already Catholics, but also for the correction of those who are not yet within the Church."[57] Suffering punishment is of itself no proof of righteousness or holiness;

men are made martyrs not by the amount of their suffering, but by the cause in which they suffer. This I would say even were I opposing men who were only involved in the darkness of error, and suffering penalties on that account most truly merited, and who had not dared to assault any one with insane violence.[58]

This seems to be the first indication that Augustine would approve of the imposition of legal penalties on those who are simply heretics and have committed no criminal acts. He notes that some of the Donatists resist conversion with "active rage" and others with "passive immobility." The Church cannot and should not refuse to use any remedies that may promote their recovery, when "seeking with a mother's anxiety the salvation of them all, and distracted by the frenzy of some and the lethargy of others." [59] The first group must be restrained and the second stirred up, and in both cases the treatment is a work of love.[60] He no longer feels that "strong measures" against heresy accomplish nothing. "For when the entrenchments of stubborn custom are stormed by fear of human authority, this is not all that is done, because at the same time faith is strengthened, and the understanding convinced, by authority and arguments which are Divine." [61] He never asserts that force and fear are methods that can be directly effective against heresy. However, he now begins to argue that the threat of punishment not only can restrain some men from their violent frenzy but also can be the means of releasing others from the fear of the violence of the fanatics; once the timid followers are freed from this fear and from the bonds of habit, it may be possible to convince them by rational arguments and scriptural authority.[62]

The long letter written in 408 to Vincentius, who had been his friend when he was a student at Carthage and who was now Bishop of Cartenna and a member of the small Rogatist faction of the Donatists, provides a clear statement of Augustine's change of heart on the problem of employing state coercion against heresy. He notes that although at first he was opposed to any use of coercion, he has changed his mind because of the examples of the effectiveness of compulsion which his colleagues have presented to him.

I have therefore yielded to the evidence afforded by these instances which my colleagues have laid before me. . . . But this opinion of mine was overcome not by the words of those who controverted it, but by the conclusive instances to which they could point. For, in the first place, there was set over against my opinion my own town, which, although it was once wholly on the side of Donatus, was brought over to the Catholic unity by fear of the imperial edicts, but which we now see filled with such detestation of your ruinous perversity, that it would scarcely be believed that it had ever been involved in your error.[63]

Nor has this success of the policy of coercion been limited to the town of Hippo.

We see not a few men here and there, but many cities, once Donatist, now Catholic, vehemently detesting the diabolical schism, and ardently loving the unity of the Church; and these became Catholics under the influence of that fear which is to you so offensive by the laws of emperors, from Constantine, before whom your party of their own accord impeached Caecilianus, down to the emperors of our own time. . . .[64]

While it is true that no one "can be good in spite of his own will," the fear of suffering the penalties imposed by the laws has compelled many persons either to give up their enmity to the Church or to investigate the truth of which they had been ignorant; such a man "under the influence of this fear repudiates the error which he was wont to defend, or seeks the truth of which he formerly knew nothing, and now willingly holds what he formerly rejected." [65] Many who were held among the Donatists by the force of habit and tradition have been converted, and, what is even more wonderful, many of the fanatically violent

Circumcellions have been brought into the Church by the whole-some fear occasioned by the imperial punishments.[66] Of course, there are among the Donatists men who have not been restrained from violent hostility to the Church nor awakened from their lethargy by the fear of punishment, but the fact that the remedy does not cure all those who are ill is no reason for not using it. "Is the art of healing, therefore, to be abandoned, because the malady of some is incurable?"[67]

Thus, Augustine states that it was the success of the policy of state coercion in bringing large numbers of Donatists back to the unity of the Church that convinced him that his original oppo-sition to this method had been wrong and that his fellow bishops who favored the appeal to the State had been right. Indeed, he now sees the conversions that have been effected as a result of the legal penalties for heresy as "conquests of the Lord."

Could I therefore maintain opposition to my colleagues, and by re-sisting them stand in the way of such conquests of the Lord, and prevent the sheep of Christ which were wandering on your moun-tains and hills—that is, on the swellings of your pride—from being gathered into the fold of peace, in which there is one flock and one Shepherd?[68]

Without the shock of alarm caused by the State's repression and correction, many of the Donatists who have been liberated from error would not have been impelled to examine the truth and so would have remained in the "bondage of custom" and "would in no way have thought of being changed to a better condi-tion."[69] Had the Catholics done nothing to alarm and correct them by this wholesome fear of temporal punishment, they would not have been good or merciful toward them but rather would have rendered unto them evil for evil. Some of the Donatists admit that they wanted to return to the Church some time before, and so they now say, "Thanks be to God, who has given us oc-casion for doing it at once, and has cut off the hesitancy of procrastination!" [70] Others thank the Lord who has broken asunder the bonds of old custom and brought them back into the bond of peace, while still others thank God for having startled them by the stimulus of fear into examining the Catholic truth of which they were ignorant and into discovering how false were the reports about the Church which their leaders gave them.

Coercion in and of itself is neither right nor wrong; what must be considered when coercion is applied to anyone is "the nature of that to which he is coerced, whether it be good or bad. . . ." [71] If it were always praiseworthy to suffer persecution, the Lord would have said, "Blessed are they which are persecuted" and would not have added "for righteousness' sake." [72] And if it were always wrong to inflict persecution, we would not be told in the Scriptures, "Whoso privily slandereth his neighbour, him will I persecute." [73] Some men who suffer persecution are wicked, and they deserve the punishment they receive; others are good men who are unjustly persecuted. Some persecutors are evil men who act out of hatred and malice, while others are good men who punish in a spirit of love and justice. Even when "the true and rightful Mother," the Church, acts with severity toward her children and they receive bitter medicine from her,

she is not rendering evil for evil, but is applying the benefit of discipline to counteract the evil of sin, not with the hatred which seeks to harm, but with the love which seeks to heal. When good and bad do the same actions and suffer the same afflictions, they are to be distinguished not by what they do or suffer, but by the causes of each: e.g. Pharaoh oppressed the people of God by hard bondage; Moses afflicted the same people by severe correction when they were guilty of impiety: their actions were alike; but they were not alike in the motive of regard to the people's welfare,—the one being inflated by the lust of power, the other inflamed by love. [74]

Although we are commanded to love our enemies, yet we must also, in the spirit of love, correct their errors.

To Vincentius's objection that nowhere in the New Testament

is there found any example of the Church asking the kings of the earth for aid or protection against her enemies, Augustine replies that while this is true, we must distinguish between the age of the apostles and the martyrs and the present age, in which the prophecy, "Be wise now, therefore, O ye kings: be instructed, ye judges of the earth. Serve the Lord with fear," [75] has been fulfilled. The actions of King Nebuchadnezzar in the Old Testament prefigure both the condition of the Church in the age of the martyrs and her present condition.[76]

In the age of the apostles and martyrs, that was fulfilled which was prefigured when the aforesaid king compelled pious and just men to bow down to his image, and cast into the flames all who refused. Now, however, is fulfilled that which was prefigured soon after in the same king, when, being converted to the worship of the true God, he made a decree throughout his empire, that whosoever should speak against the God of Shadrach, Meshach, and Abednego should suffer the penalty which their crime deserved.[77]

In another work he tells us that the reason why this story was recorded in the Scriptures and is read in front of Christian Emperors is "that an example might be set both before the servants of God, to prevent them from committing sacrilege in obedience to kings, and before kings themselves, that they should show themselves religious by belief in God" and that they should "consider what decrees they ought to make in their kingdom, that the same God . . . should not be treated with scorn among the faithful in their realm." [78]

In the period of Christ's ministry on earth and in the days of the apostles, the humble and the poor believed on Christ while the rulers, in their madness, failed to acknowledge Him and, indeed, were eager to slay Him.[79] The Lord first chose as His followers poor men rather than rich men, fishermen rather than emperors or orators, so that those who were chosen would not be proud and would not attribute their calling to their own merits.

Later, He chose rich men, men of influence and power, even emperors. When Peter and Paul were put to death, they were despised; "now, the earth having been enriched by them, and the cross of the Church springing up, behold, all that is noble and chief in the world, even the emperor himself, cometh to Rome, and whither does he hasten? to the temple of the emperor, or the memorial of the fisherman?" [80] Now the very kings who once persecuted the Church have become subject to Christ's name and serve the Lord and His Church by persecuting the false gods of the heathen and by chastising heretics.[81]

All men ought to serve God, both by virtue of their common condition and by virtue of their several gifts and earthly functions. In that a man is a man, he serves God by living faithfully, but in that he is a king he serves the Lord with fear by preventing and punishing those acts that are contrary to God's commandments; his special function, which other men cannot perform, is to serve God "by enforcing with suitable rigor such laws as ordain what is righteous [*iusta*], and punish what is the reverse." [82] For example, no private individual would have the right to command that the idols of the heathen be removed or destroyed; such action would be "the way of ill-regulated men, and the mad Circumcelliones." [83] Only those who legally possess the property where the idols are found have the right to destroy them after they have become Christians and the idols in their hearts have been broken down, or the king or ruler by virtue of his public authority has the right to order that the idols be destroyed.

If it is the duty of Christian kings to command what is righteous and to punish what is unrighteous, no sane man "could say to the kings, 'Let not any thought trouble you within your kingdom as to who restrains or attacks the church of your Lord; deem it not a matter in which you should be concerned, which

of your subjects may choose to be religious or sacrilegious.' " [84]
The Donatists are distressed because Christian rulers are roused
against heretics and schismatics. "How otherwise should they
give an account of their rule to God? Observe, beloved, what I
say, that *it concerns Christian kings of this world to wish their
mother the Church, of which they have been spiritually born, to
have peace in their times.*" [85] The gist of Augustine's view of
the proper role of kings and rulers in the correction and punishment of heresy and schism is expressed in a brief phrase in the
letter of 408 to Vincentius: "Nay verily; let the kings of the
earth serve Christ by making laws for Him and for His cause
[*immo uero seruiant reges terrae Christo etiam leges ferendo pro
Christo*]." [86]

Although Augustine sometimes speaks of the great honor and
glory which the Church now enjoys on earth as a consequence of
the aid and protection given to her by Christian kings,[87] at
other moments he flatly denies that this service and honor rendered by kings serve to make the Church glorious. Royal protection and favor constitute for the Church only "a more perilous
and a sorer temptation"; she will be truly glorious only when
the evils and troubles of this world have passed away and Christ
appears in triumph to claim His Bride, the Church. "Nor do
we put confidence in princes, but, so far as we can, we warn
princes to put confidence in the Lord. And *though we may seek
aid from princes to promote the advantage of the Church, yet do
we not put confidence in them.*" [88]

In this letter of 408 to Vincentius we also find what seems to
be Augustine's first use of the parable of the Great Supper (*Luke*
xiv, 16–24) as a justification of the use of state coercion against
heretics—the famous doctrine of *"Compelle intrare* [Compel
them to come in]." Vincentius argues that no man should be
coerced in order to deliver him from the fatal consequences of

error. This argument, Augustine replies, ignores the fact that God, "who loves us with more real regard for our profit than any other can," [89] often deals with us in this way. Moreover, Vincentius has forgotten Christ's statement that "No one can come to me unless the Father who sent me draws him." [90] The answer to Vincentius's argument that no one should be compelled to follow righteousness is found in the order given by the householder to his servant in the parable related by Luke— "Whomsoever ye shall find, compel them to come in." Although Augustine does not, at this time, discuss the rest of the parable, in his later references he uses the entire story as a figure of the Church. A certain man prepared a great supper and invited many guests, but all of them made excuses and did not appear.

The master of the house being angry said to his servant, "Go out quickly into the streets and lanes of the city, and bring in hither the poor, and the maimed, and the halt and the blind." And the servant said, "Lord, it is done as thou hast commanded, and yet there is room." And the lord said unto the servant, "Go out into the highways and hedges, and compel them to come in, that my house may be filled. For I say unto you, That none of those men which were bidden shall taste of my supper." [91]

According to Augustine's interpretation of this parable, the guests who were originally invited but refused to attend are the Jews; the poor, the maimed, the halt, and the blind, "brought in" from the streets and lanes of the city, are the Gentiles who became Christians; and those who are "compelled to come in" from the highways and hedges are those who are forced to return to the Church from heresies and schisms. [92]

For those who make hedges, their object is to make divisions. Let them be drawn away from the hedges, let them be plucked up from among the thorns. They have stuck fast in the hedges, they are unwilling to be compelled. Let us come in, they say, of our own good will. This is not the Lord's order, "Compel them," saith He, "to come in." Let compulsion be found outside, the will will arise within.[93]

"The instrument by which those who are found in the highways and hedges—that is, in heresies and schisms—are compelled to come in" is "the power which the Church has received by divine appointment in its due season, through the religious character and the faith of kings."[94] In a letter written in 416 to a Donatist priest, Donatus, Augustine reminds him that in the Gospel period the Church was only in its infancy and the prophecy, "Yea, all kings shall fall down before him: yea, all nations shall serve him,"[95] was not yet fulfilled. Now that the prophecy has, to a large extent, been accomplished,

the Church wields greater power, so that she may not only invite, but even compel men to embrace what is good. . . . Mark, now, how it was said in regard to those who came first, "bring them in;" it was not said, "compel them to come in,"—by which was signified the incipient condition of the Church, when it was only growing towards the position in which it would have strength to compel men to come in.[96]

The purpose of the State's enactments against heresy and schism and of the penalties of fines or exile imposed upon the Donatists (mild penalties compared to the punishment of death imposed upon those who perform heathen sacrifices) is to admonish the wanderers to depart from evil and to return to the Church of Christ, rather than to punish them for their crimes.[97]

In 408, after the death of Stilicho, the principal minister of state, who had been an opponent of the Donatists, Augustine wrote a letter to his murderer and successor, Olympius, requesting him to show the same zeal in enforcing the Emperor Honorius's laws against heresy and in defense of the Church. He informs Olympius that the Donatist leaders are spreading reports that the measures taken against them by Stilicho were done "without his [the Emperor's] knowledge, or against his will, and thus they render the minds of the ignorant full of seditious violence, and excite them to dangerous and vehement enmity against us." [98] This appeal was successful, since the Emperor soon confirmed the decrees that he had issued in 404.

In the next year, 409, Augustine, in a letter addressed to the Donatists as a group, made another appeal to them to return to the unity of the Church. He tells them that when the Catholics plead with them to come back to the Church or threaten them with penalties, or when the secular authorities make and enforce laws against them, or when in any way they suffer loss or trouble, it is God Himself who is doing these things to them through His agents. [99] If the emperors issued laws against the truth, "the just would be both tried and crowned by not doing what was commanded because it was forbidden by God. . . . But, when the emperors hold to the truth, in accordance with that truth they give commands against error, and whoever despises them brings down judgment on himself." [100] He tells the Donatists that they have brought upon their own heads the imperial decrees compelling them to rejoin the Church

by stirring up violence and threats whenever we wished to preach the truth, and you tried to prevent anyone from listening to it in safety or choosing it voluntarily. . . . [C]all to memory the deeds of your Circumcellions and the clerics who have always been their leaders, and you will see what brought this on you. Your complaints are baseless because you forced the enactment of all these decrees. [101]

Yet the Donatists, who are being justly punished for their evil deeds and acts of brigandage, have the audacity to claim the glory of martyrdom. [102] And in a letter to Macrobius, Augustine once more reminds the Donatists that, while they now complain of unwarranted persecution by the State, they themselves used the State and its courts to drive the Maximianists from their churches; whatever defense they will make of their actions in this matter he will now adopt as his own defense against their complaints.[103]

Thus, it is clear that before the Imperial Conference of 411 at Carthage, presided over by Marcellinus,[104] Augustine had elaborated all the major elements of his defense of the Church's right to appeal to the State to punish heretics and schismatics. Although force cannot directly change the evil or misguided wills of men, the overt expressions of those wills in sacrilegious or criminal acts can be punished; and in some cases the punishment suffered may induce those who wander in error to listen to reason and to the voice of God in the Scriptures and thus to discover the truth to which they have been blind. In any case, the secular authorities have not only the right but the duty to act with severity and with love toward those who are guilty of heresy and schism. When they act in this way, they are serving as agents and ministers of God, who through them corrects and emends the conduct of those who have gone astray and scourges with punishment those who refuse to turn from their wickedness. Compulsion and punishment serve as a warning and as an entering wedge to permit instruction and persuasion to go forward once the hindrances of violence, long-continued habit, and slothful indifference have been broken down.[105]

After the Conference of 411, Augustine was active in the effort to secure wide public attention for the proceedings and for the decision condemning the Donatists. He ordered that the Acts of the Conference (*Gesta Collationis*) be read in the churches in his diocese, and this example was followed in other districts. He prepared a short summary of the *Gesta*, entitled *Breuiculus Collationis,* and published it by the end of 411. In writing to Marcellinus in 412, he refers to the Donatists' confession of the murder of one priest and the blinding and maiming of another, and says:

My heart's desire is, that many similar Donatist cases may be tried and decided by you as these have been, and that in this way the crimes and the insane obstinacy of these men may be often brought to light; and that the Acts recording these proceedings may be published, and brought to the knowledge of all men.[106]

On a number of occasions he repeats his denial of the Donatists' charges that the Church is acting unjustly and that the Emperor has no right to impose penalties upon them.[107]

In 416 Augustine wrote to a Donatist priest, Donatus, who had been arrested and brought before the authorities after having been forcibly prevented from committing suicide by drowning. From these events he draws an analogy in defense of the policy of compelling heretics to abandon their errors.

You, with your own free will, threw yourself into the water that you might be drowned. They took you against your will out of the water, that you might not be drowned. . . . If, therefore, mere bodily safety behoves to be so guarded that it is the duty of those who love their neighbour to preserve him even against his own will from harm, how much more is this duty binding in regard to that spiritual health in the loss of which the consequence to be dreaded is eternal death! [108]

Donatus has no right to be angry because the wandering and perishing are sought out and brought home; "for it is better for us to obey the will of the Lord, who charges us to compel you to return to His fold, than to yield consent to the will of the wandering sheep, so as to leave you to perish." [109]

One of the most famous of Augustine's anti-Donatist writings is the letter written early in 417 to Boniface, tribune and later Count of Africa, urging him to apply stringently the laws against the Donatists. This letter is also known by the title, *De*

Correctione Donatistarum. The laws that the Donatists regard
as their enemies and persecutors

are in reality their truest friends; for through their operation many of
them have been, and are daily being reformed, and return God thanks
that they are reformed, and delivered from their ruinous madness.
And . . . now that they have recovered their right minds, they
congratulate themselves that these most wholesome laws were
brought to bear against them, with as much fervency as in their madness they detested them.[110]

While there are Donatists who have refused to return to the
Church, some of whom have committed suicide, they are a
minority compared to the "estates, villages, streets, fortresses,
municipal towns, cities, that are delivered by the laws under consideration from that fatal and eternal destruction." [111]

Augustine admits to Boniface that at an earlier period he had
been opposed to punishment of heretics *per se,* and had desired
that only their violent and criminal acts be punished by the imposition of fines on their clergy. But now he rejoices that the
more stringent policy of his fellow-bishops rather than his own
plan was adopted, and that the Emperor issued a law that completely outlawed Donatism and provided penalties of exile and
fines, but no capital punishment.[112] He refers to the experiences
of St. Paul to show that Christ Himself first used compulsion to
convert Paul and then gave him teaching and consolation. "He
not only constrained him with His voice, but even dashed him
to the earth with His power; and that He might forcibly bring
one who was raging amid the darkness of infidelity to desire the
light of the heart, He first struck him with physical blindness of
the eyes." [113] God's great mercy toward many of the Donatists
is demonstrated by their being rescued, against their will, from
this heretical sect by means of these imperial laws. As a result,
those who were kept in the sect by fear have been released; many

have been removed from the influence of "lying devils" who taught them evil doctrines, and have been brought into the Church, where they are exposed to good teaching and example.[114]

The Church was gravely afflicted by the furious violence of the Donatist leaders, directed both at Catholics and at their own wavering followers, many of whom wanted to return to the Church. In these straits, she sought *the assistance of God, to be rendered through the agency of Christian emperors.* [115] The purpose of her "righteous persecution," carried on in the spirit of love, is to do good to her enemies and to cause them to make advance in the truth and to move toward eternal salvation. She acts toward the Donatists as the physician acts toward the "raving madman" or the father toward the undisciplined son; the doctor restrains and the father chastises, and yet both act in love.[116] The remnants of the Donatist party who still violently rage against the Church and the State and refuse to abandon their heresy prefer to destroy themselves bodily and spiritually by suicide rather than return to the Church; they are "so in love with murder, that they commit it on their own persons, when they cannot find victims in any others." [117]

At several places in his commentaries on the Gospel of St. John,[118] Augustine refers to the Donatists' charges that they are being wrongfully persecuted. He notes that the pains inflicted upon them by the constituted authorities are justified and legitimate, and that they have been afflicted only in body, while they persecute the Spirit in Christians; at the same time, "they do not spare the flesh; as many as they were able, they slew with the sword; they spared neither their own nor strangers." [119] The Donatists hate the Emperor and the political authorities because they act according to the law. They refuse to recognize that the bodily persecutions—if such they can be called—that they have suffered have been *the scourges of the Lord, plainly administer-*

ing temporal correction, lest He should have to condemn them eternally, if they did not acknowledge it and amend themselves." [120]

He returns to this theme in his homilies on the Epistle of John.[121] The Donatists are the real persecutors, not only because of the illegal force and violence which they have so often used against both the Catholics and their own followers but because they have divided the Church.[122] To praise, commend, and flatter the evildoer is a work of hatred, while admonition, reproof, even denunciation or legal prosecution of a friend who commits evil may be acts of love and charity.[123] Provided that you hold fast to love, you need not be afraid of harming anyone, no matter how severely you may reprove or punish him, for no one can do any ill to the person that he loves.

Love, and you cannot but do well [*Dilige, non potest fieri nisi bene facias*]. You may rebuke, but that will be the act of love, not of harshness: you may use the rod, but it will only be for discipline; for the love of love itself [*amor ipsius dilectionis*] will not suffer you to pass over the lack of discipline in another. Sometimes there is a kind of contrariness apparent in the products of hatred and of love: hatred may use fair words and love may sound harshly.[124]

Despite—or perhaps because of—his shift from opposition to approval on the issue of using state power against the Donatists, Augustine repeatedly intervened with high officials of the Empire to plead for moderation in the punishment of convicted Donatists and, above all, for no use of capital punishment, even if they were guilty of murder or violence. In 409 he writes to Donatus, the proconsul of Africa; a clear echo of his early opposition to any appeal to the temporal power is heard in the opening sentence of the letter: "I would indeed that the African Church were not placed in such trying circumstances as to need the aid of any earthly power." [125] But in view of the great calamities by which the Church is assailed, it is a consolation bestowed by God that a man like Donatus, so devoted to the name of Christ, occupies the exalted post of proconsul "so that power allied with your good-will may restrain the enemies of the Church from their wicked and sacrilegious attempts." [126]

Augustine has only one fear about Donatus's administration of justice—that just because he realizes that the injury done to the Church by impious heretics is more serious and more heinous than other crimes, he may conclude that "it ought to be punished with a severity corresponding to the enormity of the crime, and not with the moderation which is suitable to Christian forbearance. We beseech you, in the name of Jesus Christ, not to act in this manner." [127] When the Church seeks aid from judges and from laws, she desires not the death of her enemies but their deliverance from error and from the penalty of eternal punishment; so, while she wishes her errant children to be corrected with suitable discipline, she is unwilling that they should suffer the more severe punishments that they deserve. Augustine implores Donatus to forget, when he is pronouncing judgment in cases affecting the Church, that he has the power of capital punishment, no matter how great the injuries may be which the accused have inflicted upon the Church. If this plea is ignored and death sentences are imposed on the Donatists, the Church will be compelled to abandon such prosecutions completely.

If, therefore, your opinion be, that death must be the punishment of men convicted of these crimes, you will deter us from endeavouring to bring anything of this kind before your tribunal; and this being discovered, they will proceed with more unrestrained boldness to accomplish speedily our destruction, when upon us is imposed and enjoined the necessity of choosing rather to suffer death at their hands, than to bring them to death by accusing them at your bar.[128]

In this letter to Donatus, Augustine explicitly states that one of his reasons for opposing the death penalty is his fear that the Donatists will make effective use of the argument that they are suffering martyrdom for their adherence to the true faith.[129]

Three years later, in a letter to Marcellinus, Augustine says that while the Church favors "the removal from these wicked men of the liberty to perpetrate further crimes," she desires that

> justice be satisfied without the taking of their lives or the maiming of their bodies in any part, and that, by such coercive measures as may be in accordance with the laws, they be turned from their insane frenzy to the quietness of men in their sound judgment, or compelled to give up mischievous violence and betake themselves to some useful labour.[130]

In this way the discipline imposed upon them by penal sentences will be truly a benefit rather than a vindictive punishment. In another letter to Marcellinus, written later in the same year, 412, he beseeches him to use his influence with the judge to have a penalty less severe than the death sentence imposed on a number of Donatists who have confessed to grievous crimes. If the judge refuses to grant this request, "let him at least allow that the men be remanded for a time; and we will endeavour to obtain this concession from the clemency of the Emperors, so that the sufferings of the martyrs, which ought to shed bright glory on the Church, may not be tarnished by the blood of their enemies." [131]

In the same year, he writes in a similar vein to Apringius, proconsul of Africa. If death were the only possible punishment available to curb the wicked acts of these desperate men, "we should prefer to let them go free, rather than avenge the martyrdom of our brothers by shedding their blood." [132] But, since other, less drastic punishments are available by which their violent excesses can be restrained, "why do you not commute your

sentence to a more prudent and more lenient one, as judges have
the liberty of doing even in non-ecclesiastical cases? . . . They
shed Christian blood with impious sword; do you, for Christ's
sake, withhold even the sword of the law from their blood." [133]
And, constantly, Augustine warns his congregation not to revile
the heretics nor to exalt themselves against them; "we pray you
to beware, whosoever ye are in the Church, do not revile them
that are not within; but pray ye rather, that they too may be
within." [134]

In the course of Augustine's great struggle against the Pelagians, which occupied the center of his attention during the
last fifteen years of his life, the issue of the use of state power
against heresy was again raised. In 416 the African bishops, under Augustine's leadership, appealed to Pope Innocent to excom-
municate Pelagius and Caelestius and to condemn their doctrines; to the great rejoicing of Augustine and his colleagues,
Innocent, early in 417, wrote back a strong condemnation of the
Pelagian errors and announced the excommunication of the leaders of the heresy.[135] However, Innocent died soon after, in March,
417, and his successor, Pope Zosimus, began to make efforts to
reinstate Pelagius and Caelestius. After examining Caelestius and
reading a written statement by Pelagius, the Pope wrote to the
African churches, criticizing them for their haste in condemning
virtuous Christians on the basis of inadequate evidence. Even
worse, Zosimus "pronounced the creed of Pelagius to be fully
orthodox and catholic." [136] The Africans, however, stood firm
in their opposition, and insisted that the issue had been closed
by Innocent's decision against the Pelagians. In September, 417,
in a sermon preached at Carthage, Augustine urged his hearers
not to protect or shield the Pelagians who were known to them,
but to bring them to the leaders of the Church. He insisted that
the two councils of the African Church, whose actions had been

approved by Pope Innocent, had settled the matter, which could not now be reopened.[137]

Late in 417 or early in 418, the African bishops again met in council and sent a formal reply to Zosimus that the case had been tried and was finished. At the end of April, 418, any plans that Zosimus might have entertained for a reversal of Innocent's condemnation of the Pelagians were suddenly frustrated when the Emperor Honorius issued a rescript condemning the Pelagians; the rescript provided penalties against the heresy and urged the Roman See to take measures of its own against its leaders. Warfield suggests that it may well have been Augustine, through his correspondence with influential friends at the imperial court, who was responsible for this decree.

There is, indeed, no direct proof that it was due to Augustin, or to the Africans under his leading . . . that the State interfered in the matter. . . . [B]ut . . . it seems, on internal grounds, altogether probable that he was the *Deus ex machinā* who let loose the thunders of ecclesiastical and civil enactment simultaneously on the poor Pope's devoted head.[138]

There is no doubt at all that Augustine heartily approved of the State's actions against the Pelagians. In one of his anti-Pelagian treatises,[139] written in 420 and dedicated to his friend, Count Valerius, he says to his Pelagian opponent:

Entertaining such impious views as these, of what use is it that you fearlessly face that which is enacted for you in order to induce salutary fear and to treat you as a human being? . . . The reason why your catholic mother alarms you is, because she fears for both you and others from you; and *if by the help of her sons who possess any authority in the State she acts with a view to make you afraid, she does so, not from cruelty, but from love.* You, however, are a very brave man; and you deem it the coward's part to be afraid of men. Well then, fear God. . . . Although I could even wish that that spirited temper of yours would entertain some little fear of human authority, at least in the present case. I could wish, I say, that it would rather tremble through cowardice than perish through audacity.[140]

After the Emperor's edict against the Pelagians, Zosimus capitulated and published a condemnation of Pelagianism, as did another influential figure at Rome, who had been suspected of favoring the Pelagians, the priest Sixtus, who later became Pope Sixtus III. In a letter to Augustine and Alypius, Sixtus clearly rejected Pelagius's "fatal dogma." Augustine was very pleased. In one of the two letters that he wrote in reply, he urged Sixtus not only to bring avowed heretics to punishment but to seek out those who were covertly spreading their wicked doctrine; even those who were now silent should be forced to defend the true doctrines with the same energy and zeal that they used to show in the defense of error.

For some of their party might be known to you before that pestilence was denounced by the most explicit condemnation of the apostolic see [Pope Zosimus's condemnation in 418], whom you perceive to have now become suddenly silent; nor can it be ascertained whether they have been really cured of it, otherwise than through their not only forbearing from the utterance of these false dogmas, but also defending the truths which are opposed to their former errors with the same zeal as they used to show on the other side.[141]

This statement has a familiar sound to modern ears. When heresy is being hunted out, especially by the State, it is fatally easy to move from punishing those who have expressed heretical opinions to requiring that those whose orthodoxy is in any way suspect publicly affirm the "truth" and denounce "error."

In 419 the Emperors Honorius and Theodosius wrote a letter to Bishop Aurelius of Carthage in which they stated that long ago—presumably in 418—it had been

decreed that Pelagius and Celestius, the authors of an execrable heresy, should, as pestilent corruptors of the Catholic truth, be expelled from the city of Rome, lest they should, by their baneful influence, pervert the minds of the ignorant. . . . Their obstinate persistence in the offence having, however, made it necessary to issue the decree a second time, we have enacted further by a recent edict, that if any one, knowing that they are concealing themselves in any part of the provinces shall delay either to drive them out or to inform on them, he, as an accomplice, shall be liable to the punishment prescribed.[142]

A letter in the same terms was also sent by the Emperors to Augustine, who, in a work written in 418, had expressed his approval of the condemnation of the Pelagians by the episcopal councils, the Apostolic See, the whole Roman Church, and "the Roman Empire itself, which by God's gracious favour has become Christian." [143] About 420, Augustine wrote to Boniface, the new Bishop of Rome, A Treatise Against Two Letters of the Pelagians (*Contra Duas Epistolas Pelagianorum*). In it he denied the Pelagians' charge that the Roman clergy had submitted to state pressure when they reversed their judgment and finally condemned the Pelagians.[144] Augustine passes over the period in which Pope Zosimus had expressed a favorable attitude toward the Pelagians; he insists that they had been condemned by Zosimus as well as by Innocent, and that there had been no shift in the position of the Bishop of Rome or of the Roman clergy.

We have followed the path by which Augustine moved from his original view that the Church must deal with schismatics and heretics only by argument and persuasion and not by threats of state coercion, to a transitional position that the Church had the right to ask the political authorities for protection against the acts of violence committed by some of the members of the Donatist sect, and, finally, to the position that the Church had a duty as well as a right to ask the State to punish heretics and schismatics *per se,* while Christian kings had an obligation to use their power to protect and support the Church against heresy and schism as well as against paganism. When he finally agreed with his colleagues that coercion and criminal penalties should be applied to the Donatists to "compel them to come in," he was not content simply to argue that state intervention was, in this case, necessary and successful. As we have seen, he went on to elaborate a general defense of the *principle* that Christian rulers are duty-bound to use their power and authority to punish those men whose views on doctrine or organization are declared to be heterodox by the leaders of the Church.

Of course, Augustine did not originate this idea. Ever since the conversion of Constantine, Emperors had issued decrees against enemies of the Church; especially during the reigns of Theodosius I and his sons there had been a steady stream of imperial laws and edicts against heretics and schismatics.[145] However, Augustine made an important contribution to this development. He not only recognized and accepted the fact that rulers were using their power to defend the Church, but he set forth, by argument and appeal to the Scriptures, a thoroughgoing defense of these activities. Perhaps without clearly recognizing the full and final consequences of his teachings, he moved in the direction of a theocratic theory of the State, a theory which was to be fully developed in the Middle Ages by a series of great Popes, from Gregory VII to Boniface VIII, and by their supporters.

The theocratic element in Augustine's teachings about the nature and functions of state power—and it is always only an element of his doctrine, which co-exists with many other different elements—[146] is a direct consequence of the view that the State ought to punish those who are guilty of heresy or schism. For heresy and schism are religious questions—questions of doctrine and of ecclesiastical organization—and it is the bishops of the Church who decide what is orthodox doctrine and correct organization and discipline within the Church and what, on the other hand, constitutes heresy and schism. No strong church, least of all the vigorous Catholic Church of the Western Empire in the fifth century, would permit secular rulers to decide for themselves these issues of doctrine and organization. In this area, at least, the State and its officials become, therefore, auxiliaries of the Church and its officers. The leaders of the Church, by their own procedures and deliberations, determine what is orthodox and what is unorthodox. The political authorities are reduced to the status of "the secular arm," the coercive instrument by which ecclesiastical decisions are enforced upon dissident and recalcitrant members. Even when the officials of the State cooperate willingly with the Church authorities, they are obviously subordinate to the Church which sets the ends that they implement. Furthermore, it is the Church as the higher authority which will decide what other matters of state activity have so close a tie with religious or moral issues that they, too, must be dealt with by the State under the direction of ecclesiastical authority.[147]

Is there a fundamental inconsistency between the view to which Augustine was driven by the exigencies of the struggle against the Donatists—that is, that Christian rulers have the obligation as well as the right to punish those whom the Church discovers to be heretics or schismatics, and, in general, that it is the duty of Christian kings to serve God by making and enforcing laws to prevent sinful men from offering insult to God's majesty and to protect and promote true religion—and Augustine's general theory of the nature and function of the State —that it is an imperfect, though essential, organization made necessary by the Fall of man, whose primary purpose is to guarantee, by the use of the external instruments of coercion and the fear of punishment, the maintenance of earthly peace, security, and justice?[148] This question is one which arose at an earlier point in my discussion and which was set aside until I had had an opportunity to examine Augustine's varying treatments of the problem of using the coercive power of the State against heresy.[149] On several occasions in his discussions of that problem, Augustine seems to be arguing that there is no conflict between his general conception of the State and his support for the principle of state punishment of heresy. In the *Contra Epistulam Parmeniani,* for example, he argues that heresies, seditions, and emulations are overt evil actions, crimes that must be punished, just as murder, violence, theft, and fraud are punished, if the external peace and order of earthly society are to be maintained.[150] Even after his complete acceptance of the principle that state power ought to be used to compel heretics to return to the fold of the Church, he clearly states that coercion can do no more than compel the heretic to abandon his open resistance and force him back into the visible Church.

In and of itself compulsion cannot make the heretic or schismatic a sincere believer or a good man.[151] It can, however, force him out of the hedges and highways and back to the unity of the Catholic Church. There he will hear true doctrine preached, and he will participate in sacraments that are not, like the "sacraments" performed outside the Church, snares to drag him down to perdition. Of course, the former heretic's mere physical presence in the Church and his participation in its rites and services do not guarantee his salvation. If most of the members of the visible Church, who have never wandered off into heresy and schism, are not destined to be among the elect chosen by God for eternal blessedness, although some of them are living in a fashion that seems to be moral and pious,[152] it certainly cannot be argued that heretics, simply by returning to the Church—especially when they return by the path of legal compulsion, because they are afraid of suffering earthly punishment—are granted the blessings of regeneration and salvation. Inside the Church, they have a chance, if only a slight chance, of true repentance and of receiving the grace of God that draws a man to salvation; outside the Church, they face nothing but certain damnation.

Augustine often tells us that when the State punishes ordinary criminals it does not, by its repressive actions, bring about any fundamental change in the evil will either of the criminal who is punished or of the man who is kept from committing crime only because he fears that he, too, may be discovered and punished. Yet, the punishment of criminals and the discouragement of would-be criminals are not, therefore, useless. Some criminal actions are prevented, and the minimum of peace and justice essential to the preservation of society is maintained.[153] The thief who has suffered imprisonment for his crimes may, after his release, refrain from further robberies because he is afraid that he will again be punished, while another man may be led by his example to give up the idea of stealing property that belongs to others. It is quite possible that neither the thief nor the would-be thief has undergone any real change in his sinful desires or aims. It is also possible, of course, that God will sometimes use punishment or the fear of punishment as instruments of His saving grace in order to lead the sinner to true repentance and to a real conversion from his evil ways. This result, however, is not one which the State itself can bring about, nor is it what it intends to accomplish when it imposes penalties for theft. Similarly, Augustine states that although the experience of punishment or the fear of suffering punishment may, in a given case, lead the heretic to genuine repentance and to a recognition of God's truth, this result is a demonstration of God's special mercy and grace toward this particular sinful man; from it we cannot conclude that punishment or fear alone will bring about sincere conversion.

Thus, Augustine might argue that there is no real conflict between his general description of the State and its legal system and his advocacy of the State's right and duty to punish heresy and schism. He may not have been guilty of inconsistency, especially if the two doctrines are considered on the formal or verbal level, although, as we have seen, it is not easy to accommodate to his general theory of the State as an external, limited, coercive instrument for repressing sinful men some of his more extravagant statements about the Christian ruler's duty to use his power and authority "for the greatest possible extension" of God's worship, or his obligation to "serve Christ by making laws for Him and for His cause" and to lead his subjects to worship God both by the example of his own piety and by his use of his political power.[154] When, however, we seek to move beyond or beneath this formal level of analysis, we can hardly avoid the conclusion that Augustine's general attitude toward the State does conflict in a fundamental way with his final position of approval of the use of political and legal weapons to punish religious dissidence. His own awareness of this basic tension is indicated not only by the statements in which he laments the necessity of persecution, but also by his frequent, almost feverish, efforts to pile up arguments to persuade his readers, and possibly himself, that the resort to compulsion can be justified rationally, morally, and, above all, on scriptural grounds.

Few men have seen as clearly as Augustine the inherent limitations and inadequacies of the political process. The instruments available to the State are rough and crude; it never has the knowledge of facts or motives that it really needs as it makes its decisions and renders its verdicts; it acts always through the agency of fallible men, who are ignorant of much that they ought to know, who are often ruled by strong passions, such as pride, avarice, and hatred, rather than by reason, and whose judgments are frequently warped by self-interest and prejudice. The weapons at the State's disposal are blunt instruments—fines, imprisonment, punishment, torture, and death—and frequently it cannot know what effects its use of these weapons will have on a given man or on the society as a whole.[155]

To introduce this imperfect instrument and the rough and partial justice that it is able to secure into the realm of men's thoughts and beliefs, especially their religious beliefs, involves Augustine in a contradiction of the most fundamental kind. The paradox that results from using the blunt weapons of the political system to deal with men's innermost thoughts is so striking that it cries out for exposure by someone who possesses Augustine's own mastery of the techniques of irony and scorn. The tragedy is heightened by the fact that he knew, at least during the first years of his struggle with the Donatists, that compulsion and legal punishment could never come to grips with thoughts and beliefs, and that even "successful" coercion could do no more than make hypocrites and surface conformists of most of the heretics.[156] Long years of discouragingly unsuccessful efforts to win back the Donatists by the use of reason, persuasion, and appeals to the Scriptures, combined with the experience of seeing that systematic, vigorous compulsion was indeed "successful" in bringing some of the Donatists back to the Church, explain, even if they do not justify, Augustine's reversal of his position. More terrible and less easy to understand than his change of attitude is his use of the doctrine of love in defense of the policy of coercion. To defend the Church's appeal to the State to punish heretics and schismatics by imprisonment, fines, and exile as a labor of love toward errant sinners, to argue for this policy on the basis of the analogy with a father's loving correction of his son, to speak of the successful results of the state's coercion as "conquests of the Lord"[157]—all these demonstrate the grim conclusions to which even a very wise man can be led by zeal for the promotion of orthodoxy.

CONCLUSION

The central theme of Augustine's realistic political theory is that the State exists to maintain earthly peace so that men can live and work together and attain the objects that are necessary for their earthly existence.[1] The State accomplishes its purpose primarily through the use of coercion and the fear of punishment. By means of these external, repressive, and essentially negative instruments of the legal system, it protects the lives, the safety, and the property of its citizens, and it keeps men from destroying one another by preventing some crimes and by punishing those that are committed.[2] The State preserves external peace and order, the peace of Babylon; this peace is absolutely necessary for all men, including the wayfaring pilgrims from the City of God, as long as they live in this world. Of course, the peace and order maintained by the State are not true peace and true concord, and the rough justice which rulers and magistrates can secure is only a shadowy reflection of the true justice found with God and in His kingdom.

Even after we have given up the hope that the State will be able to inculcate true virtue and wisdom in its citizens, we find that it can accomplish its proper tasks—the maintenance of earthly peace and the punishment of those who violate the norms of earthly justice—only in a most imperfect fashion. The two major defects of fallen man, perversity of will and ignorance (which is a result of misdirected will), infect every action that the State takes through its all too human agents. Since all those who bear political power—rulers, officials, judges, policemen, soldiers—are only men, their judgment is fallible, their information is inevitably inadequate and often incorrect, and their decisions are frequently biased by passion and self-interest.[3] Their actions, even when they are successful, never dispose of the problems that they face, whether these be domestic issues or questions of foreign relations. Since the problems persist, all that the political agent can do is to deal each day, as best he can, with the particular aspect or example of the problem that most urgently demands his attention, knowing full well that tomorrow will bring new events that will both require new decisions and destroy or weaken the solutions that were painfully pieced together today or yesterday.

Augustine's thought has no place for the vision of a politics of perfection, in which all-wise rulers devise truly good and lasting solutions for social problems and in which contented subjects live together in stable harmony. Politics is a realm in which fallible, sinful men work out imperfect, precarious solutions to recurring difficulties and tensions; Augustine would have had no difficulty in understanding Max Weber's comment that "politics is a strong and slow boring of hard boards."[4] No matter how tranquil the surface of political life may appear to be at a given moment, the peace and order that the State seeks to preserve are always liable to be shattered by sudden outbursts of greed, violence, and hostility from within or without. Above all, politics is a realm in which paradox, irony, and dark shadows abound. The legal system exists to hold in check the worst effects of human sinfulness, and yet if men were not sinful, if they did not love the things that can be taken from them against their will, the punishments and threats of punishment which the law wields would be completely ineffectual.[5] Political rulers and their subordinates often make the right decision for the wrong reasons, and, just as often, good intentions lead them to decisions that prove in the event to have been wrong or evil. The instruments which the State employs to discover crimes and to punish criminals are often morally repugnant and cruel—informers, spies, the rack, and the noose—and at the center of even the "well-regulated state" stands the grim figure of the executioner.[6] A statesman wrestles with problems of war and peace, knowing all the time that if he takes a strong stand he may set in motion a train of events that can bring about the destruction of his country and the death of many of his countrymen, while if he hesitates or shows weakness he may also invite invasion and disaster. He may even have to face the terrible necessity of choosing between the safety of his country and the preservation of its honor and good faith.[7]

However, Augustine's profound awareness of the imperfect nature of politics, his recognition that the justice and peace secured by the State are faulty and unstable, and his insight into the complexities, ambiguities, inequities, and harshnesses inherent in the political process never lead him to suggest that the State and the order it provides are unimportant or superfluous. Since even the pilgrim members of the City of God need the State and its earthly peace as long as they sojourn on this earth, they have a sacred obligation to respect and honor its rulers and its laws.[8] For sinful and unredeemed men, the great majority of the human race, the rewards and punishments of the legal system, backed by the coercive power of the State, are still more essential. Without these divinely established remedies for sin, without the rough approximation of justice which is maintained by the power of the State, the conflicting wills of sinful men would create a situation of anarchy and war in which mutual injury and common misery, if not total annihilation, would be the fate of mankind.

Augustine's conclusions agree with one of the important strands in the Christian attitude toward the State—it is a divinely established institution to repress and punish the wicked, and its rulers, who are ordained by God, are the ministers of His wrath and a terror to evildoers.[9] No matter how corrupt, wicked, or cruel rulers may be, they must be accorded absolute obedience and respect; this obedience must be given not only because of fear of their power, but for conscience's sake, since God has commanded that they be obeyed. Only when their orders are contrary to the clear commands that God Himself has given to men must kings and rulers be refused obedience. Men must always obey the commands of the superior authority; so when a king dares to order his subjects to violate God's express ordinance against, for example, the worship of idols, he must not be obeyed. Even in this case, however, the subject has no right to rebel against or to resist the ruler. He must not raise his hand against the minister of God, but must be willing to accept the punishment—fine, imprisonment, or death—that the ruler imposes upon him for disobedience to his orders and adherence to God's commandments. The subject must accept this punishment as retribution for his sins or as a trial of his devotion to God; his only recourse is to pray that God will forgive his transgressions and limit his punishment and that He will convert the ruler from his wickedness to true goodness and piety.

It is clear that Augustine accepted many of the ideas about the State and politics that he inherited from the Christian tradition, and that he clarified, deepened, and expanded these conceptions. In addition, however, he modified or rejected some elements of the Christian tradition in order to bring about an accommodation of the Church to its new role as the established religion of the Empire. The first and most obvious change is that Augustine insisted not only that Christians might take part in political activities without violating the commands of Christ, but also that they had a positive duty to participate in the State's work of governance, adjudication, punishment, and warfare, if they had the talents that fitted them for these duties.[10]

His defense of war and military service, his elaboration of a doctrine of just wars, and his efforts to demonstrate that Christ's teachings did not prevent a Christian from serving in the army or killing the enemies of the State [11] are striking examples of the differences between his views and those of the early Church and of the reconciliation that he effected between the Church's doctrines and the practical needs of the new age. Of course, Christian service in the armed forces of the State was not a novelty in Augustine's day; nor was he the first Christian thinker to accept military activity and warfare as compatible with the teachings of Christ. However, no previous thinker had elaborated so complete and detailed a defense of these activities and of Christian participation in them. Nor had anyone undertaken such a direct assault on the tradition of antimilitarism and pacifism that was embodied not only in the writings of thinkers like Tertullian and Lactantius but also in the attitudes and beliefs of many ordinary Christians, even in the fourth and fifth centuries.

Augustine's effort to harmonize the teachings of Christ with the view that the Christian is obliged to serve as a soldier and to kill in battle rested primarily, as we have seen,[12] on the argument that Christ's injunctions against the use of force and His commands to resist evil only by loving one's enemies and by turning the other cheek to those who inflict violence were meant to be interpreted spiritually rather than literally. By these commands Christ was urging His followers to act in a spirit of true love and benevolence toward their enemies; He was not enjoining upon them non-resistance and passivity in the face of evil, injustice, and violence. Augustine saw no incongruity in exhorting Christian soldiers to retain in their hearts an attitude of charity and good will toward their enemies while they were killing or wounding them, even though he recognized that most of the wars waged among states were in no sense just. He allowed to the Christian serving in the army no independent judgment of the justice or rightness of the conflict in which he fought, since he reserved for the ruler alone the decision whether another state's conduct was so flagrantly unjust that it required to be punished by war. Augustine's acceptance of war as a grim necessity if even a minimum of justice and order is to be preserved in the world, his attempt to distinguish between just and unjust wars, and his flat rejection of pacifism and merely passive resistance to evil may be more realistic and more adequate than the ethic of love and nonresistance. They represent, however, a pronounced change from the beliefs of the early Christian Church, and they mark a significant milestone in the process of relativizing and accommodating Christ's teachings to the imperatives of earthly existence and to the views of right and wrong that were generally accepted in the world into which Jesus came.

A similar process of accommodation to "reality" occurs when Augustine teaches that it is the Christian's duty to participate actively in the work of the State as emperor, official, judge, policeman, or jailer. Although he is aware of the special dangers and temptations that Christians face when they occupy positions of power and employ coercion, and although he knows that the necessities that confront the governor or the judge often compel him to act with harshness or cruelty, he insists that, like the soldier, the Christian ruler or judge must remain at his post. The Christian is guilty of no violation of Christ's commandments when he judges other men's actions or when he inflicts punishment upon those he believes to be guilty; indeed, he remains "sinless," although miserable, when he orders that the accused man whose guilt has not yet been determined or even the completely innocent witness be put to torture.[13] When we contrast these statements with the Gospel warnings against the desire for lordship over other men, with the prohibitions against recourse to the law by Christians, with the command, "Judge not lest ye be judged," and with Christ's refusal to judge the woman taken in adultery, we see a profound change in Christian attitudes toward participation in political and judicial activities. Once more, we must recognize that Augustine is not responsible for the entire movement away from the early Christian view that it was not permissible for the servants of Christ to occupy positions of authority in the State or to employ physical force even for official purposes. Nevertheless, his acceptance of the "necessities" involved in the work of public officials and his unquestioning approval of Christians who serve as rulers, judges, and officials mark a decisive moment in the relations between the Church and the world.

Augustine's most startling reversal of the traditional attitude of Christians toward the State and its rulers came when, in the course of his struggle with the Donatists, he finally took the *political* position that the political authorities had not only the right but *authorities* the obligation to use their power to punish those men who, in *(?)* the eyes of the Church, were guilty of heresy and schism.[14] During the long years of bitter controversy, the Donatists repeatedly charged that the Catholics had surrendered their Christian beliefs and had become the allies and instruments of the ungodly political authorities. They frequently referred to the traditions of the Church and especially to the writings of the great figures of African Christianity, Tertullian and Cyprian, to demonstrate that their view that the State had no right to interfere in the affairs of the Church was the orthodox and true position. These arguments were extremely effective weapons against the Catholic Church, particularly in the rural areas of Africa where religious zeal was combined with bitter hostility to the Roman State and to its officials and tax-collectors. Augustine shows his awareness of the power and appeal of the Donatists' anti-state position by his repeated efforts to prove that on a number of occasions (the original appeal to Constantine, the appeal to Julian, the use of state power against their own dissident factions) they had shown themselves willing to seek and accept state aid and protection. Although he is compelled to acknowledge that no example can be found in the New Testament of the Church appealing to the State or its officials for support, he tries to explain the change by making a distinction between the Church of the period of the apostles and the martyrs, when kings were her enemies and persecutors, and the Church of the present age, which is defended and supported by the Emperor.[15] This distinction he seeks to establish on a Biblical foundation by reference to King Nebuchadnezzar, who first persecuted the servants of God and later ordered that anyone in his kingdom who failed to worship the true God of Shadrach, Meshach, and Abednego should be punished.[16]

At the end of the previous chapter,[17] I discussed the theocratic implications of Augustine's doctrine that the State has the duty to punish those whom the Church regards as schismatics or heretics, and the fundamental inconsistency between this doctrine and his general analysis of the State's principal functions and of the means which it employs to accomplish its tasks. Here we need only note that this defense of the principle of using state coercion against heresy (including the use of the phrase, *Compelle intrare,* from the Gospel of Luke) constitutes Augustine's most important break with the outlook and beliefs of the early Church and his most influential contribution to the political thought and practice of the medieval Church. The doctrine that in compelling the Church's enemies to return to the fold rulers act as instruments of God's grace is far removed from the traditional view that rulers are established to punish the wicked and have nothing to do with the governance of Christ's Church. Moreover, the doctrine flatly contradicts that strand of Christian thought which saw the kingdoms of this world and their rulers as parts of the kingdom of the devil and as fundamentally hostile to God and His Church—a strand which, as we have seen, is one of the elements in Augustine's own thought.[18] However, in the medieval period it was the theocratic element implicit in Augustine's doctrine that the State must use its coercive powers against heresy and schism that exercised far greater influence than either his occasional acceptance of the traditional tendency to identify political authorities with the powers of darkness or the position more characteristic of his thought—a realistic recognition of the State's inherent imperfections and limitations, combined with an insistence on its absolute necessity in view of the sinful nature of fallen man.

It is not difficult to see why Augustine's political realism received little attention and no further development in the centuries that followed his death. With the downfall of the Western Empire and its replacement by a series of unstable and shifting barbarian kingdoms, the Church and its hierarchy became the only visible unifying force in the West. With each passing century the Church became more and more involved in temporal affairs; not only was she a temporal power in her own right, but her bishops and other leaders were deeply involved in governance and politics, both as royal officials and as virtually independent feudal magnates. For almost a thousand years, no state in Western Europe possessed anything that even resembled the power and authority of the Roman Empire, and at some periods the State almost ceased to exist as an entity independent of and superior to the complex network of private rights that we call feudalism. The political order was neither strong enough nor secure enough to stand much realistic examination. Even if the Church had not itself been intimately associated with the process of governance, it might well have tended to support and extol

the virtues of a stable, centralized political system rather than
to encourage a sharply critical attitude toward the State and the
means that it uses to accomplish its ends. In any case, the weak-
nesses and inadequacies of the State, as well as the cruelties and
crimes of rulers, were too obviously apparent to all observers,
especially in the early Middle Ages, to require special notice by
Christian thinkers.

I do not propose to present here an outline of medieval political doctrines or to attempt to trace the influence of the various
elements of Augustine's thought upon medieval writers.[19] I simply note that in the medieval period Augustine's attitude of pessimistic realism about the State and politics received little attention and exerted no great influence. It is possible that we hear
echoes of his thought in some of the arguments used by medieval
Popes and their supporters during their controversies with Emperors and kings and their partisans. In these polemics the papalist
writers occasionally seek to strengthen the position of the Church
and of the Pope against the imperial or royal claims that *regnum*
is an authority equal to and independent of *sacerdotium,* by the
argument that temporal power is inherently inferior and subordinate to priestly authority because the power of kings rests on
pride, cupidity, and crime, the works of the devil.

Pope Gregory VII, for example, in the famous letter to Hermann, Bishop of Metz, written in 1081, says:

Who does not know that kings and princes are sprung from those
who unmindful of God, urged on, in fact, by the devil, the prince of
the world, and by pride, plunder, treachery, murders and by almost
every crime, have striven with blind cupidity and intolerable presumption to dominate over their equals, that is to say, over men? [20]

Later, he quotes Augustine's statement in Book I of the *De
Doctrina Christiana,* "Indeed whoever strives to gain control over
those who are naturally his equals, that is men, is intolerably

proud in every way," and says that "it is unfortunately true that demons rule over all the kings and princes of the earth who do not live a godly life and do not fear God in their deeds as they ought, and they torment them with a wretched captivity." [21] It is particularly necessary for the Church and the Pope to compel kings and emperors to act with humility, since "worldly glory and secular anxiety usually do draw into pride, in particular those who rule; as a result, neglecting humility and pursuing their own glory, they perpetually yearn to dominate their brethren." [22] Gregory says that even the good and humble are made worse by the exercise of temporal power; he notes that of the countless kings who have ruled since the beginning of the world very few have been found to be saints, while almost a hundred of the occupants of the Roman See have been canonized.[23]

Even if, as Gregory's reference to Augustine suggests, statements of this kind about the vices of temporal rulers reflect the influence of Augustine's teachings about politics, they do not represent a significant continuation or development of his doctrines. A single aspect of his complex thought about politics is extracted for use as a polemical weapon. Since Gregory's primary concern is to demonstrate that priestly authority is in every way superior to temporal authority, he uses a variety of arguments or analogies that seem to support his position, but he is not interested in elaborating a coherent, realistic view of the State and political power. As the quotations from his letter to Hermann indicate, his attitude toward rulers is far more moralistic than Augustine's. His condemnation of the vices and crimes of most kings focuses attention on their wickedness, while Augustine is much more concerned to point out the inadequacies and injustices that are inherent in the very operation of the political and legal systems, whether the ruler happens to be a relatively good man or an unusually evil man.

Perhaps the most important and enduring influence that Augustine exerted on medieval political thought stems from a misinterpretation of his teaching. His great vision of the separation and conflict throughout all history between the City of God and the earthly city could quite easily be translated into the distinction between the Church and temporal authority, the sacerdotal power and the royal power, provided that the visible Church was equated with the City of God. Although Augustine himself did not make this identification and insisted that many members of the Church as organized in this world would not be members of the City of God,[24] it was perhaps inevitable that as the power of the Church and of the Papacy increased, the distinction between the hierarchically organized Church and the City of God in heaven should become increasingly blurred. Once the Church was identified with the City of God, Augustine could be used to support the view that the authority of the Church and of the Pope was immeasurably superior to the authority of temporal rulers and, indeed, that all power (*plenitudo potestatis*) rested in the hands of the Pope, who then delegated to secular authorities the power to deal with temporal affairs.

An interesting example of the use of Augustine's writings to defend an extreme version of theocracy and the doctrine of papal supremacy is found in an anonymous anti-papalist tract, the *Quaestio de potestate papae* (*Rex pacificus*), written in 1302. The author first gives a number of the familiar arguments for papal supremacy over temporal rulers and then tries to refute them. One of these arguments, probably taken from the work of the papalist writer, Egidius Romanus,[25] is based on Augustine's statement in *The City of God* that true justice exists only in that republic whose founder and ruler is Christ.[26] The quotation runs:

Moreover, true justice does not exist in the commonwealth of which Christ is not the ruler. But the commonwealth of the Christian people ought to be just and true. Therefore Christ ought to be the ruler in it. But the Pope is the vicar of Christ. . . . Therefore the Pope is the ruler of the commonwealth even in temporal affairs.[27]

It should be noted that in a theocratic theory of this kind, the State, although it is reduced to the status of an organization vastly inferior to the Church, is also "divinized" or sanctified since it is regarded as an instrument of ecclesiastical authority and, ultimately, of divine authority. The Pope as the head of the Church and the vicar of Christ is the *de jure* sovereign in respect to both spiritual and temporal matters; if he delegates to kings the exercise of temporal authority, he always retains the authority to overrule their decisions and to remove them if they misuse the power devolved upon them. Although the independence and majesty of political authority are severely limited by this doctrine, it also provides a halo of divine sanction for the State and its actions which offers little encouragement to the kind of realistic analysis of political life that Augustine undertook.

Augustine's central political insight—the idea of a politics of imperfection, a necessary consequence of human sinfulness—and his profound awareness of the inevitable limitations of a coercive political order were obscured under the impact of this "sanctification" of the State by theocratic doctrines, as well as by the revival of the classical view that the State is an organization intended to promote the good life in this world and to produce good and virtuous men. Although this classical conception of the State never reappeared in its full force, some of its elements were combined with traditional Christian political doctrine when St. Thomas incorporated important aspects of Aristotelian thought into his great philosophic synthesis. St. Thomas accepts

much more of the Greek view of the State than Augustine does;
for him, the functions of the State are far more positive than they
are for Augustine; since he places less emphasis on the sinfulness
and depravity of mankind after the Fall, he is not compelled, as
Augustine was, to regard the State as primarily a negative, repressive instrument designed to hold in check the worst consequences
of human sin. Thomas maintains, therefore, that the State is
"natural" in the sense that it alone is a "perfect" or self-sufficient
community, which allows men to carry on the division of labor
and the cooperation in intellectual activities that are essential to
their existence and to their well-being.[28] The Aristotelian elements in St. Thomas's doctrine permit a large measure of idealiza-
tion of the State and of its activities. Since its goals and purposes
are again elevated, and since it becomes, in effect, a halfway
house to salvation, there is less incentive to examine realistically
the functions that it actually performs and the ambiguous means
that it employs.

The task of reviving the tradition of political realism and
of looking once again at the darker aspects of political life was
left for thinkers of another revolutionary age, the period of war
and conflict in which the medieval order disintegrated and gave
way to the modern world—Machiavelli, Luther, Calvin, and,
above all, Hobbes. The Lutheran and Calvinist views of human
nature and of political authority carry clear marks of their
Augustinian origin, and it is difficult to believe that Hobbes's
theories were not influenced, directly or indirectly, by Augustine's
pessimism and realism. We have already seen a number of parallels between the Augustinian and Hobbesian theories.[29] Both
thinkers see man as a fundamentally self-centered creature, who
restlessly seeks the satisfaction of one desire after another. Egoism leads each man to try to assure his survival and his present
and future happiness by accumulating goods and money and by

attaining power over other men. Since the ends which each man pursues are similar to those of every other man, since the wealth and power that all men seek are both limited and comparative, and since all men are roughly equal in natural ability, the clash of their egoistic drives leads to a situation of general conflict (the Hobbesian *bellum omnium*), universal frustration and misery, and complete instability of all possessions.

Because anarchy and mutual destruction are the consequences that both Augustine and Hobbes see as inevitable if human appetites and passions are unrestrained, they both regard peace and order as the highest earthly goods and as the prerequisites of all other satisfactions and accomplishments. The task of the State, then, is to maintain peace by employing its overwhelming powers of coercion to hold in check the warring aspirations of selfish men. Its weapons are the deprivations of property, liberty, and life that it can inflict through its punishments and the fear that it is able to inspire by the prospect of punishment. By these means and by its control over the doctrines and dogmas that are publicly taught, rather than by any effort to mold or change the internal desires, attitudes, and beliefs of its citizens, the State preserves an external peace—what Augustine calls earthly peace or the peace of Babylon—even among men whose basic egoism remains unchanged. As a result, men can live and work together in relative tranquillity and in the assurance that the products of their industry will generally be protected from attacks by others. Both thinkers insist that subjects must give unquestioning obedience to the commands of the political authorities (Augustine makes the exception that rulers must be refused obedience when they order men to neglect or violate God's express commandments, while for Hobbes the subject is not bound to obey orders to destroy or injure himself). Both Augustine and Hobbes refuse to grant to the individual subject the right to decide whether the commands of the ruler are just or wise and so obligate him to obey, since they believe that such subjective decisions would lead to a disruption of the framework of order maintained by the State and a relapse into the condition of general anarchy.

It might be said that the Hobbesian theory or vision of man and society is the Augustinian vision after God and the City of God have been eliminated. Augustine's picture of the characteristics of most men, who are sinful and proud, is accepted by Hobbes as a description of the basic drives of all men, and Augustine's condemnation of this sinful nature is rejected. The Augustinian conception of the State as the guarantor of an imperfect peace during the brief period of man's pilgrimage in "this hell upon earth" becomes for Hobbes the vision of the State as the defender of peace, prosperity, and all the arts of civilization, which constitute the only heaven available to men. In addition, Hobbes's theory demonstrates the effects of the Reformation and of Calvinism by grounding the political order on the freely given consent of each member of society, whereas Augustine simply accepts political authority as inevitable after the Fall and does not inquire into its earthly origins.

This comparison between Augustine and Hobbes reminds us that the most important reason for studying the history of philosophy and, in particular, the history of political thought, is that each great thinker has emphasized and highlighted certain qualities and characteristics of human nature and of social and political life. Since each major philosopher sensitizes us to a certain range of phenomena, we must look at society and politics from all the angles of vision that they offer if we wish to achieve the fullest understanding that our tradition offers. The particular aspects of society that each philosopher selects as most significant and into which he probes deeply are the result of many influences—the time and place in which he lives, the intellectual tradition available to him (which both shapes his thought and constitutes a body of ideas against which he reacts), the circumstances of his own life, his personality, temperament, and interests, and the social, political, and moral questions that are crucial in his day.

Every great social and political philosopher offers us a theory—literally, a vision—of man and society; these visions have enduring importance because each of them provides us with a searching analysis of certain dimensions of human experience. Each theory achieves its power to penetrate far beneath the surface of human actions by concentrating on some facets of social life while ignoring or passing lightly over others. I think that John Stuart Mill was right when he said that most original political and social philosophers are, like Bentham, "one-eyed men" who sacrifice range and completeness of view in order to focus sharply on some aspect of human action.[30] Each of them then tends to see everything from this particular angle, *sub specie* of his own vision, with the consequence that other elements in social and political life are often distorted or blurred.

As far as I can see, this defect is inherent and irremediable. Certainly it cannot be attributed to the inadequate intellectual power of the philosopher, whether he be Plato, Aristotle, Hobbes, Hume, Rousseau, or Hegel, or to his naïve failure to recognize that he and his predecessors have omitted or slighted many things because of their concentration on some things. The partiality of his vision is essential to his accomplishment. Unless he is so deeply concerned about some particular problems or certain facets of human experience that he ignores others, unless he drives relentlessly forward to catch up as much of the world as he possibly can within the limited range of his vision and his leading ideas, he will not make a major contribution to social and political thought. The man who is so aware of the dangers of partial vision, of being "one-eyed," that he tries to look at everything and to understand all points of view may be an admirable man, a great teacher, or a wise counselor, but he is not likely to be a great original philosopher.

John Stuart Mill is a good example of a thinker whose early overexposure to a particular philosophic system—the utilitarianism of Bentham and of his father, James Mill—caused him to react sharply against all philosophic systems and to maintain throughout his life an attitude of eclecticism and sympathetic understanding of many divergent points of view. The result, as described by John Plamenatz, was that the younger Mill

felt the need to take into account many things that his father could safely ignore because they meant nothing to him. . . . He should have had a narrower or else a more inventive mind. He could have had either without coming any nearer to the truth than he did, but his reputation as a philosopher would have been more enviable. As it is, he was less solid and less assured than his father, while he lacked the powerful imagination that has enabled some philosophers, out of the most varied materials, to build a great system, which, however small its resemblance to the real world, yet appears coherent.[31]

On the other hand, a truly original thinker, such as Freud, is so profoundly certain that his ideas are significant that he follows their implications to the end with single-minded concentration, even though he may realize that he is neglecting other possibilities. If he is occasionally disturbed by the thought of the distortions that may result from his almost monomanic preoccupation with his leading ideas, he can always take comfort in the assurance that the lesser minds of his own and succeeding generations will, with great energy and relish, demonstrate his excesses and the limitations of his vision.

Since Augustine was a profoundly original thinker, his ideas about man, society, and the state exhibit both the power and the limitations of the great vision. He saw man in his fallen condition as completely vitiated by sin. Every human action from the most sublime expression of altruism or patriotism or the highest intellectual or artistic achievement to the most sordid or trivial action is rooted in human sinfulness—in each man's burning desire for self-aggrandizement, whether by the relentless accumulation of material goods and money, the driving lust for power over other men, or the insatiable appetite for fame and glory and, therefore, for the approbation of other human beings. Occasionally, Augustine notes that there are meaningful differences among these sinful actions and among the sinful men who perform them. The patriotic devotion and the desire for glory of the ancient Romans spurred them on to deeds of great bravery and heroic self-sacrifice which enhanced the safety and prosperity of the nation. Although Augustine recognizes that their conduct was "quasi-virtuous" [32] and far more admirable than the materialistic self-indulgence of the later Romans, he does not pursue the idea that there may be "higher" and "lower" forms of sin, better and worse actions. Since his attention is focused on the sinfulness of men's wills and deeds, he sees that even these acts of heroism and self-sacrifice are radically infected with vice—the terrible vices of pride and of vainly seeking immortality by winning the applause of deluded men.

His thought is dominated by the sharp contrast between unredeemed man, whose every action is an exhibition of sin and pride, and the man who has been saved by the gratuitous gift of God's love, and who is therefore capable of truly virtuous action since not he but the love of God now works within him. In this perspective, the varieties or gradations found in sinful actions, the fact that in the eyes of the world certain sinful deeds are "good" or "honorable," and the fact that the redeemed man may, on occasion, lapse into sinful deeds are all profoundly irrelevant. In Augustine's vision there are two clearly separated types of man

—the minority, who love God and do His will, and the great majority, who love themselves and earthly goods, wealth, power, fame, and pleasure. In consequence, there is in his thought no room for the idea that every man is a particular, complex mixture of good and evil impulses, of love and hate, or of egoism and altruism.

His basic idea that most men are sinful and self-seeking leads him directly to the vision of society as a scene of constant strife and mutual injury where each man struggles to satisfy his desires and ambitions at the expense of all other men. It is this vision which constrains him to believe that only the State, with its apparatus of laws, punishments, and coercion, can hold these conflicts within bounds and prevent men from annihilating one another. Because of the violence of men's passions and the strength of their appetites, the peace and order which the State maintains are supremely important and, at the same time, highly precarious. Augustine is so sharply aware of the need to impose a system of order on the conflicting wills of sinful men if human society is to be kept from collapsing into anarchy that he insists that the maintenance of peace is the primary function of the State. He is willing to settle for this one great accomplishment and to ask for relatively little in the way of positive benefits from the political system, because he is so acutely conscious of the importance and the fragility of earthly peace and so deeply impressed by the disastrous consequences of disorder, strife, and war.

As a result of his concentration on the necessity of preserving peace and order (which must always be the first word, though not the last, that is said about the goals of the political system), Augustine insists on absolute obedience to the commands of all rulers, no matter how wicked or corrupt they may be; he allows disobedience, with no attempt at resistance, only when the ruler's orders run counter to the clear commandments of God. Also, he completely ignores the problem of classifying and evaluating different forms of government, as well as the question of how a given system of rule can be changed so as to make it more just or more satisfactory. The worst possible government is far better than anarchy, and in any case it must be endured as a divine punishment for men's sins. Revolution and rebellion, which would destroy the framework of peace and order, would serve only to compound the evil and the suffering.

In addition to his fundamental insight into the essential function of the political order—maintaining peace by the application of coercion—Augustine also gives us penetrating analyses of the complexities of political action and of the pitfalls of ignorance, pride, and cruelty inevitably associated with the exercise of political power. No one who has read Augustine carefully can fail to be impressed by the ambiguities and limitations inherent in political action, and by the enormously difficult tasks and the almost insoluble moral dilemmas that confront the ruler at every turn.

As he surveyed the collapse of ancient institutions and the rising tide of destruction in the world around him, which led many of his contemporaries to the conclusion that the end of the world was at hand,[33] Augustine's keen sense of the perpetual power of human pride and sinfulness compelled him to reject any hope that the future would bring enduring peace or progress. Both his theological beliefs and his experience and observation of men's actions in an age of disorder enforced upon him an attitude of pessimistic realism, which would not allow him to sentimentalize or evade the darker aspects of social and political life.

In our own century, when, once more, men have been compelled to recognize the almost incredible brutalities of which human beings are capable, especially when they struggle for political power and military domination, it is no accident that

Augustinian pessimism and realism have enjoyed a considerable revival among both theologians and secular thinkers. As a result of our own experiences, we are much more prepared than our fathers were to give a hearing to the doctrine of original sin and to the view that ceaseless application of coercive power is necessary in order to hold in check human pride and the fruits of pride—aggression, avarice, and lust—and to preserve the fabric of civilization which is constantly imperiled by these forces.

We may have learned our lessons by reading Freud and by observing the new barbarism of our century rather than by listening to Christian realists. Nevertheless, the optimistic beliefs of many nineteenth-century liberals and Marxists—the certainty that the future would inevitably bring a sharp reduction, if not the complete elimination, of the need to employ coercion in social life, and the faith that men could be educated to cooperate voluntarily in a just and harmonious social order—strike us as hopelessly irrelevant as guides to present and future action and shamelessly hypocritical if offered as descriptions of present realities. We know that pride, self-assurance, and a sense of being the instruments of Providence or of historical necessity, as well as the more obvious vices of avarice, lust for domination, and hatred, can lead men and nations to perpetrate enormous crimes. We know too that we must be prepared to use awful weapons to defend ourselves and our civilization from threats of destruction, although we also recognize that our use of these weapons and techniques renders us liable to fall into the same vices. For, like Augustine, we have learned that greed, pride, aggressiveness, and hatred are not simply characteristics of other men and other states. We know that since these impulses dwell in each of us and in our society, we too are capable of translating them into action once the pressures acting upon us rise beyond a certain level.

I believe that these are some of the reasons why pessimistic analysts of human nature and of society and politics have received increasing attention during the last two decades, and why Augustine's views are entitled to our serious consideration. If we are going to preach—or listen to—neo-Augustinianism, we should be willing to examine its doctrines in their original and most compelling forms. My argument is not that grim realism is the only viable political and social doctrine for our age or that the Augustinian version of it is the closest approximation to the truth. I say only that in our era of war, terror, and sharp anxiety about man's future, when, again, a major epoch in human history may be drawing to a close, we cannot afford to ignore Augustine's sharply etched, dark portrait of the human condition. How much of that picture each of us accepts or rejects, how much he modifies it, is a problem that each man must solve for himself. Only one thing is certain. The intellectual equipment that we employ as we face our dilemmas will be needlessly restricted if it has no place for Augustine's powerful and somber vision.

Quibus parum uel quibus nimium est, mihi ignoscant; quibus autem satis est, non mihi, sed Deo mecum gratias congratulantes agant. Amen. Amen. (DCD, XXII, 30; CCSL XLVIII, 866.)

ABBREVIATIONS

The following abbreviations have been used throughout the work.

De Div. Quaest. ad Simplic.	De Diversis Quaestionibus ad Simplicianum
De Div. Quaest. 83	De Diversis Quaestionibus octoginta tribus
De Doctr. Christ.	De Doctrina Christiana
De Dono Persever.	De Dono Perseverantiae
De Fide Rerum	De Fide Rerum Quae Non Videntur
De Gratia Christi et De Pecc. Orig.	De Gratia Christi et De Peccato Originali
De Gratia et Lib. Arbit.	De Gratia et Libero Arbitrio
De Lib. Arbit.	De Libero Arbitrio
De Mor. Eccl. Cath.	De Moribus Ecclesiae Catholicae
De Mor. Manich.	De Moribus Manichaeorum
De Nupt. et Concup.	De Nuptiis et Concupiscentia
De Peccat. Meritis	De Peccatorum Meritis et Remissione et De Baptismo Parvulorum
De Perf. Iust. Hominis	De Perfectione Iustitiae Hominis
De Praedest. Sanct.	De Praedestinatione Sanctorum
De Sermone Domini	De Sermone Domini in Monte
De Util. Cred.	De Utilitate Credendi
En. in Ps.	Enarrationes in Psalmos
Ep.	Epistula
Expos. Quar. Prop. ex Ep. ad Romanos	Expositio Quarumdam Propositionum ex Epistola ad Romanos
In Epist. Ioann.	In Epistolam Ioannis ad Parthos Tractatus Decem
In Ioann. Evangel.	In Ioannis Evangelium Tractatus CXXIV
Quaest. in Hept.	Quaestionum in Heptateuchum

NOTES

NOTES TO PREFACE

1. See the remarks by John Neville Figgis in his work, *The Political Aspects of S. Augustine's 'City of God'* (London, Longmans, Green, and Co., 1921). "Like S. Paul and unlike S. Thomas, Augustine wrote only under the pressure of immediate necessity. All his writings have an apologetic character. Most of them are coloured by his intensely rich personality. Trained in rhetoric, Augustine is never abstract or impersonal. . . . Theories abound in S. Augustine's works, but the last thing he is is a theorist, pure and simple. Augustine became a theologian, as he had become a philosopher, driven by practical needs" (p. 5). "Augustine had a discursive mind, and his training in rhetoric increased this tendency. He had no great powers of construction. The architectonics even of the 'Confessions' leave much to be desired. . . . We can never understand S. Augustine if we think of him as a system-maker. Systems may have come out of him, but before all else he is a personality" (pp. 6–7).

2. Étienne Gilson, *Introduction à l'étude de saint Augustin* (3d ed., Paris, Librairie Philosophique J. Vrin, 1949). The bibliography appears on pp. 325–51; the section dealing with "Political and Social Doctrines" is on pp. 338–40. Note that the recent translation of Gilson's work, *The Christian Philosophy of Saint Augustine* (New York, Random House, 1960), has a much less complete bibliography which omits the subject-matter divisions and Gilson's comments on the works listed. Another bibliography, which lists works dealing with *The City of God,* is found on pp. ix–xx of Volume XLVII of the *Corpus Christianorum, Series Latina,* Books I–X of the *De Civitate Dei.*

3. See above, note 1.

4. There have been, of course, a number of short essays on this subject, as well as treatments of it by authors of books dealing with more general themes; e.g., Ernest Barker's Introduction to the Everyman's Library edition of John Healey's translation of *The City of God* (2 vols., London, J. M. Dent & Sons Ltd.; New York, E. P.

Dutton & Co., Inc., 1945); Norman H. Baynes's essay, "The Political Ideas of St. Augustine's *De Civitate Dei*," Historical Association Pamphlet No. 104, London, 1936; reprinted in *Byzantine Studies and Other Essays* (London, University of London, The Athlone Press, 1955), pp. 288–306; Vernon J. Bourke's article, "The Political Philosophy of St. Augustine," *Proceedings of the Seventh Annual Meeting of the American Catholic Philosophic Association,* St. Louis, 1931, pp. 45–55; Anton-Hermann Chroust's essay, "The Philosophy of Law of St. Augustine," *Philosophical Review,* LIII (March 1944), 195–202; two articles by F. Edward Cranz, "De civitate Dei, XV, 2, and Augustine's Idea of the Christian Society," *Speculum,* XXV (April 1950), 215–25, and "The Development of Augustine's Ideas on Society Before the Donatist Controversy," *Harvard Theological Review,* Vol. XLVII, No. 4 (October 1954), pp. 255–316; Leonard Hodgson's article, "Christian Citizenship: Some Reflections on St. Augustine, Ep. 138," *Church Quarterly Review,* CXLV (October 1947), 1–11; the essay by Moorhouse F. X. Millar, S.J., "The Significance of St. Augustine's Criticism of Cicero's Definition of the State," *Philosophia Perennis* (Festgabe Josef Geyser, Regensburg, Josef Habbel, 1930), I, 99–110; and Thomas M. Parker's article, "St. Augustine and the Conception of Unitary Sovereignty," *Augustinus Magister* (Paris, Études Augustiniennes, 1954), II, 951–55; also, the discussions by Charles H. McIlwain in his book, *The Growth of Political Thought in the West* (New York, The Macmillan Company, 1932), pp. 154 ff.; and by Charles N. Cochrane in *Christianity and Classical Culture* (London, New York, Toronto, Oxford University Press, 1944), esp. pp. 486–516.

5. Gilson, *Introduction à l'étude,* p. 339.
6. Paris, Librairie Plon, 1927.
7. Gilson, *Introduction à l'étude,* p. 340.
8. See esp. Chap. IV, note 61.

NOTES TO INTRODUCTION

1. See E. R. Dodds, *The Greeks and the Irrational* (Berkeley, The University of California Press, 1951), pp. 179–95.

2. Cf. Thomas Hobbes, *Leviathan,* Part 2, Chaps. XVII and XVIII (Oxford, Basil Blackwell, 1946), pp. 111, 119–20.

3. See p. 125.

4. See, e.g., Cochrane, *Christianity and Classical Culture,* pp. 327–38.

5. See, e.g., *Luke* xxii, 49 and *Acts* i, 6.

6. *Luke* xxii, 25–26 (AV).   7. See p. 143.

8. *Matthew* xxii, 21 (RSV); see pp. 148 and 172.

9. T. M. Parker, *Christianity and the State in the Light of History* (London, Adam and Charles Black, 1955), p. 18.

10. *Romans* xii, 1–5; 1 *Peter* ii, 13–14; see Chap. IV, note 86.

11. See Parker, *Christianity and the State,* p. 19.

12. "In the whole New Testament, indeed, there is nothing of the Hellenic conception of the State as existing for the good life or as being the chief or only educative influence upon human nature." (*Ibid.,* p. 19.)

13. For a brief summary and analysis of the persecutions, see *ibid.,* pp. 22–42.

14. See p. 125.   15. See p. 155.

16. Tertullian, *Apologeticus,* XXXVIII, 3; translation quoted from *Tertullian: Apology, De Spectaculis,* tr. by Gerald H. Rendall, Loeb Classical Library (London, William Heinemann, Ltd.; New York, G. P. Putnam's Sons, 1931), p. 173.

17. See esp. Chaps. IV and V.

NOTES TO CHAPTER I

1. See DCD, XII, 1; CCSL XLVIII, 356; H I, 482, and *Contra Epist. Fundamenti,* 36; CSEL XXV, 241–42; S IV, 147–48.

2. "Thus, the rational being, whether in the angelic spirit or in the human soul, is so constituted that it cannot be its own good, the source of its own happiness, but, if its changeable state is turned to the unchangeable good, it finds happiness; if it is turned away from it, it finds wretchedness. Its turning away is its sin; its turning toward God is its virtue. By nature, therefore, it is not evil, because the spiritual creation of rational life, even when it is deprived of the good whose possession makes it happy, that is, even when it is sinful, is superior to any corporeal being. . . ." (*Ep.* CXL, XXIII, 56; CSEL XLIV, 202; FCL III, 105.)

3. "For approach to God is not by intervals of place, but by likeness, and withdrawal from Him is by unlikeness." (*De Trinitate,* VII, VI, 12; PL XLII, 946; S III, 113.)

4. See *De Mor. Manich.,* II, 2 and 3; PL XXXII, 1345–46; S IV, 69–70.

5. DCD, XIV, 13; CCSL XLVIII, 435; H II, 27. See also: "The first destruction of man, was the love of himself. . . . For this is to

love one's self, to wish to do one's own will." (*Sermo* XCVI, 2; PL XXXVIII, 585; S VI, 408.)

6. "All things thus imitate thee—but pervertedly—when they separate themselves far from thee and raise themselves up against thee." (*Confess.*, II, VI, 14; CSEL XXXIII, 40; Outler, 57.)

7. *In Ioann. Evangel.*, XXV, 16; CCSL XXXVI, 256–57; S VII, 166. "You cannot therefore attribute to God the cause of any human fault. For of all human offences, the cause is pride. For the conviction and removal of this a great remedy comes from heaven. God in mercy humbles Himself, descends from above, and displays to man, lifted up by pride, pure and manifest grace in very manhood, which He took upon Himself out of vast love for those who partake of it." (*De Peccat. Meritis*, II, XVII, 27; CSEL LX, 99; S V, 55.) See, too, Augustine's detailed discussion in the *Confessions* of his own youthful transgression in stealing pears that he did not really want, where he notes that at the root of his sin was his desire to rebel against God's law simply for the sake of disobedience and rebellion, "by doing with impunity deeds that were forbidden, in a deluded sense of omnipotence. . . . Could I find pleasure only in what was unlawful, and only because it was unlawful?" (*Confess.*, II, VI, 14; CSEL XXXIII, 40; Outler, 58.) The pleasure obtained from stealing the pears came not from the pears, but from "the crime itself, enhanced by the companionship of my fellow sinners." (*Ibid.*, II, VIII, 16; CSEL XXXIII, 42; Outler, 59.) "I did not desire to enjoy what I stole, but only the theft and the sin itself. . . . It was foul, and I loved it. I loved my own undoing. I loved my error—not that for which I erred but the error itself. A depraved soul, falling away from security in thee to destruction in itself, seeks nothing from the shameful deed but shame itself." (*Ibid.*, II, IV, 9; CSEL XXXIII, 36; Outler, 54–55.)

8. DCD, XXI, 15; CCSL XLVIII, 781; H II, 441.

9. *De Div. Quaest. ad Simplic.*, I, II, 16; PL XL, 121; Burleigh, 398. See, too, *De Div. Quaest. 83*, LXVIII, 3; PL XL, 71.

10. DCD, XIII, 3; CCSL XLVIII, 387; H I, 523.

11. *Contra Faustum*, XXXII, 14; CSEL XXV, 774; S IV, 337. See, too: "Man's nature owes nothing to the Devil. But, by persuading man to sin, the Devil violated what God made well, so that the whole human race limps because of the wound made through the free choice of two human beings." (*Contra Julianum*, IV, XVI, 83; PL XLIV, 781; FC 35, 239.)

12. *Enchiridion*, VIII, 26; PL XL, 245; Outler, 354. See, too, *De Natura et Gratia*, III, 3; CSEL LX, 235; S V, 122.

13. See *De Nupt. et Concup.*, II, IX, 21; CSEL XLII, 273–74; S V, 291.

14. "For God does not compel any one to sin simply because He knows already the future sins of men. For He foreknew sins that were theirs, not His own; sins that were referable to no one else, but to their own selves. Accordingly, if what He foreknew as theirs is not really theirs, then had He no true foreknowledge: but as His foreknowledge is infallible, it is doubtless no one else, but they themselves, whose sinfulness God foreknew, that are the sinners." (*In Ioann. Evangel.*, LIII, 4; CCSL XXXVI, 453; S VII, 292.) See, too, DCD, V, 9 and 10; CCSL XLVII, 138–41; H I, 192–97.

15. See below, in this chapter, pp. 24–28. "Freedom for the race . . . was lost in the strict sense by the Fall. Men still have a choice, but only between different kinds of sinful acts." (Figgis, *The Political Aspects,* p. 41.) See, too: "a man can choose between ambition and self-indulgence, between the pride of heroism and the meanness of cowardice." (*Ibid.,* p. 46.)

16. "But by creating so many to be born who, He foreknew, would not belong to his grace, so that they are more by an incomparable multitude than those whom he deigned to predestinate as children of the promise into the glory of His kingdom,—He wished to show by this very multitude of the rejected how entirely of no moment it is to the just God what is the multitude of those most justly condemned. And that hence also those who are redeemed from this condemnation may understand, that what they see rendered to so great a part of the mass was the due of the whole of it." (*Ep.* CXC, III, 12; CSEL LVII, 146–47; S V, Intro., xlvii–xlviii.) See, too, *De Corrept. et Gratia,* XIII, 39; PL XLIV, 940; S V, 487. Augustine states that the saints within the Church are "so few in comparison with so vast a host" of sinners who are in the Church (*De Baptismo,* VII, LI, 99; CSEL LI, 371; S IV, 512). The part of the human race predestined to salvation will "fill up the loss which that diabolical disaster had caused in the angelic society." (*Enchiridion,* IX, 29; PL XL, 246; Outler, 356.)

17. "No one believes who is not called. God calls in his mercy, and not as rewarding the merits of faith. The merits of faith follow his calling rather than precede it." (*De Div. Quaest. ad Simplic.*, I, II, 7; PL XL, 115; Burleigh, 391.) Not more than three or four years before writing this work, Augustine himself had maintained that God predestinates men to salvation on the basis of His foreknowledge that they will, of their own free will, choose faith and so merit grace; see, e.g., *Expos. Quar. Prop. ex Ep. ad Romanos,* 55; PL XXXV, 2076.

18. "Those are chosen who are effectually [*congruenter*] called. Those who are not effectually called and do not obey their calling are not chosen, for although they were called they did not follow. . . . He calls the man on whom he has mercy in the way he knows will suit him, so that he will not refuse the call." (*De Div. Quaest. ad Simplic.*, I, II, 13; PL XL, 119; Burleigh, 395.) See, too, *De Corrept. et Gratia*, IX, 23; PL XLIV, 929–30; S V, 481, and *De Praedest. Sanct.*, XVIII, 36 and 37; PL XLIV, 987–88; S V, 516.

19. ". . . the grace of God, which both begins a man's faith and which enables it to persevere unto the end, is not given according to our merits, but is given according to His own most secret and at the same time most righteous, wise, and beneficent will. . . ." (*De Dono Persever.*, XIII, 33; PL XLV, 1012; S V, 538.)

20. DCD, XXI, 12; CCSL XLVIII, 778; H II, 438; italics added.

21. See *De Dono Persever.*, VIII, 17; PL XLV, 1002–3; S V, 531, and XI, 25; PL XLV, 1007–8, S V, 535. On Augustine's effort to reconcile the existence of evil in the world with God's perfect goodness and justice, see pp. 66–71.

22. DCD, XIII, 23; CCSL XLVIII, 408; H I, 551; italics added.

23. See *Contra Duas Epist. Pelag.*, II, VII, 13; CSEL LX, 473–74; S V, 397.

24. See *De Div. Quaest. ad Simplic.*, I, II, 16; PL XL, 120–21; Burleigh, 398, and I, II, 18; PL XL, 123–24; Burleigh, 401, and I, II, 22; PL XL, 128; Burleigh, 406.

25. ". . . neither does he who is saved have a basis for glorying in any merit of his own; nor does the man who is damned have a basis for complaining of anything except what he has fully merited. For grace alone separates the redeemed from the lost, all having been mingled together in the one mass of perdition, arising from a common cause which leads back to their common origin." (*Enchiridion*, XXV, 99; PL XL, 278; Outler, 398.) See, too, *Contra Duas Epist. Pelag.*, IV, VI, 16; CSEL LX, 539–40; S V, 424.

26. See *Sermo* CXLV, 4; PL XXXVIII, 793; S VI, 541–42, and *De Div. Quaest. ad Simplic.*, I, II, 17 and 18; PL XL, 122–24; Burleigh, 398 and 400–401.

27. *De Praedest. Sanct.*, V, 9; PL XLIV, 967; S V, 502. See, too, *De Doctr. Christ.*, Preface, 8; PL XXXIV, 18; S II, 521.

28. *Ep.* CXCIV, V, 19; CSEL LVII, 190; FCL IV, 313.

29. "With great eagerness, then, I fastened upon the venerable writings of thy Spirit and principally upon the apostle Paul. . . . So

I began, and I found that whatever truth I had read [in the Platonists] was here combined with the exaltation of thy grace. Thus, he who sees must not glory as if he had not received, not only the things that he sees, but the very power of sight—for what does he have that he has not received as a gift? . . . The books of the Platonists tell nothing of this. Their pages do not contain the expression of this kind of godliness—the tears of confession, thy sacrifice, a troubled spirit, a broken and a contrite heart, the salvation of thy people, the espoused City, the earnest of the Holy Spirit, the cup of our redemption." (*Confess.*, VII, XXI, 27; CSEL XXXIII, 166–68; Outler, 155–56.)

30. See Augustine's description, *De Div. Quaest. ad Simplic.*, I, II, 22; PL XL, 128; Burleigh, 406.

31. *Ibid.*

32. "From the time that I have been turned to Thee, renewed by Thee who had been made by Thee, re-created who had been created, re-formed who had been formed: from the time that I have been converted, I have learned that no merits of mine have preceded, but that Thy grace hath come to me *gratis,* in order that I might be mindful of Thy righteousness alone." (*En. in Ps.*, LXX [2], 2; CCSL XXXIX, 961; S VIII, 322.)

33. *Romans* xiii, 13–14 (RSV).

34. For the complete narrative see *Confess.*, VIII, XII, 28–30; CSEL XXXIII, 193–96; Outler, 175–77.

35. See DCD, VIII, 4 and 5; CCSL XLVII, 219–22; H I, 311–14, *Contra Academicos*, III, XVIII, 41; CSEL LXIII, 78–79; FC 1, 218, and *Ep.* CXVIII, III, 20–21; CSEL XXXIV (2), 683–85; S I, 445, and *ibid.*, V, 33; CSEL XXXIV (2), 696–97; S I, 450.

36. See DCD, X, 24; CCSL XLVII, 297; H I, 414, and X, 29; CCSL XLVII, 304; H I, 423.

37. See *Enchiridion*, XIV, 48; PL XL, 255; Outler, 368, and *De Consensu Evangel.*, I, XXXV, 53; CSEL XLIII, 59–60; S VI, 100–101.

38. Man can be cured of the universal sickness of sin, which stems from Adam's fall, only by drinking "the bitter cup, the cup of temptations, wherein this life abounds, the cup of tribulation, anguish, and sufferings. . . . And that the sick man may not make answer, 'I cannot, I cannot bear it, I will not drink;' the Physician, all whole though he be, drinketh first, that the sick man may not hesitate to drink." (*Sermo* LXXXVIII, 7; PL XXXVIII, 543; S VI, 381.)

39. 1 *Tim.* ii, 4 (AV).

40. *Enchiridion,* XXVII, 103; PL XL, 280; Outler, 401. See, too, *De Corrept. et Gratia,* XIV, 44; PL XLIV, 943; S V, 489. Since Augustine here explicitly rejects the view that God wills all men to be saved and since he often states categorically that God, in His unfathomable mercy and His incomprehensible justice, bestows the gift of grace and, thereby, salvation upon only a small number of the sons of Adam (see above, notes 16, 20, 21, and 22), I do not understand how Father Portalié can maintain that, in opposition to the opinions of the Semi-Pelagians and the Predestinationists, "Augustine formulated (not invented) the Catholic dogma, which affirms these two truths at the same time: a) the eternal choice of the elect by God is very real, very gratuitous, and constitutes the grace of graces; b) but this decree does not destroy the Divine will to save all men, which, moreover, is not realized except by the human liberty that leaves to the elect full power to fall and to the non-elect full power to rise," and that Augustine and the Catholic Faith agree in maintaining "the very sincere will of God to give to all men the power of saving themselves and the power of damning themselves." (Eugène Portalié, S.J., "Augustine of Hippo," *The Catholic Encyclopaedia* [New York, The Encyclopaedia Press, Inc., 1907], II, 97–98.)

41. See pp. 34–38.

42. See DCD, XVIII, 47; CCSL XLVIII, 645; H II, 279–80. "It follows that those ancient saints [of the Old Testament] are members of Christ through their faith in His resurrection, which had not in their day happened, but which was one day to come to pass." (*De Gratia Christi et De Pecc. Orig.,* II, XXVI, 31; CSEL XLII, 190–91; S V, 248.) See, too, *Contra Duas Epist. Pelag.,* III, IV, 8; CSEL LX, 494; S V, 405, *Ep.* CII, 12 & 15, CSEL XXXIV (2), 554 and 557; S I, 417–18, and *Ep.* CXC, II, 6 & 8; CSEL LVII, 141–43; FCL IV, 274–76.

43. See pp. 34–37.

44. ". . . sin which arises from the action of the free will turns out to be victor over the will and the free will is destroyed." (*Enchiridion,* IX, 30; PL XL, 247; Outler, 356.) "For, vanquished by the sin into which it fell by its volition, nature has lost liberty. . . . For true liberty is also real health; and this would never have been lost, if the will had remained good." (*De Perf. Iust. Hominis,* IV, 9; CSEL XLII, 8–9; S V, 161.)   45. See *ibid.*

46. *Confess.,* VIII, V, 12; CSEL XXXIII, 180; Outler, 165. "The enemy held fast my will, and had made of it a chain, and had bound

me tight with it. For out of the perverse will came lust, and the service of lust ended in habit, and habit, not resisted, became necessity." (*Ibid.*, VIII, V, 10; CSEL XXXIII, 178; Outler, 164.)

47. "Certainly, will is that by which a man sins or lives righteously. . . . But mortals cannot live righteously and piously unless the will itself is liberated by the grace of God from the servitude to sin into which it has fallen, and is aided to overcome its vices." (*Retractationum*, I, IX, 4 [on *De Libero Arbitrio*]; CSEL XXXVI, 41–42; Burleigh, 103.) See, too: "In this mortal life one thing remains for free will, not that a man may fulfil righteousness when he wishes, but that he may turn with suppliant piety to him who can give the power to fulfil it." (*De Div. Quaest. ad Simplic.*, I, I, 14; PL XL, 108; Burleigh, 382.) Later Augustine argues that even the first movements of the will in its turning back to God come from God's grace and not from man's will or power (see below, notes 54 and 57).

48. *Retractationum*, I, IX, 6 (on *De Libero Arbitrio*); CSEL XXXVI, 46; Burleigh, 104.

49. See *De Spiritu et Littera*, XVI, 28; CSEL LX, 181; Burnaby, 216.

50. *De Perf. Iust. Hominis*, IV, 9; CSEL XLII, 9; S V, 161–62.

51. "What is man, while in this life he uses his own proper will, ere he choose and love God, but unrighteous and ungodly?" (*De Patientia*, XXI, 19; CSEL XLI, 684; S III, 534.) "Our life, as ours, that is, of our own personal will, will be only evil, sinful, unrighteous; but the life in us that is good is from God, not from ourselves; it is given to us by God, not by ourselves. . . . as for man, he liveth now ill, now well. He who was living ill, was in his own life; he who is living well, is passed to the life of Christ." (*In Ioann. Evangel.*, XXII, 9; CCSL XXXVI, 228; S VII, 148.)

52. *Contra Duas Epist. Pelag.*, II, V, 9; CSEL LX, 468–69; S V, 395. ". . . if he applies his hand to fire, and if evil and death please him, his human will effects all this, but if, on the contrary, he loves goodness and life, not alone does his will accomplish the happy choice, but it is assisted by divine grace." (*De Gestis Pelagii*, III, 7; CSEL XLII, 58; S V, 186.)

53. See above, note 44.

54. "Free will is most important. It exists, indeed, but of what value is it in those who are sold under sin? . . . We are commanded to live righteously, and the reward is set before us that we shall merit to live happily for ever. But who can live righteously and do good works unless he has been justified by faith? . . . But who

can believe unless he is reached by some calling, by some testimony borne to the truth?" (*De Div. Quaest. ad Simplic.*, I, II, 21; PL XL, 126–27; Burleigh, 404–5.) "Forasmuch then as our turning away from God is our own act, and this is evil will; but our turning to God is not possible, except He rouses and helps us, and this is good will,—what have we that we have not received?" (*De Peccat. Meritis,* II, XVIII, 31; CSEL LX, 102; S V, 56.) See, too, *Contra Duas Epist. Pelag.*, I, III, 7; CSEL LX, 428–29; S V, 379, and III, VIII, 24; CSEL LX, 516; S V, 414. In the light of Augustine's repeated statements that after the Fall free will is "not of avail for good and pious living," and that fallen man, since he is in bondage to sin, is completely unable to live righteously unless and until his will is liberated by God's grace (see, e.g., notes 44, 48, and 52 above), I do not see how Father Portalié can say: "Thus, when he says that we have lost freedom in consequence of the sin of Adam, he is careful to explain that this lost freedom is not the liberty of choosing between good and evil, because without it we could not help sinning, but the perfect liberty which was calm and *without struggle,* and which was enjoyed by Adam in virtue of his original integrity." (Portalié, "Augustine of Hippo," p. 96.) Note, too, Augustine's statement in his comments in the *Retractationum* on one of his anti-Manichaean works, the *De Duabus Animabus:* "For when sin is such that it is the same as the punishment for sin, what power is left to the will when it is in bondage to desire, except, perhaps, if it is pious, to pray for help? For it is only free to the extent that it has been liberated, and it is only then that it is called a will [*Nam quando tale est, ut idem sit et poena peccati, quantum est quod ualet uoluntas sub dominante cupiditate, nisi forte, si pia est, ut oret auxilium? in tantum enim libera est, in quantum liberata est, et in tantum appellatur uoluntas*]." (*Retractationum,* I, XIV, 4; CSEL XXXVI, 75–76; author's translation.)

55. "Hence, from the fact that some infirmity remains, I venture to say that, in what measure we serve God, we are free; in what measure we serve the law of sin, we are still in bondage. Hence says the apostle, . . . 'I delight in the law of God after the inward man.' Here then it is, wherein we are free, wherein we delight in the law of God; for liberty has joy. For as long as it is from fear that thou doest what is right, God is no delight to thee. Find thy delight in Him, and thou art free." (*In Ioann. Evangel.*, XLI, 10; CCSL XXXVI, 363; S VII, 233.)

56. DCD, XIV, 11, CCSL XLVIII, 432; H II, 23.

57. *In Ioann. Evangel.*, XLI, 8; CCSL XXXVI, 362; S VII, 233.

It is God who works in the elect that they may have a good will, i.e., that they may desire to follow His commandments and to act righteously; and when through His grace they have this will, He cooperates with them when they will and when they act in accordance with that good will. See *De Gratia et Lib. Arbit.*, XVII, 33; PL XLIV, 901; S V, 458.

58. *Enchiridion*, IX, 30; PL XL, 247; Outler, 357.

59. "Our hope is this, brethren, to be made free by the free One; and that, in setting us free, He may make us His servants. For we were the servants of lust; but being set free, we are made the servants of love." (*In Ioann. Evangel.*, XLI, 8; CCSL XXXVI, 362; S VII, 232.) See, too, *De Nupt. et Concup.*, II, III, 8; CSEL XLII, 259; S V, 285.

60. See *De Gratia et Lib. Arbit.*, XV, 31; PL XLIV, 899–900; S V, 456.

61. *En. in Ps.*, LXVII, 13; CCSL XXXIX, 877; S VIII, 289. "God's grace is apart by itself, the nature of man apart by itself. Do but examine the nature of man: man is born and grows, he learns the customs of men. What does he know but earth, of earth? He speaks the things of men, knows the things of men, minds the things of men; carnal, he judges carnally, conjectures carnally: lo! it is man all over. Let the grace of God come, and enlighten his darkness . . . let it take the mind of man, and turn it to its own light; immediately he begins to say, as the apostle says, 'Yet not I, but the grace of God that is with me.'" (*In Ioann. Evangel.*, XIV, 6; CCSL XXXVI, 144–45; S VII, 96.)

62. *Ibid.*, XLI, 9; CCSL XXXVI, 362; S VII, 233.

63. *De Perf. Iust. Hominis*, IV, 9; CSEL XLII, 9; S V, 161.

64. See DCD, XXII, 30; CCSL XLVIII, 863–64; H II, 542. "Therefore the first liberty of the will was *to be able not to sin*, the last will be much greater, *not to be able to sin;* the first immortality was to be able not to die, the last will be much greater, not to be able to die; the first was the power of perseverance, to be able not to forsake good—the last will be the felicity of perseverance, not to be able to forsake good." (*De Corrept. et Gratia*, XII, 33; PL XLIV, 936; S V, 485.)

65. *Enchiridion*, XXVIII, 105; PL XL, 281; Outler, 402–3. Note, however, that in another context Augustine himself, in effect, "finds fault" with such a will and says that it is not truly a will since it is not free to choose evil, when he argues that man would have been less good had God created him with a "will" that was incapable of sin, rather than a will able to choose between good and evil.

66. See above, in this chapter, pp. 18–21. "Fear and grief, and labour and danger are unavoidable, so long as we live in this world; but the great question is, for what cause, with what expectation, with what aim a man endures these things. . . . Occasionally, however, some open their ears and hearts to the truth,—rarely in prosperity, more frequently in adversity. *These are indeed the few, for such it is predicted that they shall be.*" (*Ep.* CCIII; CSEL LVII, 316; S I, 558; italics added.)

67. See DCD, X, 7; CCSL XLVII, 279–80; H I, 392.

68. The theme of the division of mankind into two classes, "the multitude of the impious" and "the succession of the people devoted to the one God," appears as early as the year 390; see *De Vera Religione,* XXVII, 50; PL XXXIV, 144; Burleigh, 250. For Augustine's views on history and on the end of the world, see Chap. II, pp. 71–76.

69. See the famous passage in the Tenth Homily on the Epistle of St. John: "It is because the sons of God are the Body of God's only Son; because he is Head, and we are members, the Son of God is still one. Therefore to love the sons of God is to love the Son of God; to love the Son of God is to love the Father; none can love the Father unless he love the Son; and he that loves the Son, loves also the sons of God. These sons of God are the members of God's Son; and he that loves them, by loving becomes himself a member; through love he becomes a part of the structure of Christ's Body. And thus the end will be the one Christ, loving himself; for the love of the members for one another is the love of the Body for itself." (*In Epist. Ioann.,* X, 3; PL XXXV, 2055; Burnaby, 341.)

70. See DCD, VIII, 24; CCSL XLVII, 243; H I, 344, *De Baptismo,* I, XVI, 25; CSEL LI, 169; S IV, 422, *En. in Ps.,* LXXXV, 14; CCSL XXXIX, 1188; S VIII, 414, and *ibid.,* XC (2), 1; CCSL XXXIX, 1266; S VIII, 450.

71. *In Ioann. Evangel.,* CXV, 2; CCSL XXXVI, 644; S VII, 423. See, too, DCD, XV, 1; CCSL XLVIII, 454; H II, 51.

72. *Ibid.,* X, 32; CCSL XLVII, 312; H I, 433.

73. See pp. 34–36.

74. "Let those then who, being in this life, groan, and long for their country, run by love, not by bodily feet; let them seek not ships but wings, let them lay hold on the two wings of love. What are the two wings of love? The love of God, and of our neighbour. For now we are pilgrims, we sigh, we groan." (*En. in Ps.,* CXLIX, 5; CCSL XL, 2182; S VIII, 678.)

75. The sojourners are prefigured by Noah's ark in the flood (DCD, XV, 26; CCSL XLVIII, 493–94; H II, 98–99). See, too, DCD, I, Pref.; CCSL XLVII, 1; H I, 1, and XV, 1; CCSL XLVIII, 454; H II, 51, and *En. in Ps.,* LXI, 7; CCSL XXXIX, 777; S VIII, 252. "He is a Christian who, even in his own house and in his own country, acknowledges himself to be a stranger. For our country is above, there we shall not be strangers. For every one here below, even in his own house, is a stranger. If he be not a stranger, let him not pass on from hence." (*Sermo* CXI, 2; PL XXXVIII, 642–43; S VI, 446.)

76. "The Holy City is not the Church of this country only, but of the whole world as well: not that of this age only, but from Abel himself down to those who shall to the end be born and believe in Christ, the whole assembly of the Saints, belonging to one city; which city is Christ's body, of which Christ is the Head. There, too, dwell the Angels, who are our fellow-citizens: we toil, because we are as yet pilgrims: while they within that city are awaiting our arrival. Letters have reached us too from that city, apart from which we are wandering: those letters are the Scriptures, which exhort us to live well. Why do I speak of letters only? The King himself descended, and became a path to us in our wanderings: that walking in Him, we may neither stray, nor faint nor fall among robbers, nor be caught in the snares that are set near our path." (*En. in Ps.,* XC [2], 1; CCSL XXXIX, 1266; S VIII, 450.) "Nor is it a little matter that the Holy Spirit teaches us to groan, for He gives us to know that we are sojourners in a foreign land, and He teaches us to sigh after our native country; and through that very longing do we groan. He with whom it is well in this world, or rather he who thinks it is well with him, who exults in the joy of carnal things, in the abundance of things temporal, in an empty felicity, has the cry of the raven; for the raven's cry is full of clamor, not of groaning. . . . Many indeed groan by reason of earthly misery. They are shattered, it may be, by losses, or weighed down by bodily ailment, or shut up in prisons, or bound with chains, or tossed about on the waves of the sea, or hedged in by the ensnaring devices of their enemies. Therefore do they groan, but not with the moaning of the dove, not with love of God, not in the Spirit. Accordingly, when such are delivered from these same afflictions, they exult with loud voices, whereby it is made manifest that they are ravens, not doves." (*In Ioann. Evangel.,* VI, 2; CCSL XXXVI, 53–54; S VII, 39–40.)

77. "Neither does the spiritual man judge concerning that division

between spiritual and carnal men which is known to thy eyes, O God, and which may not, as yet, be made manifest to us by their external works, so that we may know them by their fruits; yet thou, O God, knowest them already and thou hast divided and called them secretly, before the firmament was made." (*Confess.*, XIII, XXIII, 33; CSEL XXXIII, 372; Outler, 320.) See, too, below, in this chapter, pp. 34–37.

78. DCD, XIV, 1; CCSL XLVIII, 414; H II, 2.

79. "For all men who love pride and temporal power with vain elation and pomp of arrogance, and all spirits who set their affections on such things and seek their own glory in the subjection of men, are bound fast together in one association; nay, even although they frequently fight against each other on account of these things, they are nevertheless precipitated by the like weight of lust into the same abyss, and are united with each other by similarity of manners and merits. And, again, all men and all spirits who humbly seek the glory of God and not their own, and who follow Him in piety, belong to one fellowship." (*De Catechiz. Rudibus,* XIX, 31; PL XL, 333–34; S III, 303.) See, too, DCD, XV, 4; CCSL XLVIII, 456; H II, 53.

80. DCD, XV, 17; CCSL XLVIII, 479; H II, 81.

81. *Ibid.,* XVIII, 2; CCSL XLVIII, 593; H II, 218. See, too, *ibid.,* XVI, 17; CCSL XLVIII, 521; H II, 130–31, where Augustine says that at the time of God's promises to Abraham "there were three famous kingdoms of the nations, in which the city of the earth-born [*terrigenarum ciuitas*], that is, the society of men living according to man under the domination of the fallen angels, chiefly flourished, namely, the three kingdoms of Sicyon, Egypt, and Assyria." See, too, *En. in Ps.,* LI, 6; CCSL XXXIX, 628; S VIII, 197, where he says: "Let us therefore speak first of the evil body of kingdom earthly [*Dicatur ergo primo de corpore malo regni terreni*]."

82. See *En. in Ps.,* LXI, 8; CCSL XXXIX, 778; S VIII, 253, and LXIV, 2; CCSL XXXIX, 823; S VIII, 268, and DCD, XI, 1; CCSL XLVIII, 321–22; H I, 437.

83. *En. in Ps.,* LXI, 8; CCSL XXXIX, 778; S VIII, 253.

84. *Ibid.*

85. *Sermo* CXXV, 7; PL XXXVIII, 694; S VI, 479. See, too: "But we cannot love God, if we love the world: if we love the world, it will separate us from the love of God which is charity. . . . Two loves there are, of the world and of God: if the love of the world dwells in us, the love of God can find no entrance. The love of the

world must depart, the love of God come in to dwell: make room for the better love. Once you loved the world, now cease to love it: empty your heart of earthly love and you shall drink of the love divine: charity will begin its dwelling in you, and from charity nothing evil can proceed." (*In Epist. Ioann.*, II, 8; PL XXXV, 1993; Burnaby, 274.)

86. *En. in Ps.*, XCI, 10; CCSL XXXIX, 1287; S VIII, 455. See, too, *ibid.*, LXX (1), 9; CCSL XXXIX, 947–48; S VIII, 318.

87. *Ibid.*, VI, 9; CCSL XXXVIII, 33; S VIII, 18.

88. See DCD, XVIII, 51; CCSL XLVIII, 649; H II, 284–85.

89. See *In Ioann. Evangel.*, XXVIII, 9; CCSL XXXVI, 282; S VII, 182.

90. "But when all time is past, then we return to our country, as after seventy years that people returned from the Babylonish captivity, for Babylon is this world; since Babylon is interpreted 'confusion.' . . . So then this whole life of human affairs is confusion, which belongeth not unto God. In this confusion, in this Babylonish land, Sion is held captive." (*En. in Ps.*, CXXV, 3; CCSL XL, 1847; S VIII, 604.) See, too, *ibid.*, LXIV, 2; CCSL XXXIX, 823; S VIII, 268.

91. *Sermo* LXXXI, 7; PL XXXVIII, 503; S VI, 355–56.

92. DCD, XV, 18; CCSL XLVIII, 481; H II, 83.

93. *Matthew* xxii, 37–39 (RSV).

94. *En. in Ps.*, XCVIII, 4; CCSL XXXIX, 1381; S VIII, 484.

95. See *ibid.*, CXXI, 4; CCSL XL, 1804; S VIII, 594.

96. *Ibid.*, CXXII, 4; CCSL XL, 1816–17; S VIII, 597.

97. See *De Sermone Domini*, II, V, 17; PL XXXIV, 1276–77; S VI, 39, and *Contra Faustum*, XXII, 67; CSEL XXV, 664; S IV, 298.

98. *In Ioann. Evangel.*, XLIX, 19; CCSL XXXVI, 429; S VII, 276 [*Ergo fides tua de Christo, Christus est in corde tuo*].

99. DCD, XV, 3; CCSL XLVIII, 456; H II, 53.

100. See above, note 79, and Chap. II.

101. "But sinners are in this life sometimes not scourged at all, or are scourged less than their deserts: because the wickedness of their heart is given over as already desperate. Those, however, for whom eternal life is prepared, must needs be scourged in this life: for that sentence is true . . . 'For whom the Lord loveth He chasteneth, and scourgeth every son whom He receiveth.'" (*En. in Ps.*, XXXVII, 23; CCSL XXXVIII, 397; S VIII, 109.)

102. See DCD, XVIII, 54; CCSL XLVIII, 656; H II, 292.

103. *Ibid.*, XV, 7; CCSL XLVIII, 461; H II, 58.

104. See *ibid.,* XX, 9; CCSL XLVIII, 716–17; H II, 365.

105. See Chap. VI.

106. "For who of the multitude of believers can presume, so long as he is living in this mortal state, that he is in the number of the predestinated?" (*De Corrept. et Gratia,* XIII, 40; PL XLIV, 940–41; S V, 488.) See, too, DCD, XI, 12; CCSL XLVIII, 333; H I, 451, and XXI, 15; CCSL XLVIII, 781; H II, 442.

107. DCD, XX, 7; CCSL XLVIII, 711; H II, 358.

108. "In that unspeakable foreknowledge of God, many who seem to be without are in reality within, and many who seem to be within yet really are without." (*De Baptismo,* V, XXVII, 38; CSEL LI, 295; S IV, 477.) See, too, *ibid.,* V, XXVIII, 39; CSEL LI, 296–97; S IV, 478. Many who have been baptized, even though they remain in the Church, fail to obtain salvation (*Ibid.,* IV, XIV, 21; CSEL LI, 246; S IV, 456). Many who are open heretics are, in God's sight, better than many good Catholics (*Ibid.,* IV, III, 4; CSEL LI, 225; S IV, 448). Yet, there is no salvation outside the visible Church (*Ibid.,* IV, I, 1; CSEL LI, 223; S IV, 447, and IV, XVII, 24; CSEL LI, 250; S IV, 458), except for those who received the "baptism of blood" instead of the usual ceremony of baptism by water, because they were killed as martyrs in the cause of Christ before they had been baptized (DCD, XIII, 7; CCSL XLVIII, 389–90; H I, 527, and *De Natura et Origine Animae,* I, IX, 11; CSEL LX, 311; S V, 319).

109. See DCD, I, 35; CCSL XLVII, 33–34; H I, 46, and XXI, 24; CCSL XLVIII, 789; H II, 452.

110. *In Ioann. Evangel.,* XLV, 12; CCSL XXXVI, 395; S VII, 254.

111. See *ibid.,* XXVII, 11; CCSL XXXVI, 276; S VII, 178, and *De Div. Quaest. ad Simplic.,* I, II, 22; PL XL, 127–28; Burleigh, 406. Obviously, this does not mean that persons who openly commit grave sins cannot or should not be excommunicated from the Church, at least until they have shown clear evidence of repentance and amendment.

112. "You see that those who forsake the unity of the Church, who try to manifest their own sinlessness by pretending to be injured by the sins of others, are themselves the greatest offenders." (*Ep.* CVIII, 12; CSEL XXXIV [2], 624; FCL II, 226.)

113. See *En. in Ps.,* CXXXVIII, 27; CCSL XL, 2009; S VIII, 640, *Contra Litt. Petil.,* III, III, 4; CSEL LII, 164–65; S IV, 598, *Sermo* LXXIII, 1; PL XXXVIII, 470; S VI, 334, and *Sermo* XLVII, 6; PL XXXVIII, 299–300.

114. DCD, XVIII, 49; CCSL XLVIII, 647; H II, 282. See, too, *De Div. Quaest. 83,* LVII, 2; PL XL, 41, and LXXXI, 3; PL XL, 97.

115. *In Ioann. Evangel.,* XIX, 18; CCSL XXXVI, 201; S VII, 130.

116. *In Epist. Ioann.,* V, 7; PL XXXV, 2016; Burnaby, 298–99. It is clear that this mixture of good and evil men in the Church applies to the clergy as well as the laity. "There are, therefore, some who hold the honourable office of shepherds in order that they may provide for the flock of Christ; others occupy that position that they may enjoy the temporal honours and secular advantages connected with the office. It must needs happen that these two kinds of pastors, some dying, others succeeding them, should continue in the Catholic Church even to the end of time, and the judgment of the Lord." (*Ep.* CCVIII, 2; CSEL LVII, 343; S I, 558.)

117. "How great the number of believers that are gathered together; how great the multitudes that flock together; many of them truly converted, many but in appearance: and those who are truly converted are the minority; those who are so but in appearance are the majority. . . ." (*En. in Ps.,* XXXIX, 10; CCSL XXXVIII, 433; S VIII, 123.) "He [a believer] would see many who do not practise the required duties; but this would not shake his faith, even though these people should belong to the same Church and partake of the same sacraments as himself. He would understand that few share in the inheritance of God, while many partake in its outward signs; that few are united in holiness of life, and in the gift of love shed abroad in our hearts by the Holy Spirit who is given to us, which is a hidden spring that no stranger can approach; and that many join in the solemnity of the sacrament." (*Contra Faustum,* XIII, 16; CSEL XXV, 395–96; S IV, 205.) See, too, *De Catechiz. Rudibus,* XIX, 31; PL XL, 333; S III, 303, where he speaks of the many who "consent unto the devil," and the few who "follow God." See, too, above, note 16, and Chap. VI, note 88.

118. See *En. in Ps.,* VII, 7; CCSL XXXVIII, 40; S VIII, 23.

119. *Ibid.,* VII, 9; CCSL XXXVIII, 42; S VIII, 24. "What do we make of all those evil men who are found mixed with the Church, and *who become more numerous as the Church extends,* and as all nations are united in Christ? . . . Patience is necessary to obey the command, 'Suffer both to grow together till the harvest.'" (*Contra Faustum,* XIII, 16; CSEL XXV, 397; S IV, 205; italics added.)

120. *In Ioann. Evangel.,* CXXII, 7; CCSL XXXVI, 672; S VII, 441–42.

121. *Ibid.,* XXV, 10; CCSL XXXVI, 252; S VII, 163.

122. See *Sermo* CXXXVII, 14; PL XXXVIII, 762; S VI, 522, and *En. in Ps.,* CXVIII (24), 3; CCSL XL, 1745.

NOTES TO CHAPTER II

1. *In Ioann. Evangel.,* XIX, 12; CCSL XXXVI, 195; S VII, 127.

2. *Ibid.*

3. DCD, XIV, 4; CCSL XLVIII, 418; H II, 6. See, too: "Dying, to thy flesh, is the losing of its life: dying to thy soul, is the losing of its life. The life of thy flesh is thy soul: the life of thy soul is thy God. As the flesh dies in losing the soul, which is its life, so the soul dieth in losing God, who is its life. Of a certainty, then, the soul is immortal. Manifestly immortal, for it liveth even when dead." (*In Ioann. Evangel.,* XLVII, 8; CCSL XXXVI, 408; S VII, 263.)

4. DCD, IX, 17; CCSL XLVII, 265–66; H I, 374.

5. "The body tends toward its own place by its own gravity. A weight does not tend downward only, but moves to its own place. Fire tends upward; a stone tends downward. They are propelled by their own mass; they seek their own places. . . . *My weight is my love.* By it I am carried wherever I am carried." (*Confess.,* XIII, IX, 10; CSEL XXXIII, 351–52; Outler, 304; italics added.) "Now the souls of men, whether good or bad, love rest, but how to attain to that which they love is to the greater part unknown; and that which bodies seek for their weight, is precisely what souls seek for their love, namely, a resting-place. For as, according to its specific gravity, a body descends or rises until it reaches a place where it can rest . . . so the soul of man struggles towards the things which it loves, in order that, by reaching them, it may rest." (*Ep.* LV, X, 18; CSEL XXXIV [2], 189; S I, 309.) "Thy affections are the steps: thy will the way. By loving thou mountest, by neglect thou descendest. Standing on the earth thou art in heaven, if thou lovest God. For the heart is not so raised as the body is raised: the body to be lifted up changes its place: the heart to be lifted up changes its will." (*En. in Ps.,* LXXXV, 6; CCSL XXXIX, 1181; S VIII, 411.) See, too, DCD, XI, 28; CCSL XLVIII, 348; H I, 472.

6. *Confess.,* XIII, IX, 10; CSEL XXXIII, 351–52; Outler, 304.

7. "Since then the majority of men are such as their loves are, and that there ought to be no other care for the regulation of our lives, than the choice of that which we ought to love; why dost thou wonder, if he who loves Christ, and who wishes to follow Christ, for the love of Him denies himself?" (*Sermo* XCVI, 1; PL XXXVIII,

585; S VI, 408.) "For every soul follows what it loves." (*In Ioann. Evangel.*, VII, 1; CCSL XXXVI, 67; S VII, 48.) "For a person lives in those things which he loves, which he greatly desires, and in which he believes himself to be blessed." (*Ep.* CXXX, III, 7; CSEL XLIV, 48; S I, 461.) Cf. Plato, *Laws* X, 904: "For as a man's desires tend, and as is the soul that conceives them, so and such, as a general rule, does every one of us come to be," A. E. Taylor, tr. (London, Everyman's Library, J. M. Dent & Sons Ltd.; New York, E. P. Dutton & Co., Inc., 1960), p. 298.

8. *In Epist. Ioann.*, II, 14; PL XXXV, 1997; Burnaby, 278; italics added. See, too: "[M]an, by worshipping the works of his own hands, may more easily cease to be man, than the works of his hands can, through his worship of them, become gods. For it can sooner happen that man, who has received an honourable position, may, through lack of understanding, become comparable to the beasts, than that the works of man may become preferable to the work of God, made in His own image, that is, to man himself." (DCD, VIII, 23; CCSL XLVII, 241; H I, 341.)

9. *De Vera Religione*, XXXVIII, 69; PL XXXIV, 153; Burleigh, 260–61; italics added. The reference to "carnal pleasures," "vain power," and "some showy spectacle" recalls Augustine's classification of the three kinds of earthly men—the lovers of the lower pleasures, the proud, and the curious. "As it is written: 'All that is in the world is lust of the flesh, lust of the eyes, and ambition of this world.' (I John 2:16.) Three classes of men are thus distinguished; for lust of the flesh means those who love the lower pleasures, lust of the eyes means the curious, and ambition of this world denotes the proud." (*Ibid.*, XXXVIII, 70; PL XXXIV, 153; Burleigh, 261.)

10. *In Ioann. Evangel.*, XLVI, 8; CCSL XXXVI, 403; S VII, 259.

11. *De Doctr. Christ.*, I, IV, 4; PL XXXIV, 21; S II, 523. "Woe to those who put their hope in the world; woe to them that cling to those things which they brought forth through hope in the world. What then should the Christian do? He should use, not serve the world." (*En. in Ps.*, XCV, 14; CCSL XXXIX, 1352; S VIII, 474.) This distinction between "using" and "serving" or "enjoying" is one of Augustine's favorites. God, the supreme and absolute good, alone is to be "enjoyed" (*frui*) or "served"; every created object is not to be "enjoyed" or "served" but rather "used" (*uti*) as a means toward the enjoyment of the highest good.

12. See DCD, XIII, 13; CCSL XLVIII, 395; H I, 534.

13. *Ibid.*, XIV, 15; CCSL XLVIII, 437; H II, 30.

14. *In Ioann. Evangel.*, XVIII, 7; CCSL XXXVI, 184; S VII, 120.

15. *En. in Ps.*, XL, 5; CCSL XXXVIII, 453; S VIII, 130.

16. See DCD, I, 9; CCSL XLVII, 8–10; H I, 12–14.

17. See *ibid.*, I, 8; CCSL XLVII, 7; H I, 10, and I, 10; CCSL XLVII, 10–12; H I, 15–16, and I, 29; CCSL XLVII, 30; H I, 41, and V, 18; CCSL XLVII, 154; H I, 214.

18. See *ibid.*, XI, 25; CCSL XLVIII, 344–45; H I, 467.

19. *En. in Ps.*, LXXII, 16; CCSL XXXIX, 995; S VIII, 337.

20. "Is not this then happiness, to have sons safe, daughters beautiful, garners full, cattle abundant, no downfall, I say not of a wall, but not even of a hedge, no tumult and clamour in the streets, but quiet, peace, abundance, plenty of all things in their houses and in their cities? Is not this then happiness? or ought the righteous to shun it? or findest thou not the house of the righteous too abounding with all these things, full of this happiness? Did not Abraham's house abound with gold, silver, children, servants, cattle? . . . What say we? is not this happiness? Be it so, still it is on the left hand. What is, on the left hand? Temporal, mortal, bodily. I desire not that thou shun it, but that thou think it not to be on the right hand. . . . For what ought they to have set on the right hand? God, eternity, the years of God which fail not. . . . Let us use the left for the time, let us long for the right for eternity." (*En. in Ps.*, CXLIII, 18; CCSL XL, 2085–86; S VIII, 656.)

21. See *Sermo* LXXX, 7; PL XXXVIII, 497–98; S VI, 352.

22. *In Ioann. Evangel.*, XL, 10; CCSL XXXVI, 356; S VII, 229; italics added. "Put we up then in the hostelry of this life as travellers passing on, and not as owners intending to remain." (*Sermo* LXXX, 7; PL XXXVIII, 497; S VI, 352.) The man in whom Christ dwells "begins to treat this world with indifference; not to be lifted up when prosperity befalls him, nor crushed when adversity, but in all things to praise God, not only when he aboundeth, but also when he loseth; not only when he is in health, but also when he is sick." (*En. in Ps.*, CXXXVIII, 16; CCSL XL, 2001; S VIII, 638.)

23. *De Mendacio*, VII, 10; CSEL XLI, 428; S III, 463.

24. See DCD, XIV, 15; CCSL XLVIII, 438; H II, 31.

25. See *Confess.*, XIII, XVII, 20; CSEL XXXIII, 359–60; Outler, 310–11.

26. *Sermo* CXXV, 11; PL XXXVIII, 698; S VI, 481.

27. *De Vera Religione*, XXI, 41; PL XXXIV, 139; Burleigh, 245.

28. *En. in Ps.*, XXXIX, 7; CCSL XXXVIII, 430; S VIII, 121–22.

29. *Ibid.*, XXXVIII, 11; CCSL XXXVIII, 412; S VIII, 115.

30. DCD, VII, 3; CCSL XLVII, 188; H I, 264.

31. The difference between Hobbes and Augustine is, of course, that the former accepts man's restless, never-ending search for satisfaction as natural and inevitable, while Augustine regards it as sinful folly, natural only to man in his fallen state. See Conclusion, pp. 234–36.

32. DCD, XVIII, 2; CCSL XLVIII, 593; H II, 218. See, too, *En. in Ps.*, VII, 16; CCSL XXXVIII, 47; S VIII, 26, and below, in this chapter, pp. 46–50 and 61–62; see, also, pp. 126 and 157–58.

33. *En. in Ps.*, LXIV, 9; CCSL XXXIX, 832; S VIII, 271.

34. *Ibid.*

35. "But the rich man is anxious with fears, pining with discontent, burning with covetousness, never secure, always uneasy, panting from the perpetual strife of his enemies, adding to his patrimony indeed by these miseries to an immense degree, and by these additions also heaping up most bitter cares." (DCD, IV, 3; CCSL XLVII, 100; H I, 138.) "Usually when we have them [mutable goods] we imagine that we do not love them, but when they begin to leave us we discover what manner of men we are. We have a thing without loving it when we can let it go without grieving." (*De Vera Religione,* XLVII, 92; PL XXXIV, 163; Burleigh, 273.)

36. *En. in Ps.*, LXIV, 9; CCSL XXXIX, 832; S VIII, 271.

37. *Ibid.*, CXXIII, 10; CCSL XL, 1833; S VIII, 600.

38. See *ibid.*, CVIII, 3; CCSL XL, 1586; S VIII, 537.

39. *Confess.*, IX, IV, 10; CSEL XXXIII, 204–5; Outler, 184.

40. See DCD, XIX, 15; CCSL XLVIII, 682; H II, 323–24, and *In Epist. Ioann.*, VIII, 6; PL XXXV, 2039; S VII, 508.

41. *De Doctr. Christ.*, I, XXIII, 23; PL XXXIV, 27; S II, 528. "Man has transgressed his proper limit: created higher than the beasts, he has let covetousness carry him away, so that he might be higher than other men. And that is pride." (*In Epist. Ioann.*, VIII, 8; PL XXV, 2040; Burnaby, 322.)

42. *De Trinitate,* XIII, XIII, 17; PL XLII, 1026–27; S III, 176.

43. *De Catechiz. Rudibus,* XIX, 31; PL XL, 333; S III, 303.

44. *En. in Ps.*, I, 1; CCSL XXXVIII, 1; S VIII, 1.

45. Hobbes, *Leviathan,* Part 1, Chap. XI; Blackwell edition, p. 64. The cause of this perpetual desire for power is that "a man cannot assure the power and means to live well, which he now has, without acquiring more." (*Ibid.*)

46. DCD, I, Preface; CCSL XLVII, 1; H I, 2.

47. See his reference to "that state which the first Romans founded

and increased by their virtues [*uirtutibus*]," and his statements that "although they did not have true devotion to the true God . . . they did preserve a certain characteristic uprightness [*quandam sui generis probitatem*], sufficient to found, increase, and preserve an earthly city. God showed in the rich and far-famed Roman Empire how much can be achieved by natural [more accurately, "civic"] virtues without true religion [*quantum ualerent ciuiles etiam sine uera religione uirtutes*]. . . ." (*Ep.* CXXXVIII, III, 17; CSEL XLIV, 144–45; FCL III, 50.) He also says that "the civic virtue" possessed by "men who have shown a Babylonian love for their earthly fatherland," "is not true virtue but resembles true virtue [*virtute civili, non vera, sed veri simili*]." (*Contra Julianum,* IV, III, 26; PL XLIV, 751; FC 35, 190.) See, too, *Contra Academicos,* III, XVII, 37; CSEL LXIII, 76; FC 1, 214. See, too, the statement that for His own reasons God "helped forward the Romans, *who were good according to a certain standard of an earthly state* [*Romanos secundum quandam formam terrenae ciuitatis bonos*], to the acquirement of the glory of so great an empire. . . ." (DCD, V, 19; CCSL XLVII, 155; H I, 216; italics added.) Yet he insists that the truly pious agree "that no one without true piety—that is, true worship of the true God—can have true virtue; and that it is not true virtue which is the slave of human praise," although earthly men "are more useful to the earthly city when they possess even that virtue than if they had not even that." (*Ibid.,* V, 19; CCSL XLVII, 155–56; H I, 216.) See, too, the comment that "although some suppose that virtues which have a reference only to themselves, and are desired only on their own account, are yet true and genuine virtues [*uerae atque honestae . . . uirtutes*], the fact is that even then they are inflated with pride, and are therefore to be reckoned vices rather than virtues." (*Ibid.,* XIX, 25; CCSL XLVIII, 696; H II, 341.) See, too, pp. 80–83 and pp. 139–42.

48. DCD, V, 12; CCSL XLVII, 142–43; H I, 198.

49. *Aeneid,* I, 279.

50. DCD, V, 12; CCSL XLVII, 144; H I, 200.

51. See *ibid.,* XVIII, 22; CCSL XLVIII, 612; H II, 241. See below, in this chapter, pp. 68–70.

52. *Ibid.,* V, 15; CCSL XLVII, 149; H I, 207.

53. *Ibid.,* V, 13; CCSL XLVII, 146–47; H I, 204. On the idea that the desire for glory and fame is a vice superior to other human vices, see Seneca's essay, "On the Shortness of Life," in Moses Hadas, tr.

and ed., *The Stoic Philosophy of Seneca* (Garden City, N.Y., Anchor Books, Doubleday & Co., Inc., 1958), pp. 47–73.

54. DCD, XV, 5; CCSL XLVIII, 457–58; H II, 54–55.

55. See Chap. V.   56. DCD, III, 14; CCSL XLVII, 77; H I, 107.

57. *Ibid.,* V, 19; CCSL XLVII, 155; H I, 215–16.

58. *Ibid.,* V, 16; CCSL XLVII, 149; H I, 208.

59. *Ibid.,* V, 17; CCSL XLVII, 150; H I, 209. "Now, what does it profit to acquire in this world any temporal and transitory thing whatsoever, be it money, or pleasure of the palate, or honor that consists in the praise of men? Are they not all wind and smoke? Do they not all pass by and flee away? Are they not all as a river rushing headlong into the sea? And woe to him who shall fall into it, for he shall be swept into the sea." (*In Ioann. Evangel.,* X, 6; CCSL XXXVI, 103; S VII, 71.)

60. *De Catechiz. Rudibus,* XVI, 24; PL XL, 329; S III, 300.

61. See DCD, V, 17–18; CCSL XLVII, 150–54; H I, 209–14.

62. See, e.g., DCD, VI, 9; CCSL XLVII, 179; H I, 249–50, and XIV, 18; CCSL XLVIII, 440–41; H II, 34, and XIV, 26; CCSL XLVIII, 449; H II, 45.

63. "You see, then, that there is a great difference between exhorting to virginity as the better of two good things, and forbidding to marry by denouncing the true purpose of marriage. . . ." (*Contra Faustum,* XXX, 6; CSEL XXV, 755; S IV, 330.) "The union, then, of male and female for the purpose of procreation is the natural good of marriage. But he makes a bad use of this good who uses it bestially, so that his intention is on the gratification of lust, instead of the desire of offspring." (*De Nupt. et Concup.,* I, IV, 5; CSEL XLII, 215; S V, 265.) See, too, *Contra Julianum,* IV, II, 12; PL XLIV, 742; FC 35, 175, where Augustine says that the married use well what celibates do better by not using.

64. See *De Nupt. et Concup.,* I, XV, 17; CSEL XLII, 229; S V, 270–71, and I, XVI, 18; CSEL XLII, 230–31; S V, 271.

65. See DCD, XIV, 23; CCSL XLVIII, 445; H II, 39.

66. *De Nupt. et Concup.,* I, VI, 7; CSEL XLII, 219; S V, 266.

67. See DCD, XIV, 23; CCSL XLVIII, 444–46; H II, 39–41.

68. ". . . we would that there should be no lusts, but we cannot hinder it. Whether we will or not, we have them; whether we will or not, they solicit, they allure, they sting, they disturb us, they will be rising. They are repressed, not yet extinguished. . . . As long then as we live here, my brethren, so it is; so is it with us even

who have grown old in this warfare, less mighty enemies it is true we have, but yet we have them. Our enemies are in a measure wearied out even now by age; but nevertheless, wearied though they be, they do not cease to harass by such excitements as they can the quiet of old age. Sharper is the fight of the young; we know it well, we have passed through it." (*Sermo* CXXVIII, 11; PL XXXVIII, 718–19; S VI, 494.)

69. "Marriage is not the cause of the sin which is transmitted in the natural birth, and atoned for in the new birth; but the voluntary transgression of the first man is the cause of original sin." (*De Nupt. et Concup.*, II, XXVI, 43; CSEL XLII, 297; S V, 300.)

70. The ardor of lust, present even in the lawful and honorable embrace of marriage, "is the carnal concupiscence, which, while it is no longer accounted sin in the regenerate, yet in no case happens to nature except from sin. It is the daughter of sin, as it were; and whenever it yields assent to the commission of shameful deeds, it becomes also the mother of many sins." (*Ibid.*, I, XXIV, 27; CSEL XLII, 240; S V, 275.) "We do not censure the honourable connection between husband and wife, because of the shame-causing lust of bodies. . . . [W]e have two distinct facts . . . the good of that laudable union of the sexes for the purpose of generating children; and the evil of that shameful lust, *in consequence of which* the offspring must be regenerated in order to escape condemnation." (*Ibid.*, II, XXI, 36; CSEL XLII, 290; S V, 297; italics added.)

71. *Confess.*, I, VI, 8; CSEL XXXIII, 7; author's translation.

72. *Ibid.*, I, VII, 11; CSEL XXXIII, 9–10; Outler, 37.   73. *Ibid.*

74. See *In Ioann. Evangel.*, XV, 21; CCSL XXXVI, 158–59; S VII, 104.

75. *Confess.*, I, IX, 15; CSEL XXXIII, 14; Outler, 39–40. See, too, DCD, XXII, 22; CCSL XLVIII, 843; H II, 519, where he notes that "parents rarely wish anything useful to be taught" to their children. In recalling the deceptions and dishonesty that he practiced as a boy, he says: "Moreover, in this kind of play, I often sought dishonest victories, being myself conquered by the vain desire for pre-eminence. And *what was I so unwilling to endure, and what was it that I censured so violently when I caught anyone, except the very things I did to others?* And, when I was myself detected and censured, I preferred to quarrel rather than yield. Is this the innocence of childhood? It is not, O Lord, it is not. I entreat thy mercy, O my God, for *these same sins as we grow older are transferred from tutors and masters; they pass from nuts and balls and sparrows, to magistrates*

and kings, to gold and lands and slaves, just as the rod is succeeded by more severe chastisements." (*Confess.,* I, XIX, 30; CSEL XXXIII, 27–28; Outler, 48–49; italics added.)

76. *En. in Ps.,* CXXXVI, 21; CCSL XL, 1977; S VIII, 632.

77. *Ibid.,* CXXVII, 15; CCSL XL, 1878; S VIII, 610.

78. *Confess.,* X, VIII–XXVI; CSEL XXXIII, 234–55; Outler, 208–24.

79. See *De Trinitate,* esp. Books X and XIII; PL XLII, 971–84 and 1013–36; S III, 134–43 and 166–82.

80. *Sermo* LXXX, 8; PL XXXVIII, 498; S VI, 352.

81. See DCD, XI, 23; CCSL XLVIII, 341–42; H I, 463–64.

82. *Ibid.,* XX, 1; CCSL XLVIII, 699; H II, 346.

83. See *ibid.,* XIX, 4; CCSL XLVIII, 668–69; H II, 307, *En. in Ps.,* CXXXVII, 12; CCSL XL, 1986; S VIII, 634–35, and *Ep.* CLV, IV, 16; CSEL XLIV, 446–47; FCL III, 317.

84. See DCD, XVII, 20; CCSL XLVIII, 589; H II, 212, and XIX, 20; CCSL XLVIII, 687; H II, 330.

85. *Ibid.,* XXII, 22; CCSL XLVIII, 845; H II, 520.

86. See *Sermo* LXXXI, 7; PL XXXVIII, 503–4; S VI, 355–56.

87. *En. in Ps.,* LXXXV, 24; CCSL XXXIX, 1196; S VIII, 418. We find "that the bad generally have great power against the good, and that the bad often oppress the good; that the wicked exult, while the good suffer; the evil are proud, while the good are humbled." (*Ibid.,* XCIII, 1; CCSL XXXIX, 1300; S VIII, 459.) "It must needs be that all men, so long as they are mortal, are also miserable. . . ." (DCD, IX, 15; CCSL XLVII, 262; H I, 369.)

88. *Sermo* LXXXIV, 2; PL XXXVIII, 520; S VI, 366.

89. DCD, XXII, 22; CCSL XLVIII, 842; H II, 518; italics added. See, too, *De Lib. Arbit.,* III, XVIII, 52, 177–79; CSEL LXXIV, 132–33; Burleigh, 201–2. See Chap. III, pp. 93–94, and Chap. IV, pp. 134–37.

90. *Enchiridion,* VII, 21; PL XL, 243; Outler, 352.

91. See DCD, XXII, 22; CCSL XLVIII, 843; H II, 519.

92. *Sermo* LVIII, 9; PL XXXVIII, 398; S VI, 287.

93. See DCD, XIX, 5; CCSL XLVIII, 669–70; H II, 307–9. See Chap. IV.

94. See DCD, XXII, 22; CCSL XLVIII, 844; H II, 520.

95. *Ibid.,* XXII, 22; CCSL XLVIII, 844; H II, 519–20.

96. See *ibid.,* XIX, 4; CCSL XLVIII, 665–66; H II, 303–4, and XIX, 4; CCSL XLVIII, 668; H II, 307.

97. See *ibid.,* XIX, 4; CCSL XLVIII, 667–68; H II, 306.

98. "Meantime the cupidities exercise their dominion tyrannically and disturb the man's whole mind and life with varying and contrary tempests, fear on one side, longing on the other; here anxiety, there vain and false rejoicing; here torture because something loved has been lost, there eagerness to obtain what it does not possess; here grief for injury suffered, there incitements to seek revenge. Wherever it turns it can be restricted by avarice, wasted by luxury, bound by ambition, inflated by pride, tortured by envy, enveloped in sloth, excited by wantonness, afflicted by subjection, suffering all the other countless emotions which inhabit and trouble the realm of lust." (*De Lib. Arbit.*, I, XI, 22, 78; CSEL LXXIV, 23; Burleigh, 126.)

99. *In Ioann. Evangel.*, XC, 2; CCSL XXXVI, 552; S VII, 360. "Every man in this life is a foreigner [*peregrinus*]: in which life ye see that with flesh we are covered round, through which flesh the heart cannot be seen. . . . [I]n this sojourning of fleshly life every one carrieth his own heart, and every heart to every other heart is shut." (*En. in Ps.*, LV, 9; CCSL XXXIX, 683–84; S VIII, 221.) "Men may speak, may be seen by the operations of their members, may be heard speaking in conversation: but whose thought is penetrated, whose heart seen into? What he is inwardly engaged on, what he is inwardly capable of, what he is inwardly doing or what purposing, what he is inwardly wishing to happen, or not to happen, who shall comprehend?" (*Ibid.*, XLI, 13; CCSL XXXVIII, 470; S VIII, 136.)

100. *In Ioann. Evangel.*, XC, 2; CCSL XXXVI, 552; S VII, 360.

101. "Whatever, therefore, be our circumstances in this world, there is nothing truly enjoyable without a friend. But how rarely is one found in this life about whose spirit and behaviour as a true friend there may be perfect confidence! For no one is known to another so intimately as he is known to himself, and yet no one is so well known even to himself that he can be sure as to his own conduct on the morrow. . . ." (*Ep.* CXXX, II, 4; CSEL XLIV, 44; S I, 460–61.)

102. DCD, XIX, 8; CCSL XLVIII, 672; H II, 311–12.   103. *Ibid.*

104. *Ibid.*, XXII, 24; CCSL XLVIII, 851; H II, 528–29. See, too, *ibid.*, XXI, 24; CCSL XLVIII, 791; H II, 454, and XXII, 21; CCSL XLVIII, 841–42; H II, 517.

105. *En. in Ps.*, XXXVIII, 7; CCSL XXXVIII, 409; S VIII, 114.

106. *Sermo* LXXXIV, 2; PL XXXVIII, 520; S VI, 366.

107. *En. in Ps.*, XXXVIII, 19; CCSL XXXVIII, 420; S VIII, 118;

see the rest of the passage. See, too, *De Trinitate,* IV, XII, 15; PL XLII, 898; S III, 77.

108. See *Sermo* LXXXIV, 1; PL XXXVIII, 519; S VI, 365–66.

109. *Ep.* CXXVII, 4; CSEL XLIV, 23; FCL II, 359.

110. DCD, XIV, 25; CCSL XLVIII, 448; H II, 43.

111. *Ibid.,* XIII, 10; CCSL XLVIII, 392; H I, 530.

112. *Ibid.,* XXI, 14; CCSL XLVIII, 780; H II, 440. "A hard condition is the life of man. What else is it to be born, but to enter on a life of toil? Of our toil that is to be, the infant's very cry is witness. From this cup of sorrow no one may be excused." (*Sermo* LX, 2; PL XXXVIII, 402–3; S VI, 290.)

113. Compare, e.g., some of the writings of St. Jerome, as discussed in Samuel Dill, *Roman Society in the Last Century of the Western Empire* (New York, Meridian Books, Inc., 1958), pp. 123–30.

114. "Did not thy Lord tell thee, the world shall be laid waste? Did not thy Lord tell thee, the world shall fail?" (*Sermo* LXXXI, 8; PL XXXVIII, 504; S VI, 356.) See, too, below, in this chapter, pp. 71–72 and 74–76.

115. DCD, XVI, 32; CCSL XLVIII, 536; H II, 147.

116. *En. in Ps.,* LX, 3; CCSL XXXIX, 766; S VIII, 249. "For every temptation is a test, and the outcome of every test has its own consequences. Because a man is often unknown even to himself, and does not know what he can or cannot bear, and sometimes presumes that he can bear what in fact he cannot, and sometimes despairs of being able to bear what in fact he can, therefore temptation comes like an interrogation, and the man discovers himself, since he had kept himself in the dark but he had not kept his Maker in the dark." (*Ibid.,* LV, 2; CCSL XXXIX, 678; author's translation.) See, too, Augustine's argument that the tribulations that men face in this world are punishments for the wicked and exercises for the righteous. "Tribulation comes; it will be as ye choose it, either an exercise, or a condemnation. Such as it shall find you to be, will it be." (*Sermo* LXXXI, 7; PL XXXVIII, 503; S VI, 356.) The servants of Christ "will not refuse the discipline of this temporal life, in which they are schooled for life eternal; nor will they lament their experience of it, for the good things of earth they use as pilgrims who are not detained by them, and its ills either prove or improve them." (DCD, I, 29; CCSL XLVII, 30; H I, 41.) Even heresies that seek to seduce men into error are useful, since they arouse the faithful to a more diligent effort to understand difficult questions and to discover the

truth. "For with less carefulness would truth be sought out, if it had not lying adversaries." (*Sermo* LI, VII, 11; PL XXXVIII, 339; S VI, 249.) "For while the hot restlessness of heretics stirs questions about many articles of the catholic faith, the necessity of defending them forces us both to investigate them more accurately, to understand them more clearly, and to proclaim them more earnestly; and the question mooted by an adversary becomes the occasion of instruction." (DCD, XVI, 2; CCSL XLVIII, 499; H II, 105.) See, too, *En. in Ps.*, LIV, 22; CCSL XXXIX, 672–73; S VIII, 217. Despite great differences in belief and attitude, one is reminded of John Stuart Mill's argument that error and controversy are necessary for the discovery and understanding of truth.

117. *En. in Ps.*, CX, 2; CCSL XL, 1622; S VIII, 545.

118. *Sermo* CXXV, 5; PL XXXVIII, 692–93; S VI, 478.

119. *Contra Faustum*, XXII, 78; CSEL XXV, 678; S IV, 303. "[A]s the judgments of God and the movements of man's will contain the hidden reason why the same prosperous circumstances which some make a right use of are the ruin of others, and the same afflictions under which some give way are profitable to others, and since the whole mortal life of man upon earth is a trial, who can tell whether it may be good or bad in any particular case—in time of peace, to reign or to serve, or to be at ease or to die—or in time of war, to command or to fight, or to conquer or to be killed? At the same time, it remains true, that whatever is good is so by the divine blessing, and whatever is bad is so by the divine judgment." (*Contra Faustum*, XXII, 78; CSEL XXV, 679–80; S IV, 303.)

120. See *ibid.*, XXII, 76; CSEL XXV, 674; S IV, 301, *De Consensu Evangel.*, I, XII, 18–19; CSEL XLIII, 17–18; S VI, 84–85, and DCD, IV, 33; CCSL XLVII, 126; H I, 175, and V, 1; CCSL XLVII, 128; H I, 177–78, and V, 11; CCSL XLVII, 142; H I, 198, and V, 26; CCSL XLVII, 162–63; H I, 226.

121. See pp. 143–50.

122. After each Biblical citation, the RSV translation of the verse in question is given: *Rom.* xiii, 1 ("For there is no authority except from God"), *Job* xxxiv, 30 ("That a godless man should not reign, that he should not ensnare the people"), *Prov.* viii, 15 ("By me kings reign, and rulers decree what is just"), and *Hos.* xiii, 11 ("I have given you kings in my anger, and I have taken them away in my wrath").

123. See *De Natura Boni*, 32; CSEL XXV, 870–71; S IV, 358.

124. See p. 53.

125. DCD, V, 19; CCSL XLVII, 155; H I, 216.

126. See *ibid.*, V, 21; CCSL XLVII, 157–58; H I, 218–19, and V, 25; CCSL XLVII, 160–61; H I, 223–24.

127. See pp. 66–67, and *Ep.* CXI, 2–3; CSEL XXXIV (2), 644–47; S I, 433–34.

128. *De Corrept. et Gratia,* XIV, 45; PL XLIV, 943–44; S V, 489–90. See, too, *De Gratia et Lib. Arbit.,* XXI, 42; PL XLIV, 907–8; S V, 462.

129. See *Sermo* CV, 13; PL XXXVIII, 624–25; S VI, 434–35, and DCD, V, 23; CCSL XLVII, 159; H I, 221–22.

130. See *Contra Faustum,* XXII, 20; CSEL XXV, 609; S IV, 279.

131. *En. in Ps.,* XCI, 8; CCSL XXXIX, 1285; S VIII, 454.

132. DCD, XI, 18; CCSL XLVIII, 337; H I, 457. See, also, *ibid.,* XI, 22; CCSL XLVIII, 340–41; H I, 461–62, and XI, 23; CCSL XLVIII, 342; H I, 464.

133. See pp. 14–15.

134. For Augustine's opposition to the theory of recurring cycles in history, see DCD, XII, 14; CCSL XLVIII, 368–69; H I, 498–99, and XII, 20–21; CCSL XLVIII, 376–77 and 379; H I, 509–10 and 513. Theodor E. Mommsen, in his interesting article, "St. Augustine and the Christian Idea of Progress," *Journal of the History of Ideas,* XII, No. 3 (June 1951), maintains that even a Christian thinker like Origen shared the cyclical theory, although in modified form, and that Augustine's argument was directed against him as well as against the pagan philosophers (see pp. 354–55). For an argument that Augustine did view secular history, in which he was not particularly interested, as essentially repetitive, see Hannah Arendt's essay on "The Concept of History," in *Between Past and Future* (New York, The Viking Press, 1961), esp. pp. 65–66.

135. See DCD, XII, 11; CCSL XLVIII, 365; H I, 494.

136. *De Trinitate,* IV, 4, 7; PL XLII, 892; S III, 73. See, also, *In Ioann. Evangel.,* IX, 6; CCSL XXXVI, 93; S VII, 65, DCD, XXII, 30; CCSL XLVIII, 865; H II, 544, and *De Div. Quaest. 83,* LVIII, 2; PL XL, 43.

137. *In Ioann. Evangel.,* XXV, 5; CCSL XXXVI, 250; S VII, 162. Mommsen contrasts Augustine's philosophy of history with the views of the Christian optimists, such as Eusebius and Ambrose, who believed in continuous progress in this world, especially after the establishment of Christianity as the official religion of the Empire ("St. Augustine and the Christian Idea of Progress," pp. 356–74).

138. See DCD, XX, 8; CCSL XLVIII, 713; H II, 361.

139. See *ibid.,* XXI, 26; CCSL XLVIII, 799; H II, 463–64, and *En. in Ps.,* CIII (3), 24; CCSL XL, 1520; S VIII, 516.

140. "For these latter will say: 'Peace and security,' so that sudden destruction will come upon them and the coming of the Lord will overtake them as a thief in the night. . . ." (*Ep.* CXCIX, XI, 37; CSEL LVII, 276; FCL IV, 385–86.)

141. See DCD, XX, 29; CCSL XLVIII, 752; H II, 405, and XX, 30; CCSL XLVIII, 758; H II, 411.

142. See *ibid.,* XVIII, 52–53; CCSL XLVIII, 652; H II, 288.

143. "Be we then willingly ignorant of that which the Lord would not have us know. . . ." (*En. in Ps.,* VI, 2; CCSL XXXVIII, 27; S VIII, 15.)

144. See his warning against falling "into a panic over present happenings as if they were the ultimate and extreme of all things," so that "we may not be laughed at by those who have read of more and worse things in the history of the world." (*Ep.* CXCIX, XI, 39; CSEL LVII, 277–78; FCL IV, 387.)

145. *Acts* i, 7 (AV).

146. See *Ep.* CXCIX, XIII, 54; CSEL LVII, 292; FCL IV, 400–401.

147. *Ibid.,* V, 15; CSEL LVII, 255; FCL IV, 367.

148. *Ibid.,* XI, 37; CSEL LVII, 275–76; FCL IV, 385–86.

149. See DCD, IV, 7; CCSL XLVII, 104; H I, 143.

150. *Sermo* LXXXI, 9; PL XXXVIII, 505; S VI, 356.

151. *Ibid.,* PL XXXVIII, 505; S VI, 357.

152. See *Sermo* CV, 9; PL XXXVIII, 622; S VI, 433, and *ibid.,* 11; PL XXXVIII, 623; S VI, 433–34.

153. *Sermo* LXXXI, 9; PL XXXVIII, 505; S VI, 357.

154. See DCD, I, 33; CCSL XLVII, 32; H I, 45, and V, 23; CCSL XLVII, 159; H I, 222, and *Sermo* CV, 12; PL XXXVIII, 623–24; S VI, 434.

155. *Sermo* CV, 8; PL XXXVIII, 622; S VI, 432–33. "Thou didst believe in Christ: why didst thou believe? What did He promise thee? If it was the happiness of this world that Christ promised thee, then murmur against Christ; yes! murmur against Him, when thou seest the wicked flourishing. What of happiness did He promise? What, save in the Resurrection of the Dead? But what in this life? That which was His portion." (*En. in Ps.,* XXXVI [1], 9; CCSL XXXVIII, 343; S VIII, 93.) "If ye are Christians, look for tribulations in this world; look not for more peaceful and better times." (*Ibid.,* XCVI, 20; CCSL XXXIX, 1371; S VIII, 480.)

156. *Sermo* LXXX, 8; PL XXXVIII, 498; S VI, 352.

157. *Ep.* CXLV, 2; CSEL XLIV, 267; S I, 495. See, too, *En. in Ps.,* LXVIII (1), 1; CCSL XXXIX, 901; S VIII, 299, where he says that felicity in human affairs is more to be feared than misery, since "felicity doth corrupt the soul with a perverse security, and giveth place for the Devil the Tempter. . . ."

158. See the letter of Cyprian to the proconsul of Africa, Demetrianus, in which he says that "the world itself announces its approaching end by its failing powers." (Quoted in Rebecca West, *St. Augustine* [New York, D. Appleton and Co., 1933], pp. 1–3.)

159. DCD, II, 18; CCSL XLVII, 50; H I, 71.

160. *Sermo* LXXXI, 8; PL XXXVIII, 504–5; S VI, 356.

161. *Ep.* CXXVII, 1; CSEL XLIV, 20; FCL II, 357.

162. *Ep.* CXXXVII, IV, 16; CSEL XLIV, 120; S I, 480.

163. *Ep.* CXXII, 2; CSEL XXXIV (2), 743–44; S I, 451. See, too, *Sermo* LX, 7; PL XXXVIII, 405–6; S VI, 292.

164. See *Ep.* CCXX, 8; CSEL LVII, 437; S I, 575.

165. *Ep.* CCXXVIII, 2; CSEL LVII, 485–86; S I, 577.

166. See Joseph McCabe, *Saint Augustine and His Age* (London, Duckworth and Co., 1902), pp. 428–29.

NOTES TO CHAPTER III

1. Compare the anticipations in the New Testament of the idea of the two cities, e.g., *Gal.* iv, 21–31; *Heb.* xi, 10 and 13–16; xii, 22, and xiii, 14; *Eph.* ii, 11–22; *Phil.* iii, 17–21; 1 *John* ii, 15–17; *Rev.* iii, 12, and xxi, 2 and 10.

2. See pp. 95–97, and Chap. IV.

3. *De Bono Coniugali,* I, 1; CSEL XLI, 187; S III, 399.

4. *Ibid.* "And therefore God created only one single man . . . that by this means the unity of society and the bond of concord might be more effectually commended to him, men being bound together not only by similarity of nature, but by family affection." (DCD, XII, 22; CCSL XLVIII, 380; H I, 514.)

5. *En. in Ps.,* LIV, 9; CCSL XXXIX, 663; S VIII, 212.

6. *Ep.* CXXX, VI, 13; CSEL XLIV, 55; S I, 463. "For, if money is a reason which makes men partners, much more is their common nature a reason to draw them together, not for business purposes but because of their birth. . . . Thus, the kinship of human souls stirs the feeling of all so naturally that every man feels himself a neighbor of every other man." (*Ep.* CLV, IV, 14; CSEL XLIV, 444–45; FCL III, 315–16.)

7. See pp. 83–84.

8. DCD, XIX, 12; CCSL XLVIII, 677; H II, 317–18 (*Quanto magis homo fertur quodam modo naturae suae legibus ad ineundam societatem pacemque cum hominibus, quantum in ipso est, omnibus obtenendam*). See pp. 101–2.

9. *Matthew* xxii, 37–39 (RSV).   10. *Matthew* xxii, 40 (RSV).

11. See pp. 50–53.   12. See pp. 16–18.

13. DCD, XIV, 13; CCSL XLVIII, 435; H II, 27.

14. "For it happens in a surprising way that the mind of man is puffed up more by false humility than it would be by open pride." (*Ep.* CXLIX, II, 28; CSEL XLIV, 374; FCL III, 261.) See Chap. I, p. 20.

15. *Ep.* CCXI, 6; CSEL LVII, 360–61; S I, 565. See, too, DCD, I, 28; CCSL XLVII, 28–29; H I, 39–40, and XXII, 23; CCSL XLVIII, 845–46; H II, 521–22.

16. *Ep.* CXVIII, III, 22; CSEL XXXIV (2), 685; S I, 446. ". . . unless humility precede, accompany, and follow every good action which we perform, being at once the object which we keep before our eyes, the support to which we cling, and the monitor by which we are restrained, pride wrests wholly from our hand any good work on which we are congratulating ourselves." (*Ibid.*)

17. "Nevertheless, they who restrain baser lusts, not by the power of the Holy Spirit obtained by the faith of piety, or by the love of intelligible beauty, but by desire of human praise, or, at all events, restrain them better by the love of such praise, are not indeed yet holy, but only less base." (DCD, V, 13; CCSL XLVII, 147; H I, 204.) See, too, *ibid.*, XIX, 25; CCSL XLVIII, 696; H II, 341, and *Contra Duas Epist. Pelag.*, III, V, 14; CSEL LX, 502–3; S V, 408–9, where Augustine states that the man who has not received the gift of faith will be condemned even if his actions seem to be more virtuous than those of a man who has the faith which works by love.

18. *En. in Ps.*, CXVIII (12), 2; CCSL XL, 1701; S VIII, 566.

19. "Sometimes, indeed, patent [*apertissima*] vices are overcome by other and hidden vices [*occultis uitiis*], which are reckoned virtues [*quae putantur esse uirtutes*], though pride and a kind of ruinous self-sufficiency are their informing principles. Accordingly, vices are then only to be considered overcome when they are conquered by the love of God, which God Himself alone gives, and which He gives only through the Mediator between God and men, the man Christ Jesus. . . ." (DCD, XXI, 16; CCSL XLVIII, 782; H II, 443.)

20. *In Ioann. Evangel.,* LXXXIII, 3; CCSL XXXVI, 536; S VII, 349.

21. *Ep.* CXLV, 4; CSEL XLIV, 269; S I, 496. "All the divine precepts, are, therefore, referred back to *love.* . . . Thus every commandment harks back to love. For whatever one does either in fear of punishment or from some carnal impulse, so that it does not measure up to the standard of love which the Holy Spirit sheds abroad in our hearts—whatever it is, it is not yet done as it should be, although it may seem to be." (*Enchiridion,* XXXII, 121; PL XL, 288; Outler, 411.)

22. See below, in this chapter, pp. 95–98 and 102–4, and Chap. IV, pp. 134–42.

23. The four primary virtues are, of course, taken over by Christian writers from Platonic and Stoic moral philosophy. "For if God is man's chief good . . . it clearly follows, since to seek the chief good is to live well, that to live well is nothing else but to love God with all the heart, with all the soul, with all the mind; and, as arising from this, that this love must be preserved entire and incorrupt, which is the part of temperance; that it give way before no troubles, which is the part of fortitude; that it serve no other, which is the part of justice; that it be watchful in its inspection of things lest craft or fraud steal in, which is the part of prudence. This is the one perfection of man, by which alone he can succeed in attaining to the purity of truth." (*De Mor. Eccl. Cath.,* XXV, 46; PL XXXII, 1330–31; S IV, 54.) "For who can truly rejoice who loves not good as the source of his joy? Who can have true peace, if he have it not with one whom he truly loves? Who can be long-enduring through persevering continuance in good, save through fervent love? Who can be kind, if he loves not the person he is aiding? Who can be good, if he is not made so by loving? Who can be sound in the faith, without that faith which worketh by love? Whose meekness can be beneficial in character, if not regulated by love? And who will abstain from that which is debasing, if he love not that which dignifies?" (*In Ioann. Evangel.,* LXXXVII, 1; CCSL XXXVI, 544; S VII, 354.)

24. *De Mor. Eccl. Cath.,* XV, 25; PL XXXII, 1322; S IV, 48. See, too, *De Div. Quaest. 83,* LXI, 4; PL XL, 51, where justice is defined as "love of God and of one's neighbor [*dilectio Dei et proximi*]." "He who has and loves the good will, and resists what is hostile to it, cannot will any evil to anybody. It follows that he injures nobody,

which must mean simply that he gives to everyone his due. This, I said, was the function of justice, and I dare say you remember you agreed." (*De Lib. Arbit.*, I, XIII, 27, 93; CSEL LXXIV, 28; Burleigh, 128–29.) See, too, DCD, XIX, 4; CCSL XLVIII, 666; H II, 304, and *De Trinitate*, VIII, VI, 9; PL XLII, 955; Burnaby, 48–49.

25. *En. in Ps.*, LXXXIII, 11; CCSL XXXIX, 1157–58; S VIII, 403.

26. See *In Ioann. Evangel.*, XXXII, 4; CCSL XXXVI, 302; S VII, 194.

27. *De Doctr. Christ.*, I, XXVIII, 29; PL XXXIV, 30; S II, 530.

28. See *En. in Ps.*, XXXIII (2), 6; CCSL XXXVIII, 285–86; S VIII, 74.

29. See *ibid.*, V, 10; CCSL XXXVIII, 24; S VIII, 13–14.

30. *Sermo* LVI, 14; PL XXXVIII, 383–84; S VI, 278.

31. *En. in Ps.*, LXXII, 18; CCSL XXXIX, 996; S VIII, 338.

32. *Ep.* CLI, 10; CSEL XLIV, 390; S I, 508. Anyone who could behold the inward parts of evil men, their torturing consciences, and "their souls racked with such mighty perturbations of desires and fears, would see them to be miserable even when they are called happy." (*En. in Ps.*, LXXII, 11; CCSL XXXIX, 993; S VIII, 336.)

33. *Ibid.*, C, 4; CCSL XXXIX, 1410; S VIII, 492.

34. *Ep.* XCI, 3; CSEL XXXIV (2), 429; S I, 377. Note his reply to the charge that Christianity undermines public morality by promising men pardon for all their sins when they are converted. The conclusion is striking: "Now therefore live well. Tomorrow, he replieth, I will live well. God hath promised the pardon; no one promised thee to-morrow." (*En. in Ps.*, CI [1], 10; CCSL XL, 1434; S VIII, 498.)

35. "Since there is a law in man's reason, written by nature in the heart of everyone who enjoys the use of free will [*lex est etiam in ratione hominis, qui iam utitur arbitrio libertatis, naturaliter in corde conscripta*], and this law suggests that a man do no evil to another which he would not wish to suffer himself, therefore, according to this law all are transgressors, even those who have not received the law given by Moses. . . ." (*Ep.* CLVII, 15; CSEL XLIV, 463; FCL III, 331.) See, too, *De Div. Quaest. 83*, LIII, 2; PL XL, 36, where he speaks of the "natural law" (*naturalis lex*) which is "transcribed upon the rational soul [*quasi transcripta . . . in animam rationalem*]," and *De Spiritu et Littera*, XXVIII, 48; CSEL LX, 203; Burnaby, 231–32, where in referring to the Jews to whom the written law or Ten Commandments were given he says, "there was in them that natural impulse [*uis illa naturae inerat eis*] which gives the rational

creature both a certain awareness of what is lawful and a certain power of doing it."

36. *In Ioann. Evangel.*, XLIX, 12; CCSL XXXVI, 426; S VII, 274 (*Quod tibi non uis fieri, alii ne feceris*). See, too, *De Ordine,* II, VIII, 25; CSEL LXIII, 164; FC 1, 302, *De Sermone Domini,* II, IX, 32; PL XXXIV, 1283; S VI, 44, and *Confess.,* I, XVIII, 29; CSEL XXXIII, 26; Outler, 48. Note that Hobbes, too, uses the negative version of the Golden Rule when he states the essential meaning of the laws of nature; see *Leviathan,* Part 1, Chap. XV, Blackwell ed., p. 103.

37. *In Ioann. Evangel.*, XLIX, 12; CCSL XXXVI, 426; S VII, 274 (*Quod non uis pati, facere noli*).

38. *En. in Ps.*, LVII, 1; CCSL XXXIX, 708; S VIII, 229 (*Quod tibi non uis fieri, ne facias alteri*).

39. *Confess.,* II, IV, 9; CSEL XXXIII, 35; Outler, 54. See, too: "For to what unjust man is it not an easy thing to speak justice? or what man if questioned about justice, when he hath not a cause, would not easily answer what is just?" (*En. in Ps.*, LVII, 1; CCSL XXXIX, 708; S VIII, 229.)

40. See pp. 92–94.

41. See *In Ioann. Evangel.*, XLIX, 12; CCSL XXXVI, 426; S VII, 274.

42. "But lest men should complain that something had been wanting for them, there hath been written also in tables that which in their hearts they read not. For it was not that they had it not written, but read it they would not." (*En. in Ps.*, LVII, 1; CCSL XXXIX, 708; S VIII, 229–30.)

43. See *Ep.* CLVII, 15; CSEL XLIV, 463; FCL III, 332.

44. *En. in Ps.*, LVII, 1; CCSL XXXIX, 708; S VIII, 230 (*Quod tibi non uis fieri, noli alteri facere*).

45. *Ibid.*   46. See above, note 35.

47. See *Sermo* LXXXI, 2; PL XXXVIII, 500; S VI, 353. There is also a slightly different use of the term "eternal law" (*lex aeterna*) in Augustine which is somewhat closer to the meaning given to it by St. Thomas; see, e.g., "And the eternal law is the divine order or will of God, which requires the preservation of natural order, and forbids the breach of it [*lex uero aeterna est ratio diuina uel uoluntas dei ordinem naturalem conseruari iubens, perturbari uetans*]." (*Contra Faustum,* XXII, 27; CSEL XXV, 621; S IV, 283.) See Alois Schubert, *Augustins Lex-aeterna-Lehre nach Inhalt und Quellen*

(*Beiträge zur Geschichte der Philosophie des Mittelalters* [Münster, Aschendorff, 1924], XXIV, 2).

48. *De Trinitate,* XIV, XV, 21; PL XLII, 1052; S III, 194–95. The section that precedes the quotation given in the text is worth noting: "And it [the mind] remembers the Lord its God. . . . And He is whole everywhere. And hence it both lives, and is moved, and is in Him; and so it can remember Him. . . . But it is reminded, that it may be turned to God, as though to that light by which it was in some way touched, even when turned away from Him. For hence it is that even the ungodly think of eternity, and rightly blame and rightly praise many things in the morals of men. And by what rules [*regulis*] do they thus judge, except by those wherein they see how men ought to live, even though they themselves do not so live? And where do they see these rules? For they do not see them in their own [moral] nature; since no doubt these things are to be seen by the mind, and their minds are confessedly changeable, but these rules are seen as unchangeable by him who can see them at all; nor yet in the character [*habitus*] of their own mind, since these rules are rules of righteousness [*justitiae*], and their minds are confessedly unrighteous [*injustas*]." See, too, *ibid.,* VIII, VI, 9; PL XLII, 953–56; Burnaby, 46–50. Righteousness or justice is a beauty of the soul which is not visible to the outward eye. "Whence then can a man not yet righteous learn the meaning of the word, and through loving the righteous become righteous himself? . . . When I say, and say with knowledge, that 'the righteous soul is that which by rational principle in life and conduct assigns to each his own' [definition given by Cicero, *De Finibus,* V, 33] . . . I perceive something *present,* perceive it in myself, though I am not myself what I perceive. . . . But then what *is* present to the soul when it sees and defines the righteous soul, and sees it entirely in itself though itself is not righteous? Our answer is, that what it sees is an *inward truth* present to the soul that has the power to contemplate it. Not all have the power; and those that have are not all themselves what they contemplate—not all themselves righteous souls, though they can see and define the righteous soul." (*Ibid.,* VIII, VI, 9; PL XLII, 954–55; Burnaby, 48–49.) See, too, p. 96.

The two quotations from the *De Trinitate* given in the preceding paragraph make plain the clear parallel that exists between Augustine's theory of moral judgment and his theory of knowledge or intellectual judgment. The norms in terms of which even sinful men make moral judgments, judgments about what is good and bad in human actions, are not to be discovered in the nature of the human mind, for the norms are changeless while the mind is mutable, nor in the characteristic functioning [*habitus*] of the mind, for the norms are norms of justice or righteousness while men's minds are clearly unjust and unrighteous. The mind that sees these norms or principles within itself sees "an inward truth," the light of God's eternal truth from which even the sinful soul is not completely cut off. The mind is illumined by a light that is outside itself, that is, by the Truth which is God ("the true Light which lighteth every man that cometh into the world" [*John* i, 9; AV]), and so God is the source of the norms of righteousness that the mind discovers in itself, even in its sinful, depraved state.

Similarly, the mind, in order to reach any understanding of truth, theoretical or practical, any knowledge of the principles of reason, and, thus, of the world, no matter how incomplete such knowledge and understanding may be, must be enlightened or illuminated by the "higher light," the Truth or Logos itself, the Son of God. This epistemological doctrine, according to which the first principles of human knowledge have their source in the unchanging truth of God, whence they pass over to the mind of man "not by transference but by impression," is often described by the term "illuminationism." Gilson says of the "Augustinian doctrine of divine illumination" that it supposes that "comme le soleil est la source de la lumière corporelle qui rend visibles les choses, Dieu soit la source de la lumière spirituelle qui rend les sciences intelligibles à la pensée. Dieu est donc à notre pensée ce que le soleil est à notre vue; comme le soleil est source de la lumière, Dieu est source de la vérité." (Gilson, *Introduction à l'étude,* p. 103), see the whole section, pp. 103–30. See also Charles Boyer, *L'idée de vérité dans la philosophie de saint Augustin* (Paris, G. Beauchesne, 1921), and Regis Jolivet, *Dieu soleil des esprits, la doctrine augustinienne de l'illumination* (Paris, Desclée de Brouwer, 1934), and Johannes Hessen, *Die Begründung der Erkenntnis nach dem hl. Augustinus* (*Beiträge zur Geschichte der Philosophie des Mittelalters* [Münster, Aschendorff, 1916], XIX, 2). The basic source of the doctrine and of the metaphor is obviously Plato's analogy between the sun and The Good or Form of Forms, which renders intelligible the whole realm of Forms or Ideas.

Following Plato and Aristotle, Augustine says that when human life is well ordered, the soul rules the body, the understanding or reason, the highest part of the soul, rules the soul, and contemplative reason is superior to practical reason (see *Contra Faustum,* XXII,

27; CSEL XXV, 621; S IV, 283). However, the distinctly Christian element appears when he says that the mind or reason is not itself divine but requires illumination by God's Truth. Those men who order all the motions of their souls and subject them to reason "become a kingdom of God: in which all things are so arranged, that that which is chief and pre-eminent in man rules without resistance over the other elements, which are common to us with the beasts; and that very element which is pre-eminent in man, i.e., mind and reason, is brought under subjection to something better still, which is the truth itself, the only-begotten Son of God. For a man is not able to rule over things which are inferior, unless he subjects himself to what is superior." (*De Sermone Domini*, I, II, 9; PL XXXIV, 1233; S VI, 5; see, too, *In Ioann. Evangel.*, XV, 19; CCSL XXXVI, 157–58; S VII, 103–4, and XV, 22; CCSL XXXVI, 159; S VII, 105.)

No creature, angelic or human, shines with his own light; each receives whatever truth or light he possesses from Christ, the one true Light. It is this gift of reason or understanding that distinguishes man from the beasts, and it is the mind and reason, or "the heart within," capable of being illuminated by God's Light and God's Truth, which is "the image of God" in man; by it we discern truth from falsehood and distinguish right from wrong (see *En. in Ps.*, XLII, 6; CCSL XXXVIII, 479; S VIII, 140). "Return to thy heart; see there what, it may be, thou canst perceive of God, for in it is the image of God. In the inner man dwelleth Christ, in the inner man art thou renewed after the image of God, in His own image recognize its author. See how all the senses of the body bring intelligence to the heart within of what they have perceived abroad; see how many ministers the one commander within has and what it can do by itself even without these ministers. . . . Thy heart sees and hears and judges all other things perceived by the senses; and, what the senses do not aspire to, discerns things just and unjust, things evil and good." (*In Ioann. Evangel.*, XVIII, 10; CCSL XXXVI, 186; S VII, 121.)

Just as the mind, when it turns away from God's light, obscures and sometimes almost effaces the norms of moral judgment which come to "the heart within" from God's Truth, so "the mind itself, though naturally capable of reason and intelligence, is disabled by besotting and inveterate vices" from abiding in or even tolerating God's light; in order to be healed and renewed, it must be "impregnated with faith, and so purified." (DCD, XI, 2; CCSL XLVIII, 322; H I, 437–38); see, too, in this chapter, pp. 93–95. Still, even in sinful man there remains some love of truth, no matter how distorted it may be; "every man prefers to grieve in a sane mind, rather than to be glad in madness." (*Ibid.*, XI, 27; CCSL XLVIII, 347; H I, 470.) Many men wish to deceive others, but no one wishes to be deceived. "Thus, thus truly thus: the human mind so blind and sick, so base and ill-mannered, desires to lie hidden, but does not wish that anything should be hidden from it. And yet the opposite is what happens—the mind itself is not hidden from the truth, but the truth is hidden from it. Yet even so, for all its wretchedness, it still prefers to rejoice in truth rather than in known falsehoods." (*Confess.*, X, XXIII, 34; CSEL XXXIII, 253; Outler, 222-23.) "Yet there is a little light in men. Let them walk—let them walk in it, lest the darkness overtake them." (*Ibid.*, X, XXIII, 33; CSEL XXXIII, 253; Outler, 222.)

Since the human mind, because of its own sin, its own turning away from its true Light, God, is "blind and sick," it must, in order to be healed, be cleansed from sin and error by the faith established by God's eternal Truth who assumed human flesh and became the Mediator between God and men. Only through this faith, which is a gift of God's grace, bestowed on only a few men, can men attain salvation and achieve true wisdom, *sapientia,* as distinguished from knowledge, *scientia* (see *De Trinitate,* XII, XV, 25; PL XLII, 1012; S III, 165). This is what Augustine means when he says: "Therefore do not seek to understand in order to believe, but believe that thou mayest understand; since, 'except ye believe, ye shall not understand' [*Isa.* vii, 9]." (*In Ioann. Evangel.,* XXIX, 6; CCSL XXXVI, 287; S VII, 184 [*ergo noli quaerere intelligere ut credas, sed crede ut intelligas; quoniam nisi credideritis, non intelligetis*].) Note that in modern editions of the Bible the text from Isaiah has a rather different meaning; cf. *Isa.* vii, 9, in the AV: "If ye will not believe, surely ye shall not be established."

Our wills and our loves are corrupt. Since we cannot know that which we do not truly love, we can come to know and understand the truth only when our sinful wills have been healed and our love redirected to its proper object, God. The only medicine by which the will can be healed is the doctrine of humility and repentance preached by Christ and transmitted by Him to His Church. These teachings must be believed so that reason and understanding may be able to function effectively (see *De Util. Cred.,* 21; CSEL XXV, 26; S III, 357, and *Ep.* CXVIII, V, 32; CSEL XXXIV [2], 695-96; S I, 449-50). Of course, Augustine does not mean that God's Truth can be attained merely by a mechanical adherence to or repetition of dogmas and formulas. Rather, the Truth can be known only by a purified will and a cleansed mind, a will and a mind freed from pride, the root of all sin. For a recent discussion of this question, see Michael B. Foster, *Mystery and Philosophy* (London, SCM Press Ltd., 1957), esp. pp. 27–28, 46, 66–67, and 81–84.

49. *De Doctr. Christ.*, I, XXVI, 27; PL XXXIV, 29; S II, 529.

50. *Ibid.*

51. Augustine also uses the term "law of nature" (*lex naturae*) in reference to laws governing the behavior of physical bodies, and maintains that God is not bound by these laws; e.g., "God will bring to pass what He has foretold regarding the bodies of men, no difficulty preventing Him, no law of nature prescribing to Him His limit." (DCD, XXI, 8; CCSL XLVIII, 773; H II, 431–32.)

52. *Contra Faustum,* XV, 7; CSEL XXV, 429; S IV, 216.

53. *De Doctr. Christ.*, I, XXVI, 27; PL XXXIV, 29; S II, 529.

54. *Contra Duas Epist. Pelag.*, III, IV, 10; CSEL LX, 496; S V, 406.

55. *Contra Faustum,* XXII, 47; CSEL XXV, 639; S IV, 289.

56. *Ibid.* "For all the arrangements that are in force among men, because they have agreed among themselves that they should be in force, are human institutions; and of these, some are matters of superfluity and luxury, some of convenience and necessity." (*De Doctr. Christ.*, II, XXV, 38; PL XXXIV, 54; S II, 548.) See, also, the remarks in *Confess.*, III, VII, 13; CSEL XXXIII, 54; Outler, 69, on "foolish men who were judging by human judgment and gauging their judgment of the mores of the whole human race by the narrow norms of their own mores." See, too, the discussion of natural law, customary law, and positive law, quoted from Book II of Cicero's *De Inventione,* in *De Div. Quaest. 83,* XXXI, 1; PL XL, 20–21.

57. *Confess.*, III, VIII, 15; CSEL XXXIII, 57; Outler, 71.

58. "But those things which are done against God's law cannot be just. It is said unto God, 'Thy law is truth': and consequently, what is against truth cannot be just. Now who can doubt that every lie is against truth? Therefore there can be no just lie." (*Contra Mendacium,* XV, 31; CSEL XLI, 512; S III, 495.) See, too: "Right [*ius*] and wrong [*iniuria*] are contraries. Right is what is just [*iustum*]. For not all that is called right, is right. What if a man lay down for you unjust right [*ius iniquum*]? nor indeed is it to be called right, if it is unjust [*iniustum*]. That is true right, which is also just." (*En. in Ps.,* CXLV, 15; CCSL XL, 2116; S VIII, 664.)

59. See pp. 147–49.

60. *De Lib. Arbit.*, I, VI, 15, 50–51; CSEL LXXIV, 15–16; Burleigh, 120–21. See also the preceding section: "If a people, then, is well balanced and serious-minded, a careful guardian of the common good; if everyone in it thinks less of his private interests than of the public interest, it would be right to pass a law allowing that people to appoint its own magistrates to administer its affairs, that is, its public affairs? *Ev.*—Quite right. *Aug.*—Now if that same people degenerated little by little, put private interests before the public interest, sold its votes and, corrupted by men who love honours, committed rule over itself to wicked and criminal men, in such a case, if there existed some good and powerful man, would he not be right to strip that people of the power to bestow honours, and to give that power into the hands of a few good men or even of one man? *Ev.*—Again entirely right." (*Ibid.*, I, VI, 14, 45–46; CSEL LXXIV, 14–15; Burleigh, 120.) See, too, *ibid.*, I, V, 11, 33; CSEL LXXIV, 12; Burleigh, 118, where he says: "For a law that is unjust does not seem to me to be a law at all [*Nam lex mihi esse non videtur, quae iusta non fuerit*]." The entire passage is quoted in Chap. V, note 22.

61. *De Vera Religione,* XXXI, 58; PL XXXIV, 148; author's translation. Note that Burleigh's translation of this passage (pp. 254–55) contains serious inaccuracies.

62. Combès, *La doctrine politique,* pp. 152 and 416. See Chap. IV, pp. 143–50.

63. *Confess.,* III, VII, 13; CSEL XXXIII, 55; Outler, 70.

64. *Ep.* CXXXVIII, I, 4; CSEL XLIV, 129; FCL III, 38.

65. *Confess.,* III, VII, 13; CSEL XXXIII, 55; Outler, 70. See, too, *Ep.* CXXXVIII, I, 8; CSEL XLIV, 132–33; FCL III, 41, and *Sermo* LI, 28; PL XXXVIII, 349; S VI, 255.

66. *In Ioann. Evangel.,* XXXV, 4; CCSL XXXVI, 319; S VII, 205. See, too, the discussion of polygamy in relation to the law in *De Doctr. Christ.,* III, XII, 20; PL XXXIV, 73; S II, 562, and see above, note 57.

67. *De Doctr. Christ.,* III, XIV, 22; PL XXXIV, 74; S II, 562–63.

68. *Ep.* LIV, V, 6; CSEL XXXIV (2), 165–66; S I, 302.

69. See pp. 46–48 and 59–66.

70. DCD, XIX, 12; CCSL XLVIII, 677; H II, 318; see above, note 8.

71. *Ibid.,* XII, 28; CCSL XLVIII, 384; H I, 520.

72. *Ibid.,* XII, 23; CCSL XLVIII, 380; H II, 514–15.

73. *De Trinitate,* IV, IX, 12; PL XLII, 896; S III, 76.

74. "And in what was he [man] made after God's image? In the intellect, in the mind, in the inner man; in that he understands truth, distinguishes between right and wrong, knows by whom he was made, is able to understand his Creator, to praise his Creator: he hath this intelligence, who hath prudence. Therefore when many by evil lusts wore out in themselves the image of God, and by perversity of their manners extinguished the very flame, so to say, of intelligence, the Scripture cried out aloud to them, 'Become not ye as the horse and mule which have no understanding.' . . . But because by sin man deserted Him whom he ought to be under, he is made subject to the things which he ought to be above." (*In Epist. Ioann.*, VIII, 6; PL XXXV, 2039; S VII, 508–9.) "Yet we must remember that the image of God in the human soul has not been so completely obliterated by the stain of earthly affections, that no faint outlines of the original remain therein; and therefore it can rightly be said even in the ungodliness of its life to do or to hold some parts of the law. . . . Just as by the new covenant there is a renewal in the mind of believers of that very image of God which ungodliness had not entirely done away—at the least there remained the essential rationality of the human soul—so even here what is written is undoubtedly that law of God which was never quite effaced by unrighteousness and now is renewed by grace." (*De Spiritu et Littera*, XXVIII, 48; CSEL LX, 202; Burnaby, 231.) See pp. 96–97.

75. See pp. 85–87.   76. See Chap. II, note 75.

77. See Chap. I, note 54.

78. "For if the law be present with its command, and the Spirit be absent with His help, the presence of the prohibition serves only to increase the desire to sin, and adds the guilt of transgression." (DCD, XXI, 16; CCSL XLVIII, 782; H II, 443).

79. *De Natura et Gratia*, II, 2; CSEL LX, 235; S V, 122. "Therefore, Christ died in vain if men without the faith of Christ through other means or power of reasoning may arrive at true faith, at true virtue, at true justice, at true wisdom." (*Contra Julianum*, IV, III, 17; PL XLIV, 746; FC 35, 182.) Augustine attempts to explain away St. Paul's reference to those who do by nature the works of the Law without the Law since they have the Law written in their hearts, by the argument that Paul is here speaking not of virtuous heathen but rather of those who came to the Gospel from the Gentiles, and not from the Jews, to whom the Law was given. See, too, *De Spiritu et Littera*, XXVII, 48; CSEL LX, 202; Burnaby, 231.

80. See pp. 26–27.

81. *Contra Julianum,* IV, III, 23; PL XLIV, 750; FC 35, 188. A few paragraphs later he continues: "You cannot prove through them what you wish to prove—that even unbelievers can have true virtues —for these men [those who came to the Gospel from the Gentiles] are believers. If they have not the faith of Christ, then they are neither just nor pleasing to God, since without faith it is impossible to please God. Their thoughts will defend them on the day of judgment thus: that they may receive a more tolerable punishment, because in some way they did naturally the works of the Law, having the work of the Law written in the hearts to the extent that they did not to others what they did not want done to themselves. But those men without faith sinned in that they did not refer their works to the end to which they should be referred. Fabricius will be punished less than Catiline, not because Fabricius was good, but because Catiline was more evil. Fabricius was less wicked than Catiline, not because he had true virtues, but because he did not deviate so much from the true virtues." (*Ibid.,* IV, III, 25; PL XLIV, 750–51; FC 35, 189–90.) See pp. 50–52, and pp. 81–82.

82. See pp. 19–20, 23–24, and 37–38.

83. "But for the sake of the necessities of this life we must not neglect the arrangements of men that enable us to carry on intercourse with those around us." (*De Doctr. Christ.,* II, XXXIX, 58; PL XXXIV, 62; S II, 553.) See, too, *ibid.,* II, XXV, 40; PL XXXIV, 55; S II, 548. Note the comment made by A. J. Carlyle in *A History of Mediaeval Political Theory in the West* (4th impression, Edinburgh and London, Wm. Blackwood and Sons, Ltd., 1950), I, 120: "[T]he Fall, in bringing corruption into the world, made necessary institutions which should correct and control the sinfulness of human nature."

84. See above, note 48. The Platonic origin of this idea that earthly justice, order, and peace are "copies," "images," "reflections," or "impressions" of God's true and immutable justice, order, and peace, and that the former exist only by virtue of their "participation" in the real being of the latter, is obvious.

85. See above, note 75.

86. *De Trinitate,* XIV, XVI, 22; PL XLII, 1053; Burnaby, 120.

87. See *De Div. Quaest. ad Simplic.,* I, II, 16; PL XL, 120; Burleigh, 397–98. Note, however, that for Augustine God's true equity and justice are beyond the comprehension of man, even if he is "just." For example, God's decision to extend mercy to some men and to "harden" many more "belongs to a certain hidden equity that can-

not be searched out by any human standard of measurement. . . ."
God's "standard of equity . . . is most secret and far removed from
human powers of understanding." (*Ibid.*) See, too, *ibid.*, I, II, 22;
PL XL, 127–28; Burleigh, 405–6.

88. *De Vera Religione,* XXVI, 49; PL XXXIV, 143; Burleigh,
249.

89. *De Div. Quaest. ad Simplic.,* I, II, 16; PL XL, 120–21; Burleigh, 398. "For all this justice of men [*omnis ista hominum justitia*],
which the human soul is able to possess by acting rightly and to
lose by sinning, would not be graven upon the soul [*non imprimere-
tur animae*], unless there existed a certain unchangeable justice
[*aliqua incommutabilis justitia*]. . . . And this unchangeable justice
surely comes from God [*Quae justitia incommutabilis utique Dei
est*]. . . ." (*De Div. Quaest. 83,* LXXXII, 2; PL XL, 98; author's
translation.) See, too, *In Ioann. Evangel.,* XIX, 11–12; CCSL XXXVI,
194–96; S VII, 126–27, *Sermo* IV, 6–7; PL XXXVIII, 35–36; and *En.
in Ps.,* LXI, 21; CCSL XXXIX, 789, and *ibid.,* LXIII, 11; CCSL
XXXIX, 814.

90. See pp. 134–42.

91. *In Ioann. Evangel.,* VIII, 2; CCSL XXXVI, 82–83; S VII, 58.
See, too: "If this faith be taken away from human affairs, who but
must observe how great disorder in them, and how fearful confusion
must follow? For who will be loved by any with mutual affection,
(being that the loving itself is invisible,) if what I see not, I ought
not to believe? Therefore will the whole of friendship perish, in that
it consists not save of mutual love. . . . [T]o that degree are human
affairs thrown into disorder, if what we see not we believe not, as
to be altogether and utterly overthrown, if we believe no wills of
men, which assuredly we cannot see. . . . [I]f we believe not those
things which we cannot see, human society itself, through concord
perishing, will not stand." (*De Fide Rerum,* II, III, 4; PL XL,
173–74; S III, 338–39.)

92. "For a community is nothing else than a harmonious collection of individuals [*cum aliud ciuitas non sit quam concors hominum
multitudo*]." (DCD, I, 15; CCSL XLVII, 17; H I, 24.)

93. See Ernest Barker's comments in his Introduction to the Every-
man's Library edition of *The City of God* (London, J. M. Dent and
Sons, Ltd.; New York, E. P. Dutton and Co., Inc., 1945), p. xviii:
"Absolute righteousness [*justitia*] is a system of right relations to
God—relations which are at once religious, moral, and, if you will,
legal: relations which are, in a word, *total.* . . . Relative righteous-

ness is a system of right relations mainly in the legal sphere, and it is a system of right relations reckoning with, and adjusted to, the sinfulness of human nature. It is the best possible, *granted the defect of sin;* but again, and just because that defect has to be assumed, it is only a second best. This is the basis of St. Augustine's conception of the State and all the institutions of the State—government, property, slavery. All of these institutions are forms of *dominium*—the *dominium* of government over subjects, the *dominium* of owners over property, the *dominium* of masters over slaves. All *dominium* is a form of *ordo,* and to that extent good; but the order is an order conditioned by, and relative to, the sinfulness which it has to correct, and it is therefore only relatively good." Gilson is even less laudatory when he discusses the order and the peace found in the earthly city: "Certes, l'ordre de cette cité n'est au fond qu'une dérision de l'ordre véritable contre lequel elle est en révolte permanente; mais enfin si les voleurs, les bêtes fauves même, obéissent à des sortes de loi et respectent une certaine sorte de paix, à plus forte raison des êtres raisonnables ne sauraient-ils vivre sans engendrer une sorte de société. Si mauvaise soit-elle, elle est, et en tant qu'elle est, elle est bonne; ne nous étonnons donc point qu'elle conserve, jusque dans sa dépravation même, une apparence de beauté. Ajoutons toutefois que cette paix des impies est une fausse paix et que, comparée à celle des justes, elle n'en mérite pas même le nom. Au fond, son ordre apparent n'est qu'un désordre." (Gilson, *Introduction à l'étude,* pp. 228–29.)

94. See Chap. II.

95. *En. in Ps.,* LXXXIV, 10; CCSL XXXIX, 1170; S VIII, 407.

96. *Ibid.;* CCSL XXXIX, 1170–71; S VIII, 407.

97. DCD, XIX, 27; CCSL XLVIII, 697; H II, 342.

98. *In Ioann. Evangel.,* LXXVII, 4; CCSL XXXVI, 522; S VII, 340.

99. *Ibid.,* XXXIV, 10; CCSL XXXVI, 316; S VII, 203.

100. *Ibid.*

101. *En. in Ps.,* XLVIII (2), 6; CCSL XXXVIII, 570; S VIII, 175; italics added.

102. DCD, XVII, 13; CCSL XLVIII, 578; H II, 198.

103. *In Ioann. Evangel.,* LXXVII, 5; CCSL XXXVI, 522; S VII, 340.

104. DCD, XIX, 12; CCSL XLVIII, 677–78; H II, 318; italics added.

105. *Ibid.,* XIX, 12; CCSL XLVIII, 675; H II, 315–16; italics added.

106. *Ibid.*, XIX, 17; CCSL XLVIII, 684; H II, 326. "Peace between man and man is well-ordered concord. Domestic peace is the well-ordered concord between those of the family who rule and those who obey. Civil peace is a similar concord among the citizens. . . . The peace of all things is the tranquillity of order. Order is the distribution which allots things equal and unequal each to its own place." (*Ibid.*, XIX, 13; CCSL XLVIII, 679; H II, 319–20.)

107. *Ibid.*, XIX, 17; CCSL XLVIII, 684; H II, 326.

108. *Ibid.*, XIX, 17; CCSL XLVIII, 684; H II, 327. See pp. 82–83.

109. *Ibid.*, XIX, 26; CCSL XLVIII, 697; H II, 341. See, too, *ibid.*, III, 9; CCSL XLVII, 71; H I, 98.

110. *Ibid.*, XIX, 17; CCSL XLVIII, 685; H II, 328. See, too, *Expos. Quar. Prop. ex Ep. ad Romanos,* 72; PL XXXV, 2083, and *En. in Ps.,* LV, 2; CCSL XXXIX, 677–78. Note the similarities between this idea of earthly peace and the conceptions of peace in the writings of Marsilius, Hobbes, and Spinoza.

111. *De Catechiz. Rudibus,* XXI, 37; PL XL, 337; S III, 306.

112. See esp. Chaps. IV and V.

113. See Carlyle, *History of Mediaeval Political Theory,* Vol. I, esp. pp. 132–46, and Ernst Troeltsch, *The Social Teaching of the Christian Churches* (translated by Olive Wyon; 3d impression, London, George Allen & Unwin Ltd; New York, The Macmillan Company, 1950), Vol. I, esp. pp. 115–18.

114. See, for example, the quotations from St. Ambrose given in Carlyle, *History of Mediaeval Political Theory,* I, 136–37.

115. *In Ioann. Evangel.,* VI, 25–26; CCSL XXXVI, 66–67; S VII, 47–48; italics added.

116. *Ep.* XCIII, XII, 50; CSEL XXXIV (2), 493; S I, 400.

117. *Ibid.,* XII, 50; CSEL XXXIV (2), 494; S I, 400.

118. *Ep.* CLIII, VI, 26; CSEL XLIV, 426; FCL III, 302.

119. *Ibid.*

120. See Carlyle, *History of Mediaeval Political Theory,* I, 140.

121. Gilson, quite correctly, comments: "Il ne serait pas difficile de trouver des propriétaires injustes obligés de rendre ce qu'ils ont, mais trouver les justes possesseurs capables d'en bien user serait plus difficile." (Gilson, *Introduction à l'étude,* p. 233, note 1).

122. *Ep.* CLIII, VI, 26; CSEL XLIV, 426–27; FCL III, 302; italics added. I would interpret the following passage from *Sermo* L in the same way, i.e., as a formulation of a moral judgment rather than a legal rule. "Gold belongs to him who uses it rightly, and so it is more truly God's. Gold and silver, therefore, belong to the man who

knows how to use gold and silver. For even among men, a man is properly said to possess something only when he uses it rightly. For what is not employed justly is not held rightly. And if a man calls his own that which he does not possess rightly, his voice will not be that of a just possessor but the wickedness of a shameless usurper." (*Sermo* L, II, 4; PL XXXVIII, 327; author's translation.) See, too, *ibid.*, I, 2; PL XXXVIII, 326–27, where he says that since gold and silver belong to God and not to man, he who gives to the poor is giving what is God's and not what is his own, and so he has no reason for pride in himself. Clearly, Augustine is not suggesting that legally the money does not belong to the man who possesses it or, later, to the poor man to whom it is given.

123. See pp. 45–46.

124. *En. in Ps.*, CXXXI, 25; CCSL XL, 1924; S VIII, 621.

125. "Thou dost possess these riches. I blame it not: an inheritance hast come to thee, thy father was rich, and he left it to thee. Or thou hast honestly acquired them: thou hast a house full of the fruit of just labour; I blame it not. Yet even thus do not call them riches." (*Sermo* CXIII, 4; PL XXXVIII, 650; S VI, 451.) See, too: "[F]or to have these things [wealth, etc.,] without cleaving to them is much more admirable than not to have them at all." (*De Mor. Eccl. Cath.*, XXIII, 42; PL XXXII, 1329; S IV, 53.)

126. See *Ep.* CLVII, IV, 39; CSEL XLIV, 486; FCL III, 352.

127. See *Ep.* XCVI, 1; CSEL XXXIV (2), 514; S I, 404–5, and *Contra Adimantum*, 20; CSEL XXV, 178.

128. *En. in Ps.*, CXXXI, 25; CCSL XL, 1924; S VIII, 621. "Let us, therefore, brethren, abstain from the possession of private property; or from the love of it, if we may not from its possession; and we make a place for the Lord." (*Ibid.*, CXXXI, 6; CCSL XL, 1914; S VIII, 617.)

129. *Ep.* CXXX, II, 3; CSEL XLIV, 43; S I, 460. See, too, *Ep.* CCXI, 9; CSEL LVII, 362; S I, 565.

130. *En. in Ps.*, LXVIII (2), 18; CCSL XXXIX, 929; S VIII, 311.

131. *Ep.* CLVII, IV, 35; CSEL XLIV, 482; FCL III, 348–49. "It could happen that some public official would say to a Christian: 'Either you will stop being a Christian, or, if you persist in being one, you shall have no house or property.' That will be the time when those rich men, who had decided to keep their riches in order to win merit with God by using them for good works, will choose to give them up for Christ's sake rather than Christ for their sake, so as to receive the hundredfold in this world . . . and everlasting life in

the world to come, lest by giving up Christ for the sake of riches they be cast into everlasting death." (*Ibid.*, IV, 32; CSEL XLIV, 479–80; FCL III, 346–47.)

132. *Matthew* xix, 24 (RSV).

133. *En. in Ps.*, LI, 14; CCSL XXXIX, 634; S VIII, 201. "This is intended to show us that on the one hand it was not poverty in itself that was divinely honored, nor, on the other, riches that were condemned, but that the godliness of the one and the ungodliness of the other had their own consequences, and, as the torment of fire was the lot of the ungodly rich man, so the bosom of the rich Abraham received the godly poor man." (*Ep.* CLVII, IV, 23; CSEL XLIV, 473; FCL III, 340–41.)

134. *En. in Ps.*, LXXXV, 3; CCSL XXXIX, 1178; S VIII, 410.

135. 1 *Tim.* vi, 17 (AV).

136. *En. in Ps.*, LXXXV, 3; CCSL XXXIX, 1178; S VIII, 410.

137. *Ep.* CLVII, IV, 29; CSEL XLIV, 477; FCL III, 344.

138. 1 *Tim.* vi, 8 (AV).

139. *Sermo* LXXXV, 5; PL XXXVIII, 522; S VI, 367–68.

140. DCD, XXI, 27; CCSL XLVIII, 801; H II, 465–66.

141. *En. in Ps.*, CXXXI, 26; CCSL XL, 1925; S VIII, 621. "But those who have none of this wealth, but only desire it, are counted also among rich men who will be rejected; for God takes account not of power, but of will." (*Ibid.*, LXXXIII, 3; CCSL XXXIX, 1147; S VIII, 400.)

142. *Ibid.*, LXXXIII, 3; CCSL XXXIX, 1147; S VIII, 400.

143. *Sermo* CXIII, 4; PL XXXVIII, 650; S VI, 451.

144. If you worship God for the sake of these goods, "thy feet will totter, thou wilt suppose thyself to worship without cause, when thou seest those things to be with them who do not worship Him. All these things, I say, He giveth even to evil men, Himself alone He reserveth for good men." (*En. in Ps.*, LXXIX, 14; CCSL XXXIX, 1119; S VIII, 390.)

145. *Sermo* LXXXV, 6–7; PL XXXVIII, 522–23; S VI, 368.

146. *Ep.* CIV, I, 3; CSEL XXXIV (2), 583; S I, 427.

147. *Psalms* xv, 5 (AV).

148. *En. in Ps.*, XXXVI (3), 6; CCSL XXXVIII, 372; S VIII, 99.

149. See *ibid.*, CXXVIII, 6; CCSL XL, 1884; S VIII, 612, and *Ep.* CLIII, 25; CSEL XLIV, 425–26; FCL III, 301–2.

150. *Sermo* LXXXVI, 3; PL XXXVIII, 525; S VI, 369.

151. *De Sermone Domini*, II, IV, 16; PL XXXIV, 1276; S VI, 39.

152. "Now let not the lord disdain to have his slave for a brother,

seeing the Lord Christ has vouchsafed to have him for a brother."
(*Sermo* LVIII, 2; PL XXXVIII, 393; S VI, 285.)

153. *En. in Ps.,* CXXIV, 7; CCSL XL, 1841; S VIII, 602. The only
exception to this rule of complete obedience to one's master that
Augustine would probably allow would be parallel to the sole exception that he makes to the duty of absolute obedience to political
rulers or to parents—when the commands of human authority are
contrary to God's commands, king, master, or father must be dis-
obeyed. On the subject of obedience to political authorities, see, also,
Chap. IV, pp. 143–50. On obedience to parents, note: "In this case
alone a son ought not to obey his father, if his father should have
commanded anything contrary to the Lord his God. For indeed the
father ought not to be angry, when God is preferred before him.
But when a father doth command that which is not contrary to God;
he must be heard as God is: because to obey one's father God hath
enjoined." (*Ibid.,* LXX [1], 2; CCSL XXXIX, 941; S VIII, 315.)

154. DCD, XIX, 15; CCSL XLVIII, 682; H II, 324–25. See, too,
In Epist. Ioann., VIII, 6; PL XXXV, 2039; S VII, 508, and see above,
p. 49.

155. DCD, XIX, 15; CCSL XLVIII, 682; H II, 324.

156. *Ibid.,* XIX, 15; CCSL XLVIII, 682; H II, 325.

157. *Quaest. in Hept.,* II, 77; CSEL XXVIII (2), 142.

158. DCD, XIX, 15; CCSL XLVIII, 683; H II, 325.

159. *Ibid.,* XIX, 15; CCSL XLVIII, 682; H II, 324–25.

160. *In Epist. Ioann.,* VIII, 14; PL XXXV, 2044; Burnaby, 327.
"Each one of you doth need the other. Therefore neither of you is
truly lord and neither of you truly servant." (*En. in Ps.,* LXIX, 7;
CCSL XXXIX, 938; S VIII, 314.)

161. *De Sermone Domini,* I, XIX, 59; PL XXXIV, 1260; S VI,
26.

162. *Ibid.*

NOTES TO CHAPTER IV

1. See esp. Chap. II.

2. "But while those are better who are guided aright by love, those
are certainly more numerous who are corrected by fear." (*Ep.*
CLXXXV, VI, 21; CSEL LVII, 19; S IV, 641). See, too, pp. 28–31
and 34–38.

3. See DCD, XII, 9; CCSL XLVIII, 364; H I, 493, and XXII, 30;
CCSL XLVIII, 863; H II, 541–42.

4. *Ibid..* II, 21; CCSL XLVII, 53; H I, 75.

5. *Ibid.*, II, 21; CCSL XLVII, 55; H I, 77.   6. *Ibid.*

7. *Ibid.*, XIX, 21; CCSL XLVIII, 688; H II, 331.

8. See Chap. III, note 24.

9. DCD, XIX, 21; CCSL XLVIII, 688; H II, 331.

10. *Ibid.*, XIX, 21; CCSL XLVIII, 689; H II, 332.

11. McIlwain, *The Growth of Political Thought,* pp. 154–60. I have selected McIlwain's interpretation for discussion here not only because it has had great influence (see, e.g., the statements in George H. Sabine's *A History of Political Theory* [Rev. ed., New York, Henry Holt and Co., 1950], p. 192, which are based on McIlwain's analysis), but because I regard it as more persuasive and more scholarly than other versions of the "clericalist" interpretation. If it can be shown that his treatment of Augustine is not satisfactory, other statements of the view that Augustine believed that only a Christian state can be truly just and, therefore, a true commonwealth can be ignored.

12. McIlwain, *The Growth of Political Thought,* pp. 155–56; see below, notes 20 and 35.

13. *Ibid.*, pp. 158–59. Compare Figgis's statement: "So far is S. Augustine from giving a clericalist definition of the State, that he definitely discards it, and shows us that he does so with intention, and gives his grounds. It is contrary to the facts of life" (Figgis, *The Political Aspects,* p. 64).

14. DCD, II, 21; CCSL XLVII, 55; H I, 77.

15. *Ibid.*, XIX, 23; CCSL XLVIII, 695; H II, 339; italics added.

16. *Ibid.*, II, 21; CCSL XLVII, 55; H I, 77; see p. 118.

17. *Ibid.*, XIX, 24; CCSL XLVIII, 695; H II, 339–40; italics added.

18. McIlwain, *The Growth of Political Thought,* p. 157.

19. See pp. 40–41.

20. A state "is nothing else than a multitude of men bound together by some associating tie [*ciuitas, quae nihil est aliud quam hominum multitudo aliquo societatis uinculo conligata*]." (DCD, XV, 8; CCSL XLVIII, 464; H II, 63.) "For what is a republic but a commonwealth? Therefore its interests are common to all; they are the interests of the State. Now what is a State but a multitude of men bound together by some bond of concord? [*quid est autem ciuitas nisi hominum multitudo in quoddam uinculum redacta concordiae?*]" (*Ep.* CXXXVIII, II, 10; CSEL XLIV, 135; S I, 484.) "For the happiness of the state has no other source than the happiness of man, since the state is merely a unified group of men [*concors hominum multitudo*]." (*Ep.* CLV, III, 9; CSEL XLIV, 439–40; FCL III, 312.)

"For a people is composed of men associated under one law, a temporal law, as we have said." (*De Lib. Arbit.*, I, VII, 16, 52; CSEL LXXIV, 16; Burleigh, 121.) "A population forms a city, and dissension is full of danger for it: to dissent [*dis-sentire*]—what is that, but to think diversely? An army is made up of many soldiers. And is not any multitude so much the less easily defeated in proportion as it is the more closely united? In fact, the joining is itself called a coin, a co-union, as it were." (*De Ordine*, II, 18, 48; CSEL LXIII, 181; FC I, 325.) See, too, DCD, XVII, 14; CCSL XLVIII, 578; H II, 199, and *De Genesi ad Litteram*, IX, 9; CSEL XXVIII (1), 277.

21. See the statement by Gerd Tellenbach in his *Church, State and Christian Society at the Time of the Investiture Contest* (Oxford, Basil Blackwell, 1948), p. 31: Augustine "never even drew a clear distinction between the heathen and the Christian Empire."

22. DCD, II, 19; CCSL XLVII, 51; translation and italics by author.

23. Cochrane, *Christianity and Classical Culture,* pp. 327–36.

24. Note that after his statement that the first Romans "did preserve a certain characteristic uprightness, sufficient to found, increase, and preserve an earthly city," he does not go on to say that if true religion is added the earthly state becomes truly righteous, but rather that men can then become citizens of the only truly just community, the City of God. "God showed in the rich and far-famed Roman Empire how much can be achieved by natural [i.e., civic; *ciuiles*] virtues without true religion, so that we might understand how, with this added, men can become citizens of another state whose king is truth, whose law is love, whose measure is eternity." (*Ep.* CXXXVIII, III, 17; CSEL XLIV, 145; FCL III, 50.)

25. See pp. 96–104.

26. DCD, XVII, 14; CCSL XLVIII, 578; H II, 199.

27. *De Vera Religione,* XXVI, 48; PL XXXIV, 143; Burleigh, 249.

28. *Ibid.* This reference to kings or princes as the rulers of "a well-ordered earthly city" suggests that McIlwain's distinction between a city [*civitas*] and a kingdom [*regnum*] is not one that Augustine actually follows. See, too: "So then where a king, where a court, where ministers, where commonalty are found, there is a city [*ciuitas*]." (*En. in Ps.,* IX, 8; CCSL XXXVIII, 62; S VIII, 35.) McIlwain's attempt to draw an even sharper line of cleavage between a *res publica,* on the one hand, and a *civitas* or *regnum,* on the other, is, I think, forced and, ultimately, unconvincing.

29. *En. in Ps.,* IX, 8; CCSL XXXVIII, 62; S VIII, 35. "You must see how plainly the sacred writings show that the happiness of the

state has no other source than the happiness of man. . . . Thus, in order to . . . place happiness where it truly exists, he [the Psalmist] says: 'Happy is the people whose God is the Lord.'" (*Ep.* CLV, II, 7–8; CSEL XLIV, 437 and 439; FCL III, 310–11.)

30. *En. in Ps.,* VII, 16; CCSL XXXVIII, 47; S VIII, 26.

31. See pp. 34–38.

32. ". . . and if the justice of the ungodly is not true justice, then whichever they have of the virtues allied with it are not true virtues (because failure to refer the gifts of God to their Author makes the evil men using them unjust); thus, neither the continence of the ungodly nor their modesty is true virtue." (*Contra Julianum,* IV, III, 17; PL XLIV, 746; FC 35, 182.) See, too, DCD, XIX, 25; CCSL XLVIII, 696; H II, 340–41, and see pp. 50–51 and, also, p. 80.

33. See *Ep.* CXXXVIII, III, 17; CSEL XLIV, 144; FCL III, 50, and see pp. 50–52.

34. See the discussion by Christopher Dawson, "St. Augustine and His Age," in M. C. D'Arcy *et al., Saint Augustine* (New York, Meridian Books, 1957), p. 63.

35. DCD, IV, 4; CCSL XLVII, 101; H I, 139–40; italics added.

36. Professor McIlwain admits the force of this paragraph, but, as we have seen, he argues that a *regnum* or a *civitas,* which can exist without justice, is essentially different from a *res publica,* which must possess the bond of justice and law which Cicero required (McIlwain, *The Growth of Political Thought,* pp. 155–56). Note the similarity between Augustine's views and those set forth by Cardinal Newman in "Sanctity the Token of the Christian Empire," in *Sermons on Subjects of the Day,* p. 273 (first edition), cited by Dawson, "St. Augustine and His Age."

37. DCD, IV, 4; CCSL XLVII, 101–2; H I, 140. "*Manus et ipsa hominum est, imperio principis regitur, pacto societatis astringitur, placiti lege praeda diuiditur. Hoc malum si in tantum perditorum hominum accessibus crescit, ut et loca teneat sedes constituat, ciuitates occupet populos subiuget, euidentius regni nomen adsumit, quod ei iam in manifesto confert non dempta cupiditas, sed addita inpunitas. Eleganter enim et ueraciter Alexandro illi Magno quidam comprehensus pirata respondit. Nam cum idem rex hominem interrogaret, quid ei uideretur, ut mare haberet infestum, ille libera contumacia: Quod tibi, inquit, ut orbem terrarum; sed quia ⟨id⟩ ego exiguo nauigio facio, latro uocor; quia tu magna classe, imperator.*"

38. *Ibid.*, IV, 6; CCSL XLVII, 103; H I, 142. *"Inferre autem bella finitimis et in cetera inde procedere ac populos sibi non molestos sola regni cupiditate conterere et subdere, quid aliud quam grande latrocinium nominandum est?"*

39. *Ibid.*, XIX, 12; CCSL XLVIII, 676; H II, 316; italics added.

40. "But if it were not that, as a defender of the basest cause, you are hindered by the desire of building up falsehood . . . there can be no doubt that you could, without any difficulty, recall some good kings as well as some bad ones, and some friendly to the saints as well as some unfriendly. . . . Why then did you thus run headlong with your eyes shut, so that when you said, 'What have you to do with the kings of this world?' you did not add, In whom Christianity has often found envy towards herself, instead of boldly venturing to say, 'In whom Christianity has never found anything save envy towards her?'" (*Contra Litt. Petil.*, II, 92, 204; CSEL LII, 127–29; S IV, 579.)

41. *En. in Ps.*, LI, 6; CCSL XXXIX, 627; S VIII, 197. "For how many faithful, how many good men, are both magistrates in their cities, and are judges, and are generals, and are counts, and are kings? . . . And as if they were doing bond-service [*angariam*] in the city which is to pass away, even there by the doctors of the Holy City they are bidden to keep faith with those set over them, 'whether with the king as supreme, or with governors as though sent by God for the punishment of evil men, but for the praise of good men': or as servants, that to their masters they should be subject, even Christians to Heathens, and the better should keep faith with the worse, for a time to serve, for everlasting to have dominion. For these things do happen until iniquity do pass away." (*Ibid.*, LXI, 8; CCSL XXXIX, 779; S VIII, 253.) See p. 31.

42. DCD, V, 19; CCSL XLVII, 156; H I, 216–17. "Wherefore if the true God is worshipped, and if He is served with genuine rites and true virtue, it is advantageous that good men should long reign both far and wide. Nor is this advantageous so much to themselves, as to those over whom they reign. . . . In this world, therefore, the dominion of good men is profitable, not so much for themselves as for human affairs." (*Ibid.*, IV, 3; CCSL XLVII, 101; H I, 139.)

43. Since the believer "by making progress in Christian faith and well-doing," becomes "so much the more faithful and useful in the administration of public business" (*Ep.* CLI, 14; CSEL XLIV, 392; S I, 509), "those who, by a talent for business, are fitted for govern-

ment, must for the public benefit consent to bear the burden and suffer the hardships of public life. . . ." (*Contra Faustum,* XXII, 58; CSEL XXV, 653; S IV, 294.)

44. See *Ep.* CLV, IV, 17; CSEL XLIV, 447; FCL III, 317–18, and *En. in Ps.,* II, 9–10; CCSL XXXVIII, 6.

45. DCD, V, 24; CCSL XLVII, 160; H I, 223.

46. For examples and discussion of "Mirror of Princes" literature, especially in the period before Augustine, see Ernest Barker, *From Alexander to Constantine* (Oxford, Oxford University Press, 1956), pp. 236–38, 253–56, 303–8, 361–73, and 477–79, and *Social and Political Thought in Byzantium* (Oxford, Oxford University Press, 1957), pp. 20–21, 54–63, and 151–59.

47. DCD, V, 24; CCSL XLVII, 160; H I, 223.

48. *Ep.* CLV, III, 10; CSEL XLIV, 440; FCL III, 312.

49. *Ibid.,* CSEL XLIV, 440–41; FCL III, 312–13. See, too, *ibid.,* III, 12; CSEL XLIV, 441–42; FCL III, 313–14: "If you recognize that you have received the virtues which you have, and if you return thanks to Him from whom you have received them, directing them to His service even in your secular office; if you rouse the men subject to your authority and lead them to worship God, both by the example of your own devout life and by your zeal for their welfare, whether you rule them by love or by fear; if, in working for their greater security, you have no other aim than that they should thus attain to Him who will be their happiness—then yours will be true virtues, then they will be increased by the help of Him whose bounty lavished them on you, and they will be so perfected as to lead you without fail to that truly happy life which is no other than eternal life."

50. See Chap. VI, esp. pp. 214–20.

51. DCD, XIX, 17; CCSL XLVIII, 684; H II, 326.

52. *Ibid.,* XIX, 17; CCSL XLVIII, 685; H II, 328. See Chap. III, pp. 102–03.

53. *Ibid.,* V, 26; CCSL XLVII, 162; H I, 226.

54. *De Trinitate,* III, IV, 9; PL XLII, 873; S III, 58; italics added.

55. See below, in this chapter, pp. 147–50.

56. See below, in this chapter, pp. 139–40.

57. "How deep and dark a question it is to adjust the amount of punishment so as to prevent the person who receives it not only from getting no good, but also from suffering loss thereby! Besides, I know not whether a greater number have been improved or made worse when alarmed under threats of such punishment at the hands of

men as is an object of fear. What, then, is the path of duty, seeing that it often happens that if you inflict punishment on one he goes to destruction; whereas, if you leave him unpunished, another is destroyed?" (*Ep.* XCV, 3; CSEL XXXIV [2], 508; S I, 402.)

58. "All or almost all of us men love to call or consider our suspicions knowledge [*cognitiones*], since we are influenced by the credible evidence of circumstances; yet some credible things are false, just as some incredible ones are true." (*Ep.* CLIII, VI, 22; CSEL XLIV, 421; FCL III, 298.)

59. See *Sermo* CCCXLII, 5; PL XXXIX, 1504.

60. Augustine recognizes that the true Christian should avoid all recourse to legal proceedings; when St. Paul says that it is permissible to have cases between Christians decided by brethren within the Church (though not by the regular courts), "it is clear that some concession is being made here for the infirmities of the weak." (*Enchiridion,* XXI, 78; PL XL, 270; Outler, 387.) Nevertheless, Augustine not only believes that social necessity compels the judge to continue at his post, despite the inadequacies and the fallibilities of the legal system and of his own powers of judgment, he does not object if a Christian buys the right to judicial office, provided that he uses his office for the good of society and in the service of justice. "You wish to be a judge, even if you do it by money since you cannot by your merits—still I do not condemn you. For perhaps you seek to be of service in human affairs, and you buy that you may be of service; in order that you may serve justice, you do not spare your money." (*Sermo* XIII, 6–7; PL XXXVIII, 110; author's translation.) But he insists that once he occupies the office, the judge must give judgment impartially and without regard to popularity; see *En. in Ps.,* XXV (2), 13; CCSL XXXVIII, 149–50. Above all, judges and witnesses must never accept payments from the parties to a case. "But when verdicts and testimony are sold, they are unfair and untrue, because just and true ones are not to be sold, and it is much more infamous for money to be taken when it is infamously even if willingly paid." (*Ep.* CLIII, VI, 23; CSEL XLIV, 423; FCL III, 300.)

61. DCD, XIX, 6; CCSL XLVIII, 670–71; H II, 309–10; italics added. See, too, *Ep.* CXX, IV, 19; CSEL XXXIV (2), 720–21; FCL II, 315–16. Note too Augustine's expressions of his abhorrence of the use of torture in judicial inquiries in connection with outrages perpetrated by the Donatists. "Resolving, however, not to institute inquiry in regard to the instigators, because these, perhaps, could not

be ascertained without recourse to the use of tortures, from which we shrink with abhorrence, as utterly inconsistent with our aims." (*Ep.* CIV, IV, 17; CSEL XXXIV [2], 594; S I, 433.) See, too, his comment on the question of investigating the instigation of the attack on Christians and the Church by the pagans of Calama: "We think that we have a suspicion of this instigation, but no truth; so let us not discuss things which cannot be found out in any other way than by putting to torture those who could be examined." (*Ep.* XCI, 9; CSEL XXXIV [2], 433–34; FCL II, 48.) However, it is not accurate to say, as Combès does (*La doctrine politique,* pp. 192–95), that Augustine "condemned" torture. While it is clear that he did not want torture to be used in any investigation or trial in which the Church was involved, particularly in proceedings against the Donatists, he never denies that the use of torture to obtain information from accused persons and witnesses is a grim necessity of criminal justice; the judge who orders the use of torture is not committing a sin and is not to be condemned (see pp. 135–36).

At several points we shall have to indicate reservations or objections to Combès's interpretations of Augustine's political doctrines. However, quite apart from any differences in interpretation of Augustine, it should be noted that Combès's volume must be used with care by the student, since it contains many errors and inaccuracies in the references to Augustine's writings. I note only a few examples: *1*) on p. 77, the phrase *"ut se interim tutos ab injuriis facerent"* does not occur in the source cited, *Ep.* LIX; PL XXXIII, 226; 2) on pp. 46 and 91, Combès says that in DCD, II, 21, Augustine "adopts Scipio's thesis" and "uses the speech of Scipio in [Cicero's] *De Republica* to illustrate his own thesis" that a state cannot exist without justice; the text makes it clear that Augustine is simply reporting the arguments set forth by Scipio and Laelius; *3*) on p. 92, a definition of justice is attributed to Augustine and the reference is given to *Opus imperf. contra Julianum,* I, 35; PL XLIV [should be XLV], 1063; examination of the text shows that it is Julian and not Augustine who is speaking at this point; *4*) on p. 93, the phrase quoted at note 3 does not occur in DCD, XIX, 11, and the phrase quoted at note 7 is not found in *Sermo* XCII, 3; PL XXXVIII, 573; *5*) on pp. 135–36, the long quotation from *Contra Faustum,* XIX, 2; PL XLII, 347–48, is from Faustus the Manichaean and not from Augustine; *6*) on p. 138, note 4, the citation should be to *De Vera Religione,* XXXI, 58; PL XXXIV, 148, not to XXVI, 48; PL XXXIV, 143; *7*) on p. 149, at note 1, Combès quotes Augustine as referring to the treasury as a "dragon qui dévorait tout"; the text of *En. in Ps.*, CXLVI, 17; CCSL XL, 2135, reads: "A 'fisc' is a purse. . . . Do *not* think that a fisc is some kind of dragon, because the collector of the fisc is heard with terror; the fisc is a purse—the public purse [translation and italics by author]"; *8*) on p. 152, at note 2, the reference is to *Ep.* CXCV, 8; this letter is from Jerome to Augustine (see CSEL LVII, 214–16), has no paragraph 8, and does not refer to the subject mentioned; *9*) on p. 176, at note 4, the reference is to *Ep.* CLIV, 6; this letter contains no paragraph 6, and column 667 of PL XXXIII contains paragraphs 1–3 of *Ep.* CLV.

62. See DCD, XX, 2; CCSL XLVIII, 700; H II, 347.

63. See *De Lib. Arbit.*, I, V, 12, 34–36; CSEL LXXIV, 12; Burleigh, 118–19. The punishments imposed upon children by parents and teachers and the more severe punishments imposed upon grown-ups by the legal and political system are necessary to guard us against ignorance and to bridle our evil desires—"these evils with which we came into the world"—but the punishments themselves are "full of labour and sorrow." (DCD, XXII, 22; CCSL XLVIII, 843; H II, 518–19.)

64. *Ep.* CLIII, VI, 26; CSEL XLIV, 426–27; FCL III, 302. See, too, pp. 139–40.

65. *Ep.* CXXXIV, 3; CSEL XLIV, 86; FCL III, 10.

66. See *En. in Ps.*, CV, 34; CCSL XL, 1566; S VIII, 531.

67. Combès, e.g., concludes his discussion of *l'état Chrétien* by saying: "L'État chrétien, en effet, n'est pas celui où le Christ règne extérieurement sur la nation par les représentants de son culte; c'est celui où il règne intérieurement dans la conscience du chef, des magistrats et de *tous les citoyens.*" (Combès, *La doctrine politique,* p. 112; italics added.) All that one needs to add is that therefore, according to Augustine, such a state has never existed, does not now exist, and never will exist in this world.

68. "Those who are happy on account of their love of eternal things I hold act under obedience to the eternal law, while on unhappy men the temporal law is imposed. . . . [T]hose who serve the temporal law cannot be set free from subjection to the eternal law. . . . *But those who with a good will cleave to the eternal law do not need the temporal law,* as apparently you well understand." (*De Lib. Arbit.*, I, XV, 31, 107; CSEL LXXIV, 32; Burleigh, 131; italics added.)

69. *Ep.* CXXXVIII, II, 15; CSEL XLIV, 141–42; S I, 486; italics added. *"Yet, were our religion listened to as it deserves, it would es-*

tablish, consecrate, strengthen, and enlarge the commonwealth [*consecraret, firmaret augeretque rem publicam*] in a way beyond all that Romulus, Numa, Brutus, and all the other men of renown in Roman history achieved." (*Ibid.,* II, 10; CSEL XLIV, 135; S I, 484; italics added.) In another of his letters where he is defending Christianity against pagan attacks, Augustine says that in the two great commandments of Christ—"You shall love the Lord your God with all your heart, and with all your soul, and with all your mind," and "You shall love your neighbor as yourself" (*Matt.* xxii, 37–39, RSV)—are contained all natural science, all ethics, all logic; "herein is the praiseworthy security of the state [*laudabilis rei publicae salus*], for the best city is erected and safeguarded on no other foundation than the bond of faith and unbreakable concord [*neque enim conditur et custoditur optima ciuitas nisi fundamento et uinculo fidei firmaeque concordiae*]. This happens when the common good is loved, when God is the highest and truest good, and when men love each other most sincerely because they love themselves for the sake of Him from whom they cannot hide the true sentiment of their hearts." (*Ep.* CXXXVII, V, 17; CSEL XLIV, 122; FCL III, 34.) Again, Augustine is insisting that the only basis for "the bond of faith and unbreakable concord" which is the foundation of "the best city" is the sincere love of its members for God, the highest good, and for one another in God. Since no earthly city or state will ever be made up entirely, or even predominantly, of men who love God and their fellow men in this way, no earthly city can be maintained by "the law of love" but must rely on coercion and the fear of punishment. Only "the best city," the City of God, has as its citizens only pious and good men who are ruled by the law of love.

70. *Ep.* CLIII, VI, 16; CSEL XLIV, 413–14; FCL III, 293; italics added. "Who is so blind in mind that he does not see what an ornament the human race is to the earth, even though few men live rightly and praiseworthily, and *how great is the value of the order of the state which coerces even sinners into the bond of its earthly peace?* For men are not so thoroughly depraved that they are not even better than the beasts and the birds." (*De Genesi ad Litteram,* IX, 9; CSEL XXVIII [1], 277; translation and italics by author). See Chap. III, pp. 102–3.

71. *De Lib. Arbit.,* I, XV, 32, 108; CSEL LXXIV, 32; Burleigh, 131.

72. See pp. 104–7.

73. See *Sermo* XIII, 8–9; PL XXXVIII, 110–11.

74. *De Lib. Arbit.*, I, XV, 32, 111; CSEL LXXIV, 33; Burleigh, 132. See, too, *ibid.*, I, V, 13, 40–41; CSEL LXXIV 13–14; Burleigh, 119.

75. *Ibid.*, I, XV, 33, 112; CSEL LXXIV, 33; Burleigh, 132.

76. See pp. 67–70.

77. *Sermo* CXXV, 5; PL XXXVIII, 693; S VI, 478.

78. *De Ordine*, II, 4, 12; CSEL LXIII, 155; FC 1, 287. See, too, *De Div. Quaest. 83*, LIII, 2; PL XL, 36, where he notes that the executioner kills the condemned person in accordance with the law, although it is his cupidity that has led him to assume the office; thus, too, his cruelty, which might otherwise be directed against the innocent, is used in the service of law and justice.

79. For example, a good law can be made by a man who is not good and who acts, in making it, for wrong motives; see *De Lib. Arbit.*, I, V, 12, 35–36; CSEL LXXIV, 12; Burleigh, 118–19.

80. *De Sermone Domini*, I, XX, 63; PL XXXIV, 1262; S VI, 27. See, too, *Sermo* XIII, 4 and 7–9; PL XXXVIII, 108–11.

81. See pp. 163–66.

82. *Ep.* CXXXVIII, II, 14; CSEL XLIV, 140; S I, 485. See, too, pp. 135–36.

83. "To be innocent, we must not only do harm to no man, but also restrain him from sin or punish his sin, so that either the man himself who is punished may profit by his experience, or others be warned by his example." (DCD, XIX, 16; CCSL XLVIII, 683; H II, 326.)

84. "The very avengers of crime, who are not to be influenced by their personal anger but are to act as agents of the law, and those who enforce the law against proved injuries done to others, not to themselves, as judges should do, all these quail before the divine judgment, recalling that they have need of the mercy of God for their own sins, and they do not think they do an injury to their office if they show mercy to those over whom they have the lawful power of life and death." (*Ep.* CLIII, III, 8; CSEL XLIV, 404; FCL III, 286.) "Yet be not negligent in correcting those who belong to you, who in any way appertain to your charge, by admonition, or instruction, by exhortation, or by threats. Do it, in whatsoever way ye can. . . . But then in the correction and repression of other men's sins, one must take heed, that in rebuking another he do not lift up himself. . . . Let the voice of chiding sound outwardly in tones of terror, let the spirit of love and gentleness be maintained within." (*Sermo* LXXXVIII, 19–20; PL XXXVIII, 549–50; S VI, 385.)

85. In the *Confessions* Augustine recognizes that, as a man who wields authority in society, he is exposed to the special temptation of "the desire to be feared and loved of men, with no other view than that I may find in it a joy that is no joy. . . . And yet certain offices in human society require the office-holder to be loved and feared of men, and through this the adversary of our true blessedness presses hard upon us, scattering everywhere his snares of 'well done, well done'; so that while we are eagerly picking them up, we may be caught unawares and split off our joy from thy [God's] truth and fix it on the deceits of men. In this way we come to take pleasure in being loved and feared, not for thy sake but in thy stead." (*Confess.,* X, XXXVI, 59; CSEL XXXIII, 271; Outler, 236.) "Men seek them [the vanities of this life] at first through imprudence, and give them up at last with disappointment and remorse." (*Ep.* CCIII; CSEL LVII, 316; S I, 558.) See, too, DCD, XIX, 15; CCSL XLVIII, 682; H II, 324–25, and see pp. 150–51.

86. *Romans* xiii, 1–5 (RSV). See, too, 1 *Peter* ii, 13–14.

87. *Contra Litt. Petil.,* II, 20, 45; CSEL LII, 45; S IV, 540. See, too, *Sermo* CCCLVIII, 6; PL XXXIX, 589.

88. *John* xix, 11 (RSV), cited by Augustine, e.g., in *Contra Faustum,* XXII, 20; CSEL XXV, 609; S IV, 279.

89. See *Expos. Quar. Prop. ex Ep. ad Romanos,* 72; PL XXXV, 2083.

90. See *ibid.,* 74; PL XXXV, 2084, and *Sermo* CCCII, 19; PL XXXVIII, 1392–93.

91. "Although we are called to that kingdom where there will be no power of this sort, nevertheless while we are in the midst of the journey, and until we arrive at that age when every principality and power passes away, let us endure our condition in the measure of that very order of human affairs, doing nothing feignedly and by that very fact obeying not so much men as God, who orders this." (*Expos. Quar. Prop. ex Ep. ad Romanos,* 72; PL XXXV, 2084; author's translation.)

92. *De Catechiz. Rudibus,* XXI, 37; PL XL, 337; S III, 306.

93. See DCD, V, 19; CCSL XLVII, 155; H I, 216, and V, 21; CCSL XLVII, 157–58; H I, 218–19. See, too, pp. 68–69.

94. *De Bono Coniugali,* XIV, 16; CSEL XLI, 209; S III, 406.

95. *En. in Ps.,* CXXIV, 7; CCSL XL, 1840; S VIII, 602.

96. See pp. 68–70.

97. *En. in Ps.,* LXV, 14; CCSL XXXIX, 850–51; S VIII, 279.

98. See *ibid.,* LXI, 8; CCSL XXXIX, 779; S VIII, 253.

99. *Ibid.,* CXXXVII, 7; CCSL XL, 1984; S VIII, 634.

100. *Confess.,* III, VIII, 15; CSEL XXXIII, 57; Outler, 71; italics added. While the king or emperor is the source of law and is not limited in his enactments by his own previous law-making, the power of his subordinates is clearly limited and bounded by the law. Augustine writes to an imperial official: "By whose authority and command you carried off Faventius is something for you to look to for yourself, but this I know, that *all authority set up under the power of the emperor is subject to law.* . . . However, I am now sending it [the law] again in this letter, not to threaten you, but to ask you . . . that you would kindly grant this favor to your own reputation and to my request, and not refuse to do, at my prayer and intercession, what the law of the emperor commands, since you are a public official in his service." (*Ep.* CXIV; CSEL XXXIV [2], 660–61; FCL II, 257–58; italics added.) Once laws have been enacted and promulgated, "it is not lawful for a judge to pass judgment upon them, but only to give judgment in accordance with them." (*De Vera Religione,* XXXI, 58; PL XXXIV, 148; author's translation.) See, too, p. 90.

101. See pp. 147–50.

102. 1 *Tim.* ii, 1–2 (RSV).

103. *Sermo* LI, 14; PL XXXVIII, 341; S VI, 250.

104. If your parents are "bringing thee up for Christ; they are to be heard in all things, they must be obeyed in every command; let them enjoin nothing against one above themselves, and so let them be obeyed. . . . Thy country again should be above thy very parents; so that whereinsoever thy parents enjoin aught against thy country, they are not to be listened to. And whatsoever thy country enjoin against God, it is not to be listened to." (*Sermo* LXII, 8; PL XXXVIII, 418; S VI, 300–301.) See also *Confess.,* III, VIII, 15; CSEL XXXIII, 56–57; Outler, 71. See, too, Chap. III, note 154.

105. *Sermo* LXII, 13; PL XXXVIII, 421; S VI, 302; italics added.

106. The Doctrine of the Two Swords was set forth by Pope Gelasius I in 494 in a letter to the Eastern Emperor, Anastasius I; Gelasius I, *Ep.* XII, 2 (see Carlyle, *History of Mediaeval Political Theory,* I, 190–93).

107. *Expos. Quar. Prop. ex Ep. ad Romanos,* 72; PL XXXV, 2083: "We consist of body and soul. So as long as we are in this temporal life, we use temporal things for the support of this life. With respect to that part of us which pertains to this life, it behooves us to be subject to the powers, i.e., to the men who administer human affairs in some preferment or other. But with respect to that part of us by

which we believe in God and are called to His kingdom, it does not behoove us to be subject to any man who seeks to subvert in us that very gift which God has deigned to give us for achieving eternal life." (Author's translation.)

108. *Matthew* xxii, 21 (RSV).

109. *Expos. Quar. Prop. ex Ep. ad Romanos,* 72; PL XXXV, 2083–84; author's translation.

110. See *Sermo* CCCXXVI, 2; PL XXXVIII, 1450.

111. See *Ep.* CV, 7; CSEL XXXIV (2), 599–600; FCL II, 200, and *Ep.* CLXXXV, II, 8; CSEL LVII, 7–8; S IV, 636. See, too, his comments on the contrast between the attitude of the Christian martyrs toward unjust laws and the attitude of Apuleius when he was accused of magic arts (DCD, VIII, 19; CCSL XLVII, 236; H I, 333–34). On the whole question of disobedience to earthly rulers and their laws, note the very different position ascribed to Augustine by Combès, *La doctrine politique,* pp. 153–54, when he says that according to Augustine orders or regulations that *1)* are "clearly immoral" or *2)* "violate a natural liberty" or *3)* "seriously injure the interests of the citizens" are not true laws and need not be obeyed, and when, on p. 157, he states that Augustine *"ne dénie à personne le droit de supprimer l'injustice par les armes,* mais il préfère la décourager, comme l'a fait l'Église, par la révolte obstinée des âmes." (Italics added.) See, too, pp. 88–91.

112. *En. in Ps.,* CXXIV, 7; CCSL XL, 1841–42; S VIII, 602–3. See the rest of this paragraph.

113. *Ibid.,* CXVIII (31), 1; CCSL XL, 1770; S VIII, 586.

114. See *Ep.* CXXXVII, V, 20; CSEL XLIV, 124–25; S I, 481. "But who, even though he be a stranger to our religion, is so deaf as not to know how many precepts enjoining concord, not invented by the discussions of men, but written with the authority of God, are continually read in the churches of Christ?" (*Ep.* CXXXVIII, II, 11; CSEL XLIV, 136; S I, 484.) See, too, *ibid.,* II, 17; CSEL XLIV, 144; S I, 487.

115. *De Mor. Eccl. Cath.,* XXX, 63; PL XXXII, 1336; S IV, 58.

116. *Ep.* CXXX, VI, 12; CSEL XLIV, 53; S I, 463.

117. *En. in Ps.,* CXXXVII, 9–10; CCSL XL, 1984–85; S VIII, 634. "For it is expedient for you, that ye should be under Him, by whom understanding and instruction are given you. And this is expedient for you, that ye lord it not with rashness, but that ye 'serve the Lord' of all 'with fear,' and 'rejoice' in bliss most sure and most pure, with all caution and carefulness, lest ye fall therefrom into pride." (*Ibid.,* II, 9; CCSL XXXVIII, 6; S VIII, 4.)

118. DCD, VI, 1; CCSL XLVII, 166; H I, 231.

119. *Ibid.,* X, 32; CCSL XLVII, 309; H I, 430.

120. *Contra Faustum,* XXII, 76; CSEL XXV, 674–75; S IV, 301.

121. DCD, IV, 5; CCSL XLVII, 102; H I, 141.

122. *Ibid.,* V, 17; CCSL XLVII, 149; H I, 208; italics added.

123. The true kings and rulers of the earth are not those who reign over "exceeding wide provinces," but those who rule over and subdue their own earthly desires (see *En. in Ps.,* LXXV, 18; CCSL XXXIX, 1051; S VIII, 360).

124. *De Vera Religione,* LV, 111; PL XXXIV, 171; Burleigh, 281. "For to the just all the evils imposed on them by unjust rulers are not the punishment of crime, but the test of virtue. Therefore, the good man, although he is a slave, is free; but the bad man, even if he reigns, is a slave, and that not of one man, but, what is far more grievous, of as many masters as he has vices. . . ." (DCD, IV, 3; CCSL XLVII, 101; H I, 139.)

125. *Ep.* CIV, II, 7; CSEL XXXIV (2), 587; S I, 429; italics added. The last sentence might better be translated as follows: "What becomes of that virtue, which even your own [i.e., pagan] literature commends,—the virtue of the ruler of his country who seeks to promote the welfare rather than the wishes of his people?"

NOTES TO CHAPTER V

1. See pp. 76–77.

2. DCD, III, 14; CCSL XLVII, 76; H I, 106.

3. *Ibid.,* V, 17; CCSL XLVII, 150; H I, 208–9. See, too, *ibid.,* III, 18; CCSL XLVII, 85–86; H I, 117–18.

4. See C. John Cadoux, *The Early Christian Attitude to War* (London, Headley Bros. Publishers, Ltd., 1919), esp. pp. 49–66, 102–60, and 255–57. For a discussion of the Roman Catholic Church's doctrine of just war since the time of Augustine, see Robert H. W. Regout, *La doctrine de la guerre juste de saint Augustin à nos jours* (Paris, Éditions A. Pedone, 1934).

5. DCD, XVII, 13; CCSL XLVIII, 578; H II, 198–99.

6. *Ep.* CXCIX, X, 35; CSEL LVII, 274; FCL IV, 384.

7. *En. in Ps.,* XLV, 13; CCSL XXXVIII, 527; S VIII, 159.

8. See Chap. III, pp. 95–97, and Chap. IV, pp. 134–36 and 138–41.

9. DCD, XIX, 7; CCSL XLVIII, 672; H II, 311.

10. See *Sermo* XXV, 1; PL XXXVIII, 168–69.

11. DCD, VII, 14; CCSL XLVII, 198; H I, 277.

12. The Romans who captured and destroyed Jerusalem were

wicked and impious, but nevertheless they acted as the instrument of God in bringing vengeance upon the Jews (see *En. in Ps.,* LXXIII, 7–8; CCSL XXXIX, 1010–11). The barbarian invasions of the Empire are a punishment of the corrupt morals of the wicked and a trial and test for the righteous (see DCD, I, 1; CCSL XLVII, 2; H I, 3).

13. DCD, XVIII, 2; CCSL XLVIII, 593; H II, 218. "Thus also the durations of wars are determined by Him as He may see meet, according to His righteous will, and pleasure, and mercy, to afflict or to console the human race, so that they are sometimes of longer, sometimes of shorter duration." (*Ibid.,* V, 22; CCSL XLVII, 158; H I, 220.) God, "when the human race is to be corrected and chastised by wars, regulates also the beginnings, progress, and ends of these wars. . . ." (*Ibid.,* VII, 30; CCSL XLVII, 211; H I, 298.)

14. *Ibid.,* XIX, 12; CCSL XLVIII, 675, H II, 315–16; see, too, pp. 101–2.

15. *Ibid.,* XV, 4; CCSL XLVIII, 457; H II, 54.

16. *Ibid.,* XV, 4; CCSL XLVIII, 456–57; H II, 53–54; it is difficult to understand how Combès, in discussing this passage, can say that if the second alternative is followed "cette modération . . . assurera . . . une paix solide et durable." (Combès, *La doctrine politique,* p. 297.) See, too, DCD, XVIII, 2; CCSL XLVIII, 593; H II, 218.

17. "And on this principle, if the commonwealth [lit., "this earthly commonwealth"] observe the precepts of the Christian religion, even its wars themselves will not be carried on without the benevolent design that, after the resisting nations have been conquered, provision may be more easily made for enjoying in peace the mutual bond of piety and justice." (*Ep.* CXXXVIII, II, 14; CSEL XLIV, 140; S I, 485.) See pp. 165–66.

18. *Ep.* CLXXXIX, 6; CSEL LVII, 135; S I, 554. Yet Augustine regards it as legitimate to employ ruses, traps, and ambushes against the enemy when one is waging a just war. He notes God's commands to Joshua to place his soldiers in ambush in order to surprise the enemy (cf. *Joshua* viii, 1–23), and says: "Thereby we are shown the legitimacy of the use of ruses by those who wage a just war. . . . The moment one has undertaken a just war, it is of no consequence to its justice whether one triumphs in an open battle or by ambushes." (*Quaest. in Hept.,* VI, 10; CSEL XXVIII [2], 428; author's translation.)

19. *Ep.* CCXXIX, 2; CSEL LVII, 497–98; S I, 581–82: written to Darius in 429.

20. *Quaest. in Hept.,* VI, 10; CSEL XXVIII (2), 428; author's translation.

21. DCD, XV, 4; CCSL XLVIII, 457; H II, 54. "Therefore, to carry on war and extend a kingdom over wholly subdued nations seems to bad men to be felicity, to good men necessity. But because it would be worse that the injurious should rule over those who are more righteous, therefore even that is not unsuitably called felicity. But beyond doubt it is greater felicity to have a good neighbour at peace, than to conquer a bad one by making war. Your wishes are bad, when you desire that one whom you hate or fear should be in such a condition that you can conquer him. If, therefore, by carrying on wars that were just, not impious or unrighteous, the Romans could have acquired so great an empire, ought they not to worship as a goddess even the injustice of foreigners? For we see that this has co-operated much in extending the empire, by making foreigners so unjust that they became people with whom just wars might be carried on, and the empire increased." (*Ibid.,* IV, 15; CCSL XLVII, 111; H I, 153.)

22. See the discussion in the *De Libero Arbitrio:* Augustine says, "I think we ought first to discuss whether an attacking enemy or an armed lier-in-wait can be slain in defence of life or liberty or chastity, without any lust." Evodius hesitates, and asks how men can be void of lust who fight for things which they can lose against their will. Augustine continues: "Then the law is not just which gives the traveller authority to kill a brigand lest he should himself be killed by him. Or the law that allows any man or woman to slay, if he can, any one who comes with intent to ravish, even before the crime has been committed. The law also bids the soldier to slay the enemy. If he abstains from killing he is punished by the general. Shall we dare to say that these laws are unjust or rather null and void? For a law that is unjust does not seem to me to be a law at all." Evodius then replies: "It is, however, evident that this law is well prepared against such an accusation, for in the state where it is in force it allows lesser evil deeds to prevent worse being committed. It is much more suitable that the man who attacks the life of another should be slain than he who defends his own life; and it is much more cruel that a man should suffer violation than that the violator should be slain by his intended victim. In killing an enemy the soldier is a servant of the law and can easily avoid lust in performing his duty." (*De Lib. Arbit.,* I, V, 11–12, 32–34; CSEL LXXIV, 11–12; Burleigh, 118.) See, too, DCD, I, 21; CCSL XLVII, 23; H I, 32. But, in regard

to the right of the private citizen to kill in self-defense, contrast the following: "As to killing another in order to defend one's own life, I do not approve of this, unless one happen to be a soldier or public functionary acting, not for himself, but in defence of others or of the city in which he resides, if he act according to the commission lawfully given him, and in the manner becoming his office." (*Ep.* XLVII, 5; CSEL XXXIV [2], 135; S I, 293.)

23. See DCD, III, 10; CCSL XLVII, 71; H I, 100. See, too, above, note 21.

24. "If some nation or some state which is warred upon has failed either to make reparation for an injurious action committed by its citizens or to return what has been wrongfully appropriated." (*Quaest. in Hept.*, VI, 10; CSEL XXVIII [2], 428; author's translation.)

25. *Ibid.*, IV, 44; CSEL XXVIII (2), 353; author's translation; cf. *Numbers* xxi, 21–25.

26. *Contra Faustum*, XXII, 74; CSEL XXV, 672; S IV, 301.

27. *Ibid.* I have retranslated the first three sentences.

28. "Let necessity, therefore, and not your will, slay the enemy who fights against you." (*Ep.* CLXXXIX, 6; CSEL LVII, 135; S I, 554.) See, too, *Contra Faustum*, XXII, 78; CSEL XXV, 678–80; S IV, 303, and *Ep.* CXXXVIII, II, 14; CSEL XLIV, 140–41; S I, 485–86.

29. *Contra Faustum*, XXII, 75; CSEL XXV, 673; S IV, 301.

30. "Since, therefore, a righteous man, serving it may be under an ungodly king, may do the duty belonging to his position in the State in fighting by the order of his sovereign . . . how much more must the man be blameless who carries on war on the authority of God . . . ?" (*Ibid.*; CSEL XXV, 673–74; S IV, 301.)

31. *Ibid.*

32. DCD, I, 26; CCSL XLVII, 27; H I, 37. He explains the saying in the Gospel of Matthew, "He that taketh the sword shall perish by the sword," in the following way: "To take the sword is to use weapons against a man's life, without the sanction of the constituted authority." (*Contra Faustum*, XXII, 70; CSEL XXV, 667; S IV, 299.) There are exceptions made by God to His own prohibition against taking another man's life. "These exceptions are of two kinds, being justified either by a general law, or by a special commission granted for a time to some individual. And in this latter case, he to whom authority is delegated, and who is but the sword in the hand of him who uses it, is not himself responsible for the death he deals. And,

accordingly, they who have waged war in obedience to the divine command, or in conformity with His laws have represented in their persons the public justice or the wisdom of government, and in this capacity have put to death wicked men; such persons have by no means violated the commandment, 'Thou shalt not kill.'" (DCD, I, 21; CCSL XLVII, 23; H I, 32.)

33. "Do not think that it is impossible for any one to please God while engaged in active military service." (*Ep.* CLXXXIX, 4; CSEL LVII, 133; S I, 553.) "For not soldiering but malice militates against benevolence [*Non enim benefacere prohibet militia, sed malitia*]." (*Sermo* CCCII, 15; PL XXXVIII, 1391; author's translation.)

34. *Ep.* XLVII, 5; CSEL XXXIV (2), 135; S I, 293. See, too, his statement that the injunction to turn the other cheek or the command to give the man who sues you for your coat your cloak also "is rightly understood as a precept having reference to the preparation of heart, not to a vain show of outward deed." (*De Sermone Domini*, I, XIX, 59; PL XXXIV, 1260; S VI, 26.) See, too, p. 142.

35. *Ep.* CXXXVIII, II, 13; CSEL XLIV, 138–39; S I, 485.

36. *Ibid.* See, too, *In Ioann. Evangel.*, CXIII, 4; CCSL XXXVI, 639; S VII, 420, *De Mendacio*, XV, 27; CSEL XLI, 447; S III, 470, and *Contra Faustum*, XXII, 76; CSEL XXV, 674; S IV, 301. "For if the Christian religion condemned wars of every kind, the command given in the gospel to soldiers asking counsel as to salvation would rather be to cast away their arms, and withdraw themselves wholly from military service; whereas the word spoken to such was, 'Do violence to no man, neither accuse any falsely, and be content with your wages,' the command to be content with their wages manifestly implying no prohibition to continue in the service." (*Ep.* CXXXVIII, II, 15; CSEL XLIV, 141; S I, 486.) For a modern Christian pacifist's rejection of the argument that Jesus meant his followers to adopt the "spirit" of his non-resistance teaching, without being bound by the "letter," see Cadoux, *The Early Christian Attitude*, pp. 22–24.

37. See Chap. VI, esp. pp. 189–90 and 207–8.

38. *Ep.* CXXXVIII, II, 14; CSEL XLIV, 140; S I, 485.

39. *Ep.* CLXXXIX, 6; CSEL LVII, 135; S I, 554.

40. See DCD, III, 20; CCSL XLVII, 88–89; H I, 121–23, and XXII, 6; CCSL XLVIII, 814; H II, 482–83.

41. *Ibid.*, III, 20; CCSL XLVII, 88; H I, 121.

42. Cicero, *De Republica*, as quoted by Augustine, *ibid.*, XXII, 6; CCSL XLVIII, 814; H II, 482.

43. *Ibid.*, XXII, 6; CCSL XLVIII, 814; H II, 482–83.

44. *Ibid.*, XXII, 6; CCSL XLVIII, 814; H II, 483.

45. *Ibid.*, XVI, 4; CCSL XLVIII, 505; H II, 113.

46. *Ibid.*, XIX, 7; CCSL XLVIII, 671; H II, 310–11.

47. *Ibid.*, XIX, 7; CCSL XLVIII, 671; H II, 311.   48. *Ibid.*

49. *Ibid.*, XIX, 7; CCSL XLVIII, 671–72; H II, 311.

50. *Ibid.*, XVIII, 45; CCSL XLVIII, 643; H II, 276.

51. *Ibid.*, I, 30; CCSL XLVII, 31; author's translation. See, too, pp. 50–53.

52. *Ibid.*, III, 21; CCSL XLVII, 90; H I, 124.

53. *Ibid.*, IV, 3; CCSL XLVII, 100; H I, 138.   54. *Ibid.*

55. *Ibid.*, III, 10; CCSL XLVII, 71; H I, 99.

56. *Ibid.*, IV, 15; CCSL XLVII, 111; H I, 153.

57. *Ibid.*, V, 17; CCSL XLVII, 150; H I, 208.

NOTES TO CHAPTER VI

1. See Chap. IV, pp. 148–49, and the references there to *Expos. Quar. Prop. ex Ep. ad Romanos,* 72; PL XXXV, 2083–84.

2. See pp. 147–49.   3. *Matthew* xxii, 21 (RSV).

4. *John* xix, 15 and 19 (RSV).

5. *En. in Ps.,* LV, 2; CCSL XXXIX, 677–78; author's translation.

6. See Chap. IV, pp. 136–38, and especially the reference to *Ep.* CXXXIV, 3; CSEL XLIV, 86; FCL III, 10.

7. DCD, V, 26; CCSL XLVII, 162; H I, 226.

8. See below, in this chapter, pp. 198–200, for Augustine's discussions of the new position of the Church now that kings have ceased to persecute her and have become her children.

9. See pp. 37–38.

10. "I have difficulty in obtaining even a very little leisure, amidst the accumulation of business into which, in spite of my own inclinations, I am dragged by other men's wishes or necessities; and what I am to do, I really do not know." (*Ep.* CXXXIX, 3; CSEL XLIV, 153; S I, 490.) "I would much rather every day at certain hours, as much as is appointed by rule in well-governed monasteries, do some work with my hands, and have the remaining hours free for reading and praying, or some work pertaining to Divine Letters, than have to bear these most annoying perplexities of other men's causes about secular matters, which we must either by adjudication bring to an end, or by intervention cut short." (*De Opere Monachorum,* XXIX, 37; CSEL XLI, 587; S III, 521.) "Certainly, on account of those who carry on law suits pertinaciously with one another, and, when they harass the good, scorn our judgments, and cause us to

lose the time that should be employed upon things divine; surely, I say, on account of these men we also may exclaim in the words of the Body of Christ, 'Away from me, ye wicked! and I will search the commandments of my God.'" (*En. in Ps.,* CXVIII [24], 3; CCSL XL, 1745; S VIII, 579.) See, too, *Ep.* CCXIII, 5; CSEL LVII, 377; S I, 570, and *Sermo* CCCII, 17; PL XXXVIII, 1391–92. Cf. Parker, *Christianity and the State,* pp. 61–63.

11. This outline is based primarily on two recent English works on Donatism—G. G. Willis, *Saint Augustine and the Donatist Controversy* (London, S.P.C.K., 1950), and W. H. C. Frend, *The Donatist Church* (Oxford, Clarendon Press, 1952). The former gives a clear and penetrating account of the ecclesiastical aspects of the conflict between the Catholics and the Donatists, while the latter, based on archaeological as well as literary evidence, shows the connections between Donatism and widespread social protest in North Africa, especially in the only superficially Romanized areas remote from the coast. Frend also gives a valuable account of the place of Donatism in the whole history of Christianity in North Africa, and offers some intriguing hypotheses about the connections between Donatist beliefs and actions and the Berbers' pre-Christian worship of Saturn and Caelestis, and the Islamic sects to which they were converted in the seventh century.

Another recent study that is useful to the student of Donatism and of Augustine is B. H. Warmington, *The North African Provinces from Diocletian to the Vandal Conquest* (Cambridge, Cambridge University Press, 1954). Paul Monceaux's *Histoire littéraire de l'Afrique chrétienne depuis les origines jusqu'à l'invasion arabe* (7 vols., Paris, Leroux, 1901, 1902, 1905, 1912, 1920, 1922, 1923), is still an important work on the Donatist movement and on Augustine's struggle with it (esp. vols. III and VII). Edward F. Humphrey's *Politics and Religion in the Days of Augustine,* Columbia University Ph.D. dissertation (New York, 1912), is useful because it relates the intervention of the State against the Donatists to the political scene in Italy and in the Empire as a whole, and because it gives the texts, together with translations, of many of the Imperial decrees against Donatism.

12. Frend, *The Donatist Church,* pp. 144–46.

13. Willis, *St. Augustine,* p. 7.

14. Frend, *The Donatist Church,* p. 159.

15. "The main division between the Churches is shown to be that between the Donatism of the inland plains and the Catholicism of

the cities and towns on the Tell [i.e., in Proconsular Africa]. To a less marked degree there is also a difference between the Berber-speaking areas of North Africa which were mainly Donatist, and the Latin- and Punic-speaking areas which were mainly Catholic." (Frend, *The Donatist Church*, p. 52.)

16. Warmington, *The North African Provinces*, pp. 87–88, argues that they were a distinct social class of "free agricultural workers who went from estate to estate offering their labour," and that their violence and their attachment to Donatism "very likely result from pressure by the authorities and the landowners to fix them to the soil; a change of status would soon mean a loss of personal freedom." Frend, on the other hand, while agreeing that they were peasants from Upper Numidia and Mauretania, who terrorized the owners of great estates and creditors, insists that they "were, above all, religious fanatics," who "derived their name from the fact that they lived 'around the shrines' (*circum cellas*) whence they got their food." (Frend, *The Donatist Church*, p. 173.) They were "*agonistici* or *milites Christi*—soldiers of Christ," whose lives "were in fact devoted to martyrdom." (*Ibid.*, p. 174.)

17. Willis, *St. Augustine*, p. 17.

18. Frend, *The Donatist Church*, p. 227. Warmington, *The North African Provinces*, pp. 91–92, also notes that Donatism made considerable headway among the educated; he says: "It is clear that for much of the fourth century Donatism attracted the best intellects among the African Christians."

19. See *Ep.* CLXXXV, VII, 25–26; CSEL LVII, 23–25; S IV, 642–43.

20. For the texts, see Humphrey, *Politics and Religion*, pp. 115–20.

21. Marcellinus became one of Augustine's close friends, and it was to him that *The City of God,* the *De Peccatorum Meritis,* and the *De Spiritu et Littera* were dedicated.

22. For the text, see Humphrey, *Politics and Religion*, pp. 177–78.

23. Frend, *The Donatist Church*, pp. 309–12.

24. See p. 176.   25. See pp. 34–37.

26. *Ep.* XXIII, 7; CSEL XXXIV (1), 71–72; S I, 244; italics added. Father Hugh Pope, in his detailed but partisan examination of the question of Augustine's attitude toward state intervention against the Donatists, refers to this letter, but he makes no mention of the all-important sentences that I have quoted; see his *Saint Augustine of Hippo* (London, Sands & Co. Ltd., 1937), p. 315. Likewise, he does not give the quotation from *Ep.* XXXIV referred to in note 27, al-

though he twice refers to the letter (see p. 316). On page 342, he quotes Augustine's statement in the *Retractations* that in 397 when he wrote the *Contra partem Donati* he was opposed to the use of secular power to force schismatics back into the Church (see below, note 28), but he does not admit that there was a clear and frankly admitted change in Augustine's views between 397 and, e.g., 408 (see below, note 32). In fact he says: "But these moderate views Augustine had held consistently throughout his life" (p. 342), and "Augustine has no doubt whatever about the right of the State to intervene in the organization of religious affairs" (p. 325). It is difficult to see how he can admit that Augustine argued that men "were to be driven into the fold by coercive laws" (p. 359), and at the same time say that Augustine, "while fully conceding the right of the State to punish violators of the established form of religion, maintained that this should only be done in the last resort, that *no compulsion was to be used in order to make a man change his religious beliefs.* . . ." (P. 345; italics added.)

Augustine's views on the subject of using the power of the State to punish schism and heresy have been the subject of extended, and sometimes sharp, controversy. Many Roman Catholic writers have attempted to present apologies for Augustine's teachings, while some Protestant and secular commentators have bitterly condemned him as the father of the Inquisition. For this reason, I have set forth, in considerable detail, the passages from Augustine's writings that show the various positions that he adopted on the question of using coercion against the Donatists and the arguments that he employed in defense of his views. My own evaluation of his doctrines is postponed until I have presented the relevant material from his works (see esp. pp. 214–20).

27. *Ep.* XXXIV, 1; CSEL XXXIV (2), 23; S I, 262. In the same year Augustine notes that he had forbidden a father to use force to compel his daughter, who had been converted to Donatism and had become one of their nuns, to return to the Church. "Now her father wished to compel her by severe treatment to return to the Catholic Church; but I was unwilling that this woman, whose mind was perverted, should be received by us *unless with her own will, and choosing, in the free exercise of judgment, that which is better:* and when the countryman began to attempt to compel his daughter by blows to submit to his authority, I immediately forbade his using any such means." (*Ep.* XXXV, 4; CSEL XXXIV [2], 30; S I, 264–65; italics added.)

28. *Retractationum,* II, V; CSEL XXXVI, 137; author's translation. In the same year Augustine in writing against the Manichaeans says that since for a long time he had shared their delusions, he of all men must not rage against them, but must deal with them with great patience. "Let those rage against you who know not with what labor the truth is to be found and with what difficulty error is to be avoided. . . . Let those rage against you who know not with what sighs and groans the least particle of the knowledge of God is obtained. And, last of all, let those rage against you who have never been led astray in the same way that they see that you are. For my part, I . . . by whom, in fine, all those fictions which have such a firm hold on you . . . were diligently examined, and attentively heard, and too easily believed, and commended at every opportunity to the belief of others, and defended against opponents with determination and boldness,—I can on no account rage against you; for I must bear with you now as formerly I had to bear with myself, and I must be as patient towards you as my associates were with me, when I went madly and blindly astray in your beliefs." (*Contra Epist. Fundamenti,* 2 and 3; CSEL XXV, 194–95; S IV, 129–30.)

29. *Ep.* XLIII, VIII, 21; CSEL XXXIV (2), 103; S I, 283.

30. "For they themselves [the Donatists] had constituted the Emperor the arbiter and judge in this question regarding the surrender of the sacred books, and regarding the schism, by their sending petitions to him, and afterwards appealing to him; and nevertheless they refuse to acquiesce in his decision. If, therefore, he is to be blamed whom the magistrate absolved, though he had not himself applied to that tribunal, how much more worthy of blame are those who desired an earthly king to be the judge of their cause!" (*Ibid.,* IV, 13; CSEL XXXIV [2], 95; S I, 280.)

31. *Ep.* XLIV, V, 10–11; CSEL XXXIV (2), 117–18; S I, 288–89; italics added.

32. *Ep.* XCIII, V, 17; CSEL XXXIV (2), 461; S I, 388. Note, too, the comments in the letter written to Count Boniface in 417 (*Ep.* CLXXXV or *De Correctione Donatistarum*), in which he says that before the repressive laws had been successfully enforced against the Donatists, his position had been that there should be no punishment of heretics *per se,* but that only the violence of the Donatists should be punished by fines levied on their clergy (*Ep.* CLXXXV, VII, 25; CSEL LVII, 23–24; S IV, 642–43). This midway position between his original opposition to any appeal to the authorities and his final complete approval of the use of state power against heresy, is

one to which he moved in the years 399 to 405; see pp. 188–93.

33. *Ep.* LI, 3; CSEL XXXIV (2), 146–47; S I, 297. "If you were acting according to the law of Christ, how much more consistently do certain Christian emperors frame ordinances in accordance with it? . . . But, in point of fact, you have chosen to expel them [the Maximianists] under laws which have been passed against heretics, and against yourselves among their number." (*Contra Litt. Petil.,* II, 58, 132; CSEL LII, 93–94; S IV, 563.)

34. Willis puts it at 398 (*St. Augustine,* p. 42); see Pope's reasons for assigning the later date (*St. Augustine of Hippo,* p. 374).

35. "My question is, since the Apostle enumerates the manifest 'works of the flesh'—which are, he says, fornications, uncleannesses, . . . strifes, emulations, animosities, dissensions, heresies, envies, drunkenness, feasting, and other things like these—, why do they think that the crime of idolatry is justly punished by the emperors, or if they do not approve of this, why do they admit that the force of the laws is rightly brought to bear on poisoners, and yet are not willing to admit that it should be applied to heretics and to impious dissensions, since by apostolic authority these are included among the same fruits of iniquity? Or can it be that they do not permit the powers of that human constitution they speak of to oversee such matters?" (*Contra Epist. Parmeniani,* I, X, 16; CSEL LI, 37; author's translation.)

36. "Therefore, not everyone who has been punished by the emperor in some matter of religion is made a martyr. . . . On this reasoning even the demons themselves could claim the glory of martyrdom, because they suffer this persecution by Christian Emperors. . . . Therefore, righteousness is not proved by suffering, but by righteousness suffering is made glorious. Thus the Lord, to prevent anyone from obscuring this issue and from seeking in his own damnation the praise of the proven martyrs, does not say in general: 'Blessed are those who suffer persecution,' but he adds an important distinction by which piety is truly differentiated from sacrilege, for he says: 'Blessed are those who suffer persecution for righteousness' sake.' Those in no way suffer for righteousness' sake who have divided Christ's Church, and with their pretended righteousness seek to separate the grain from the chaff before the time, make divisions by their false accusations, and are by this fact themselves separated like the lightest chaff by the inconstant winds of rumor." (*Ibid.,* I, IX, 15; CSEL LI, 36; author's translation.)

37. *Contra Litt. Petil.,* II, 83, 184; CSEL LII, 114; S IV, 573.

38. The same note is struck by Augustine in a letter written in 402 to Crispinus, a Donatist. He reminds him that according to the imperial decree ten pounds of gold could be demanded of him. However, his conclusion is: "But . . . we do not bid you be afraid of man: rather let Christ fill you with fear." (*Ep.* LXVI, 1; CSEL XXXIV [2], 235; S I, 323.) See the remark by Willis, *St. Augustine,* p. 130: "When dealing in the year 417 with this development [i.e., the Catholic appeal to the State for defense against Donatist aggression], Saint Augustine says explicitly that the object was not that all Donatists should be fined under the edict, but that the power of prosecution should be available to the Church in those areas which suffered most severely from Circumcellion depredations."

39. *Contra Litt. Petil.,* II, 84, 184; CSEL LII, 112–13; S IV, 572. In the same work, Augustine also states that the war waged by spiritual men against carnal men is carried on not with the sword, but with the word of God (*ibid.,* II, 68, 154; CSEL LII, 100; S IV, 566–67). See pp. 137 and 139, and *Sermo* LXII, 18; PL XXXVIII, 423; S VI, 304.

40. See pp. 138–42.

41. *Contra Litt. Petil.,* II, 84, 186; CSEL LII, 115-16; S IV, 574. "Whatever we do in our dealings with you, though we may do it contrary to your inclination, yet we do it from our love to you, that you may voluntarily correct yourselves, and live an amended life. For no one lives against his will; and yet a boy, in order to learn this lesson of his own free will, is beaten contrary to his inclination, and that often by the very man that is most dear to him. And this, indeed, is what the kings would desire to say to you if they were to strike you, for to this end their power has been ordained of God. But you cry out even when they are not striking you." (*Ibid.,* II, 94, 217; CSEL LII, 139; S IV, 585.) "There is no other question requiring solution, except whether you have been pious or impious in separating yourselves from the communion of the whole world. For if it shall be found that you have acted impiously, you would not be surprised if there should be no lack of ministers of God by whom you might be scourged, seeing that you suffer persecution not from us, but as it is written, from their own abominations." (*Ibid.,* II, 19, 43; CSEL LII, 44-45; S IV, 540.) See, too, *Contra Cresconium,* III, LI, 57; CSEL LII, 463.

42. *Contra Litt. Petil.,* II, 80, 178; CSEL LII, 110; S IV, 571.

43. *Ibid.,* II, 47, 110; CSEL LII, 84; S IV, 559.

44. See pp. 143–47.

45. *Contra Litt. Petil.*, II, 98, 226; CSEL LII, 144; S IV, 587.

46. See *Ep.* LXXVI, 4; CSEL XXXIV (2), 328; S I, 344. See, too, *Contra Epist. Parmeniani,* I, VIII, 13; CSEL LI, 34.

47. See pp. 179–80.

48. *Ep.* LXXXVI; CSEL XXXIV (2), 396–97; S I, 365.

49. See above, note 38; see, too, below, note 51.

50. Willis, *St. Augustine,* p. 64, dates it 405 to 411; Pope, *St. Augustine of Hippo,* p. 264, places it between 406 and 411.

51. *Ep.* LXXXVII, 8; CSEL XXXIV (2), 404; S I, 368; italics added. See, too, *Contra Cresconium,* III, XLIII, 47; CSEL LII, 453–55, and III, XLIX, 54; CSEL LII, 461.

52. *Ep.* LXXXVII, 8; CSEL XXXIV (2), 404; S I, 368.

53. *Ep.* LXXXVIII, 6; CSEL XXXIV (2), 412; S I, 371.

54. *Ibid.,* 8; CSEL XXXIV (2), 414–15; S I, 372.

55. *Ibid.,* 9; CSEL XXXIV (2), 415–16; S I, 372.

56. "And now, what other law is in force against your party than that decision of the elder Constantine, to which your forefathers of their own choice appealed, which they extorted from him by their importunate complaints, and which they preferred to the decision of an episcopal tribunal? If you are dissatisfied with the decrees of emperors, who were the first to compel the emperors to set these in array against you?" (*Ibid.,* 5; CSEL XXXIV [2], 411; S I, 370–71.)

57. *Ep.* LXXXIX, 1; CSEL XXXIV (2), 419; S I, 373.

58. *Ibid.,* 2; CSEL XXXIV (2), 419; S I, 374.

59. *Ibid.,* 6; CSEL XXXIV (2), 423–24; S I, 375.

60. "Both are provoked, but both are loved; both, while they continue under their infirmity, resent the treatment as vexatious; both express their thankfulness for it when they are cured." (*Ibid.*)

61. *Ibid.,* 7; CSEL XXXIV (2), 424; S I, 376.

62. "When, however, wholesome instruction is added to means of inspiring salutary fear, so that not only the light of truth may dispel the darkness of error, but the force of fear may at the same time break the bonds of evil custom, we are made glad . . . by the salvation of many, who with us bless God, and render thanks to Him. . . ." (*Ep.* XCIII, I, 3; CSEL XXXIV [2], 448; S I, 383.) See Frend's comment: "Limited by his environment and class, Augustine failed to appreciate the religious ideas and background of his Donatist opponents. He thought he was dealing with mental aberrations hardened into custom, from which people could be jolted by mild perse-

cution. He was in fact faced with a 'communal' issue of the bitterness which characterizes religious faith in the Near East." (Frend, *The Donatist Church,* p. 234.)

63. *Ep.* XCIII, V, 17; CSEL XXXIV (2), 461–62; S I, 388. Augustine was guilty of exaggeration or of a measure of self-delusion in his statement about the complete "conversion" of Hippo to Catholicism. After Stilicho's execution in August, 408, the successor of the Donatist Bishop who had been driven out after the Edict of Unity of 405 returned to Hippo in triumph with an escort of Circumcellions. See Frend, *The Donatist Church,* pp. 265, 270, and 272, and the references there to Augustine's letters, *Ep.* CVIII, V, 14, *Ep.* CVI, and *Ep.* CXXIV, 2.

64. *Ep.* XCIII, V, 16; CSEL XXXIV (2), 461; S I, 388. Note, however, that Frend in discussing the results of the persecution from 405 to 411 says that "on the whole the Catholic gains were local and partial, depending very much on the personal qualities of the individual Catholic bishop, and to a surprising extent they were balanced by losses to Donatism. The division of North Africa into fixed, watertight areas, the Catholics predominating in the settled urban country and the Donatists on the Numidian High Plains, became more pronounced. Each side evidently concentrated on eliminating the minorities of the other in his own territory." (Frend, *The Donatist Church,* p. 265; see also pp. 267 and 272.)

65. *Ep.* XCIII, V, 16; CSEL XXXIV (2), 461; S I, 388.

66. "Oh, if I could but show you how many we have even from the Circumcelliones, who are now approved Catholics, and condemn their former life, and the wretched delusion under which they believed that they were doing in behalf of the Church of God whatever they did under the promptings of a restless temerity, who nevertheless would not have been brought to this soundness of judgment had they not been as persons beside themselves, bound with the cords of those laws which are distasteful to you! As to another form of most serious distemper,—that, namely, of those who had not, indeed, a boldness leading to acts of violence, but were pressed down by a kind of inveterate sluggishness of mind, and would say to us: 'What you affirm is true, nothing can be said against it; but it is hard for us to leave off what we have received by tradition from our fathers,'—why should not such persons be shaken up in a beneficial way by a law bringing upon them inconvenience in worldly things, in order that they might rise from their lethargic sleep, and awake to the salvation

which is to be found in the unity of the Church?" (*Ibid.*, I, 2; CSEL XXXIV [2], 447; S I, 382–83.)

67. *Ibid.*, I, 3; CSEL XXXIV (2), 447; S I, 383.

68. *Ibid.*, V, 19; CSEL XXXIV (2), 463; S I, 389; see, too, *Ep.* CXLIV, 1; CSEL XLIV, 262–63; S I, 494. "Was it my duty to be displeased at the salvation of these men, and to call back my colleagues from a fatherly diligence of this kind, the result of which has been, that we see many blaming their former blindness?" (*Ep.* XCIII, I, 1; CSEL XXXIV [2], 446; S I, 382.)

69. *Ibid.*, I, 1; CSEL XXXIV (2), 445–46; S I, 382. They feared "lest, if without profit, and in vain, they suffered hard things at the hands of men, for the sake not of righteousness, but of their own obstinacy and presumption, they should afterwards receive nothing else at the hand of God than the punishment due to wicked men who despised the admonition which He so gently gave and His paternal correction." (*Ibid.*)

70. *Ibid.*, V, 18; CSEL XXXIV (2), 463; S I, 388.

71. *Ibid.*, V, 16; CSEL XXXIV (2), 461; S I, 388. "Wicked men, evil doers, housebreakers, adulterers, seducers, all these suffer many evils, yet there is no wrong [*iniuria*]. It is one thing to suffer wrong; it is another to suffer tribulation, or penalty, or annoyance, or punishment. . . . Right and wrong are contraries. Right is what is just. For not all that is called right, is right. What if a man lay down for you unjust right? nor indeed is it to be called right, if it is unjust. That is true right, which is also just. Consider what thou hast done, not what thou art suffering. If thou hast done right, thou art suffering wrong; if thou hast done wrong, thou art suffering right." (*En. in Ps.*, CXLV, 15; CCSL XL, 2116; S VIII, 664.)

72. See above, note 36.

73. *Psalms* ci, 5. The AV Translation of this verse is "Whoso privily slandereth his neighbour, him will I cut off."

74. *Ep.* XCIII, II, 6; CSEL XXXIV (2), 450–51; S I, 384. "In some cases, therefore, both he that suffers persecution is in the wrong, and he that inflicts it is in the right. But the truth is, that always both the bad have persecuted the good, and the good have persecuted the bad: the former doing harm by their unrighteousness, the latter seeking to do good by the administration of discipline; the former with cruelty, the latter with moderation; the former impelled by lust, the latter under the constraint of love." (*Ibid.*, II, 8; CSEL XXXIV [2], 452; S I, 384–85.) "Therefore Martyrs, not the punish-

ment, but the cause maketh, for if punishment made Martyrs, all the mines would be full of Martyrs, every chain would drag Martyrs, all that are executed with the sword would be crowned. Therefore let the cause be distinguished; let none say, because I suffer, I am righteous." (*En. in Ps.*, XXXIV [2], 13; CCSL XXXVIII, 320; S VIII, 85.) "For even among the heretics, they who for their iniquities and errors have suffered any trouble, vaunt themselves in the name of martyrdom, that with this fair covering disguised [*dealbati*] they may plunder the more easily, for wolves they are. . . . Lo, they have come to suffering, come even to the shedding of blood, yea come to the burning of the body; and yet it profiteth them nothing, because charity is lacking." (*Sermo* CXXXVIII, 2; PL XXXVIII, 764; S VI, 523.)

75. *Psalms* ii, 10–11 (AV).   76. See *Daniel* iii, 1–30.

77. *Ep.* XCIII, III, 9; CSEL XXXIV (2), 453; S I, 385.

78. *Contra Litt. Petil.*, II, 92, 211; CSEL LII, 136; S IV, 584. See, too, *In Ioann. Evangel.*, XI, 14; CCSL XXXVI, 119; S VII, 80.

79. See *ibid.*, XXXI, 7; CCSL XXXVI, 297; S VII, 191. As the Scriptures foretold, kings first persecuted the Church and later they believed in Christ; and so it came to pass that "kings believed, peace was given to the Church, the Church began to be set in the highest place of dignity, even on this earth, even in this life. . . ." (*En. in Ps.*, LXIX, 4; CCSL XXXIX, 933; S VIII, 312.)

80. *Ibid.*, CXL, 21; CCSL XL, 2042; S VIII, 647. "But better is it, that when an Emperor hath come to Rome, he should lay aside his crown, and weep at the monument of a fisherman, than that a fisherman should weep at the monument of an Emperor." (*Ibid.*, LXV, 4; CCSL XXXIX, 841; S VIII, 274-75.) See, too, *ibid.*, LXXXVI, 8; CCSL XXXIX, 1205; S VIII, 422.

81. See DCD, XVIII, 50; CCSL XLVIII, 648; H II, 283, *En. in Ps.*, CI (2), 5; CCSL XL, 1441; S VIII, 500, and *De Catechiz. Rudibus*, XXVII, 53; PL XL, 346; S III, 313.

82. *Ep.* CLXXXV, V, 19; CSEL LVII, 17; S IV, 640. "Accordingly, when we take into consideration the social condition of the human race, we find that kings, in the very fact that they are kings, have a service which they can render to the Lord in a manner which is impossible for any who have not the power of kings." (*Contra Litt. Petil.*, II, 92, 210; CSEL LII, 136; S IV, 583.) "For in this matter kings, as they have been commanded by divine authority, serve God insofar as they are kings if in their kingdoms they ordain good actions and forbid evil actions, not only those which pertain to

human society but also those which affect divine religion." (*Contra Cresconium*, III, LI, 56; CSEL LII, 462; author's translation.)

83. *Sermo* LXII, 17; PL XXXVIII, 422; S VI, 303.

84. *Ep.* CLXXXV, V, 20; CSEL LVII, 18; S IV, 640. "For why, when free-will is given by God to man, should adulteries be punished by the laws, and sacrilege allowed?" (*Ibid.*, V, 20; CSEL LVII, 19; S IV, 641.) "We have taught also that free will is given to man on such terms that punishments for grave sins are most justly enacted by divine and human laws, and that it concerns religious kings on earth not only to deal with adulteries and murders or other crimes of this kind, but also to restrain acts of sacrilege with fitting severity." (*Ep.* CCIV, 4; CSEL LVII, 319; FCL V, 5.)

85. *In Ioann. Evangel.*, XI, 14; CCSL XXXVI, 119; S VII, 80; italics added. See, too, *ibid.*, XI, 13; CCSL XXXVI, 118–19; S VII, 79–80.

86. *Ep.* XCIII, V, 19; CSEL XXXIV (2), 464; S I, 389.

87. See *En. in Ps.*, CI (2), 5; CCSL XL, 1441; S VIII, 500. See, too, above, note 79.

88. *Contra Litt. Petil.*, II, 97, 224; CSEL LII, 141; S IV, 586; italics added. "Because it is not so much when the Church is involved in so many evils, or amidst such offences, and in so great a mixture of very evil men, and amidst the heavy reproaches of the ungodly, that we ought to say that it is glorious, because kings serve it,—*a fact which only produces a more perilous and a sorer temptation;*—but then shall it rather be glorious, when that event shall come to pass of which the apostle also speaks in the words, 'When Christ, who is your life, shall appear, then shall ye also appear with Him in glory.'" (*De Perf. Iust. Hominis*, XV, 35; CSEL XLII, 35–36; S V, 172; italics added.) See, too: "In this wicked world, in these evil days, when the Church measures her future loftiness by her present humility, and is exercised by goading fears, tormenting sorrows, disquieting labours, and dangerous temptations, when she soberly rejoices, rejoicing only in hope, there are many reprobate mingled with the good. . . ." (DCD, XVIII, 49; CCSL XLVIII, 647; H II, 281.)

89. *Ep.* XCIII, II, 5; CSEL XXXIV (2), 449; S I, 383.

90. *John* vi, 44 (RSV).   91. *Luke* xiv, 21–24 (AV).

92. See *Contra Gaudentium*, I, XXV, 28; CSEL LIII, 226–27.

93. *Sermo* CXII, 8; PL XXXVIII, 647–48; S VI, 449.

94. *Ep.* CLXXXV, VI, 24; CSEL LVII, 23; S IV, 642.

95. *Psalms* lxxii, 11 (AV).

96. *Ep.* CLXXIII, 10; CSEL XLIV, 647; S I, 547. In 423, in a letter to the Lady Felicia, who had been converted from Donatism, Augustine reminds her of God's mercy in compelling her to return to the Church. "Although, however, you owe sincerest affection to those good servants of His through whose instrumentality you were compelled to come in, yet it is your duty, nevertheless, to place your hope on Him who prepared the banquet, by whom also you have been persuaded to come to eternal and blessed life." (*Ep.* CCVIII, 7; CSEL LVII, 346–47; S I, 559–60.)

97. See *Ep.* XCIII, III, 10; CSEL XXXIV (2), 454; S I, 385.

98. *Ep.* XCVII, 2; CSEL XXXIV (2), 517; S I, 406.

99. See *Ep.* CV, IV, 13; CSEL XXXIV (2), 604; FCL II, 205.

100. *Ibid.,* II, 7; CSEL XXXIV (2), 599–600; FCL II, 200–201. See, too, *Ep.* CXXIX, 4; CSEL XLIV, 36; FCL II, 372.

101. *Ep.* CV, II, 3; CSEL XXXIV (2), 596–97; FCL II, 197.

102. "If you, private citizens, so boldly and violently force men either to accept error or to remain in it, how much greater right and duty have we to resist your outrages by means of the lawfully constituted authority, which God has made subject to Christ, according to His prophecy, and so to rescue unfortunate souls from your tyranny, to free them from long-continued false teaching and let them breathe the clear air of truth! As for those who, according to you, are compelled to join us against their will, many of them wish to be compelled, as they admit to us both before and after conversion, for only thus can they escape your oppressive treatment." (*Ibid.,* II, 5; CSEL XXXIV [2], 598; FCL II, 199.)

103. See *Ep.* CVIII, VI, 17; CSEL XXXIV (2), 631; FCL II, 233, and *Ep.* CXXIX, 5; CSEL XLIV, 37; FCL II, 373.

104. See above, in this chapter, p. 180.

105. See above, in this chapter, pp. 194–97.

106. *Ep.* CXXXIX, 1; CSEL XLIV, 149; S I, 488.

107. See *Ep.* CXLI, 8; CSEL XLIV, 242; FCL III, 142.

108. *Ep.* CLXXIII, 4; CSEL XLIV, 642–43; S I, 545.

109. *Ibid.,* 3; CSEL XLIV, 642; S I, 545. "You are angry because you are being drawn to salvation, although you have drawn so many of our fellow Christians to destruction. . . . You think, however, that even what we have done to you should not have been done, because, in your opinion, no man should be compelled to that which is good. . . . The aim towards which a good will compassionately devotes its efforts is to secure that a bad will be rightly directed. . . . Nevertheless, it does not follow from this that those who are loved

should be cruelly left to yield themselves with impunity to their bad will; but in so far as power is given, they ought to be both prevented from evil and compelled to good." (*Ibid.*, 1–2; CSEL XLIV, 640–41; S I, 544.)

110. *Ep.* CLXXXV, II, 7; CSEL LVII, 6; S IV, 635.

111. *Ibid.*, VIII, 33; CSEL LVII, 31; S IV, 645. Some have been recalled from the path of destruction by the sermons of Catholic preachers, others by the edicts of Catholic princes; but "whosoever refuses to obey the laws of the emperors which are enacted in behalf of truth, wins for himself great condemnation." (*Ibid.*, II, 8; CSEL LVII, 7; S IV, 636.)

112. See *ibid.*, VII, 25–26; CSEL LVII, 23–25; S IV, 642–43. "It is not, therefore, those who suffer persecution for their unrighteousness, and for the divisions which they impiously introduce into Christian unity, but those who suffer for righteousness' sake, that are truly martyrs." (*Ibid.*, II, 9; CSEL LVII, 8; S IV, 636.)

113. *Ibid.*, VI, 22; CSEL LVII, 21; S IV, 641.

114. See *ibid.*, III, 13; CSEL LVII, 12; S IV, 638.

115. *Ibid.*, IV, 18; CSEL LVII, 17; S IV, 640; italics added.

116. "But if they were to neglect their charge, and allow them to perish, this mistaken kindness would more truly be accounted cruelty." (*Ibid.*, II, 7; CSEL LVII, 6; S IV, 635.)

117. *Ibid.*, II, 11; CSEL LVII, 10; S IV, 637.

118. *In Ioannis Evangelium Tractatus CXXIV,* written *ca.* 416. Pope, *St. Augustine of Hippo,* p. 378, argues that the first fifty-four Tractates were preached in 413, while the remainder (LV to CXXIV) were completed in 418 but never delivered.

119. *In Ioann. Evangel.,* V, 12; CCSL XXXVI, 47; S VII, 35. "These men, too, dare to say that they are wont to suffer persecution from catholic kings, or from catholic princes. What persecution do they bear? Affliction of body: yet if at times they have suffered, and how they suffered, let themselves know, and settle it with their consciences; still they suffered only affliction of body: the persecution which they cause is more grievous. . . . For if this baptism is true, he who would give thee another would be mocking thee. Beware of the persecution of the soul. For though the party of Donatus has at times suffered somewhat at the hands of catholic princes, it was a bodily suffering, not the suffering of spiritual deception." (*Ibid.,* XI, 13; CCSL XXXVI, 118; S VII, 79.)

120. *Ibid.,* V, 12; CCSL XXXVI, 47; S VII, 35; italics added. See, too, the argument that when the good persecute the wicked, they

"may be rightly said to do so both for righteousness' sake, in their love for which they persecute the wicked, and for that wickedness' sake which they hate in the wicked themselves. . . ." (*Ibid.*, LXXXVIII, 3; CCSL XXXVI, 547; S VII, 357.)

121. *In Epistolam Ioannis ad Parthos Tractatus Decem,* delivered *ca.* 416.

122. "The sword of the tongue is more powerful than any blade of steel. Hagar, Sarah's maid, was proud; and because of her pride she was afflicted by her mistress. That was discipline, not punishment. . . . Even so you, carnal souls like that proud maidservant, have no cause for your fury, though you may for discipline's sake have suffered some vexation. Return to your mistress, keep the Lord's peace [*dominicam pacem*]." (*In Epist. Ioann.,* X, 10; PL XXXV, 2062; Burnaby, 347.)

123. "Thus we may see hatred speaking softly, and charity prosecuting; but neither soft speeches nor harsh reproofs are what you have to consider. Look for the spring, search out the root from which they proceed. The fair words of the one are designed for deceiving, the prosecution of the other is aimed at reformation." (*Ibid.,* X, 7; PL XXXV, 2059; Burnaby, 344.)

124. *Ibid.,* X, 7; PL XXXV, 2059; Burnaby, 343; italics added. "When we look at differing actions, we find that charity may cause a man to be fierce, and wickedness to speak smoothly. A boy may be struck by his father, and have fair words from a slave-dealer. . . . Many things can be done that look well, yet do not issue from the root of charity. . . . Some actions seem harsh or savage, but are performed for our discipline at the dictate of charity. Thus a short and simple precept is given you once for all: Love, and do what you will [*Dilige, et quod vis fac*]." (*Ibid.,* VII, 8; PL XXXV, 2033; Burnaby, 316; italics added.) See, too, *ibid.,* VII, 11; PL XXXV, 2034–35; Burnaby, 318, and VIII, 9; PL XXXV, 2041; Burnaby, 322–23. Note also: "Let nothing be done through desire of hurting, but all through love of helping, and nothing will be done cruelly, inhumanly." (*Ep.* CLIII, VI, 19; CSEL XLIV, 418; FCL III, 296.)

125. *Ep.* C, 1; CSEL XXXIV (2), 535; S I, 411. Note also the sad comment made in 417: "It is indeed better (as no one ever could deny) that men should be led to worship God by teaching, than that they should be driven to it by fear of punishment or pain; but it does not follow that because the former course produces the better men, therefore those who do not yield to it should be neglected." (*Ep.* CLXXXV, VI, 21; CSEL LVII, 19; S IV, 641.)

126. *Ep.* C, 1; CSEL XXXIV (2), 536; S I, 411.   127. *Ibid.*

128. *Ibid.,* 2; CSEL XXXIV (2), 537; S I, 412.

129. "You will, however, most effectively help us to secure the fruit of our labours and dangers, if you take care that the imperial laws for the restraining of their sect, which is so full of conceit and of impious pride, be so used that they may not appear either to themselves or to others to be suffering hardship in any form for the sake of truth and righteousness. . . ." (*Ibid.,* 2; CSEL XXXIV [2], 538; S I, 412.)

130. *Ep.* CXXXIII, 1; CSEL XLIV, 81; S I, 470.

131. *Ep.* CXXXIX, 2; CSEL XLIV, 151; S I, 489. For examples of Augustine's attempts to win from the political authorities recognition of the right of episcopal intercession for the purpose of requesting pardon or reduction of punishment for condemned criminals, see *Ep.* CLII, 2; CSEL XLIV, 394; FCL III, 279, *Ep.* CLIII, 1–6; CSEL XLIV, 395–401; FCL III, 281–84, *ibid.,* 10; CSEL XLIV, 406–7; FCL III, 287–88, and *ibid.,* 16; CSEL XLIV, 413–14; FCL III, 293.

132. *Ep.* CXXXIV, 4; CSEL XLIV, 87; FCL III, 11.

133. *Ibid.,* 4; CSEL XLIV, 87–88; FCL III, 11–12. It is clear that Augustine is firmly opposed to the use of capital punishment against the Donatists, no matter what crimes they may have committed, and that he believes that in all criminal cases the death sentence should be used only when it is absolutely necessary, since it cuts off the possibility that the criminal may live to repent his crimes and to reform his conduct (see *Sermo* XIII, 8; PL XXXVIII, 110). On the other hand, it is not correct to say that he was opposed to capital punishment in all cases. As we have already seen, he regards the office of the hangman as essential to the peace and order of a well-regulated state (see Chap. IV, pp. 138–39 and 141–42). Note, too, the following statement: "For the judge is often compelled to draw the sword, although he is unwilling to strike. For as far as he is concerned personally, he would prefer that his reputation be kept without blood; but he is not willing to take the chance that public discipline may be destroyed. This involves his office, his power, his necessity." (*Sermo* CCCII, 16; PL XXXVIII, 1391; author's translation.)

134. *En. in Ps.,* LXV, 5; CCSL XXXIX, 843; S VIII, 275.

135. See *Ep.* CLXXXI and *Ep.* CLXXXII; CSEL XLIV, 701–23; FCL IV, 121–32.

136. John Ferguson, *Pelagius* (Cambridge, W. Heffer & Sons Ltd., 1956), p. 106.

137. "My Brethren, share with me in my sorrow. When ye find

such as these, do not hide them; be there no such misdirected [*perversa*] mercy in you; by all means, when ye find such, hide them not. Convince the gainsayers, and those who resist, bring to us. For already have two councils on this question been sent to the Apostolic see; and rescripts also have come from thence. The question has been brought to an issue; would that their error may sometimes be brought to an issue too! [*Causa finita est: utinam aliquando finiatur error!*]" (*Sermo* CXXXI, 10; PL XXXVIII, 734; S VI, 504.) It is a nice piece of irony that this last sentence, which in the context is clearly intended as a warning to the Pope not to reopen the issue, is often quoted to prove that Augustine was a strong defender of the absolute primacy of the Roman See and of the Pope as its Bishop over all churches.

138. Benjamin B. Warfield, Introductory Essay to *Saint Augustin: Anti-Pelagian Writings* in Philip Schaff, ed., *A Select Library of the Nicene and Post-Nicene Fathers of the Christian Church* (1st series, Grand Rapids, Mich., Wm. B. Eerdmans Publishing Company, 1956), V, xlii. Ferguson, *Pelagius,* p. 110, says flatly that it was Count Valerius, one of Augustine's personal friends, who persuaded the weak Emperor Honorius to act, and adds, "No doubt he [Valerius] took the initiative at the instigation of Augustine." See, too, Humphrey, *Politics and Religion,* pp. 209-11.

139. *De Nupt. et Concup.,* Book II.

140. *Ibid.,* II, III, 9; CSEL XLII, 262; S V, 286.

141. *Ep.* CXCI, 2; CSEL LVII, 164-65; S I, 555. In this and in a later letter to Sixtus (*Ep.* CXCIV) Augustine expresses his approval of the measures against the Pelagians taken by the Roman Church.

142. *Ep.* CCI, 1; CSEL LVII, 296-97; S I, 556.

143. *De Gratia Christi et de Pecc. Orig.,* II, XVII, 18; CSEL XLII, 179; S V, 243.

144. *Contra Duas Epist. Pelag.,* II, III, 5; CSEL LX, 463-64; S V, 392-93.

145. See, e.g., Cochrane, *Christianity and Classical Culture,* esp. pp. 328-37 and 346-57.

146. See pp. 217-20.

147. See the remarks of Figgis, *Political Aspects,* p. 78: "If the civil Governor is to persecute heresy, who is to advise him? He cannot do so on his own motion. Obviously, the Church, organised through its governors, will advise him. The moment you accept persecution as a policy, you tend to a religious tyranny. . . . But if it

[the State] be bound to take orders from the Church in regard to religious matters, it will not be long before there will be a claim to direct the State in regard to any policy that may have a religious, or a moral, or an ecclesiastical bearing. How much will be left out?"

148. See esp. Chap. IV, pp. 117 and 136–41.

149. See pp. 131–33. 150. See p. 188.

151. See above, in this chapter, e.g., pp. 195 and 204.

152. See esp. Chap. I, pp. 35–38. 153. See pp. 138–42.

154. See pp. 131–33; see also, in this chapter, pp. 197–200. Certainly Augustine believes that "it concerns Christian kings of this world to wish their mother the Church . . . to have peace in their times" (see above, note 85); they must make and enforce laws against false religion (e.g., paganism), sacrilege, heresy, and schism, they must protect the Church and her ministers against violence, and they must give material aid to the work of the Church by means of state subventions, remission of taxes and other duties, and exemption from certain general civic obligations. Apart from these means, which are either negative or ancillary, there does not seem to be anything that a ruler can do to lead his subjects to true piety by the use of political power.

155. See Chap. IV, esp. pp. 134–37.

156. See above, in this chapter, pp. 185–87. 157. See esp. p. 196.

NOTES TO CONCLUSION

1. See pp. 102–4, and Chap. IV, esp. pp. 117, 133, and 138–41.

2. See pp. 138–43. 3. See esp. Chap. IV, pp. 134–37.

4. Max Weber, "Politics as a Vocation," in H. H. Gerth and C. Wright Mills, eds., *From Max Weber: Essays in Sociology* (New York, Oxford University Press, 1946), p. 128.

5. See pp. 140–41. 6. See pp. 141–42.

7. See pp. 166–68. 8. See pp. 143–46.

9. See pp. 6–7. 10. See pp. 130, 135–36, and 142.

11. See Chap. V, esp. pp. 155–57 and 160–66.

12. See pp. 161 and 163–65. 13. See pp. 135–36.

14. See Chap. VI, esp. pp. 194–202. 15. See pp. 197–99.

16. See p. 198. 17. See pp. 214–20.

18. Note, e.g., the references to the kingdoms of this earth as parts of the earthly city (p. 31) and the famous comparison between kingdoms and bands of brigands (pp. 126–28).

19. Two works that deal with Augustine's influence on medieval

thought are: Ernst Bernheim, *Mittelalterliche Zeitanschauungen in ihrem Einfluss auf Politik und Geschichtschreibung* (Tübingen, Verlag J. C. B. Mohr, 1918) and H.-X. Arquillière, *L'augustinisme politique* (2d ed., Paris, Librairie Philosophique J. Vrin, 1955).

20. Translation quoted from Sidney Z. Ehler and John B. Morrall, eds., *Church and State Through the Centuries* (London, Burns and Oates, 1954), p. 33.

21. *Ibid.,* p. 34.   22. *Ibid.,* p. 36.   23. See *ibid.,* pp. 37–38.

24. See pp. 24 and 34–37.

25. See Richard Scholz, *Die Publizistik zur Zeit Philipps des Schönen und Bonifaz' VIII* (Stuttgart, Verlag von Ferdinand Enke, 1903), p. 262. See Egidius Romanus (Colonna), *De ecclesiastica potestate,* ed. by G. Boffito and G. U. Oxilia (Florence, 1908), I, IV, p. 14; II, VII, p. 60; and III, XI, p. 161.

26. DCD, II, 21; see p. 119.

27. *Quaestio de potestate papae (Rex pacificus), Proponitur quaestio,* X, in Pierre Dupuy, *Histoire du différend d'entre le pape Boniface VIII et Philippes le Bel Roy de France* (Paris, Sebastian & Gabriel Cramoisy, 1655), p. 665; author's translation. The Latin text runs: *Vera autem justitia non est in republica cujus Christus non est rector. Sed respublica populi Christiani debet esse recta et vera. Ergo Christus in ea debet esse rector. Sed papa est Christi vicarius. . . . Ergo papa est rector reipublicae etiam in temporalibus.*

28. See, e.g., Dino Bigongiari's Introduction to his *The Political Ideas of St. Thomas Aquinas* (New York, Hafner Publishing Company, 1953), p. x.

29. See pp. 46–47 and 50; see, also, p. 144.

30. F. R. Leavis, ed., *Mill on Bentham and Coleridge* (New York, George W. Stewart, Inc., 1950), p. 65. Mill writes: "For our own part, we have a large tolerance for one-eyed men, provided their one eye is a penetrating one: if they saw more, they probably would not see so keenly, nor so eagerly pursue one course of inquiry. Almost all rich veins of original and striking speculation have been opened by systematic half-thinkers. . . ."

31. John Plamenatz, *The English Utilitarians* (Oxford, Basil Blackwell, 1949), p. 124.

32. See pp. 50–52 and 80–82.   33. See pp. 72–74.

BIBLIOGRAPHY

For the titles of all the extant works of Augustine see vols. XXXII to XLVII of J.-P. Migne, *Patrologiae cursus completus . . . series Latina.*

For a chronological table, in English, of the works of Augustine in the order of their composition, see Father Hugh Pope, *Saint Augustine of Hippo,* pp. 368–87; note his reference (p. 378) to S. M. Zarb, O.P., "Chronologia Operum S. Augustini," *Angelicum,* X (1933), 359–96, 478–512.

For a bibliography of works about Augustine which is annotated and divided into a number of subject-matter categories, see Étienne Gilson, *Introduction à l'étude de saint Augustin* (3d ed., Paris, Librairie Philosophique J. Vrin, 1949), pp. 325–51.

The brief bibliography given here lists in alphabetical order by author 1) the works dealing with Augustine that have been cited or referred to in the notes, 2) all other works cited or referred to in the notes.

WORKS DEALING WITH AUGUSTINE CITED OR REFERRED TO
IN THE NOTES

Barker, Ernest. Introduction, Everyman's Library edition of *The City of God.* 2 vols. London: J. M. Dent & Sons Ltd.; New York: E. P. Dutton & Co., Inc., 1945.

Baynes, Norman H. "The Political Ideas of St. Augustine's *De Civitate Dei,*" Historical Association Pamphlet No. 104. London, 1936. Reprinted in *Byzantine Studies and Other Essays.* London: University of London, The Athlone Press, 1955.

Bourke, Vernon J. "The Political Philosophy of St. Augustine," *Proceedings of the Seventh Annual Meeting of the American Catholic Philosophic Association,* St. Louis, 1931, pp. 45–55.

Boyer, Charles. L'idée de vérité dans la philosophie de saint Augustin. Paris: G. Beauchesne, 1921.

Chroust, Anton-Hermann. "The Philosophy of Law of St. Augustine," *Philosophical Review,* LIII (March 1944), 195–202.

Cochrane, Charles N. Christianity and Classical Culture. London, New York, Toronto: Oxford University Press, 1944, esp. pp. 486–516.

Combès, Gustave. La doctrine politique de saint Augustin. Paris: Librairie Plon, 1927.

Cranz, F. Edward. "De civitate Dei, XV, 2, and Augustine's Idea of the Christian Society," *Speculum,* XXV (April 1950), 215–25.

—— "The Development of Augustine's Ideas on Society Before the Donatist Controversy," *Harvard Theological Review,* Vol. XLVII, No. 4 (October 1954), pp. 255–316.

Dawson, Christopher. "St. Augustine and His Age," in M. C. D'Arcy *et al., Saint Augustine.* New York: Meridian Books, 1957.

Figgis, John Neville. The Political Aspects of S. Augustine's 'City of God.' London: Longmans, Green, and Co., 1921.

Gilson, Étienne. Introduction à l'étude de saint Augustin. Paris: Librairie Philosophique J. Vrin, 1949. (Eng. tr., The Christian Philosophy of Saint Augustine. New York: Random House, 1960).

Hessen, Johannes. Die Begründung der Erkenntnis nach dem hl. Augustinus. *Beiträge zur Geschichte der Philosophie des Mittelalters.* Münster: Aschendorff, 1916. Vol. XIX, 2.

Hodgson, Leonard. "Christian Citizenship: Some Reflections on St. Augustine, Ep. 138," *Church Quarterly Review,* CXLV (October 1947), 1–11.

Jolivet, Regis. Dieu soleil des esprits, la doctrine augustinienne de l'illumination. Paris: Desclée de Brouwer, 1934.

McCabe, Joseph. Saint Augustine and His Age. London: Duckworth and Co., 1902.

McIlwain, Charles H. The Growth of Political Thought in the West. New York: The Macmillan Company, 1932, pp. 154 ff.

Millar, Moorhouse F. X., S.J. "The Significance of St. Augustine's Criticism of Cicero's Definition of the State," *Philosophia Perennis,* Festgabe Josef Geyser. Regensburg: Josef Habbel, 1930. Vol. I.

Mommsen, Theodor E. "St. Augustine and the Christian Idea of Progress," *Journal of the History of Ideas,* Vol. XII, No. 3 (June 1951), pp. 346–74.

Parker, Thomas M. "St. Augustine and the Conception of Unitary Sovereignty," *Augustinus Magister.* Paris: Études Augustiniennes, 1954. Vol. II.

Pope, Hugh. Saint Augustine of Hippo. London: Sands & Co. Ltd., 1937.

Portalié, Eugène, S.J. "Augustine of Hippo," *The Catholic Encyclopaedia.* New York: The Encyclopaedia Press, Inc., 1907. Vol. II.

Schubert, Alois. Augustins Lex-aeterna-Lehre nach Inhalt und Quellen. *Beiträge zur Geschichte der Philosophie des Mittelalters.* Münster: Aschendorff, 1924. Vol. XXIV, 2.

Warfield, Benjamin B. Introductory Essay to *Saint Augustin: Anti-Pelagian Writings,* Vol. V in Philip Schaff, ed., A Select Library of the Nicene and Post-Nicene Fathers of the Christian Church. 1st series. 14 vols. Grand Rapids, Mich.: Wm. B. Eerdmans Publishing Company, 1956.

West, Rebecca. St. Augustine. New York: D. Appleton and Co., 1933.

Willis, G. G. Saint Augustine and the Donatist Controversy. London: S.P.C.K., 1950.

ALL OTHER WORKS CITED OR REFERRED TO IN THE NOTES

Arendt, Hannah. Between Past and Future. New York: The Viking Press, 1961.

Arquillière, H. X. L'augustinisme politique. 2d ed. Paris: Librairie Philosophique J. Vrin, 1955.

Barker, Ernest. From Alexander to Constantine. Oxford: Oxford University Press, 1956.

—— Social and Political Thought in Byzantium. Oxford: Oxford University Press, 1957.

Bernheim, Ernst. Mittelalterliche Zeitanschauungen in ihrem Einfluss auf Politik und Geschichtschreibung. Tübingen, Verlag J. C. B. Mohr, 1918.

Bigongiari, Dino, ed. The Political Ideas of St. Thomas Aquinas. New York: Hafner Publishing Company, 1953.

Cadoux, C. John. The Early Christian Attitude to War. London: Headley Bros. Publishers, Ltd., 1919.

Carlyle, A. J. A History of Mediaeval Political Theory in the West. 4th impression. Edinburgh and London: Wm. Blackwood and Sons, Ltd., 1950.

Dill, Samuel. Roman Society in the Last Century of the Western Empire. New York: Meridian Books, Inc., 1958.

Dodds, E. R. The Greeks and the Irrational. Berkeley: The University of California Press, 1951.

Dupuy, Pierre. Histoire du différend d'entre le pape Boniface VIII et Philippes le Bel Roy de France. Paris: Sebastian & Gabriel Cramoisy, 1655.

Egidius Romanus (Colonna). De ecclesiastica potestate. Ed. by G. Boffito and G. U. Oxilia. Florence, 1908.

Ehler, Sidney Z., and John B. Morrall, eds. Church and State Through the Centuries. London: Burns and Oates, 1954.

Ferguson, John. Pelagius. Cambridge: W. Heffer & Sons Ltd., 1956.

Foster, Michael B. Mystery and Philosophy. London: SCM Press Ltd., 1957.

Frend, W. H. C. The Donatist Church. Oxford: Clarendon Press, 1952.

Gerth, H. H., and C. Wright Mills, eds. From Max Weber: Essays in Sociology. New York: Oxford University Press, 1946.

Hadas, Moses, tr. and ed. The Stoic Philosophy of Seneca. Garden City, N.Y.: Anchor Books, Doubleday & Co., Inc., 1958.

Hobbes, Thomas. Leviathan. Oxford: Basil Blackwell, 1946.

Humphrey, Edward F. Politics and Religion in the Days of Augustine. Columbia University Ph.D. dissertation. New York, 1912.

Leavis, F. R., ed. Mill on Bentham and Coleridge. New York: George W. Stewart, Inc., 1950.

Monceaux, Paul. Histoire littéraire de l'Afrique chrétienne depuis les origines jusqu'à l'invasion arabe. 7 vols. Paris: Leroux, 1901, 1902, 1905, 1912, 1920, 1922, 1923.

Parker, T. M. Christianity and the State in the Light of History. London: Adam and Charles Black, 1955.

Plamenatz, John. The English Utilitarians. Oxford: Basil Blackwell, 1949.

Plato. Laws. A. E. Taylor, tr. London: J. M. Dent & Sons Ltd.; New York: E. P. Dutton & Co., Inc., 1960.

Regout, Robert H. W. La doctrine de la guerre juste de saint Augustin à nos jours. Paris: Éditions A. Pedone, 1934.

Sabine, George H. A History of Political Theory. Rev. ed. New York: Henry Holt and Co., 1950.

Scholz, Richard. Die Publizistik zur Zeit Philipps des Schönen und Bonifaz' VIII. Stuttgart: Verlag von Ferdinand Enke, 1903.

Tellenbach, Gerd. Church, State and Christian Society at the Time of the Investiture Contest. Oxford: Basil Blackwell, 1948.

Tertullian. Apology: De Spectaculis. Gerald H. Rendall, tr. Loeb
    Classical Library; London: William Heinemann, Ltd.; New York:
    G. P. Putnam's Sons, 1931.
Troeltsch, Ernst. The Social Teaching of the Christian Churches.
    Olive Wyon, tr. 3d impression. London: George Allen & Unwin
    Ltd.; New York: The Macmillan Company, 1950.
Warmington, B. H. The North African Provinces from Diocletian
    to the Vandal Conquest. Cambridge: Cambridge University Press,
    1954.

INDEX